God, Sex, and Gender

God, Sex, and Gender

An Introduction

Adrian Thatcher

WILEY-BLACKWELL

A John Wiley & Sons, Ltd., Publication

Library of Congress Cataloging-in-Publication Data

Thatcher, Adrian.
  God, sex, and gender : an introduction / Adrian Thatcher.
     p. cm.
   Includes bibliographical references and index.
   ISBN 978-1-4051-9369-6 (hardback) – ISBN 978-1-4051-9370-2 (pbk)
   1. Sex–Religious aspects–Christianity. 2. Sex role–Religious aspects–Christianity. I. Title.
   BT708.T444 2011
   233'.5–dc22

                                                                    2010049297

A catalogue record for this book is available from the British Library.

This book is published in the following electronic formats: ePDFs 9781444396362; Wiley Online Library 9781444396386; ePub 9781444396379

Set in 10/13pt Minion by Thomson Digital, Noida, India
Printed in Singapore by Ho Printing Singapore Pte Ltd

1   2011

Contents

Introduction – Or, a Welcome to My Readers

Who Are You?

"Hello." When I write books, I like to envisage who will read them. Writing and reading form a powerful means of communication, but with one defect. A dialogue between the speaker and the reader can never become an audible or spoken exchange. Readers cannot complain to an author's face if he or she is unclear (as we Theology authors often are). Nor can they interrupt if they disagree. And authors miss all those looks of surprise, bewilderment, discovery, or rejection that accompany class discussion. So it helps this author, at least, to imagine who his readers are, why they are reading this book, what they hope to get from it, how much they already know, even the countries where they live and the religious backgrounds (if any) which may already be shaping them.

It is a safe bet that many of you will be students, studying sexuality and gender as part of a larger degree or diploma program which might be in Theology, or Religious Studies, or Ethics, or subjects closely related to these. You may be studying in a Church or denominational seminary, or in a Theology department in a secular or Christian university, or in a secular Religious Studies department in a secular University, or some other institution. Often these places are mixed up anyway (in more senses than one). There is a huge range of approaches out there to questions of belief and practice: some institutions would not permit you to study this book at all. If you have a Church allegiance, your Church will already have firm teaching about sex and gender, but there will be arguments raging, overtly or covertly, about its adequacy or its ability to remain relevant to the sex lives and "gender performances" of Christians (see Section 2.1.2 for more on this). Students of Philosophy of Religion and/or Ethics will be interested in the arguments offered here. The strange theological territory we will pass through may provide unusual features not found among the more familiar landscapes of Ancient, or Enlightenment or Modern Philosophy.

Women students in Theology and Religious Studies now outnumber men (at least in the United Kingdom, by 40%) (HESA, 2007–2008). That fact has not only enriched the study of these subjects: it is a revealing indicator of the breathtaking changes to sex and gender roles in the past 50 years, not only in higher education but nearly everywhere else. Basic theological reflections on these remarkable changes, in down to earth language, are attempted here. Not all readers will be students. That category "general reader," loved by publishers, includes clergy, ministers, and Church leaders; Christians concerned with sex and gender issues because of pastoral concerns or perplexity about their own sexualities and what their Christian commitment may require of them as sexual persons; or "Church leavers," who according to some accounts outnumber actual Church attenders, whose membership of Churches has collapsed while their interest in Theology has remained constant or intensified. We are all unavoidably sexual beings. Many of us want to make sense of our sexuality by listening to what religious traditions have to say, or could yet say, about sexuality. Many are curious why there is still such an enormous fuss among Christians about sex.

You can read this book with little or no knowledge of Theology or Religion. Ideally you might have studied either subject for a year or two years as an undergraduate. If you are already in your twenties you will almost certainly have had some sexual experience (whatever that means! – see Section 1.3) and this book will help you reflect on it, however ecstatic, or traumatic, or just boring, it might have been. I worry a lot about potential readers who will never see the book because they, and their countries and colleges cannot afford books. Yet problems to do with sexuality and gender are rife in those countries too. Inevitably the book will be read only by readers who can afford to buy it. We will need to be sensitive to this problem throughout.

Who am I?

I am curious about my readers. They may be curious about me. I have been teaching Theology and Philosophy to students, and they have been teaching me, since 1974, and I am still learning much from them at the University of Exeter, in the United Kingdom. This is not my first book, and several of the earlier ones have been about sexuality, marriage, families, living together, relationships, and how to read the Bible in a very different world from the one in which it was written. I am a Christian, an Anglican (or Episcopalian, depending on where you live). What biases, hidden agendas, can you expect?

Well, no one can set aside who they are, especially if they are writing about sex and gender! Feminist theologians, lesbian and gay theologians, evangelical theologians, Catholic theologians (traditional and revisionist), queer theologians, and others are all writing in part out of their experiences. I am no exception. It is often overlooked though, that the Christian tradition about these matters is already profoundly shaped by partisan experience, that of single, powerful, European males who were (in the main) celibate, many of whom were profoundly troubled by their desires and what to do about them. Their often tortuous utterances say as much about their unhappy troubles as they do about the tradition that "informs" them.

This author will not disguise that he is male, straight, and a grandparent. It will become clear his sympathies generally lie with progressive or revisionist themes, as long as these are deeply rooted in traditional theological sources and doctrines. A whole range of issues, perspectives, ideas are presented, as fairly as I can, yet without attempting to hide my own beliefs and practices between the lines or behind the text. I will never claim to be right – only to offer arguments and compare one argument with another. What matters most is that clear reasons and arguments are offered in support of any and every position adopted. Not all of them will convince, but at least they will be open to inspection, criticism, and eventually amendment. Some, of course, will be found wanting.

I hope it will be possible for readers to be intrigued and exhilarated by the strange yet lively material that makes up theologies of sexuality and gender. That is why I have written this book. I am intrigued and exhilarated myself by its themes and their relevance to readers and writer alike.

My Aims?

There are three main aims:

1. To introduce students and general readers to the exhilaration of thinking theologically about sex, sexuality, sexual relationships, and gender roles.
2. To introduce students and general readers to a comprehensive and consistent theological understanding of sexuality and gender, which is broad, contemporary, undogmatic, questioning, inclusive, and relevant to readers' interests, needs, and experience.
3. To offer to university and college lecturers a comprehensive core text that will provide them with an indispensable basis for undergraduate and postgraduate courses and modules in and around the topics of Theology, Sexuality, and Gender.

What's in the Book?

There are five parts. Part I, "Sex, Gender, and Theology", contains a separate chapter on each of the three topics, Sex, Gender, and Theology. Part I is introductory. An attempt is made to understand the construction of sex, sexuality, and gender in biblical times and in late-modern Western societies (Chapters 1 and 2), and to discover how some of the churches and some theologians identify and use theological sources for thinking about them (Chapter 3).

Part II, "Being Theological about Sex," contains chapters on Desire, and on Marriage. Chapter 4 analyses desire, distinguishes between different forms of desire, and links sexual desire with desire for God. Chapter 5 raises the question whether marriage must remain the framework within Christian thought for thinking about and having sex. Chapter 6 taps into the rich resources of meaning with which theological thought is able to invest marriage, at least in its egalitarian form.

Part III, "Being Theological about Gender," occupies Chapters 7 and 8. A crucial issue is whether the God of Christian faith is to be thought of as masculine, and if so, whether the male sex images God in a way the female sex does not. Can Mary, Mother of God help to restore the self-respect of women in a male-dominated Church? Chapter 8 finds the core doctrine of the "Body of Christ" crucial to thinking theologically about gender, and depicting it in such a way that "in Christ there is neither male nor female."

Part IV, "Being Theological about Same-Sex Love," closely examines passages in the Bible which have been used to condemn all same-sex contact, and concludes, perhaps controversially, that these passages can no longer be used in this way (Chapter 9). Chapter 10 examines the use of Tradition, Reason, and Natural Law in condemning homosexual practice, and concludes, again perhaps controversially, that these uses are unjustified, and that the public arguments put forward by the churches in support of these uses are frankly poor ones.

Part V, "Learning to Love," has four chapters, and develops an inclusive theology of sexual love informed by the gender awareness that a contemporary faith can provide. Chapter 11 develops theological understandings of virginity, chastity, and celibacy that may be embraced in the twenty-first century. Chapter 12 handles the practices of contraception inside and outside marriage, and in the time of HIV/AIDS. Chapter 13 shows that marriages do not begin with the ceremony of a wedding, and sketches out how couples who are having "pre-ceremonial" sex may nonetheless behave chastely. The final chapter draws together the theology of the previous chapters and briefly applies it to sexual minorities, and to the further transformation of relations of gender.

How to Use the Book

Because I am writing both for students and general readers I have tried to incorporate features that both readerships expect. The five parts are arranged in a sequence that can be easily followed. But the book need not be read from the beginning. Each of the chapters is self-contained. There are many cross-references so moving forwards and backwards through the book should be easy.

There are plenty of subheadings to identify themes and arguments. The definitions of key terms are clearly set out in the margins. Key quotations are also clearly displayed. There are also questions for discussion or an activity, sometimes followed by a comment. There are several ways of using these. They can be ignored. If the book is used in a class they can be used to generate class or group discussion. If the book is used for pre-reading prior to lectures, responses to the questions may be written down beforehand. Some of the questions may make good essay questions. If you want to use the questions as a prompt for your own thinking, you might like to use a masking card initially in order to prevent the comments being seen.

Reference

HESA (Higher Education Statistics Agency) (2007–2008) www.hesa.ac.uk/index.php/component/option,com_datatables/Itemid,121/task,show_category/catdex,3/#subject (accessed November 12, 2010).

Part I

Sex, Gender, and Theology

1

Sex

Sexuality, the Sexes, Having Sex

This chapter is about sex. It asks how the terms "sex" and "sexuality" are used (Section 1.1). It shows that until recently men and women thought of themselves as united in a single sex, even with the same sex organs, but disunited by belonging to two different genders (Section 1.2). Since there are many sexual activities in which people engage, it asks what "having sex" amounts to (Section 1.3). These topics prepare the way for a similar analysis of gender in Chapter 2.

1.1 Sexuality

Nothing can be taken for granted in the theology of sex and gender. Take for example the truism (something that looks obvious) that we are either women or men. There are at least three reasons for doubting even this.

First, if we are adults, we have *become* either men or women, as a result of a comprehensive process. It may take half a lifetime to discover the pervasive influences on us that helped to make us the men and women we now are. We are more than our biology.

Second, there are many adults who are unable to identify with either label. There are *intersex*, and *transsexual* or *transgender*, people who cannot easily say they identify with this *binary* (twofold) division of humanity into separate biological sexes (see Section 1.2).

God, Sex, and Gender: An Introduction, First Edition. Adrian Thatcher.
© 2011 Adrian Thatcher. Published 2011 by Blackwell Publishing Ltd.

Third, for most of Christian history, people were inclined to believe that there was a single sex, "man," which existed on a continuum between greater (male) and lesser (female) degrees of perfection (see Sections 1.2 and 2.3). That is something quite different from the now common assumption that there are two, and only two, sexes. If we are to understand the biblical and traditional sources for thinking about sex and gender, we will be well advised not to smother them with our modern assumptions.

Defining terms In a moment I will be suggesting a definition of sexuality, but first it may be helpful to say something about what we are doing when we define something. Throughout the book we will notice that experts sometimes disagree even over the meaning of basic terms. When coming to define sexuality, it is important to tackle the problem of definition head-on. Experts disagree about what sexuality is. Within psychology and psychoanalysis, there is a large diversity of influences and schools, and new sub-disciplines such as evolutionary psychology and sociobiology have become popular. Philosophers of language have something to teach us about how to manage this problem. They might advise us not to worry too much about definitions, that is, to look not for the fixed meaning or meanings of a word but for its *use* within its "language-game" or context where it is employed. That is what I shall be doing with definitions. I shall follow the philosopher Wittgenstein (1889–1951) in his dictum "For a *large* class of cases – though not for all – in which we employ the word 'meaning' it can be defined thus: the meaning of a word is its use in the language" (Wittgenstein, 1972, p. 20, para. 43; emphasis in original).

> **Sex:** Sex is the division of a species into either male or female, especially in relation to the reproductive functions. Whatever else sex is, it is about the ability of species to reproduce.

Sometimes it is helpful to offer a *stipulative* definition, that is, a description of the meaning of a general term combined with the author's stipulation of its meaning or use. Some of the definitions in the book, found in the margins, are stipulative.

However, even the link between sex and reproduction can be sensibly doubted, can't it? For most people most of the time, having children is the last thing on their minds when they are "having sex" (see Section 1.3). There is much more to sex than biology. It is OK to *begin* discussing sex from a biological or reproductive point of view, provided it does not end there. *Sex,* or being sexed, is a condition we share with fish, insects, birds, and other animals. Sometimes the term refers to the biological drive within species to reproduce. Since that drive can be overwhelming it requires regulation. That regulation is sexual morality.

> **Sexuality:** "Sexuality refers to a fundamental component of personality in and through which we, as male or female, experience our relatedness to self, others, the world, and even God" (USCCB, 1991, p. 9).
>
> "Sexuality especially involves the powers or capacities to form deep and lasting bonds, to give and receive pleasure, and to conceive and bear children. Sexuality can be integral to the desire to commit oneself to life with another, to touch and be touched, and to love and be loved. Such powers are complex and ambiguous. They can be used well or badly. They can bring astonishing joy and delight. Such powers can serve God and serve the neighbor. They also can hurt self or hurt the neighbor. Sexuality finds expression at the extreme ends of human experience: in love, care, and security; or lust, cold indifference, and exploitation.
>
> Sexuality consists of a rich and diverse combination of relational, emotional, and physical interactions and possibilities. It surely does not consist solely of erotic desire" (ELCA, 2009, section 3).

Our *sexuality* is more interesting. In the margin, there are two stipulative definitions of sexuality provided by churches, one Roman Catholic, the other Lutheran, both of them American.

Question: Were there any particular emphases in these descriptions with which you particularly agreed?

Comment: Both descriptions mention that we discover our sexuality in *relationship* to others. I liked the emphases on the complexity and ambiguity of sexuality. These emphases need to be placed alongside the more obvious ones about pleasure, joy, and having children, don't they?

An alternative take on sexuality The term "sexuality" is very recent, and should not be read back into pre-modern times. It began to be used in the 1860s, as part of a "discourse" of sex which was invented by the medical profession. By now it is deeply embedded in the English language and has attracted many meanings. The British Christian writer Jo Ind provides a more erotic, personal definition of sexuality. I have included it in order to discuss the issues it raises. She says:

> When I am talking about sexuality I am talking about the glorious, wide-ranging, intriguing, predictable and surprising business of being aroused. I am talking about the way we are moved by breasts, by kindness, by red toenails peeping through open-toed sandals, by wind skimming across water, by kindred spirits, by kissing down between the breasts, down around the belly button, down, down towards the groin. I am talking about the way our bodies are changed through memories, fantasies, yearnings, sweet nothings, the biting of buttocks, the word understood, the semen smelt, the integrity cherished. When I am talking about sexuality I am talking about the multi-dimensional, richly textured, embarrassingly sublime, muscle-tighteningly delicious capacity to be turned on. (Ind, 2003, p. 33)

Questions: How did you react to this understanding of sexuality? What particular features of it, if any, struck you as unusual?

Comment: It was written by a woman who makes no attempt to conceal her own sexuality and separate it from her writing about sex. It is *gynocentric* (woman-centered) not *androcentric* (man-centered).

It links sexuality to arousal. The author holds that women are likely to be aroused in more diffuse and complex ways than men, and they are better able than men to integrate the erotic dimension of their lives with all the other dimensions.

Ind links the discussion of sexuality to her experience of desiring, of being aroused, of giving and receiving pleasure. The Lutherans would agree with her about this. It is an important emphasis since much writing about sexuality is detached from the experience of sex. Whether Theology should incorporate our experience into a theology of sexuality and gender remains a contested issue (for the arguments, see Section 3.2.3).

What did you make of the metaphor of being "turned on"? The quotation was part of a chapter entitled "Whatever Turns You On." That phrase sounds too much like a glib 1960s colloquialism (in use when I was a teenager) that appeared to sanction debauchery. The suggestion that we are like taps or machines which can be turned on and off is also unfortunate but the phrase has been deliberately chosen. There is recognition that our sexualities are formed by complex and still little-known processes, which the successors of Freud and Jung are still busily researching. Ind notes "our childhood experiences have a key role in the sexual adults we become" (2003, p. 60). We have had no control over these processes, and so we are importantly not responsible for them. What arouses us, the "trigger-mechanisms" that get us thinking about and wanting sex, vary considerably from person to person and we cannot help being endowed with the sexualities we have. Ind's fine insight is that we should resist any temptation to feel guilty about what turns us on because we did not choose to be this, or any other, way. (This is a point that can be convincingly linked to the theological teaching both that God loves sinners however sinful they are, and that to love ourselves, as well as God and our neighbors, is a Gospel requirement.)

Do you have any reservations about the quotation? I have two. I thought it was a pity she did not say more about how we like turning others on. The enormous effort and expense that some people (generally women) put into their social appearance might indicate that they are just as concerned about arousing others as they are with becoming aroused themselves.

Did you feel a bit nervous about accepting as good *all* sexualities? The Lutherans were right to stress the ambiguity and hurt that attaches itself to sexuality, weren't they? There are some kinds of eroticism, for example those involving bondage or sado-masochism which many Christians will find problematic. Other kinds are unequivocally patholog-ical, such as pedophilia. If I had been abused as a child, and now desired to abuse children in my adult life, that compulsion would be understandable, but it could never be actionable or acceptable. It would be a distortion of my sexuality that required compassionate treatment.

1.2 How Many Sexes are There?

It may come as a big surprise to learn how different are our contemporary ways of thinking about sex and gender, from the ways of the ancient world and of the Christian tradition down to at least the end of the seventeenth century. The differences are so great that it takes a concerted effort to set aside what we now take for granted about biological sex and gender in order to try to understand how earlier generations understood them. Some beliefs we would probably never think to question are very recent. For example, what we now call the process of ovulation remained undiscovered until the early 1930s (see Section 1.2.3). It took another 30 years for a pill that suppressed ovulation to become available.

Why should we want to re-enter this pre-modern and pre-scientific intellectual universe and actively "un-learn" some of our modern assumptions? Here are three reasons.

First, the strangeness of earlier beliefs about sex and gender, and the discontinuity between those beliefs and many of our own, should help us to see the fragility of our own assumptions and constructions. Our knowledge may be more sound and more broadly based, but we should not assume that we have arrived at the complete truth about sex or anything else.

Second, a better understanding of the history and tradition concerning sex and gender aids contemporary believers in developing it and fashioning it into something believable for ensuing generations.

Third, even in the past 20 years there have been major contributions to the study of gender from the academic disciplines of Classics and Medical History. Theologians would be daft not to take advantage of these, even if the findings appear to make theological trouble for them.

1.2.1 Have there always been two sexes?

The standard view is that there are two sexes, male and female. This view is so securely lodged in Western religion and culture that it may appear devious even to question it. The two sexes are "opposite." Through the rise of the Women's Movement and successive waves of feminism, the "second" or "weaker" sex has successfully challenged the first or stronger sex in its claim to be first and stronger, but it has not until recently sought to challenge the basic premise that there are two and only two, human sexes. The campaigning issue has not been the *number* of sexes, but whether the two sexes received equal treatment, equal rights, and equal respect.

The churches too appear confident that there are two sexes. In the twentieth century, a verse from the opening chapter of the Bible was pressed into service to confirm the cultural truth of two sexes and to proclaim that that is how God intended the human race to be. "So God created man in his own image, in the image of God he created him; male and female he created them" (Gen. 1:27). The greatest Protestant theologian of the twentieth century, Karl Barth (1886–1968) led the way (Barth, 1961, pp. 153–154). It was but a short step to give the two sex doctrine an official title – the doctrine of the "complementarity" of the sexes (see Sections 3.2.1, 10.2.2 and 10.3). A second short step introduces the assumption that each member of the different sexes should desire only members of the other one.

In the face of apparently sealed and settled views, religious and secular, that there are two sexes, it may come as a great shock to learn that for the greater part of Christian history, *it did not occur to anyone even to think that there were two distinct sexes*. There is now a strong challenge to the two-sex theory that is gaining ground in classics, medical history, histories of sexuality and gender, and at last in theology. The idea that there is only *one* sex is of course an incredible suggestion, one to raise the collective eyebrow of any student class. So what lies behind it?

1.2.2 Is one sex enough?

It is probable that Greeks, Romans, Jews, and Christians actually held that there was one sex, not two. That sex was called "man." Christians may actually be more familiar with this than they realize. An instructive way into the one-sex theory can be found in the easy, unexamined sexism of thousands of Christian hymns, still not finally shredded, which provide primary, lingering evidence of the single, male sex. Liturgies proclaim it. Creeds announce it ("We have sinned against you and against our fellow *men*": "For us *men* and for our salvation he came down from heaven." "He became incarnate of the Virgin Mary, and was made *man*."). Vatican texts still require it. We will linger a little in

> **Sexism:** Sexism is the privileging of one sex and its interests over the other sex and interests. Any assumption that one sex is more perfect, or more valuable, or more representative than the other, or is to be included within the other, is sexist.

thinking about sexism, not just to denounce it, but more importantly to understand it as *preserving for us an earlier way of thinking about male and female.*

Activity: Can you think of any examples of sexism in hymns? What messages do your examples convey? Are they evidence for the old view that there is one sex, not two?

Comment: Mine include "Good Christian men rejoice," and "Brothers, this Lord Jesus shall return again." They are embarrassingly exclusive, aren't they? And "I cannot tell why He, whom angels worship, should set His love upon the sons of men," really sticks in my throat. If there are two sexes, then it is clearly sexist to privilege one over the other. But the important point to take from these and your own examples of sexism in hymns is the recognition that their authors would not have considered themselves sexist (the term would have been unfamiliar to them) or exclusive, or demeaning to women. They were just perpetuating the unexamined assumptions that there was one sex – man – and that women were included in this sex as silent, imperfect, and inferior members. In a strange way, then, the one-sex theory *is* inclusive. It must be, for "man" is the single generic term that includes men and women within itself.

Two genders, one sex? Let's go into this claim about a single sex in a bit more depth. What does it mean to say that for the greater part of Christian history, and before, there lay a world "where at least two genders correspond to but one sex, where the boundaries between male and female are of degree and not of kind" (Laqueur, 1990, p. 25)? As we shall see, there were plenty of people who were thought to be neither male nor female, or even to have shifted from one to the other. A useful way into the one-sex theory is through ancient ideas about human reproduction. How did the ancient world think it made babies?

Ancient conceptions of conception To start with, the Greek doctor Galen (*c.*129–*c.*216 CE) taught that men and women had the same set of genitals. This belief was already old in Galen's time, yet it continued in the West until around 1750. A principal sexual difference between women and men was that women held their genitals within their bodies; men displayed them outside. A woman had a penis, but it is turned inwards. (The word "vagina", which is Latin for "sheath," did not begin to be adopted in a medical context until about 1700.) A woman had testicles. That was why she was always wanting sex. We now know her testicles are ovaries. And her womb was "really" a scrotum tucked away.

There were two main classical theories about human reproduction. The earlier one is found in Aristotle (384–322 BCE) who held that the male provided the "form" of the newly conceived child, while the mother provided the "matter." The Latin for mother, *mater*, derives from the one who provides the *materia* for the child to grow in the womb. However, Aristotle had little idea what *sperma*, or seed, was. He thought the male body "was able to concoct food to its highest, life-engendering stage, into true sperma" (Laqueur, 1990, p. 30). There was no fertilization, of course, since there was no egg to fertilize. Sperm conveyed the "sensitive soul" or life, and the *hotter* the ejaculate, the more likely was the resulting child to be male. The matter the female provided was her *catamenia*, or menstrual blood. Since the process of menstruation was not understood for more than two millennia, discharged blood was thought to be "a plethora or leftover of nutrition." Pregnant women did not menstruate because their blood was nourishing the child in the womb.

Aristotle's theory of conception, and indeed his thought generally, was lost to most of the first millennium of Christendom, but it was reintroduced in the thirteenth century CE, through translations of Arabic editions of Aristotle's works, which greatly influenced Thomas Aquinas (*c.*1225–1274). Through Aquinas, Aristotle came to influence Roman Catholic, and to a lesser extent Protestant thought. However, the medical professions of Europe largely held to Galen's teachings.

The Christian Lactantius (*c.*250–*c.*325 CE) taught that when a masculine seed entered the right part of a uterus, or a feminine seed entered the left part, a boy or a girl respectively, with the potential gender characteristics of male and female, would be born. However, when a masculine seed entered the left part, or a feminine seed entered the right part, then the boy would acquire feminine characteristics or the girl male ones (Kuefler, 2001, pp. 21–22). Here then is an ancient speculation about the biological origins of intersex and transgender people (see Section 1.2.4).

Galen thought that a child was concocted from the sperm of men *and women.* Just as a man ejaculates when he has an orgasm, so does a woman. (Remember: women have the same equipment.) Male and female provide two versions of the same substance. Their efforts concur: their sperms coagulate, and these are what the female retains and nourishes in her body. The woman's orgasm is therefore essential to conception. This later view of conception became dominant in Western medicine. But there is a vital difference between his sperm and hers. His sperm has greater *heat* than hers; and his sperm is more *perfect.*

1.2.3 Hot men – cool women

Laqueur says the belief in men's greater heat operates like "a great linguistic cloud" (1990, p. 27) that mists over the entire phenomenon it enshrouds. Men are hotter than women because they are more perfect. That they carry their genitals outside their bodies is an instance of their greater heat. Bodies were believed to be filled with four basic substances called "humors." "Women were governed by cold and wet humors, men by hot and dry humors, with the result that all people were on a scale of male to female, according to the quantity and quality of humors they had" (Shaw, 2007, p. 223).

Men's semen was thought to be thicker than women's because it was hotter (as its bubble-like, foam-like, white hot appearance was thought to convey). It was thought that the hotter the semen, the greater the likelihood of a male child. Men troubled by reaching orgasm too quickly ("premature ejaculation") or at all (during "nocturnal emissions") were to avoid spicy foods (as well as lustful thoughts) that heated their bodies unnecessarily. For the purpose of reproduction, a short penis was preferred to a long one, because the longer the distance the semen traveled, the more likely it was to cool before it mingled with its female counterpart.

Women having difficulty with ejaculation were counseled to attend to their "chief seat of delight," which "by rubbing thereof the seed is brought away" (Fletcher, 1995, p. 37). When it became known that ovulation was a silent, natural process, it became obvious that women's orgasms were not, as had been thought for thousands of years, *necessary* for conception to happen. Grant the widespread premise that the purpose of sex was having children, and the further (accurate) premise that women's orgasms were unnecessary for the purpose of sex to be achieved, it was but a short step to the conclusion (of men) that women's orgasm was also undesirable, and preferably avoidable. As Laqueur observes,

> For women the ancient wisdom that "apart from pleasure nothing in mortal kind comes into existence" was uprooted. We ceased to regard ourselves as beings "compacted in blood, of the seed of man, and the pleasure that [comes] with sleep." We no longer linked the loci of pleasure with the mysterious infusing of life into matter. Routine accounts, like that in a popular Renaissance midwifery text of the clitoris as that organ "which makes women lustful and take delight in copulation," without which they "would have no desire, nor delight, nor would they ever conceive," came to be regarded as controversial if not manifestly stupid. (1987, p. 1)

The assumption, held until at least the end of the seventeenth century was that

> Woman was seen as a creature distinct from and inferior to man, distinguished by her lesser heat. For heat was the source of strength, and strength, whether of mind, body or moral faculties, was in this formulation what gender was all about. (Fletcher, 1995, p. xvi)

Again, the influence of Aristotle and Galen is clearly traceable. Galen thought heat was "the immortal substance of life." The male body was not only stronger; it was firmer. Male strength and firmness extended to his greater powers of understanding and discernment.

The cloud of mystery which surrounded the superstition about male heat seems to have enveloped Alexander Ross's medical textbook of 1651:

> The male is hotter than the female because begot of hotter seed . . . and because the male hath larger vessels and members, stronger limbs, a more porie skin, a more active body, a stronger concoction, a more courageous mind and for the most part a longer life; all which are effects of heat . . . the fatness, softness and laxity of the woman's body, beside the abundance of blood which cannot be concocted and exhaled for want of heat argue that she is a colder temper than men . . . her proneness to anger and venery argue imbecility of mind and strength of imagination not heat. (Fletcher, 1995, p. 61)

Perfect men – imperfect women Aristotle and Galen both made the assumed link between *heat* and *perfection*. It remained unchallenged for many centuries. Galen echoes Aristotle in stating "Now just as mankind is the most perfect of all animals, so within mankind the man is more perfect than the woman, and the reason for his perfection is his excess of heat, for heat is Nature's primary instrument" (Conway, 2008, p. 165).

The assumption that the bodies of men were more perfect than those of women goes some way towards explaining why it would have provoked incredulity in the ancient world for the Incarnation of God to have occurred in the imperfect body of a woman. The vital link to human perfection would have been lacking.

The single continuum The male, socially and biologically superior, was expected to exercise control over his body, an achievement more difficult or even impossible for women whose unruly behavior and desires required constant male surveillance. In the one-sex model of men and women, biological sex exists on a *single continuum*, from male to female. Not only did men and women have similar sex organs. Their bodies were thought to contain the same fluids (blood, milk, fat, sperm, among them) which were "fungible," that is, they "turn into one another" (Laqueur, 1990, pp. 19, 31). But there was a greater worry about fungibility. This too is a strange feature of the one-sex theory. People believed that it was possible for men to become women and for women to become men by sliding down or climbing up the "gender gradient" (see Section 2.3).

The ancient world took for granted that men were capable of erotic response to other men and to women. The worry was that when men became passive partners in sexual exchanges, they importantly failed to remain men. Women were for penetration: men were penetrators. Men who behaved in a camp or effeminate manner were in danger of becoming "feminized." Conversely, women who actively took the initiative in sexual experience, or who enjoyed sex too enthusiastically, were held to be usurping masculine roles.

Discussion: Students sometimes ask what the difference is between the ancient assumption that there is a single sex on a single continuum from male to female, and the modern assumption that male and female are two sexes. Isn't it just playing with words? Is that your reaction to the one-sex theory as well?

Comment: It is tempting to think the one-sex theory really is a lot of fuss about little or nothing; that it is words, rather than bodies, that are "fungible." I think that would be an understandable, though hasty, mistake for several reasons.

One sex, two genders First, the one-sex theory helps us to get behind modern assumptions that there are two sexes; that these are "opposite," and that all individuals should be assigned to one or the other. Sexual difference has not always been construed in ways we now take for granted, even if our modern way is to be preferred. The main difference between ancient and modern views is not principally numerical, but "spectral" (Swancutt, 2006, p. 71). That is, there existed a single spectrum from male to female, which assumed many gradations of power, strength, excellence, virtue, heat, status, and so on.

Second, if there is only one sex, all discussion about the *equality* of the sexes is simply misplaced and misconceived, because there are not two sexes to start with, and so no serious conversation can start about the relations between them. Indeed any "battle of the sexes" only serves to reinforce the idea that there are two sexes slogging it out. That does not mean that all the campaigning done by women for equality has been in vain. It *does* mean that, *if* there is only one sex, the arguments about sexual difference are really about *gender*. That is an important conclusion, since gender (see Chapter 2) is about what we do with the sexual differences we have. These issues are far from settled.

Third, then as now, becoming a man or a woman is an achievement that has as much to do with the social and cultural influences upon us and the opportunities open to us as it does with our own strivings.

Fourth, there was a real fear that in the ancient world, a man, by inappropriate sexual and social behavior, might cease to be regarded as a man: indeed if he were to become an effeminate man then in a real sense he would have already ceased to be a man. He would have become "unmanly." The ancient body "lacked stability." There was "no certainty that a masculinity earned was a masculinity saved. The specter of lost manliness, of a slide into effeminacy, was frequently raised before the eyes of the literate male audience" (Conway, 2008, p. 17).

Fifth, our belief in opposite sexes may have led to a weakening of our sense of commonality in being flesh and blood. The earlier belief in near-identical reproductive systems (even though it was wrong), and in our common experiences of sexual pleasure, may have combined into a solidarity which the division of human nature into two sexes has undermined.

Despite the arguments which favor the one-sex theory, it is important to register a caveat against it. The belief in the imperfection and inferiority of women in relation to men in the pre-modern world still caused a deep division between them. This division is similar to, and as sharp as, any of the divisions occurring in the modern battle of the sexes. That is why another leading classical scholar, Mathew Kuefler, who accepts the theory of a single continuum, warns against reading too much into the assumed biological sameness of men and women. "It has been suggested," he says, "that this notion implied a single sex, but it is more true to say that men and women were perceived as 'opposite sexes' in a very literal manner" (Kuefler, 2001, p. 20; see also p. 90).

1.2.4 Three sexes or more?

Suppose modern culture has it right: there is not one sex in two kinds; there are two separate sexes. Do not intersex and transgendered people add the sexes up to three or more?

Intersex and transgender people

These definitions are supplied in part by intersex and transgender people themselves (Intersex Society of North America, 2009). How many intersex people are there? Problems of definition, classification, and disclosure make that question difficult to answer. In 2000 the leading expert on the condition offered an "order-of-magnitude estimate" based on available medical literature in the United States of America: *1.7% of all births* (Fausto-Sterling, 2000, p. 51). There are several conditions that count as "intersex," with names such as Congenital Adrenal Hyperplasia, Androgen Insensitivity Syndrome, and Gonadal Dysgenesis (Fausto-Sterling, 2000, pp. 52–54; and see Dreger, 1998).

The intersex condition has been known from time immemorial, but the term "intersexuality" was not introduced until 1920 (Hird and Germon, 2001, p. 175). Before then the classical hybrid word "hermaphroditism" was used to cover

Intersex: A general term used for a variety of conditions in which a person is born with a reproductive or sexual anatomy that doesn't seem to fit the typical definitions of female or male. For example, a person might be born appearing to be female on the outside, but having mostly male-typical anatomy on the inside. Or a person may be born with genitals that seem to be in-between the usual male and female types – for example, a girl may be born with a noticeably large clitoris, or lacking a vaginal opening, or a boy may be born with a notably small penis, or with a scrotum that is divided so that it has formed more like labia.

Transgender: People who identify as transgender or transsexual are usually born with typical male or female anatomies but feel as though they've been born into the "wrong body." For example, a person who identifies as transgender or transsexual may have typical female anatomy but feel like a male and seek to become male by taking hormones or electing to have sex reassignment surgeries. Some transgender people are cross-dressers. Others are not. They sometimes wear clothing associated with a sex their bodies are not.

all intersex people, and the use of that term still lingers.

Until the nineteenth century, lawyers and judges were the "primary arbiters of sexual status" (Fausto-Sterling, 2000, p. 40). When there was doubt they decided whether a child was a boy or a girl, and they consulted with doctors and priests when necessary. By the 1930s however, "medical practitioners had developed a new angle: the surgical and hormonal suppression of intersexuality." Many intersex people who had and still have "corrective" surgery as babies, come greatly to resent the operations performed on them. Fausto-Sterling advocates an immediate cessation of the practice. "Stop infant genital surgery," she demands, "We protest the practices of genital mutilation in other cultures, but tolerate them at home" (Fausto-Sterling, 2000, p. 79).

> **Hermaphrodite:** In Greek mythology, Hermaphroditos was the child of Aphrodite and Hermes. After being seduced by the nymph Salmacis, he was transformed into an androgynous being, that is, s/he had both masculine and feminine characteristics and so had an ambiguous sex.

Fausto-Sterling sees corrective surgery as a sociocultural enforcement of the two-sex theory. The cultural imperative to correct and improve on nature is cruel and mistaken. "Unruly bodies" which are literally "between" the sexes challenge the rigid binary of male and female. In 1990, she argued, tongue-in-cheek, for a *five*-sex system, adding "herms," "merms," and "ferms" to male and female (Fausto-Sterling, 2000, p. 78) (A "merm" identified himself as a male with mixed anatomy; a "ferm" identified herself as a female with mixed anatomy.) Fausto-Sterling no longer advocates this because it perpetuates the classification of people according to their genitals (Fausto-Sterling, 2000, p. 110). Nonetheless the suggestion drew attention to the sexual diversity nature bestows upon us.

> *Question:* Do you think that intersex people (some of whom *have* suffered cruelly by being "gender assigned" in order to conform to a compulsive and uncritical adoption of the two-sex theory in societies that can afford surgeons) are entitled to be regarded as a *third* sex?

> *Comment:* The question is, of course, a loaded one, but it raises highly complex issues. It may even be wrong to assume two sexes before asking whether a third might be added. The people whose opinion counts are intersex people themselves, and some of them are very critical of attempts to "normalize" them. It is surely right to point out that intersex people would be subject to less pressure to become normal if they lived in societies that were less insistent on opposite sex norms (Cornwall, 2008, 2010). The two-sex theory reinforces surgical procedures and in some versions, religious teaching sanctions it.

Two-spirit people Anthropologists sometimes speak of a "third sex" (Farley, 2006, pp. 152–153). Some Native American tribes contained *berdaches*, men and women, now called "two-spirit" people, who adopted the gender roles associated with the biological sex that they were not. There are *leiti* in Tonga, and *fa'afafine* in Samoa. These are "men who identify themselves as women" (Halapua, 2006, p. 26). The *kathoeys* of Thailand, the "ladyboys" of Brazil, and many other groups of people throughout the world, are regarded by some anthropologists as a third sex. A two-spirit person who is also an indigenous

American, an Episcopalian priest, and in a covenanted relationship with a female partner, has spoken candidly of her spiritual journey and gender identity. She explains how "some Native (North) American cultures understand a multi-gendered system valuing gender diversity – male, female, male females, female males and non-specific genders and a balance of male and female known to some as 'Two Spirit'" (Galgalo and Royals, 2008, p. 244). She declares that:

> Being Two-Spirit is as much about spirituality as it is about sexuality. The ambiguity of these roles and identities poses a challenge for understanding them in the context of predominant cultures who identify sexuality as only male or female and spirituality as a relationship with God defined through religion. (Galgalo and Royals, 2008, p. 245)

Being "Two-Spirit" helps straight people to gain a glimpse of what it is like to live in a world where the binary-sexed world is not the only real world (Cornwall, 2008, 2010). Indeed, Two-Spirit people can remind the rest of us that they, and other sexual minorities, undergo real oppression by being treated as strange.

1.3 Having Sex

I hope you agreed that the question "How many sexes are there?" was worth asking, and, if it did not receive a simple answer, it raised important issues about how we view sexuality at the present time. "What is it to 'have sex'?" similarly undermines standard answers yet helps us to re-think sexual practices. In 1997–1998 that question confused half the world. Bill Clinton, the President of the United States, denied having "sexual relations" with a White House employee, Monica Lewinsky. They had had (to say the least) mouth-to-penis sexual contact, but, according to the official report into the affair, Clinton "maintained that there can be no sexual relationship without sexual intercourse, regardless of what other sexual activities may transpire. He stated that 'most ordinary Americans' would embrace this distinction" (Starr Report, 1998, p. 1C1b). Sexual relations happen, according to the definition Clinton used,

> when the person knowingly engages in or causes . . . contact with the genitalia, anus, groin, breast, inner thigh, or buttocks of any person with an intent to arouse or gratify the sexual desire of any person . . . "Contact" means intentional touching, either directly or through clothing.

Clinton was able to deny having sexual relations with Lewinsky, not just because he had not penetrated her, but because she had used her *lips* on his penis, and lips are not included in the definition of sexual relations that Clinton used. (The old Latin name for this practice is *fellatio.*) She had had sexual relations with him (she had had contact with his "genitalia" by "fellating" him). He had not had sexual relations with her.

Having sex: students have their say The confusion about what constitutes having sex was shared and confirmed by 600 college students who, in 1999, were asked "Would you say you 'had sex' with someone if the most intimate behavior that you engaged in was …?" (Sanders and Reinisch, 1999, pp. 275–277). They answered a questionnaire inviting them to say whether they thought a range of activities including oral sex (mouth to penis or mouth to vagina contact) and anal sex (penile–anal intercourse) amounted to having sex. (The old Latin name for mouth to vagina contact is *cunnilingus*). Of the respondents 60% thought that having oral sex was not having sex, and 20% thought even penile–anal intercourse was not having sex either. I have repeated the questionnaire in classes with similar results. All the students thought that penile–vaginal intercourse was having sex.

The students' replies invite several comments. First, by identifying "having sex" with "having sexual intercourse," students may be expressing a long-held Christian view – that the purpose of having sex *is* to be open to the possibility of conception. Students who think that having anal sex is having sex (without necessarily approving of it) do so on the basis of the invasiveness involved. The few who think it is not having sex seem to do so again on the ground of it being a sterile act.

Second, there is a wide range of activities or behaviors that people engage in, which involve physical intimacy, but which they do not regard as having sex.

Third, while no-one doubted that penile–vaginal intercourse *is* having sex, even that small conclusion could be sensibly doubted. In Roman Catholic canon law, a marriage is not consummated just by a husband penetrating his wife (with his penis). The spouses must "have in a human manner engaged together in a conjugal act in itself apt for the generation of offspring" (Code of Canon Law, 1983, p. 1061.1). He must ejaculate while he is still inside her. The oldest known (and unreliable) contraceptive method is the withdrawal of a penis from a vagina before ejaculation (the old Latin name for this practice is *coitus interruptus*). That is not consummation. Is it having sex? I would say so. Would you?

Questions: What do *you* mean by the expression "having sex?"
Was President Clinton right to say there can be no sexual relationship without sexual intercourse?

Comment: The fact that we may be initially puzzled about what constitutes having or not having sex, suggests we may be thinking of an important boundary or threshold in our shared intimacies which having sex crosses. I suggest a straight fertile couple crosses that boundary when they have penile–vaginal sexual intercourse. Sexual activity that may result in bringing a child into the world is most definitely in a class of its own. That is why, of course, Christian teaching limits having sex to marriage. (In future chapters the term "sexual intercourse," like the Latin expressions just used, will be avoided. It is coy and cumbersome. "Having sex" is better; it is no longer an offensive expression, and it is in common use.) It is probably better left to people themselves whether they think their shared erotic activities constitute having sex or not.

In this chapter we have thought about the meaning of sexuality, and discovered that it is a recent term with broad, rich meanings, but it is also complicated and ambiguous. We compared ancient and modern theories of sex and of reproduction, and found an unexpected disjunction between many of our modern assumptions and those held in ancient times. We noted that the two-sex theory is undermined by people who do not, and do not wish, to conform to it. By asking what we think we do when we have sex, we began to raise questions about the different forms of intimate behavior and the meanings we give them. Behind all these topics, of course, lies *gender*, the subject of the next chapter.

References

Barth, K. (1961) *Church Dogmatics*, III/4, T&T Clark, Edinburgh.

Code of Canon Law (1983) www.catholicdoors.com/misc/marriage/canonlaw.htm (accessed November 3, 2010).

Cornwall, S. (2008) The *kenosis* of unambiguous sex in the body of Christ: intersex, theology and existing "for the other." *Theology and Sexuality*, 14(2), 181–200.

Cornwall, S. (2010) *Sex and Uncertainty in the Body of Christ: Intersex Conditions and Christian Theology*, Equinox, London.

Conway, C.M. (2008) *Behold the Man – Jesus and Greco-Roman Masculinity*, Oxford University Press, Oxford.

Dreger, A.D. (1998) *Hermaphrodites and the Medical Invention of Sex*, Harvard University Press, Cambridge.

ELCA (Evangelical Lutheran Church of America) (2009) Human Sexuality: Gift and Trust. www.elca.org/What-We-Believe/Social-Issues/Social-Statements/JTF-Human-Sexuality.aspx (accessed November 3, 2010).

Farley, M. (2006) *Just Love: A Framework for Christian Sexual Ethics*, Continuum, New York/London.

Fausto-Sterling, A. (2000) *Sexing the Body: Gender Politics and the Construction of Sexuality*, Basic Books, New York.

Fletcher, A. (1995) *Gender, Sex & Subordination in England 1500–1800*, Yale University Press, New Haven/London.

Galgalo, J., and Royals, D. (2008) Christian spirituality and sexuality, in *The Anglican Communion and Homosexuality* (ed. P. Groves), SPCK, London, pp. 239–265.

Halapua, W. (2006) *Moana* waves: Oceania and homosexuality, in *Other Voices, Other Worlds – The Global Church Speaks Out on Homosexuality* (ed. T. Brown), Darton, Longman and Todd, London, pp. 26–39.

Hird, M.J., and Germon, J. (2001) The intersexual body and the medical regulation of gender, in *Constructing Gendered Bodies* (eds. K. Backett-Milburn and L. McKie), New York, Palgrave, pp. 162–178.

Ind, J. (2003) *Memories of Bliss: God, Sex, and Us*, SCM Press, London.

Intersex Society of North America (2009) What is intersex? www.isna.org/faq/what_is_intersex (accessed November 3, 2010).

Kuefler, M. (2001) *The Manly Eunuch: Masculinity, Gender Ambiguity, and Christian Ideology in Late Antiquity*, University of Chicago Press, Chicago/London.

Laqueur, T. (1987) Orgasm, generation, and the politics of reproductive biology, in *The Making of the Modern Body: Sexuality and Society in the Nineteenth Century* (eds. C. Gallagher and T. Laqueur), University of California Press, Berkeley, pp. 1–41.

Laqueur, T. (1990) *Making Sex: Body and Gender from the Greeks to Freud*, Harvard University Press, Cambridge, MA/London.

Sanders, S.A., and Reinisch, J.M. (1999) Would you say you "had sex" if...? *JAMA: Journal of the American Medical Association*, 281(3) (Jan.), 275–277.

Shaw, J. (2007) Reformed and enlightened Church, in *Queer Theology: Rethinking the Western Body* (ed. G. Loughlin), Blackwell, Malden, MA/Oxford, pp. 215–229.

Starr Report (1998) www.time.com/time/daily/scandal/starr_report/files/ (accessed November 3, 2010).

Swancutt, D. (2006) Sexing the Pauline body of Christ: scriptural sex in the context of the American Christian culture war, in *Toward a Theology of Eros – Transfiguring Passion at the Limits of Discipline* (eds. V. Burrus and C. Keller), Fordham University Press, New York, pp. 65–98.

USCCB (United States Conference of Catholic Bishops) (1991) *Human Sexuality: A Catholic Perspective for Education and Lifelong Learning*, USCCB, Washington, DC.

Wittgenstein, L. (1972) *Philosophical Investigations*, 3rd edn. (trans. E. Anscombe), Blackwell, Oxford.

2

Gender

Language, Power, and History

This second introductory chapter asks what gender is and how the term is used. It draws on ancient and contemporary thought. It examines the contention that gender is a verb, something to be *done*, or *undone*, and so not a conceptual noun to be grasped. The workings of gender are illustrated from a "gendered" passage from the New Testament (Section 2.1). Relations of gender rely heavily on the use of *language*, and on the exercise of types of social *power* that some people have over others. These are explained and analyzed (Section 2.2). Section 2.3 continues the analysis of gender in the time of Jesus that was begun in Chapter 1.

2.1 Gender

The ancient Greeks and Romans thought that the bodies of men were *hotter* than the bodies of women (see Section 1.2.2). Modern American slang still has a use for these "caloric" (about heat) metaphors, especially "cool" and "hot" in relation to sexed bodies. "Dudes" are *cool*: but "chicks" are *hot*! These strange and contradictory surmisings about the relative temperatures of male and female bodies illustrate well the principal meaning of a core concept for this book: *gender*. For at least 2,500 years the dubious conceptual move was made from apparent *biological* facts about male and female bodies to apparent *moral* facts about male–female *relations*. While various facts *can* be discerned about, say, the general size and physical strength of male bodies when compared with female ones, the attempt to ground alleged *moral* facts about the ontological or hierarchical inferiority of women upon the existence of their cooler, inferior bodies, is, to say the least far-fetched. (But there may be some silliness in our perspectives too.)

Most theorists agree with Laqueur that "no historically given set of facts about 'sex' entailed how sexual difference was in fact understood and represented at the time;" and his

God, Sex, and Gender: An Introduction, First Edition. Adrian Thatcher.
© 2011 Adrian Thatcher. Published 2011 by Blackwell Publishing Ltd.

more general claim "that no set of facts ever entails any particular account of difference" (Laqueur, 1990, p. 19). How men and women think about their relations with each other should not be based on biology, and when appeals to biology are made, the inferences drawn are likely to be misleading. These claims help us to see that culture borrows from nature, often illegitimately. Of course there are biological differences between men and women. Problems arise when actual or alleged biological differences entail assumptions about degrees of greater or less in the interpersonal realms of value, dignity, worth, greater capacities of intellect, soul or spirit, or greater entitlements to the exercise of power and control, and so on.

Gender – some characteristics   What, then, is "gender?" Let's now examine some statements about gender from Harriet Bradley's recent book, *Gender*.

> Gender refers to the relations between women and men. (2007, p. 1)

> [G]ender is a social construct; it is a category used by human beings as a way of dividing up the world they perceive around them and making sense of it. (2007, p. 3)

> Gender affects every aspect of our personal lives. Whether we identify as a man or a woman determines how we look, how we talk, what we eat and drink, what we wear, our leisure activities, what jobs we do, how our time is deployed, how other people relate to us. (2007, p. 6)

> [A]ll the institutions which make up our society (marriage, families, schools, workplaces, clubs, pubs, political organizations) are themselves *gendered* and are locations in which the *gendering* of individuals and relationships takes place. (2007, p. 6)

The statements confirm that relations of gender are *universal*. They are *constructed*, like the discourse of gender that analyzes them. They are *pervasive*, percolating down to habits of dress and speech. And they are *mediated by institutions*. (They are also conveyed by class and what sociologists call worlds of production, reproduction, and consumption. See Bradley, 2007, pp. 88–167.)

Churches, like mosques and synagogues, are hugely important institutions in "gendering" the people who attend them, in shaping them as men and women, in mediating to us beliefs and practices about ourselves in relation to people of the other sex. Some of these beliefs and practices are so deeply embedded in ourselves and the various groups we belong to that we may never question them. Bradley does not mention religious institutions in her list of examples. Perhaps in "post-religious" societies like Scandinavia or Britain, she thinks the gendering influence of Christianity has become too weak to deserve a mention?

However, all religions have teachings about the relations between men and women, and how these are to be conducted. When Christians lacking a penis are, for that reason, deemed unfit to represent the male Christ as priests, or become preachers, deacons or elders in Nonconformist Churches, or even read the Gospel in others; or when mosques arrange worship for men only; or when synagogues segregate men and women; or when women must cover themselves with a veil in public places; these are practices which already "speak" volumes about how these communities think and practice gender.

We have moved from sex, to sexuality and now in this chapter to gender, and so to a widening of perspectives – from biology, to psychology and now sociology; or from bodies and persons to societies. It is important to notice that these perspectives overlap. In fact they overlap to the extent that while they are separable in *thought*, in actuality they belong together. It is not just that moral conclusions cannot be derived from biological facts. Biology is grounded in the history of science, and factual claims about male and female, based on the possession of XX and XY chromosomes, already belong to the historical and social context where there were strong political pressures to maintain the social distinctions between the biological sexes (Laqueur, 1987). Our sexuality finds expression in relations with other people and so is never only individualized by and in "me." These relations occur in a social context laden with assumptions about gender.

Question: If you attend a place of worship, in what sense might that place already be "gendered." How does "gendering" take place within it?

2.1.1 Doing and undoing gender

Religions which have sacred, foundational texts all have difficulty in interpreting these as their origins become ever more historically distant. Suppose you were to grant the premises that the Divine breaks into the human world, and that the world's major religions testify to original divine revelation. It still would not follow that the pattern of relations between men and women in the social worlds into which divine revelation comes, and which is preserved in those sacred texts, should be preserved as part of the revelation; indeed, there are hints that original revelation queries and starts to transform these relations. Typically religions are *essentialist* about gender, and secular discussions of gender are *constructionist*. These terms have important uses, to be explored next.

Gender essentialism   For Plato (429–347 BCE), essences were more real than "particulars," or existing things. So the essence of beauty, or justice, was prior to beautiful objects or just acts, and somehow inhered or participated in them. On this view, essence is superior to existence. Essences do not change. They are eternal. For Aquinas, the essence of a thing answers the question: what is a thing *for*? The essence of a thing is its *telos*, meaning its "end" or "purpose." He thought the purpose of sexual organs was reproductive. To use them for the purpose of pleasure was contrary to their "essential nature."

"Essentialism" in modern gender theory picks out certain features of early views of essence, in particular, that an essence is something fixed, eternal, fundamental, and utterly basic to the existence of something. Essentialism then becomes a view of gender that almost all secular writers want to throw rocks at. It is the opposite of the more fashionable "constructionism," which replaces it.

There can be little doubt that modern theological views of gender, are essentialist, in that they assert the fixity of two sexes, the dominant–subordinate relations between them, and much else. God creates the two sexes the way they are meant to be, and that is their essence, male and female. God intends members of each sex to desire only members of the opposite

Essentialism: In theological discussions of gender, essentialism is the doctrine that God created humanity in two distinct sexes. Each is made for the other. Our created nature is to be either male or female. Our natures cannot change. Our desires are intended to be for the opposite sex. Same-sex desire cannot conform to our created nature.

Constructionism: This is the view that nothing about gender is fixed; everything is *constructed*. Constructionism is the name given to theories that assume that relations of gender are neither revealed by God nor read off nature, but are historical constructions which are produced by societies and social groups.

sex. While creation is distorted because of the primal sin of Adam and Eve (the "Fall"), creatures still display their essential natures, because they are created by God to be what they are. Heterosexuality is the way we are meant to be. But not all Christians are essentialists, and not all essentialists will be happy with the accompanying definition. Nonetheless it is a start.

Gender constructionism Constructionism stands at the opposite end of a continuum with essentialism. On this view, men and women relate to each other in complex and different ways which are relative to their social and cultural conditions and contexts. These relations are constructed by the societies that produce them. Those societies that appear to have fixed and rigid rules about gender cannot validly appeal to essentialist norms that come from God, or nature, or sacred text, for the rules remain constructions, politically and socially sanctioned and administered.

Theology is able to draw upon each of these opposing positions (Cahill, 1996, pp. 73–107). The basic belief of theism, that God is the Creator, entails another, that we are (the distortion of sin excepted) much as God intended. As a species of created being, God has given us the means of reproducing ourselves. Many of us then, in accordance with the intentions of God, will be powerfully drawn to members of the other sex with one or more of whom we will have sex and possibly children. There is good reason to think that desire and reproduction have existed throughout anthropological time, and so are constant, though not eternal. While there may always have been desire and arousal, there will have been considerable variation in what was found to be desirable and arousing.

It does not follow from this moderate position that God has created *everybody* so that they *must* use their bodies in this way. It is not *essential* for all of us to find sexual fulfillment through intimacy with the other sex, or indeed through intimacy with anyone at all. All species of being can reproduce, but it is not necessary for every individual member of a species to reproduce in order that the species should reproduce.

Essentialism also teaches us to look beyond the shifting and ephemeral fads and fashions of any given culture. Are there not more permanent values to be prized by all generations, past, present, and future? Surely fidelity, commitment, constancy, mutual, reciprocal love, and so on, represent unchanging goods for individuals in any age? But constructionism is also useful to theology. That God should grant to the peoples of the earth responsibility for developing just relations with one another, leaving it to us to construct how these are to work out in practice, is a good example of created freedom that we may exercise in God's name.

Churches too are free to construct new relations of gender which conform to the new life which flows from their being "in Christ" (see Sections 8.1, 8.2, 8.3, 8.4). They do not appear to be in much of a rush. However, it does not follow from a moderate constructionist position that all relations of gender are constructed. Our bodies equip us for different tasks, and our desires are not always directed to the other sex.

Men are generally stronger than women, so in general they may be better suited to tasks requiring strength. Women's bodies are better equipped for bonding with and nurturing children. These are not constructions. They are all too obvious facts about bodies that cannot be ignored. Men and women are likely to respond differently in different cognitive, social, personal, and emotional situations. A very popular book, *Men are from Mars, Women are from Venus* (Gray, 1992) made these points well. It is safe to assume there is something basic about having and being a sexed human body that leads us to respond in the ways we do.

2.1.2 The trouble with gender

The social theorist and constructionist, Judith Butler, in her book *Gender Trouble* (1990) and subsequent volumes, sets out to make "gender trouble" by means of "the mobilization, subversive confusion, and proliferation of precisely those constitutive categories that seek to keep gender in its place by posturing as the foundational illusions of identity" (1990, p. 33). Her targets included the very concepts of sex and gender and their derivatives like heterosexuality and homosexuality. She pioneered and made popular the sense that gender was not to be thought of as something essential, natural or innate, but something that is *performed*, done.

Performing gender?   The idea of *performativity* comes from the philosophy of language.

When a spouse says "With this ring I thee wed," the utterance, along with an activity, accomplishes a performance. A politician declares a new hospital wing open by saying something like "I declare this new hospital wing open." As Butler would have it, we

> **Performativity:** This is the idea that certain things we say perform certain functions just by saying them.

become the women and men we are through the repetition of countless gendered acts every day of our lives. We *perform* our genders through our actions.

We should not jump too quickly to the conclusion that we are *free* to perform gender just as we choose.

> If gender is a kind of a doing, an incessant activity performed, in part, without one's knowing and without one's willing, it is not for that reason automatic or mechanical. On the contrary, it is a practice of improvisation within a scene of constraint. (Butler, 2004, p. 1)

Our wearing that suit, this make-up and perfume, using this coarse expression, making that gesture, and so on, are all learned performances, with peer groups exerting very strong influences on us. Much of our performance is likely to be unthinking, unreflective. When we "do" or perform gendered actions, there are underlying assumptions that we are individual subjects, free to do what we do but, the idea of performativity is a bit trickier. It implies that there is all this performing going on without us being aware of the constructed, repetitive, unreflective character of it. When we *do* become aware of how we are interacting with our peers, friends, families, and so on, we may make our actions more our own by self-consciously affirming, modifying or repudiating them. In this sense freedom begins to make a difference.

The appeal of the phrase "*doing* gender" lies in the contrast between *doing*, an activity, with *being*, a more abstract term with an implication of something passive and static. "Doing gender" draws attention to the constructed, yet pervasive influences that shape us, and our freedom to challenge these. But, as the title of a more recent book of Butler's, *Undoing Gender* (2004), suggests, doing gender is just as much an *un*doing as a doing. There are social arrangements, she calls them "schemes of recognition" (p. 2), which *withhold* recognition from sexual minorities or from transsexual and transgender people, and these are manifestly to be *un*done. But, I suggest, *being* is important too. Only as this man or woman, with these parents and these genes, and this body, can "I" perform any act at all.

2.1.3 Reading gendered texts

We are going to examine an extract from the New Testament letter, 1 Timothy, chapter 2, notorious for its gendered view of women, and ask some questions about how the author constructs male/female relations in his prescriptions for their behavior. (Unless otherwise stated, the translation of the Bible used is the New International Version.)

[8]I want men everywhere to lift up holy hands in prayer, without anger or disputing.

[9]I also want women to dress modestly, with decency and propriety, not with braided hair or gold or pearls or expensive clothes, [10]but with good deeds, appropriate for women who profess to worship God.

[11]A woman should learn in quietness and full submission. [12]I do not permit a woman to teach or to have authority over a man; she must be silent. [13]For Adam was formed first, then Eve. [14]And Adam was not the one deceived; it was the woman who was deceived and became a sinner. [15]But women will be saved through childbearing – if they continue in faith, love and holiness with propriety. (1 Tim. 2:8–15)

Questions:

1. How does gender appear in the passage?
2. What evidence of constructionism is there?
3. What evidence of essentialism is there?
4. How does the author appeal to doctrine in order to substantiate his view of the inferiority of women?
5. Today there are times when many women wear revealing clothes. Should they take this author's insistence on dress codes for Christian women seriously as a counter-cultural alternative?

Comment:

Question 1 Perhaps you looked back at the list of characteristics of gender in Section 2.1 above? Many of them occur here.

First, the passage is clearly about gender because it is about "the relations between women and men."

Second, these relations are a social – or more accurately – a *religious*, "construct." We can watch them in the very act of being set up. They "divide up the world," or rather in this case the Church.

Third, they affect "every aspect" of women's lives. The gendered instructions dictate how women "look," how they "talk" (they don't), and what they wear.

Fourth, the instructions also dictate what women do ("good deeds, appropriate for women . . ."). And they are to have babies.

Fifth, they are to "perform" their gender in a manner "appropriate for women who profess to worship God."

The passage is striking confirmation, is it not, that the Church is a "gendered" institution, a location in which the *gendering* of individuals and relationships takes place?

Question 2   Constructionism is overt, isn't it? Women were taking part in worship, prayer and ministry, and are now told not to. They were the arbiters of how they looked, and are now reproved. New roles are being constructed for them, by a powerful man, consistent with *his* view of women.

Question 3   Essentialism is overt as well, isn't it (indicating that it is often found in religious constructions)? The writer finds timeless values from Genesis 1–3, which he uses for his own pastoral purposes. He probably thought that male authority (p. 12) and female submission were timeless values, eternal truths endorsed by nature.

Question 4   The author uses the story of the Fall (Gen. 3:1–24) in order to legitimize from Scripture, and to deepen his prior view of the inferiority of women. The argument is bizarre, isn't it? Because Adam was created *temporally* prior to Eve (first in order of time), Adam is *ontologically* prior to Eve (first in order of being). (A similar argument is found in 1 Cor. 11:8–10.) He has authority over her. Because Eve was the first to be deceived, all her descendants must take the blame for leading Adam and his descendants into sin. (One might imagine the author had overlooked that Adam had sinned at all.) The answer is an appeal to the essential natures of men and women which doctrine is thought to provide. Most of Christendom remains essentialist about the ministry of women.

Question 5   Christians ought, of course, to think about what they wear. In a culture that flaunts the body and routinely and excessively inflames sexual desire, there is a good case for dressing "counter-culturally." However, those decisions would be based on an alert and informed theology of the body, rather than because this author has insisted on silencing women and rendering them docile?

The point of this activity was not to rail against this male author and his apparent prejudices. It is to provide an example which illustrates how real gendered relations are stated and religiously justified. The exclusion of Christian women from ministry, their dress codes and much else have been influenced for millennia by passages such as these, reinforced by essential norms that are alleged to have come from God.

2.2 Gender, Language, and Power

Language is fundamental to most human activities. We need language to think with. The language we inherit is never just neutral or natural. It already makes assumptions and prompts us to make more assumptions about how and what we think. This is particularly true when we are thinking about sex and gender. The role of language in this area is a vast topic, so I will select a few basic points about it relevant to the argument in the rest of the book.

2.2.1　What's in a name?

First, naming is a primary characteristic of language. Wittgenstein opened his famous *Philosophical Investigations* by describing "a particular picture of the essence of human language. It is this: the individual words in language name objects – sentences are combinations of such names" (1972, p. 2). This is called the reference theory, or the picture theory of language. It is interesting that he connects the theory with an "essence." While he goes on to show that the reference theory is unsatisfactory, it works well for some language uses. Words name objects. Personal names refer to people. When someone says "Adrian," I look round.

Second, naming is a form of "power-over" (Mackey, 1994, p. 38). When Adam named the animals and birds, "the LORD God . . . brought them to the man to see what he would name them; and whatever the man called each living creature, that was its name" (Gen. 2:19). When the infant John the Baptist was circumcised on the eighth day of his young life, his dumb father Zechariah "asked for a writing tablet, and to everyone's astonishment he wrote, 'His name is John'" (Luke 1:63–64). These examples of naming are also fine examples of *performatives* (see Section 2.1.2). The people doing the naming have the power and authority to do so. They name the named by speaking their names. And the named cannot object or refuse their names.

Third, naming is part of a wider discourse. A "discourse" can just be a language people use, but in its more technical sense discourses are "practices that systematically form the objects of which they speak" (Foucault, 1972, p. 149). Sexuality and gender also form discourses. The names given to people to describe their sexual orientation, preferences, and activities, belong to a *medical* discourse. They "form the objects of which they speak," in particular ways.

A good example of the power of medical discourse is the invention of the categories "heterosexual" and "homosexual." The term "homosexual" was coined only in 1869 (Cameron and Kulick, 2003, p. 21). "Heterosexual" is even later, occurring first in German in 1887, and in English in 1892 (Loughlin, 2004, p. 87). A "heterosexual" was at first a term of *deviance*. It named people who had straight sex for pleasure, not just for procreation. Alongside "homosexual" it soon became a *norm*, in fact *the* norm against which most sexual deviance is measured.

About 140 years ago homosexual people were given new labels. They were defined by a medical establishment, and like the animals named by Adam they were unable to refuse these names. A homosexual person came to be identified by his or her sexual orientation and pronounced abnormal. Homosexual and bisexual people were marginalized and rendered both strange and immoral in a sexual system where only one type of desire was to be legitimately expressed. Perhaps intersex people were stigmatized the most by the imposition of this discourse (see Section 1.2.4).

Fourth, vernacular words for having sex also convey meanings about it. Medics and moralists do not have a monopoly on discourse. All sexual groups have an "in" language which they use to speak about themselves and those outside their groups. There are powerful heterosexual sexual discourses among men about women, and among women about men. This too conveys meanings by conflating values with descriptions of body parts and sexual acts. Bradley writes:

> Vernacular words for sexual intercourse, for example, describe the act from the point of view of the penetrative male: banging, shafting, screwing, poking, fucking. Within the tyranny of this phallocentric language, women can only read the universe through the male gaze. (2007, p. 41)

Here again, the power of naming is evident. Here is a discourse of violence, of objectification, of otherness, of contempt, of casual disposal, of heterosexual male camaraderie. This language expresses thoughts and attitudes that reduce people to things, and it reinforces the ancient prejudice that having sex consists of the active male partner doing something impersonal to the passive female partner. There are obvious moral objections to a discourse of this kind.

Fifth, name-calling can sometimes be accepted by minorities who are stigmatized by the names majorities give them and turned into means of resistance against them. Tom Robinson did this for the terms "gay" and "queer" with his 1978 hit song "Sing if You're Glad to be Gay" (still available on YouTube):

> The British Police are the best in the world.
> I don't believe one of these stories I've heard,
> 'Bout them raiding our pubs for no reason at all,
> Lining the customers up by the wall —
> Picking out people and knocking them down,
> Resisting arrest as they're kicked on the ground,
> Searching their houses and calling them queer,
> I don't believe that sort of thing happens here.
>
> Chorus:
> Sing if you're glad to be gay,
> Sing if you're happy that way.

Originally an abusive, derogatory term, aimed at almost any non-conforming, non-heterosexual person, "queer" became accepted, adopted, and reflected back on its users. The use of parody became important in refusing contempt and building self-affirmation, much as "gay pride" marches still do today (Robinson wrote his song for one of these).

Activity: Think of some more vernacular words which groups of people use to describe people who are in other groups. It might be people not just of another sex, or orientation, but another race, or religion, or enemy in war. You might like to discuss these, tactfully, and examine how language works in these cases. How is meaning conveyed, and otherness dealt with?

2.2.2 Gender and power

"Power" is another key concept crucial to the study of sexuality and gender. There are common yet contradictory meanings associated with power. If you "empower" me you enable me to do something freely, yet if you exercise power *over* me you may require me to do something whether I want to or not. For our purposes there are three discernible levels on which power operates – the level of relations between men and women (gender); the level of interaction between social institutions and individuals; and at the transformative level where relations of power can become relations of mutuality.

At the first level it is obvious that gender relations are relations of power, and historically in almost all societies men have had more of it.

This first definition indicates that power is *causal*. Its exercise brings about effects, which those affected may not choose. When this happens, power becomes "power-over."

In relations of gender, power-over often takes the form of *patriarchy*.

"Power-over" in the gendered sense can protect women from predation (as in honor killings when a woman is shamed) but protection comes at a very high price. It reinforces women's vulnerability and their need for protection. Worse, this causal power has historically been used against women to deny them legal and moral rights, and to coerce them into submission, as in cases of domestic violence and rape. This is patriarchal power. "Power-with" is a different exercise of power. It requires power to be shared among those who have it. It relies on cooperation, consultation, co-agency, mutuality, and the achievement of consensus.

Power: This is "a phenomenon which brings about states of affairs and which can be located on a continuum between the extremes of force and authority" (Mackey, 1994, p. 7).

Power-over: Power-over is to be contrasted with "power-with." Power-over is domination. Where there is domination, there is subjugation. Domination requires violence or the threat of violence to maintain itself (Cooper-White, 1995, p. 33).

Power-with: Power-with is "the power of an individual to reach out in a manner that negates neither self nor other. It prizes mutuality over control and operates by negotiation and consensus" (Cooper-White, 1995, p. 33).

Patriarchy: Patriarch is the *archè* (Gr. *rule*) of the *pateres* (*fathers*). It is a type of "power-over." It is a term used in descriptions of the multiple structures, beliefs and practices which ensure that men exercise power over women.

Pervasive social power   The French philosopher Michel Foucault (1926–1984) has been very influential in discussions of sexuality and gender since the publication of his *History of Sexuality* between 1976 and the year of his death. Foucault's understanding of power is more subtly pervasive than patriarchal power and more determining in its operations and effects. This is the second of the three levels. Of the many available summaries of Foucault's understanding of power, Graham's (below) is incisive. As there are complex ideas in the quotation, some words of explanation will follow:

> The rise of the State has involved a series of coercive measures and *institutions* which control the population via a series of *discourses*, which may be medical, moral, theological or

psychotherapeutic . . . knowledge, mediated by powerful scientific practices, becomes a crucial component of the state's maintenance of social control. But *ideology* is exerted at a *somatic* level as well as that of consciousness or propaganda: *hegemonic* institutions operate to coerce physically, via discourses of medicine, sexuality and morality. Definitions of sickness, perversion, insanity and sin are produced by influential institutions that reflect emergent forms of knowledge which serve to maintain strong (but culturally variable) lines of definition between the *normal* and mainstream, and the *marginal* and transgressive. (Graham, 1995, p. 132; emphases added)

Some of this is already familiar to us. *Discourses* (see Section 2.2.1) define their objects without seeking their permission.

The discourse of sexuality began as a medical one, which makes authoritative distinctions between "the normal and the mainstream" and "the marginal and transgressive." Hate-language is also a discourse.

The State operates its power-over us not simply by its police force and its judicial system, but by the *institutions* it operates or permits. Foucault was interested in how madness was defined, how and why people were punished, how religious sanctions were used against believers who pursued apparently sinful practices, and so on. These are all obvious examples of power.

Ideology is a term that may imply that the beliefs that people accept and that influence their behavior, are, if not actually false, powerful constructions which misrepresent their interests (Eagleton, 1991).

The "*somatic level*" is the level that affects bodies, whether the effect is, say, to refuse contraceptive practice because one's Church considers it a sin, or to be incapable of work because the workplace has injured us physically or driven up our stress levels beyond toleration.

A "*hegemonic institution*" is one that occupies a place of predominant influence or social esteem within a society. A university is a good example, exercising power not merely by conferring awards (and also withholding them), but by the expectations it creates, its innumerable regulatory requirements, the research it undertakes, and the knowledge it selects (and therefore also the knowledge it excludes) for its courses.

For Foucault, "power is everywhere. It is not, in itself, either good or evil, it is the sum of actions that constitute social fields, social relations and even subjective understandings of oneself" (Cameron and Kulick, 2003, p. 112). I think it is helpful to extend this broad account of power to the institutions on which we rely heavily for our social and private lives, our entertainment, and especially our music. Huge corporations influence what films we see, what food we eat, what programs we watch on television, what music we download, what branded tracksuits and trainers we work out in, the clothes we wear for work, home and leisure, and so on. However, the *economic* power wielded by global corporations in controlling markets is greatly intensified by the *social* or *imitative* power that they have in influencing us in what we buy, and conferring upon us a principal identity as consumers.

Activity: Think of more examples of pervasive social power and ask yourself how you may be shaped by them.

Foucault's analysis of power, like Butler's analysis of gender, is persuasive, but it leaves several difficulties in its wake. Catherine MacKinnon berates him for failing, in his three-volumed *History of Sexuality*, to identify sufficiently the overt and unrelenting abuse of women as a form of patriarchy or power-over (1989, pp. 126–154). Anthony Giddens complains he "puts too much emphasis upon sexuality at the expense of gender" (1992, p. 24).

Another important criticism of Foucault is the sheer pervasiveness of his understanding of power. If power shapes our thoughts, how can we resist it, since the tools given to us to do this are themselves a product of power? If resistance too is also a power, how do we acquire it? What room is there for freedom if our thoughts are themselves deposits of power that we have sedimented in our minds?

Finally, there may be an issue about whether Foucault's pervasive account of power undermines what are sometimes called "micropractices." These are actual uses of power, in places of work or worship, in partner and family relations, and so on, which are also sites, battlegrounds even, for domination. While it is always helpful to understand how power is diffused and exercised in these places, it can be *disempowering* to regard choices, outcomes and transformations as already determined by previous struggles for power.

Christians *should* be able to make a strong contribution to the social understanding of power because they believe Jesus Christ revealed God's power through the powerlessness of the Cross. They may agree with St. Paul that "the message of the cross is foolishness to those who are perishing, but to us who are being saved it is the power of God" (1 Cor. 1:18). The Gospels and the New Testament letters alike depict Jesus (often, but not always) as a servant (see Section 8.3), rather than a master, powerless rather than powerful, one who co-existed uneasily with powerful institutions like the Temple, the synagogue, the family.

The issue of power and how it is exercised will become central in Chapter 8. There remains the possibility that there still remains a "level of transformation" where suggestions are made about how Christian practice can and does contribute to transformations of power, albeit in the limited areas of sexuality and gender. "Power-over" must become "power-with" if gender relations are to become relations of mutuality. Relations of power must become relations of love.

2.3 Gender in the Time of Jesus

We have already given some attention to gender in the classical world (see Section 1.2). A Christian sexual theology has at least two horizons – the late modern world in which Christians find themselves and the ancient world in which their faith was planted. Sex and gender are intertwined with each other in both worlds. It is important to understand how gender was considered and practiced in the ancient world in order to see how the nascent Christian faith mingled with it and opened up possibilities for its transformation. The task in this section is more simple: to describe some of the features of gender in the ancient world, and so to be in a better position to understand some key passages of the New Testament and subsequent Tradition when we get to them. (Theologians are greatly helped by the new research conclusions of several classicists working in this area, as my indebtedness to them in the present section will show.)

2.3.1 Hard or soft?

Men, we know (see Section 1.2.2) were assumed to have greater *heat*. Another key masculine quality was "hardness" (*duritia, robur*). This was not wholly a phallic characteristic. It "referred to the muscularity of the ideal male body; it also symbolized the moral uprightness and self-discipline that men were presumed to embody" (Kuefler, 2001, p. 21). The opposite quality assigned to women was "softness" or "delicateness" (*mollitia*) which "represented not only their delicate bodies, but also their love of luxury, the languor of their minds, the ease with which they gave themselves to their emotions, and their dissolute morals" (p. 21).

Again, we find the illicit move made from certain assumed biological facts about men to certain moral conclusions, this time about the active and passive sexual roles of men and women:

> The hardness of men marked not only their moral austerity but also their role as sexual penetrators and sexual aggressors. In a complimentary (*sic*) way, the *mollitia* or softness of women denoted their role as sexually penetrated, and beyond that, the passive role they were expected to play not only in sexual relations but also in society generally. (Kuefler, 2001, p. 22; see also Halperin, 1990, p. 30)

The term "spectrum" (see Section 1.2.3) expresses well the elevation of men over women in the ancient world. Diana Swancutt, a strong advocate of the one-sex theory, explains

> ancients did not conceive of the people assigned to the ends of the spectrum as referring to two genetically differentiated sexes, male, and female. Rather, ancients constructed the human physique on a one-body, multigendered model with the perfect body deemed "male/man" (2003, p. 197).

Greek and Roman men were thought to embody "physical and political strength, rationality, spirituality, superiority, activity, dryness, and penetration." Women were thought to embody the negative qualities of "physical and political weakness, irrationality, fleshliness, inferiority, passivity, wetness, and being penetrated" (p. 198). Swancutt stresses that these "opposite" qualities do not at all reflect two opposite sexes. Rather,

> because all bodies were thought to contain more- (masculine) and less-perfect (feminine) elements that required constant maintenance to produce the perfect male/masculine body, females/women and the other gendered beings (e.g., androgynes, *kinaidoi* [effeminates], and *tribades* [dominatrices]) were deemed differently imperfect versions of the male body, versions whose imperfections (e.g., breasts, fat, menstruation, weak sperm, inverted internal penises) were manifestations of their impaired physiological health. (p. 198; emphases and brackets in original)

Élite men, Swancutt says (in a more recent essay) were defined as "hard, rational penetrators" at the top of the social ladder, while "Women occupied its lowest rungs

Androgyne: From the Greek *anèr*, *andros*, "man," and *gunè*, "woman," an androgyne was someone who possessed both male and female sexual characteristics and/or sexual organs.

Kinaidoi (or *Cinaedi*): In Greek, the term was used "to signify an effeminate dancer who used a tambourine and moved his buttocks in suggestively sexual ways" (Conway, 2008, p. 41). It was an offensive, insulting term, associated "with the effeminate sexual role of being penetrated" (Williams, 1999, p. 177; see also Conway, 2008, p. 41).

Tribades (*tribas*, singular): "[A]ll we know about *tribades* is that they [women] were characterized as physically mannish and sexually aggressive … and the reasons for their denunciation are similar to the womanish *cinaedi*, gender transgression (mannish sexual domination) and indulgence of desire" (Swancutt, 2003, p. 200).

because they were soft, leaky, and wild – the least perfect male-bodies, their vaginas deemed undescended penises" (Swancutt, 2006, p. 71).

2.3.2 The gender gradient

Heat, hardness, and perfection, then, were key marks of masculinity. The one-sex male–female species, man, also belonged within a broader social, even cosmic, hierarchy. Greeks and Romans ranked higher than other people of other nationalities; men were ranked higher than women, and women, as Colleen Conway explains, belonged with slaves and animals in the requirement of submission to male authority:

> slaves, too, were like animals, women, and foreigners insofar as they lived lives of submission. In short, understanding what it meant to be a man in the Greco-Roman world meant understanding one's place in a rationally ordered cosmos in which free men were placed at the top and what fell beneath could all be classified as "unmen." (2008, p. 15)

Real men   In contrast with all the unmen, "True men," continues Conway, were set high above all others, "whether these 'others' were slaves, women, boys, foreigners, or men who assumed a passive role in sexual relations" (p. 36). With regard to sexual activity men were definitely on top " acting like a man required one to assume the active role in private sexual practice as well as one's public life" (Conway, 2008, p. 22).

In private sexual practice, Kuefler shows that men expected to receive oral sex, but not to provide it, since it was their prerogative to take pleasure, not to provide it (2001, p. 98). It was understood "quite literally that one must be the actor, rather than one acted upon." "to be active often involved expressing one's dominion over another. To be passive meant to submit to this domination." Aristotle is cited for the assumption that men are more "godlike" than women because, being active, their activity "was linked to the creative activity of the gods" (Conway, 2008, pp. 22, 36).

Michel Foucault, speaking of classical Greece, finds there the same model of active/ passive, or dominant/dominated. Sexual relations, he writes,

> always conceived in terms of the model act of penetration, assuming a polarity that opposed activity and passivity – were seen as being of the same type as the relationship between a superior and a subordinate, an individual who dominates and one who is dominated, one who commands and one who complies, one who vanquishes and one who is vanquished … This suggests that in sexual behavior there was one role that was intrinsically honorable and valorized without question: the one that consisted in being active, in dominating, in penetrating, in asserting one's superiority. (Foucault, 1987, p. 215; *valorize* – give a value to)

The slippery slope   Finally, the gender spectrum was seen as a terrifying gradient – "the gender gradient" (Conway, 2008, p. 50) – down which men could readily slide. There was believed to be a slippery slope to be avoided, from masculinity, through effeminacy, to femininity. Men were haunted by the question "If women were not different in kind, but simply a lesser, incomplete version of men, what was there to keep men from sliding down the axis into the female realm?" (p. 18). Manhood involved constant recognition in public and private behavior, since it was "not a state to be definitely achieved but something always under construction and constantly open to scrutiny" (Gleason, 1995, p. xxii). Evidence for the gender slide could be found not simply in the ambiguous bodies of intersex or hermaphroditic people, but in lapses in the routine behavior of dominating males. In a similar way active, aggressive or "butch" behavior among women led to the accusation that they were attempting to elevate themselves above their social status by becoming men.

This chapter brings our preliminary inquiries into sex and gender to an end. I hope you will agree some small inroads have been made into secular understandings of sex and gender in both ancient and modern worlds. Theological interests straddle both worlds. What does theology say about sex and gender? What are its sources? How does it use them? In the next chapter these questions are taken up.

References

Bradley, H. (2007) *Gender*, Polity Press, Cambridge, UK/ Malden, MA.

Butler, J.C. (1990) *Gender Trouble: Feminism and the Subversion of Identity*, Routledge, London/New York.

Butler, J. (2004) *Undoing Gender*, Routledge, New York/ London.

Cahill, L.S. (1996) *Sex, Gender and Christian Ethics*, Cambridge University Press, Cambridge.

Cameron, D., and Kulick, D. (2003) *Language and Sexuality*, Cambridge University Press, Cambridge.

Conway, C.M. (2008) *Behold the Man – Jesus and Greco-Roman Masculinity*, Oxford University Press, Oxford.

Cooper-White, P. (1995) *The Cry of Tamar: Violence against Women and the Church's Response*, Fortress Press, Ausberg Fortress, MN.

Eagleton, T. (1991) *Ideology. An Introduction*, Verso, London/New York.

Foucault, M. (1972) *The Archaeology of Knowledge and the Discourse on Language*, Pantheon, New York.

Foucault, M. (1987) *The Use of Pleasure (The History of Sexuality, Vol. 2)*, Penguin, Harmondsworth, UK.

Giddens, A. (1992) *The Transformation of Intimacy: Sexuality, Love and Eroticism in Modern Societies*, Polity Press, Cambridge, UK.

Gleason, M.W. (1995) *Making Men: Sophists and Self-Presentation in Ancient Rome*, Princeton University Press, Princeton, NJ.

Gray, J. (1992) *Men are from Mars, Women are from Venus*, Thorsons, London.

Graham, E. (1995) *Making the Difference: Gender, Personhood and Theology*, Mowbray, London.

Halperin, D. (1990) *One Hundred Years of Homosexuality*, Routledge, New York/London.

Kuefler, M. (2001) *The Manly Eunuch: Masculinity, Gender Ambiguity, and Christian Ideology in Late Antiquity*, University of Chicago Press, Chicago/London.

Laqueur, T. (1987) Orgasm, generation, and the politics of reproductive biology, in *The Making of the Modern Body: Sexuality and Society in the Nineteenth Century* (eds. C. Gallagher and T. Laqueur), University of California Press, Berkeley, pp. 1–41.

Loughlin, G. (2004) Pauline conversations: Rereading Romans 1 in Christ. *Theology and Sexuality*, 11(1) (Sept.), 72–102.

Mackey, J. (1994) *Power and Christian Ethics*, Cambridge University Press, Cambridge, UK.

MacKinnon, C. (1989) *A Feminist Theory of the State*, Harvard University Press, Cambridge, MA.

Swancutt, D. (2003) "The disease of effemination:" The charge of effeminacy and the verdict of God (Romans 1:18–26), in *New Testament Masculinities* (eds. S.D. Moore and J. C. Anderson), Society of Biblical Literature, Atlanta, GA, pp. 193–234.

Swancutt, D. (2006) Sexing the Pauline body of Christ: Scriptural sex in the context of the American Christian culture war, in *Toward a Theology of Eros – Transfiguring Passion at the Limits of Discipline* (eds. V. Burrus and C. Keller), Fordham University Press, New York, pp. 65–98.

Williams, C.A. (1999) *Roman Homosexuality: Ideologies of Masculinity in Classical Antiquity*, Oxford University Press, New York.

Wittgenstein, L. (1972) *Philosophical Investigations*, 3rd edn. (trans. Elizabeth Anscombe), Blackwell, Oxford.

3

Theology

Sources and Applications

This chapter concludes Part I. In it, we get familiar with some of the sources the churches use for thinking theologically about sex. Section 3.1 names the sources. Section 3.2 identifies some problems with their use. Section 3.3 considers the ambiguous conclusions of case studies where the sources are applied to contemporary sexual practices.

3.1 Explaining the Sources: Scripture, Tradition, Reason

How do we think *theologically* about sex and gender?

Thinking about sex here means thinking about our obligations to ourselves and our sexual partners. It is not fantasizing about it. It is sexual *ethics*. Philosophical discussions of sexual ethics usually have theories about what is right, or what we ought to do, and these are applied to the possible range of sexual behavior and practice. But thinking *theologically* about sex? How does that go? Insofar as theology is a discipline of thinking done by believers for believers, it will consult some sources that would normally be avoided in philosophical or secular discussions. These sources are crucial for religious understanding. But what are they?

Scripture and Tradition   Of the world's population, 33.32% is Christian (CIA, 2009). Roman Catholics consist of 16.99% of the global population (more than half the world Christian total); Protestants are 5.78%; Orthodox 3.53%, and Anglicans 1.25% of the world population. All Christians believe that divine revelation happened in and through Jesus Christ. They differ over how they appropriate this knowledge 2,000 years later.

The Roman Catholic Church often uses the word "transmission" in relation to the conveying of past revelation to the present day. "Transmission" is a metaphor drawn from communication between satellites, broadcasting stations, and so on, and receivers of their signals. That Church believes there are "two distinct modes of transmission" of the revelation – "Sacred Tradition and Sacred Scripture" (*Catechism of the Catholic Church*, 1994, para. 80). Scripture "is the speech of God as it is put down in writing under the breath of the Holy Spirit" (para. 81). Tradition "transmits in its entirety the Word of God which has been entrusted to the apostles by Christ the Lord and the Holy Spirit." Catholics derive "certainty" from both, and each "must be accepted and honored with equal sentiments of devotion and reverence" (para. 82).

How are Scripture and Tradition to be interpreted? The Magisterium, or teaching office, does that on behalf of all Catholics. "The task of giving an authentic interpretation of the Word of God ... has been entrusted to the living teaching office of the Church alone. Its authority in this matter is exercised in the name of Jesus Christ" (*Catechism of the Catholic Church*, 1994, para. 85). Catholics have little official room to dissent from the Magisterium: "the faithful receive with docility the teachings and directives that their pastors give them in different forms" (para. 87). Finally, there is "the supernatural sense of faith," (the *sensus fidei*) which involves all Catholics, and "manifest[s] a universal consent in matters of faith and morals" (para. 92).

A three-legged stool?   Episcopalians (or Anglicans) state that they too base their beliefs on Scripture and Tradition. (Anglicans worldwide are organized into 44 regional and national churches, and have over 80 million members. The "Church of England" is one of these.) The basis of Anglicanism, their "Articles of Religion," says "Holy Scripture containeth all things necessary to salvation: so that whatever is not read therein, nor may be proved thereby, is not to be required of any man" (Book of Common Prayer, Article 6). For Anglicans there is "a core of commonly held beliefs about human sexuality," the "first" of which is "that God's intention for human sexual activity has been made known to us primarily in Holy Scripture" (House of Bishops' Group on *Issues in Human Sexuality*, 2003: paras. 1.2.4–5).

Anglicans admit difficulties in interpreting the meaning of biblical texts for today, and add Tradition (like Roman Catholics) and Reason to their sources of understanding. This is sometimes called the Anglican "three-legged stool." They admit the term "Tradition" has different meanings: it can mean the Anglican tradition; the creeds of the Church; even "the way in which the Holy Spirit brings the truth about our relationship with God in Christ to which the Scriptures testify alive in a fresh way for the Church of today" (House of Bishops' Group on *Issues in Human Sexuality*, 2.4.15).

The Episcopal Church of the United States helpfully distinguishes four historical meanings of Tradition. Originally, it referred simply to that which had been "handed down to the church from the prophets and the apostles concerning belief in God and God's redemptive work in Christ" (The Episcopal Church, 2010). Next, the term "took on different meanings to include, for example, the authorized teaching of church councils and commonly accepted creedal formulations." Next, it became "an authentic body of teaching in addition to scripture." Episcopalians and Protestants generally rejected this sense, and gave priority to Scripture. Finally Article 34 of the Articles of Religion took "a mediating position," admitting the authority "of the Traditions of the Church," as long as they were not "repugnant to the Word of God, and be ordained and approved by common authority."

Scripture is more authoritative than Tradition. In Catholicism, each is equally important. The Anglicans are clear that Tradition does not require Christians to be facing back in time. Tradition is dynamic, and Christians "need to test tradition against the Scriptures themselves and against the moral convictions of contemporary society, and remember that even the most venerable traditions can be wrong or inappropriate for today" (House of Bishops' Group on *Issues in Human Sexuality*, 2003, 2.4.17). Article 34, just cited, states

> It is not necessary that Traditions and Ceremonies be in all places one, or utterly like; for at all times they have been divers, and may be changed according to the diversity of countries, times, and men's manners, so that nothing be ordained against God's Word.

Changes to Traditions here are clearly authorized, and sometimes required by fidelity to the message of the Bible.

Reason   Reason too has several meanings, and that makes handling it difficult. Anglican bishops discern "two distinct senses" of reason. First, it refers to "the exercise of the human capacity for rational thought" (House of Bishops' Group on *Issues in Human Sexuality*, 2.4.3). Second, it refers to "the moral awareness that human beings have because of their being created in the image and likeness of God" (2.4.4). There is a "basic awareness that all human beings have of what God requires of them in terms of service to him and to their neighbors."

On the one hand, then, Reason is the ability to think, or to think critically. On the other hand Reason is the name given to an alleged universal awareness of God, whether or not the people having it are theists or even religious at all. Catholics have a different name for this: Natural Law.

There is also a third sense given to Reason, where, along with Revelation, it is one of the two modes of human knowledge. There are things that God has supernaturally revealed (Revelation), and there are things that God allows us to find out for ourselves by the use of Reason. On this broad view, Reason rightly embraces the sum of human knowledge, yet with the proviso that human knowledge is relative and contextual. It is also limited by the state of universal wickedness which is thought to taint real knowledge of the world. That is why it requires supplementation by Revelation.

A fourth leg?   Methodists add a fourth leg to the Anglican stool and call it a "Quadrilateral" (Outler, 1980). That fourth leg is Experience. Every moment of our waking lives (not to mention our dreams) is an experience of something, so this fourth category looks to be too broad to be useful. But that would be an unfair judgment. Methodism has always stressed the importance of conversion, of direct experience *of God*. St. Paul wrote that "if anyone is in Christ, the new creation has come: The old has gone, the new is here!" (2 Cor. 5:17). The experience here is one of personal transformation, which in turn may lead to a reordering of personal life, its goals and priorities. That is why the

Methodist Church of Great Britain says "Methodism particularly stresses the importance of our own experience of God's grace working in our lives. We gain wisdom and maturity from life experience, especially when we pray and reflect about our story with other Christians" (Methodist Church, 2009). It links Reason to the command of Jesus to love God with all our mind, and calls Tradition "the wisdom and creativity of Christians over time and across the world."

Finally, the Southern Baptist Convention of the United States. Since Baptists are not strictly speaking denominations or churches in the usual sense, but unions of local churches acting together, it is difficult for Baptists to speak unitedly about very much. But the Southern Baptist Convention has "basic beliefs," the first of which is about the Bible. The Bible "was written by men divinely inspired and is God's revelation of Himself to man. It is a perfect treasure of divine instruction. It has God for its author, salvation for its end, and truth, without any mixture of error, for its matter. Therefore, all Scripture is totally true and trustworthy" (Southern Baptist Convention, 2009).

This appears to be a *one*-legged stool! There is no mention of Reason, or Tradition. Experience is clearly valued by Baptists because of their stress on the need for individual conversion, but it is not mentioned as a means of arriving at theological understanding.

3.1.1 The Churches and the sources

Members of all Churches have to decide for themselves how they are to going to respond to their Church's teachings and their implications for practical living. There seem to be advantages and disadvantages in the positions of all four Churches just mentioned about the sources of theological teaching. In this section we are going to look at some of the problems that any Church is going to encounter if and when it tries to base its teaching about sex and gender on these sources.

The Roman Catholic Church is the oldest Church. Sacred Scripture is the source of its doctrine, while Tradition, equally important, provides unbroken continuity between the faith of the apostles and our own. The perilous work of interpreting Scripture and Tradition faithfully, attractively and convincingly, is done for us. Freedom is to be found in the reception of God's truth, revealed to the apostles, set down in Scripture, handed on by the Tradition, and interpreted by the Church, which has the Holy Spirit to guide it.

3.1.2 Problems with Scripture and Tradition

Activity: Can you think of any problems with this way of using the sources?

Comment: First, you might have wondered whether this view, reassuring though it undoubtedly is for those who embrace it, overlooks obvious facts about the embeddedness of the 66 books of the Bible in a time, a history, and a culture which is importantly different from our own? The fruits of two and a half centuries of historical, critical scholarship help us to appreciate these books in their historic context, yet much of this effort would seem to be wasted if the biblical text is to be invested with some trans-historical and pre-critical meaning.

Second, you might have wondered, together with Anglicans, Protestants, and liberal Catholics, whether the Magisterium always gets the interpretation of Scripture and Tradition right. We shall see that the Magisterium has needed to shift its position on many topics throughout history (see Sections 10.1–10.2), and so may not be able to provide the certainty for believers that it assumes for itself.

Third, with regard specifically to sexuality, it is not disrespectful to ask of the Magisterium whether its members have, or ever could have, the sexual experience that would qualify them to make pronouncements about the sex lives of all Christian people.

Fourth, might we not worry whether this way of presenting faith and doctrine fails to respect the autonomy of believers? Christians *enter* a faith: they cannot make one up and then call it Christian, but they *can* be given a more positive role in coming to conclusions about how to apply it to their lives, and in particular, their sex lives.

3.1.3 Problems with Tradition and Reason

The three-legged stool of the Anglicans seems to support some weight, even if it is less secure than a four-legged chair. The Anglicans do not issue authoritative documents that expect assent. They are more likely to issue *discussion* documents, intended as resources to help Anglicans, *in discussion*, to make up their minds for themselves.

Activity: Can you think of any problems with the Anglican/Episcopalian way of describing the sources?

Comment: It may be difficult to answer that question on the basis of the short preceding paragraphs. There are as many difficulties in interpreting and using Tradition and Reason, as there are in using Scripture. I wonder first, whether you might have thought that the categories are too broad to be used effectively, or even at all? Since the terms have so many different meanings, it becomes difficult to say whether one's thinking is guided by them or not.

Second, while Tradition provides important lines of continuity from the present to the time of Christ and the birth of the Church, these lines also pass through many bloody disputes, cruel practices, intolerant attitudes, and (probably to our minds) superstitious and damaging beliefs. It then becomes more difficult for us to have confidence in the routes through history that those lines have taken.

Similar difficulties attend the use of Reason as a source.

First, there are *many* uses of "Reason", not just the "two distinct senses" which the bishops propose.

Second, "Reason" translates the Greek *Logos*, which also has a huge range of meanings in classical philosophy and theology. The bishops do not mention that, in standard Anglican thought in the nineteenth century, Reason was a synonym for "Spirit," "the Source and Substance of Truths above Sense" (Reardon, 1966, p. 242). It was contrasted with a narrower term, "Understanding," which was sense-bound and concerned only with truths verifiable by the senses. Neither term is used like this today. The bishops think of Reason rather as previous generations would have thought of Understanding.

Third, a function of Reason is criticism, and this function is often directed *against* the claims of faith. Faith and Reason are often set up as opposites, set to do battle with each other. How critical should Reason be when it is used in the *service* of Faith? What is its role as critic? These questions are answerable, but they cannot just be set aside.

Fourth, isn't there something fanciful about associating Reason with a general moral awareness of God, not least because many morally aware people do not associate their moral sensitivity with *any* sense of God? Not only is this an unusual use of the term "Reason," it is contentious, and better expressed by the idea of Natural Law, or perhaps by the idea of Conscience.

Perhaps a way forward is to see Reason in theology as principally that gift of God which enables us to understand the world and ourselves within it? It is the faculty we press into service in the divinely given task of loving God "with all your mind" (Mark 12:30). A green light is then given to the explorations of the sciences and the social sciences, and to have some confidence in what they say. But reason is also critical, and can be used not just to demolish poor arguments but to offer new ones which enable us to love God better.

3.1.4 The problem of Experience

We have seen that Methodists include "Experience" in their "quadrilateral" of sources. This would seem to be an important positive development. Theological reflection on people's experience seems essential. Our sense of loving and being-in-love can lead to a discovery of the divine love. Our sense of how good a good marriage is, or how bad an intolerable marriage is, or what our sexual orientation is, must count for something. Divorced Christians still feel stigmatized: lesbian and gay Christians are still mainly marginalized and in several countries fear for their lives.

For James Nelson and others, experience provides a crucial difference between "sexual theology" and the "theology of sexuality" (Nelson, 1991, pp. 21, 67–71). "A theology of (or about) sexuality tends to argue in a one-directional way: What do scripture and tradition say about our sexuality and how it ought to be expressed?" But sexual theology begins at the other end and asks "What does our experience as human sexual beings tell us about how we read the scripture, interpret the tradition, and attempt to live out the meanings of the gospel?"

Activity: Can you think of any problem about using our experiences as a source of theological reflection?

Comment: I think the Methodists and Nelson are right to insist on the theological value of Experience. But their inclusion of experience among the sources of theology is much disputed. Whether Experience is a valid source matters, and influences greatly what is considered relevant. What follows is a list of arguments from those theologians who would leave it out. There are six. Each of these is met with a counter-argument. The conclusion to be drawn is that Experience is a valid source of Theology. If you want to skip these arguments, feel free to move straight to Section 3.2.

People who oppose an appeal to Experience are likely to argue along these lines:

1. Different groups in the church use the appeal to experience in arguments against one another (Rogers, 2002, p. xx). Experience must always conform to what God wills, and this conformity, not our experience of it, is what matters.
2. There is no such thing as experience in the abstract. Experience is always *of something*. Experience then, can be as wide as life itself. All moments (not just wakeful ones either) provide experiences.
3. Experiences of say, a constricting marriage, a growing awareness of a particular sexual orientation, or of insistent desire, occur over long periods and inevitably demand much interpretation. This interpretation, it is pointed out, does not come from the experience but is brought to it and may distort it.
4. Our experiences can seriously mislead us. Many people have come to believe in God because they have had a life-changing experience of God, often a conversion. But some people come to regret and renounce their conversions. They come to think their experience of God was an experience of something else instead. Experience is not "self-authenticating." We might be mistaken.
5. Theologians with a sense of history sometimes claim that the appeal to experience requires and reflects a turn inwards to the individual subject, against the teachings and traditions of the church. It promotes "individualism." The Protestant churches have split countless times because individuals have privileged their alleged experiences of God above those of other Christians.

In the rest of the book, the assumption will be made that Experience *does* count as a distinct source of theology. The difficulties just listed, unlike the ones that attach to Scripture, Tradition and Reason, can be cleared up without difficulty. In reply, it might be pointed out that:

1. Different groups also use the *Bible* against one another. That is not an argument for not using the Bible. It is an argument for using it well. It is the same with Experience. God's will can be known through our experience.
2. If Experience must be given a determinate meaning (it must be *of* something), fine. It does not need to be considered in the abstract. Sexual theology is about experiences of desire and love. If Experience is removed, sexual theology cannot function.
3. Yes, Experience has to be interpreted. But that hardly counts against it. So does everything else (by means of language). It reminds us that we must do the interpreting carefully.
4. Yes, we can be mistaken, but we can also get things right. We may be easily deceived, but there is no point in even thinking we may be deceived, if there are not times when we are *not* deceived.

5. Yes, "individualism" is a charge often made against people who live selfishly without consideration for others, but that is quite a different matter from taking the experiences of individuals seriously.

So I conclude that Experience *is* an important source for theology. A four-legged stool is more secure than a three-legged one. Particular emphasis must nonetheless be placed on Scripture because it is "primary Tradition" (Thatcher, 2008, pp. 163–165). It takes us nearer to the historic revelation of God in Christ. That is why the furniture metaphor of a stool is of limited value. A real four-legged stool must be symmetrical and each of its legs must be capable of bearing equal weight. The four sources of theology do *not* bear equal weight.

Other sources?   Before we leave our discussion of the sources of theology, it is important to ask whether there are other sources available to help us. There are.

Activity: Can you think of any other sources than those listed?

Comment: Conscience is one. Religious and secular thought alike hold to a faculty which helps us to distinguish between right and wrong actions, and leads to feelings either of rectitude or remorse. Conscience (in Latin, Greek and English) is literally a "knowing together with," which rather belies the popular understanding that conscience is an internal faculty or a private "inner voice." It is rather the ability to acquire moral knowledge in cooperation with other people, and especially with people who are affected by our actions. Conscience helps us to turn regret into resolve – into an opportunity not to repeat past mistakes and vices.

Several theologians have turned to *wisdom* as a theological source. Wisdom is common in the Hebrew Scriptures. Jesus was a teacher of wisdom. David Ford develops a "wisdom interpretation" of Scripture, and this is "gained from reading scripture alert both to its origins, reception and current interpretations and also to contemporary understanding and life" (Ford, 2007, p. 3).

All Christians make much of the promise of Jesus that "when he, the Spirit of truth, comes, he will guide you into all truth" (John 16:13). On the one hand the many competing claims to the truth suggest a poor discernment of the Spirit's guidance; on the other hand, *openness to divine guidance* remains a hope for the global Christian community.

3.2 Applying the Sources

Church writings about sexuality and gender take biblical and traditional teaching and relate it, sometimes qualified, sometimes not, to contemporary issues. This is what is meant here by "applying" the sources. This section leads to a regrettable and unsettling conclusion. It takes some examples from Scripture (3.2.1), Tradition (3.2.2), and Experience (3.2.3) and shows that, almost inevitably, application leads to ambiguous, if not contradictory, results.

3.2.1 Examples from Scripture

Here are two passages from the Bible clearly relevant to our questions about sex and gender.

Two equal sexes

> [26]Then God said, "Let us make mankind in our image, in our likeness, so that they may rule over the fish of the sea and the birds in the sky, over the livestock and all the wild animals, and over all the creatures that move along the ground."
> [27]So God created mankind in his own image, in the image of God he created them; male and female he created them. (Gen. 1:26–27)

We have seen how the churches officially regard the Bible, and how this passage illustrated "essentialism" earlier (see Section 1.3.1). Recent Catholic and Anglican thought has no hesitation in assuming the truth of the two-sex theory from the sixth day of creation onwards, just on the basis of these verses; or in claiming that God has made us male and female such that men should desire only women, and women should desire only men.

In a direct comment on this text the *Catechism of the Catholic Church* teaches that "Everyone, man and woman, should acknowledge and accept his sexual *identity*. Physical, moral and spiritual *difference* and *complementarity* are oriented toward the goods of marriage and the flourishing of family life" (1994, p. 2333; emphases added). The words in italics have narrow, specific meanings. Our sexual identity is male or female, nothing else. Identities such as "lesbian," "bisexual," and so on are excluded. Howsoever the two sexes may differ (no account of this is offered), the differences enrich or "complement" one another so that marriages can work better and families can be better nurtured and supported.

Anglicans canvass an almost identical view. This text (and Gen. 2:18–25) is the basis for their second "core belief" about sexuality, that "the division of humankind into two distinct but complementary sexes is not something accidental or evil but is, on the contrary, something good established by God himself when he first created the human race" (House of Bishops' Group on *Issues in Human Sexuality*, 2003, section 1.2.9). They provide a definition of "complementarity": "By complementary (*sic*) what is meant is that the differences between men and women were intended for the mutual good of each." Both churches associate this view with Tradition. It is assumed to be the "traditional" or "historical" view of our sexed human natures, such that any critical analysis or alternative formulation of it is frequently dismissed as revisionist, just because it parts company with what is advanced as the traditional view (Shaw, 2007, p. 226).

The great Protestant theologian Karl Barth adopted a similar position. The words of Genesis 1 and 2 provide the basis for his claim that all men and women have a "vocation" that can only be realized with respect to the other sex (Barth, 1961, pp. 165–166). A more recent Barthian theologian casually asserts "If God has made us as male and female, then that is the relationship we need . . . We will be restless until then" (Roberts, 2007, p. 214). So the Bible teaches that God has made men for women, and women for men, however much the experience of countless individuals is otherwise. That is also the clear teaching of churches and several respected theologians.

Activity: Do you think the churches are right to think that men are created for women, and women are created for men? Can such a belief be plausibly based on this passage?

Comment: First, the earlier question "How many sexes are there?" (see Section 1.2.1) cast doubt on the assumption that Scripture and Tradition have a bipolar attitude to the sexes. Barth and his followers may be wrongly assuming that there is "a seamless line from the world of Genesis to the early twenty-first century" (Shaw, 2007, p. 227).

Second, there is the question of "essentialism" (see Section 1.3.1). It may be possible to define the essential natures of men and women so precisely that they can only find fulfillment in the opposite sex, but would we really be justified in doing so on the basis of this text? The opening chapter of Genesis assumes the world was made in six days. There is no trace of the barely imaginable length of time that modern cosmology assumes. The pre-scientific worldview assumes that the different species of things are fixed, and so cannot evolve. (This objection was raised against Darwin's theory of evolution.)

The narrative even assumes a vegetarian diet for humans, prior to their expulsion from the Garden of Eden (Gen. 3). Christians are in no apparent hurry to condemn the carnivorous Western diet that the earth cannot sustain, on the basis of Genesis 1:29: "Then God said, 'I give you every seed-bearing plant on the face of the whole earth and every tree that has fruit with seed in it. They will be yours for food.'" But why not, if literal meanings can be read off the first chapter of the Bible and inserted directly into contemporary discussions?

It has been a painful journey for Christians, having been made to re-think the literal interpretation that served the Church well in the pre-scientific era, to reclaim Genesis 1 as theological "narrative" or "story." Would we not expect an exceptionally convincing argument to be made that, in the particular case of human sexuality, God has written, authorized and used this text to declare an essential, eternal rule, when other factual claims the narrative assumes, have long been abandoned?

Third, did you wonder why, if God has made us as complementary sexes, the oldest churches have placed such a high value on celibacy, and on single-sexed communities such as monasteries and convents? If there really are two sexes, and one sex is to find fulfillment in union with the other, it is hard to imagine why this essential condition is to be suspended when men serve God by becoming priests.

Fourth, you might think (as I do) that there is truth in this twentieth century doctrine of complementarity. God has sexed the human species so that it can reproduce and raise its offspring co-operatively. But why should that affect *every member* of the human species? It is not necessary for every member of a species to be procreative for the species itself to be procreative. Could not complementarity be affirmed as a general or species-rule while allowing for different individuals within the species to be different, and to opt out of what I call the "procreative imperative?" Why this all-or-nothing stance?

Fifth, there may be a further, scarcely hidden, reason why Genesis 1:27 is interpreted in this way. That is because homosexuality is a profound problem for the churches at present. We shall examine their arguments in detail in Chapters 9 and 10. However, the text "male and female he created them," is being made to confirm not merely an essential sexual difference, but an exclusive orientation of each for the other. Genesis 1:27 might be a convenient proof-text for theologians looking for new arguments to bolster old positions.

There are good reasons, then, for thinking that this passage may not bear the extraordinary weight that some interpreters place upon it (for yet more reasons, see Moore, 2003, pp. 118–150; Mein, 2007). Could Reason be God's way of telling us about homosexuality? Since churches have changed their mind over many different issues in the past, the time may be ripe for the developing Tradition to arrive at a more inclusive account of homosexual experience. We might also want to say that if the Wesleyan Quadrilateral is taken seriously, the experience of millions of people who do not identify themselves as straightforwardly heterosexual is itself a serious contribution to the deliberations of the churches.

The lustful eye   The second passage to help us think about *how* the Bible may become a source of revelation for us is from the Sermon on the Mount (Matt. 5–7):

[27]"You have heard that it was said, 'Do not commit adultery.' [28]But I tell you that anyone who looks at a woman lustfully has already committed adultery with her in his heart. [29]If your right eye causes you to sin, gouge it out and throw it away. It is better for you to lose one part of your body than for your whole body to be thrown into hell. [30]And if your right hand causes you to sin, cut it off and throw it away. It is better for you to lose one part of your body than for your whole body to go into hell. (Matt. 5:27–30)

On a conventional understanding of this saying of Jesus, the commandment against adultery is extended to even thinking about it. "Adultery of the heart" is as bad as adultery of the body. The law of Moses forbidding adultery is now to cover the innermost thoughts of the followers of Jesus. Drastic action is needed to avoid the sin. While some allowance for the colorful hyperbole of self-mutilation may be granted, the mention of hell can be assumed to have scared millions of believers through the ages. Divine punishment will be meted out to continual offenders. Even their private fantasies deserve damnation. This interpretation seems to be confirmed by what is going on elsewhere in the chapter where Jesus several times compares what was once said (in the law of Moses) and what is being said *now* (by Jesus, now the Reign of God has arrived).

Questions: The passage may give rise to highly unsettling questions for contemporary Christians to deal with, for example,

1. How are straight men to avoid lustful looks when the dress codes of a culture remorselessly present the female body to be alluring, revealing, available?
2. For men eager to follow the teaching of Jesus, do not these words too often result in guilt at failure and misery in the attempted repression of irrepressible desire?

Comment: It may come as a relief to learn that this standard interpretation is not the only, or even the most likely one. Two linguistic points about how the Greek is to be translated and a philosophical point about "adultery of the heart" indicate that the standard reading may actually be misconceived.

First, the word for "woman" in verse 28 is *gunè*, which also means "wife." Since Jesus is talking here of adultery, the reading "wife" is likely to be the correct one.

Second, Jesus seems to be drawing on the tenth commandment (Exod. 20:27), which in the popular Greek version of the day began "You shall not covet your neighbour's wife" (Keener, 1999, p. 187). The word for "coveting" and "lusting" is the same (from *epithumeò*).

Third, there is an assumption in the standard interpretation about there being two distinct worlds, the inner and private world, and the outer and public world. The searchlight of divine scrutiny is now to be directed on the inner world. But this assumption rests on a dualism between soul and body which the teaching of Jesus does not support.

Fourth, whatever adultery of the heart is, it is not adultery of the body with a married woman. The meaning may be best conveyed by the English phrase "His heart was [or was not] in it." It means being determined to carry some action through. Many of our fantasies we do not wish to carry through. The warning of Jesus is probably directed against predatory male behavior against married women. Gareth Moore comments,

> If I imagine committing adultery with my neighbor's wife, it may be because I want to commit adultery with her – because I am committing adultery in my heart. But no such thing need be in question. It may just be a pleasant way to idle away a few spare moments; in this case it is not a very laudable thing for me to do, and I should probably be discouraged from doing it, but it is not adultery of the heart." (2001, p. 22)

Moore thinks "it is not primarily sexual desire that Jesus is criticizing as out of place here, but the desire to have, to possess" (2001, p. 16). Jesus

> is not aiming to promote something that might be called "inner purity", if by that is meant a putative mental state divorced from any reference to activity. Neither is he merely wanting to stop particular thoughts and fantasies going through people's heads. He wants to stop people being unjust to each other. (p. 17)

This interpretation may be liberating for people who entertain sexual fantasies, perhaps several times a day. But the task at present is not to take sides in any argument about what the text "really means." It is to note that, in this case and in the previous one, an appeal to the Bible does not yield clear or unambiguous results. "Re-visionary" or revisionary accounts may be placed alongside more traditional ones. They are not always to be preferred, but there may be good grounds (in this case textual and philosophical) why they should be. And this troubling ambiguity extends to other sources of revelation too.

3.2.2 Examples from Tradition

We will consider next two extracts which belong, in some sense, to Tradition. The first is from the most famous historical theologian, Thomas Aquinas, and concerns the reasons he gives for thinking fornication a mortal sin. The second belongs to a liturgy within the Book of Common Prayer (1549) called The Order for the Visitation of the Sick.

Why is "fornication" a sin?   Aquinas writes:

> every sin committed directly against human life is a mortal sin. Now simple fornication implies an inordinateness that tends to injure the life of the offspring to be born of this union. For we find in all animals where the upbringing of the offspring needs care of both male and female, that these come together not indeterminately, but the male with a certain female, whether one or several; such is the case with all birds: while, on the other hand, among those animals, where the female alone suffices for the offspring's upbringing, the union is indeterminate, as in the case of dogs and like animals. Now it is evident that the upbringing of a human child requires not only the mother's care for his nourishment, but much more the care of his father as guide and guardian, and under whom he progresses in goods both internal and external. Hence human nature rebels against an indeterminate union of the sexes and demands that a man should be united to a determinate woman and should abide with her a long time or even for a whole lifetime. Hence it is that in the human race the male has a natural solicitude for the certainty of offspring, because on him devolves the upbringing of the child: and this certainly would cease if the union of sexes were indeterminate. (Aquinas, 1947, 2.2q.154.2)

The passage from Aquinas is interesting to the present-day Church, not because it *classifies* a particular sexual sin as a mortal one, but for its sensitive account of the reasons for the magnitude of its wrongness. Having straight sex outside marriage runs the risk of conception (the purpose of having sex, Aquinas thought, is to bring this about). At least one partner in a couple who fornicates is by definition unmarried, and so is not bonded in what Aquinas calls a "determinate union."

Aquinas thinks all male birds assist their female partners in the rearing of chicks, but only some male animals do. In the human species, he thinks it obvious that a child's father should play the greater part in the upbringing and education of his children. It is "natural" for human fathers to do this, and he thinks it explains their natural anxiety about paternity. A father wants to know that any child he helps to bring up is his.

There are obvious discontinuities between Aquinas' time and our own, not least the ages at which men and women first marry; reliable contraception; state schools, and so on. But are there not also remarkable connections to be made between his thoughts about children and the social situation in which we find ourselves?

Children need fathers. Generally, they do not like it when their parents split. When this happens they are likely, on almost every measure, to perform less well than children raised in intact families (Thatcher, 2007, pp. 115–132). Children who live with their birth mother and her unmarried partner are at hugely greater risk of abuse than if they were in the home of their natural parents. Aquinas' remarks on fornication are capable of reminding a whole generation that bringing unwanted children into the world is a sin against the children; and to speak of this sin as a mortal sin is to speak on behalf of the children who have no choice over whether to be brought into the world, or by whom.

Question: You may think I have expressed my support for Aquinas' view rather too strongly. For the present, please grant the premise that risking the conception of an unwanted child is an offence against the (possible) child. Why is that? Is it an offence because:

a – Aquinas says so?
b – Aquinas offers a good argument in support of his conclusion?
c – there is much contemporary evidence to support Aquinas' conclusion, and this is why his argument is persuasive?

Discussion:

a. I would rule out this one. Aquinas was a hugely talented theologian but he was not God! He cannot be believed just because it is Aquinas who is telling us. In this part of the *Summa Theologiae* he comes to much more contentious conclusions than those just cited, for example, that kisses and caresses are also mortal sins if indulged in for pleasure, or that men's emission of semen while asleep sometimes happens "when by the work of a devil the sleeper's phantasms are disturbed so as to induce the aforesaid result" (Aquinas, 1947, 2.2q.154.5).

b. This is right, isn't it? Aquinas always argues to his conclusion, and the conclusion is a good one. A wider reading of the passage shows how he always considers alternative arguments before rejecting them, then stating his own, and then dealing with objections. But arguments also have to have premises that are acceptable. Aquinas accepted that devils disturbed human sleep: we don't.

c. Perhaps this is the most persuasive. The crises in our time over fatherhood and single-parent families, and the separation of marriage from parenthood, provide real problems for children, and Aquinas has an argument here that is particularly relevant in our context. He could not have known our context of course, but we are surely justified in appropriating insights which he powerfully articulated for our own times.

Christians committed to using Tradition as their working materials for practical theology, need to appropriate it critically. There is much in the Tradition that no longer registers for us. There are "texts of terror" such as Luther's *On the Jews and Their Lies*, and the handbook on the interrogation of witches, the *Hammer of Witches* (or *Malleus Maleficarum*) (see Thatcher, 2008, pp. 96–106). But today's Christians have much in common with previous generations, not least their intention to witness faithfully to God's self-revelation in Jesus Christ. It is possible to stand within the Christian tradition and serve it faithfully, while cringing at some of the beliefs and practices of our ancestors. Our descendents will certainly cringe at some of the things we said, and did, and believed, in the name of Christ. The same ambivalence can be found in our second example.

Is sickness "sent?"

> Dearly beloved, know this, that Almighty God is the Lord of life and death, and of all things to them pertaining, as youth, strength, health, age, weakness, and sickness. Wherefore, whatsoever your sickness is, know you certainly, that it is God's visitation. And for what cause soever this sickness is sent unto you; whether it be to try your patience for the example of others, and that your faith may be found in the day of the Lord laudable, glorious, and honourable, to the increase of glory and endless felicity; or else it be sent unto you to correct and amend in you whatsoever doth offend the eyes of your heavenly Father; know you certainly, that if you truly repent you of your sins, and bear your sickness patiently, trusting in God's mercy, for his dear Son Jesus Christ's sake, and render unto him humble thanks for his fatherly visitation, submitting yourself wholly unto his will, it shall turn to your profit, and help you forward in the right way that leadeth unto everlasting life. (Book of Common Prayer, 1549)

The Christian tradition *does* assert the close association of sickness and sin. Sickness *is* "God's visitation." There are reasons why God sends it (even if they are known only to God) and they include the learning of exemplary patience, the increase in and witness of faith, and opportunities for repentance and growth in grace. This prayer was discussed during a recent "global theological conversation" on HIV Prevention in Johannesburg, and it was pointed out there that the theology that comes to expression in the prayer is the same sort of theology that stigmatizes sufferers of HIV/Aids and has been a major reason why people with symptoms do not seek testing or help (Thatcher, 2009).

But before the prayer is angrily rejected for the offence it clearly causes, let us remember that in the sixteenth century, when it was written, people believed in evil spirits; they believed that illnesses and all manner of malevolence could strike as the result of a spell, or a stare from an "evil eye" or the calling up of magic. People had no idea about viruses, no access to the medical understanding that we take for granted. In those circumstances they would have found *genuine comfort* in the assurance that *God* had sent a sickness, because that ruled out that it was not the consequence of a curse or an evil spirit.

Our use of this example of Tradition leaves us in a dilemma. On the one hand these pious authors were attempting to make commendable theological sense of sickness in a pre-scientific world. On the other hand this prayer is almost useless for pastoral purposes today. The conceptual world of their authors is long gone, and cannot conceivably be ours. We can still stand in the tradition of caring for and praying with people who are ill. We can still comfort them in our prayers, but not by using this one.

These two examples illustrate that Tradition must be understood in the context in which it is set, and valued for the wisdom it may still provide. It does not automatically command acceptance or require rejection. It is capable of generating remarkable insights today of which its authors could not possibly have been aware. It is there as a source of learning and sometimes of example. Christians in every generation must grapple with new problems, to which the Tradition is more likely to offer insights than solutions. Both continuity and discontinuity are necessary parts of a growing Tradition.

3.2.3 Examples from Experience

It was noted in Section 3.1 that Reason is a very broad category with different senses, so an example of a philosophical argument, or a scientific hypothesis, or any truth-claim whatever could suffice as an example. Instead let us turn to the use of Experience as a source of revelation. Methodists, we noted, include experience among their sources, so it comes as no surprise to discover that when the Methodist Church of Great Britain set up a Commission to produce a Report on Human Sexuality, they *included Methodists from sexual minorities*, and whose lifestyles did not accord with traditional Methodist teaching (Methodist Church, 1990, p. 9). The rationale for doing this was typically Methodist:

> Any discussion of what is right or ideal or acceptable or tolerable within the Church or society needs to be prefaced with a careful listening to the experience of people's lives. It is particularly important for those who belong to the majority heterosexual community to listen to those whose life styles do not conform to that pattern. (Methodist Church, 1990, p. 8)

Nearly 30 quotations and longer descriptions provided by practicing Methodists followed and they still make fascinating reading. Here are parts of two of them:

> *Example 1:* I have sexual desires and these have remained with me through a long life . . . These desires are almost equally heterosexual and homosexual, with both heterosexual and homo-sexual fantasies. Although separated from my wife for shorter and longer periods, I have not "given in" to homosexual desires. In this I have been strangely helped by my Christian faith – and, also, by fear of sexually transmitted diseases and of public disclosure and of the censure of society. I have known well homosexuals who are living in a stable relationship with each and others who have moved from partner to partner, and I continue to value them as friends. I would not want, however, their relationships to be "blessed" as a homosexual marriage, nor would I want an active homosexual admitted to the Ministry with the imprimatur that would be given by ordination. (p. 11)

> *Example 2:* At University I seemed to be "hot property," which surprised and frightened me. Men seemed to think it appropriate to comment on my anatomy from 100 yards away. I chose a close and steady heterosexual relationship early on – to prove to myself I was capable of it, and to protect myself from predatory, sexist males, of which there were many. I soon realized that "Christian" taboos on sex outside of marriage were nonsense, and had a full sexual relationship for two or three years within that committed relationship. In retrospect, I didn't enjoy penetrative sexual intercourse much, and often did it out of a sense of duty and loving commitment to the man I was in love with. When that relationship ended, I was devastated. My concept of myself had become very much bound up with being part of socially acceptable coupledom. I felt pressure to become part of a couple again – as if I was somehow incomplete being alone.
>
> However, the intense feelings I'd felt for the older woman a few years before resurfaced in relation to two or three women I knew well. Both were inaccessible, so it was safe but unhelpful to fall in love with them. I confronted my feelings of attraction and decided I was capable of "loving women," and needed to explore what that meant for me. Soon after that I met a woman nearly my own age, and took the plunge of a lesbian relationship. In the space of a few months I've become closer to her than I've ever been to anyone else in my life. Sex is wonderful, and I

never make love out of a sense of "duty." Those who condemn lesbian relationships don't know what they're missing" (p. 12) (for more recent lists of examples of testimonies of men and women of sexual minorities, see Trisk and Burns, 2008; Hagger-Holt and Hagger-Holt, 2009).

The Methodist Church did not use the stories of its members to express approval or disapproval of them. Rather it did not want to consider sexuality "purely in the abstract and to ignore the actual realities of sexual relationships" (Methodist Church, 1990, p. 8). It recognized the variety of sexual experiences and beliefs about sex in the Church (and compared these with the variety of beliefs in the Methodist Church about politics and war). It admitted that "God works through contemporary society *and experience* as well as through the tradition of the Church" (p. 14; emphasis added). Pastorally its emphasis was clear:

> we believe that people need to be affirmed not undermined, brought in not left out. The problem with too rigid statements of rules or ideals is that people are not given the space to explore and learn from their experience. We can see this in some of the sexual sub-cultures where the suppression itself leads to reactive life styles. (Methodist Church, 1990, p. 30)

The use of Experience by the Methodists in this Report is amply justified. Unlike Scripture and Tradition there is an immediacy about it that does not require scholarly endeavor and imagination in order to arrive at a particular interpretation. A climate of acceptance and honesty is provided. The admission of Experience as a source enables contact to be made between people as they are, and the Christian Gospel that may reshape them in various ways. It does not endorse any or every sexual experience, but incorporates them into the wider framework of reflection.

3.3 Using the Sources Well

I hope this trawl through the sources of Christian sexual theology may have demonstrated the distinctiveness of Christian thought about sex, but you may think we are now left with as many problems as when the chapter began.

Question: Can you suggest what some of these problems may be?

Comment: The basic problem is that the churches place considerable faith in the power of these sources to control their teaching about sex. But it isn't clear that these sources *do* control their teaching. For example, Protestant churches appear to have little trouble with divorce and further marriage. How do they square that with Scripture and Tradition?

Or again, it is important that any development in the churches' teaching about *anything* should be shown to be consistent with Scripture, Tradition, Reason, and Experience. But, notoriously, groups of Christians have been adept at proclaiming heresy and hatred when they have advocated doctrines and ethical teachings, believing them to be fully consistent with Scripture and Tradition. The related question *how* a new doctrinal or moral proposal can be shown to be both an innovation yet consistent with the traditional norms is difficult to answer. (It is attempted in Section 10.1.1.)

The two biblical passages just examined (Section 3.2.1) illustrate the difficulty. The first, Genesis 1:26–27, is pressed into service by official teaching, to condemn all same-sex sexual practices. But this is a strikingly new way of reading these texts. It shows that the churches are capable of new teaching, even if it is frankly reactionary and accompanied by a familiar claim that they have always thought this way.

The second, Matthew 5:27–30, had its guilt-inducing sting removed from it by showing that it may refer to predatory moves on married women by men who should know better, than to harmless sexual fantasies which should *not* be regarded as tantamount to adultery.

Now there are many biblical texts in the pages that follow that will attract plausible yet conflicting interpretations. If contradictory interpretations of Scripture are alike consistent with Scripture, Scripture clearly cannot control how Scripture is understood. Students on one of my courses examine scurrilous religious websites where polygamy, polyamory (having many lovers), anal sex for virgins awaiting marriage, godly threesomes, and much else, are advocated by Christian groups who justify their practices by their own eccentric readings of the Bible. Of course these opinions are bizarre, but showing *why* they are bizarre is why we look at them. The right recourse to Scripture requires much else as well, not least the history of the reception of Scripture by Christians and churches through the centuries. This, of course, is notoriously subject to historic changes.

There is a similar problem with Tradition. The study of Tradition is capable of yielding up deep insights for guiding the contemporary Church, and at the same time yielding up examples of (what appear to us to be) cruelty, violence, ignorance, and even chronic pastoral incompetence. The Christian Tradition is anti-Jewish almost from its beginning. Does this unbroken tradition justify anti-Semitism now on the grounds that it cannot change? Of course not, yet that is just the argument advanced in support of discrimination of lesbian and gay people.

Reason and experience are each open categories which generate many uses. They are elastic, and that constitutes both an opportunity and a danger.

Thinking theologically about sex   But problems with handling the sources must be tempered by several considerations.

First: perhaps the model the churches adopt for thinking about sex does not quite fit? It may be misleading to think of "sources" which present themselves conveniently to Christians, or theologians, or churches, to be used for the task in hand. This sounds like assembling the required tools for putting up a book shelf, or preparing the ingredients of our favorite recipe before we cook it. This is an "agent-based" approach to performing tasks, sometimes critiqued as "masculinist," as the use of a distinctive "male reason" (Lloyd, 1984).

Thinking theologically about sex may be more like placing ourselves in those parts of a religious tradition which inspire us, give us joy, explain ourselves to ourselves, strengthen us in our commitments, and fill us with wonder at our capacities for love, tenderness and sharing. That is a life-giving space worth occupying. There are other religious ways of doing (and knowing) that rest on trusting our most deeply held values. Ultimately this "basic trust" is, for theists, trust in God (Küng, 1981, pp. 569–573), the source of all our values. Quiet *contemplation* can replace vigorous rational action. Our *wisdom* and *intuition* can guide us too, especially when it is informed by experience and knowledge.

Second, some Christian readers may have good reason to say there are ecclesial or sacramental experiences that deserve to be given much more weight than this chapter has done. They might insist that their baptism has initiated them into a new *corporate* reality – "the paschal mystery of Christ's death and resurrection" – where one's faith and life is continually "renewed and nourished" by participation in the Eucharist (Stuart, 2003, p. 1). While the reception of divine grace is always subjective, that grace comes through the objectivity of the sacraments through which the action of God is mediated.

Several scholars insist that the experience of life-in-community is the vital character-forming ingredient that shapes one's life. Labels such as "communitarian ethics," "virtue ethics" (Hursthouse, 1999), and "ecclesial ethics" (Guroian, 1994) name these important approaches. Virtuous people learn virtue from virtuous communities. The person who immerses herself in the worship of the Church, may find she is to some extent transformed by the Holy Spirit. Some even say she has no need for "ethics," a subject that came into existence only in the modern period when the Church made a misguided attempt to bridge the gap between "contemporary debates" and its own "practices" (Hauerwas and Wells, 2004, p. 28)

Conversion, devotion, the sacraments, worship, Christian fellowship, spiritual growth, and so on count hugely in the lives of individual Christians. It is hard to see how it could be otherwise. Nevertheless these considerations can be over-emphasized. Local congregations may be places of vibrant welcome, friendship, and community, but they may not be. Are they not also known sometimes for their indifference to visitors, their intolerance, their in-fighting?

Is there not a similar problem about worship too? There are services and liturgies which invite, even compel, an overwhelming sense of the sacred, or God. But there are hymns and liturgies that compel boredom or sleep, and sermons that take triteness and irrelevance to new lows. Again it would seem unwise to place too much emphasis on these important considerations.

One difficulty with virtue or ecclesial ethics is that it underestimates the task of communication with people outside its own in-group or in-groups. Another is that it undermines that broad human commonality that is needed to reach a genuine global understanding by insisting on narrow versions of Christian identity (Klemm and Schweiker, 2008, pp. 124, 190).

3.3.1 Two principles

When I use the Bible and Tradition in Christian ethics, I try to keep two principles in the foreground of my thinking. (For a longer list see Thatcher, 2007, pp. 44–50). The first is: *Treat the Bible as a Witness to the Revelation of God in Christ.*

It may be helpful to identify two principal types of Bible use current among Christians. The *first* type assumes that God has made Godself known to humanity through the human being, Jesus Christ. The Bible *witnesses* to the truth of God revealed in Jesus. Christians think everyone can know God through Jesus, and the Bible has been, and remains, the indispensable witness to the divine self-disclosure that was Christ. This might well be called "the witness principle." The most famous Protestant theologian of the twentieth century made a succinct statement of the witness principle:

> The Word of God is God Himself in Holy Scripture. For God once spoke as Lord to Moses and the prophets, to the Evangelists and apostles. And now through their written word He speaks as the same Lord to His Church. Scripture is holy and the Word of God, because by the Holy Spirit it became and will become to the Church a witness to divine revelation. (Barth, 1963, p. 457)

The second type of Bible use, in practice if not always overtly in theory, assumes that God has made Godself known to humanity equally through the human being, Jesus Christ, *and* in Scripture. In this second type, the Bible does not merely witness to the truth of God revealed in Jesus. It shares the truth of God which is Jesus. Jesus *and* the Bible *together* constitute God's truth. On this view the Bible becomes, or is in constant danger of becoming, a co-equal source of God's revelation. The Bible on this view is not unfairly regarded as an inspired Guidebook to supernatural realities and earthly ethical practices.

The Word of God in its fullness is God's self-communication to humanity. That self-communication is supremely Jesus Christ, but not of course confined exclusively to Him. God can "speak" in countless ways to people. Problems arise within the "guidebook view" when all Scripture is regarded "in equal measure as the Word of God" (Barth, 1963, p. 480). Still worse problems arise when the text of Scripture is assumed to *be* the Word of God, even when it is clearly and offensively inconsistent with the divine Love revealed in Jesus Christ. If the Bible is to be called "the Word of God" (as Barth also does), then it is in a derivative and secondary sense that it is "a witness to divine revelation."

The Anglicans combine both these views, and their combination may be responsible for many difficulties among them (Thatcher, 2008, pp. 25–27). Appeals to the authority of the Bible as a source may be less ambiguous if the Bible was differently understood, not as a guidebook, but as a witness, as a testimony of the People of God to the One the Bible exists to commend. The first principle is to *treat the Bible as a witness to God's revelation in Christ*, and not as a moral handbook to be consulted on sexual matters. It will influence subsequent discussions of biblical passages later on.

The second principle is: *Focus on the* development *of Tradition at least as much as on its repetition.*

A similar shift in the Church's understanding of the role of Tradition might also help to minimize ambiguities in its use. "The faith rediscovers itself in the debate with tradition . . .," and this debate ought to be less an appeal to, or an authoritative repetition of tradition, but rather a reworking of tradition in the context of contemporary questions and problems" (Turner, 2004, p. 21). New generations of believers are tradition-*makers* as much as they are tradition-*receivers*. That is why the second proposal focuses on the *development* of tradition, at least as much as on its preservation and handing on. As Christians engage with new questions, both the Bible and the Tradition shed new light on those questions, and upon themselves. But more remains to be said (and will be said; see Section 10.1) about how developments of Tradition can be accepted.

In this chapter we have reviewed the sources for thinking theologically about sex and uncovered some of the problems associated with using them. The Bible and Tradition are essential to the enterprise of Theology, but we have preferred particular accounts of their purpose and use which will inevitably remain controversial. Experience as a source has been cautiously vindicated. But the greatest need is to supplement the "stool" or quadrilateral of sources with a theological framework that makes good sense of sexuality, the body, and gender. The best way of writing and thinking in a distinctively Christian way is to let oneself be immersed in the Christian doctrines of the Incarnation and the Trinity, and the practices of love which can be shown to flow from these. This framework is proposed in Part II.

References

Aquinas, T. (1947) *Summa Theologica*, Benziger Bros. edn. www.assumption.edu/users/gcolvert/summa/SS/SS154.html#SSQ154A2THEP1 (accessed November 3, 2010).

Barth, K. (1961) *Church Dogmatics*, III/4, T&T Clark, Edinburgh.

Barth, K. (1963) *Church Dogmatics*, 1.2, T&T Clark, Edinburgh.

Book of Common Prayer (1549).

Catechism of the Catholic Church (1994) Geoffrey Chapman, London, www.vatican.va/archive/catechism/ccc_toc.htm (accessed November 3, 2010).

CIA (Central Intelligence Agency) (2009) *The World Factbook*, www.cia.gov/library/publications/the-world-factbook/geos/xx.html#People (accessed November 3, 2010).

Episcopal Church (2010) *Tradition*, www.episcopalchurch.org/109399_15496_ENG_HTM.htm (accessed November 8, 2010).

Ford, D. (2007) *Divine Wisdom: Desiring God and Learning in Love*, Cambridge University Press, Cambridge.

Guroian, V. (1994) *Ethics after Christendom: Toward an Ecclesial Christian Ethic*, Eerdmans, Grand Rapids, Michigan/Cambridge, UK.

Hagger-Holt, R., and Hagger-Holt, S. (2009) *Living It Out: A Survival Guide for Lesbian, Gay and Bisexual Christians and their Friends, Families and Churches*, Canterbury Press, London.

Hauerwas, S., and Wells, S. (2004) Why Christian ethics was invented, in *The Blackwell Companion to Christian Ethics* (eds. S. Hauerwas and S. Wells), Blackwell, Malden, MA/Oxford.

House of Bishops' Group on *Issues in Human Sexuality* (2003) *Some Issues in Human Sexuality – A Guide to the Debate*, Church House Publishing, London.

Hursthouse, R. (1999) *On Virtue Ethics*, Oxford University Press, Oxford.

Keener, C.S. (1999) *A Commentary on the Gospel of Matthew*, Eerdmans, Grand Rapids, Michigan/Cambridge, UK.

Klemm, D.E., and Schweiker, W. (2008) *Religion and the Human Future: An Essay on Theological Humanism*, John Wiley and Sons, Ltd, Chichester, UK.

Küng, H. (1981) *Does God Exist? An Answer for Today*, Random House, New York.

Lloyd, G. (1984) *The Man of Reason: "Male" and "Female" in Western Philosophy*, Methuen, London.

Mein, A. (2007) Threat and promise: the Old Testament on sexuality, in *An Acceptable Sacrifice? Homosexuality and the Church* (eds. D. Dormor and J. Morris), SPCK, London, pp. 22–32.

Methodist Church (2009) *The Methodist Quadrilateral*, www.methodist.org.uk/ (accessed November 3, 2010).

Methodist Church of Great Britain (1990) *Report of Commission on Human Sexuality*, Methodist Publishing House, Peterborough, UK.

Moore, G., OP (2001) *The Body in Context: Sex and Catholicism*, Continuum, London/New York.

Moore, G., OP (2003) *A Question of Truth: Christianity and Homosexuality*, Continuum, London/New York.

Outler, A.C. (1980) *John Wesley*, Oxford University Press, New York.

Reardon, B.M.G. (1966) *Religious Thought in the Nineteenth Century*, Cambridge University Press, Cambridge, UK.

Roberts, C.C. (2007) *Creation and Covenant: The Significance of Sexual Difference in the Moral Theology of Marriage*, T&T Clark International, New York/London.

Rogers, E.F., Jr. (ed.) (2002) *Theology and Sexuality: Classic and Contemporary Readings*, Blackwell, Malden, MA/Oxford.

Shaw, J. (2007) Reformed and enlightened Church, in *Queer Theology: Rethinking the Western Body* (ed. G. Loughlin), Blackwell, Malden, MA/Oxford, pp. 215–229.

Southern Baptist Convention (2009) *Basic Beliefs*, www.sbc.net/aboutus/basicbeliefs.asp (accessed November 3, 2010).

Stuart, E. (2003) *Gay and Lesbian Theologies: Repetitions with Critical Difference*, Ashgate, Aldershot, UK/Burlington, VT.

Thatcher, A. (2007) *Theology and Families*, Blackwell, Malden, MA/Oxford.

Thatcher, A. (2008) *The Savage Text – The Use and Abuse of the Bible*, John Wiley and Sons, Ltd, Chichester.

Thatcher, A. (2009) The virus and the Bible: how living with HIV helps the Church to read it, in *HIV Prevention: A Global Theological Conversation* (ed. G. Paterson), Ecumenical Advocacy Alliance, Geneva, pp. 100–112.

Trisk, J., and Burns, S. (2008) Sexuality and identity, in *The Anglican Communion and Homosexuality* (ed. P. Groves), SPCK, London, pp. 217–237.

Turner, D. (2004) Tradition and faith. *International Journal of Systematic Theology*, 6(1) (Jan.), 21–37.

Part II

Being Theological about Sex

4

Desiring

In this chapter we will be thinking about the range of human desires. The first section begins narrowly with lust. The second section sets out ways of thinking about desire more broadly. The third section poses and answers the question what it is to desire *God*. The fourth section utilizes the work on desire in the earlier sections by exploring the remarkable theological claim that God desires *us*.

4.1 Learning from Lust

In this section two stories from the Hebrew Scriptures will be used to illustrate what might be called lust, and to make a moral judgment about the place of lust in sexual life.

4.1.1 Bathsheba's bath

Desire is a consuming human trait that includes sexual desire, but is also much broader. Lust is a name for *sexual* desire. The box contains two, contradictory, definitions of lust:

The first of these is official Roman Catholic teaching. It indicates a deep suspicion of sexual pleasure. "Order" and "purpose" are key concepts in Catholic sexual morality, and several times in these two sentences, lust is linked to a lack of these. Since the procreative and unitive purposes of sex (Pope Paul VI, 1968, p. 12) may only be exercised within marriage, all lust

> **Lust:** Lust is disordered desire for or inordinate enjoyment of sexual pleasure. Sexual pleasure is morally disordered when sought for itself, isolated from its procreative and unitive purposes. (*Catechism of the Catholic Church*, 1994, para. 2351)
>
> Lust is "the enthusiastic desire, the desire that infuses the body, for sexual activity and its pleasures for their own sake" (Blackburn, 2004, p. 19).

God, Sex, and Gender: An Introduction, First Edition. Adrian Thatcher.
© 2011 Adrian Thatcher. Published 2011 by Blackwell Publishing Ltd.

outside marriage, and too much lust inside marriage, are both morally wrong. The second definition is offered by an English philosopher who thinks the Christian record on lust is deplorable. He thinks lust "is not merely useful but essential. We would none of us be here without it" (Blackburn, 2004, p. 3). Against Christianity he sets out "to lift it from the category of sin to that of virtue" (2004, p. 3). One of his complaints is that Christianity teaches the control of lust through the exercise of the power of the will. An inescapable feature of lust, he thinks, is that it is involuntary. It invites an abandonment to one's desires. You cannot give in to your desires and control them at the same time.

Two stories from the Hebrew Bible admirably demonstrate what we may take lust to be:

> [2]One evening David got up from his bed and walked around on the roof of the palace. From the roof he saw a woman bathing. The woman was very beautiful, [3]and David sent someone to find out about her. The man said, "Isn't this Bathsheba, the daughter of Eliam and the wife of Uriah the Hittite?" [4]Then David sent messengers to get her. She came to him, and he slept with her. (She had purified herself from her uncleanness.) Then she went back home. [5]The woman conceived and sent word to David, saying, "I am pregnant." (2 Sam. 11:2–5)

The narrative is shamelessly erotic in detail, and moralistic in its conclusion: "But the thing David had done displeased the LORD" (2 Sam. 11:27).

King David finds himself aroused by the sight of a young, beautiful, and naked woman. He is complicit in his act of voyeurism. Bathsheba is unaware of his gaze, and David is aroused both by her and her apparent lack of awareness of his arousal. David has complete "power-over" Bathsheba (see Section 2.2.2). He learns of her married status but the sanction of God's Commandment against adultery (Exod. 20:14), and the knowledge that he was about to commit a capital offence (Deut. 22:22) does not deter him. Because this is a story and must be read as a story, historical questions about whether the laws of Israel as we find them in the Hebrew Scriptures were known at the time, are ignored here. Only getting Bathsheba matters. The narrative assumes her powerlessness and lack of consent. She is acquired by force and required to satisfy the king's lust.

Other translations of the passage admit "she was still purifying herself after her period" (2 Sam. 11:4, Revised English Bible). In that case David's eagerness also caused him to break the law forbidding sex during or immediately after menstruation (Lev. 15:19–24).

In a further development, the loyalty of Uriah, who refused to visit his wife while he was briefly on leave from the battle-front, for fear of distraction from the military campaign (Lev. 15:6–13), is contrasted with the King's adulterous and murderous ways. On his return to the battle front, the blameless Uriah, unknown to himself, is made to carry his own death warrant to his commanding officer (Lev. 15:14). It ordered the officer to "'Put Uriah opposite the enemy where the fighting is fiercest and then fall back, and leave him to meet his death'" (Lev. 15:15).

In this narrative lust is depicted as a near-uncontrollable power. It is no respecter of persons, of human conventions, or of divine commands. "Power-over" is exercised to obtain gratification, however murderous the consequences may turn out to be.

> *Activity:* Read 2 Samuel 11 in a modern translation. David murders the innocent husband of an innocent wife. Does the story tell us anything about the dangerous consequences of lust in contemporary societies? How is the gratification of lust linked to power in the story?

4.1.2 Susanna's stroll

A second story, which comprises the book Daniel and Susanna (found in the Roman Catholic Bible and the Protestant Apocrypha), tells of two judges each of whom was determined to have sex with Susanna, a devout Jew, and the beautiful wife of a rich aristocrat, Joakim. These judges regularly frequented their home which functioned as a court house.

> [7]At noon, when the people went away, Susanna would go and walk in her husband's garden. [8]Every day the two elders used to see her entering the garden for her walk, and they were inflamed with lust. [9]Their minds were perverted; their thoughts went astray and were no longer turned to God, and they did not keep in mind the demands of justice. [10]Both were infatuated with her; but they did not disclose to each other what torments they suffered, [11]because they were ashamed to confess they wanted to seduce her. [12]Day after day they watched eagerly for a sight of her.
>
> [13]One day, having said, "Let us go home; it is time to eat," [14]they left and went off in different directions; but turning back they found themselves face to face, and on questioning each other about this, they admitted their passion. Then they agreed on a time when they might find her alone. (Quotations from Daniel and Susanna are taken from the Revised English Bible.)

That time comes when, one very hot day, Susanna decides to have a bath in the garden pool and sends her servants away. The concealed judges pounce on Susanna and tell her if she does not consent to having sex with them they will ensure her death by giving evidence that they have seen her having sex with a young man in the garden. Susanna refuses to yield to them and cries out "at the top of her voice" (Deut. 22:24), knowing that an audible cry is the only defense against the assumption of consent (Deut. 22:24).

But the stronger voices of the startled judges drown out her desperate shouts for help. The judges carry out their threat to bring false charges against her (Deut. 22:34–40). At her trial she is humiliated by being unveiled, and the false evidence of the judges is believed, without her being given an opportunity to defend herself. According to the law of Moses, she is condemned to death. Raising her voice to God, she cries out in a last despairing cry for justice.

The young Daniel persuades the people to reopen the trial while he interrogates the judges. He establishes Susanna's innocence by eliciting from each of the judges irreconcilable statements about where in the garden Susanna and her fictitious lover had been seen. The judges are then executed and Susanna is "found innocent of a shameful deed" (Deut. 22:63).

The narrative bursts with opportunities for meaning-making. It may be read as God's vindication of women from male oppression, as an exposure of injustice by a just God (Deut. 22:53), or even as a salacious story whose moralistic ending justifies male readers' concealed enjoyment of the lurid details of feminine beauty and nakedness, of vicarious voyeurism and attempted rape. We shall draw from it both what lust is, and how lust (in both stories) is "framed." (Readers searching for a story where female lust leads similarly to injustice, deceit and lies, should consider the attempted seduction of Joseph by Potiphar's wife – Gen. 39:6–23.)

The metaphor of "inflammation" (Gen. 39:8) indicates a *burning pain*, something beyond pleasure, what the storyteller calls the suffering of "torments." The minds of the judges were "perverted:" in Latin this is a "turning inward," a concentration on the immediate satisfaction of what burns within, without thought for the long-term outward consequences which involve the violation of another's body.

Peeping   "Their thoughts went astray." That detail is similar to the remark of the existentialist philosopher Jean-Paul Sartre (1905–1980) that the intensity of desire is a "clogging of consciousness" (Sartre, 1969, p. 391), so that nothing else can be thought clearly while desire remains unsatisfied. Christian men may be uncomfortably reminded of the hard saying of Jesus: "But I tell you that anyone who looks at a woman lustfully has already committed adultery with her in his heart" (Matt. 5:28; see Section 3.2.1).

The judges were trusted, privileged, wise, appointed, senior officials. Their inflamed minds and clogged thoughts allowed them to put all this at risk. Their sexual gratification could not be reconciled with "the demands of justice" (Matt. 5:9). Each judge caught the other "peeping" (Matt. 5:14). Sartre describes how he peeped through a key-hole, only to be observed by someone else. He then sees himself as the voyeur he is. "I see *myself* because *somebody* sees me" (p. 260).

The two stories seem to confirm the first definition of lust just considered. The New Testament seems to provide further support for it. It contains many lists of virtues (2 Cor. 6:6–7; Gal. 5:22–3; Eph. 4:2–3, 32; Phil. 4:8; Col. 3:12; 1 Tim. 4:12, 6:11; 2 Tim. 2:22, 3:10; 2 Pet. 1:5–7) and vices (Mark 7:21–2; Rom. 1:29–31, 13:13; 1 Cor. 5:10–11, 6:9–10; 2 Cor. 12:20–1; Gal. 5:19–21; Eph. 4:31, 5:3–5; Col. 3:5, 8; 1 Tim. 1:9–10; 2 Tim. 3:2–5; Titus 3:3; 1 Pet. 2:1, 4:3, 15; Rev. 21:8, 22:15). Several of the vices (by no means all) concern sexual sins.

Lust is one of the seven deadly sins, the list of which weighed heavily on the European mind prior to the Reformation. Both of the narratives we considered link lust to a theological framework, where the will of God is paramount, and where the justice of God prevails over the misuse of social power for sexual gratification. David "displeased the Lord." God is the Savior of Susanna "and of those who trust in him" (verse 60), and the judges are executed according to the just law of a just God.

Activity: Go back to the two definitions of lust. Can you find anything inadequate about them? Do you think there is a way of reconciling them?

The continuum of desire

Comment: You may want to conclude that the first definition over-emphasizes the control and restriction of almost all sexual desire, and to an intrusive and unrealistic extent. But isn't it hard to sympathize with Blackburn's attempt to make a virtue out of lust too? A middle way might be found between these two positions by positing a continuum between strong sexual desire which seeks closer union with the other and desire which seeks merely gratification.

Even Blackburn is unable to escape allowing for some sort of continuum, in his case between virtuous and vicious lust. For if, as he says, lust is the reason why any of us is here, then he lacks the vital distinction between the mutual desire of having consensual sex and the desire for non-consensual sex, for which lust remains an appropriate term. The idea of a continuum of desire is found in the Letter of James: "but each person is tempted when they are dragged away by their own evil desire and enticed. Then, after desire has conceived, it gives birth to sin; and sin, when it is full-grown, gives birth to death" (1:14–15). On James' view, not all desires are evil, but the ones that are, give rise to temptation. Once yielding occurs, the danger of habituation or even addiction may arise.

A middle way might commend Judaism and Christianity for their emphasis on the need for the control of lust. Do not these two vignettes from the Hebrew Bible demonstrate this rather powerfully? Christianity names and understands the dark, deep, and deceiving elements of human desiring. The first definition helpfully defends *order*. Both the stories illustrate that there are personal, social, marital, moral, and religious orders that are necessary for corporate human life to subsist, and that lust leads to the damaging fracture of these. But the same tradition has undoubtedly over-emphasized the evils associated with sexual desire, to the point of making sexual desire and evil more or less identical. The second definition reacts against the suspicion of lust, and works towards reinstating lust within the realm of virtuous feelings and practices.

Realism about lust   I think a positive account of sexual desire must maintain a sad realism about its destructive potential, while refusing the shadow of suspicion and frustration that has too often extinguished the joy and spiritual meanings of sexual love. Do you agree? Lust is not an uncontrollable power that compels lustful people (usually men) into committing acts of sexual aggression or rape: such an admission would absolve responsibility for all sexual violence on the grounds of its unfortunate inevitability. It is, however, a consuming state of the whole person that renders him or her a danger to self, to the one desired, and to the social fabric on which it is played out. If desire causes us to lose control, we can at least choose to lose control before we do.

Activity: Before starting the next section, what do you think about the following statements? How far do you agree with them?

1. It is morally necessary to distinguish between creative and destructive forms of sexual desire.
2. There is a continuum between "ordinate" and "inordinate" desire, or between creative and destructive forms of sexual desire.
3. Lust operates at one end of the continuum. Love operates at the other end.

4.2 Desiring

In this section desire is extended, and it is suggested that the social stimulation of desire may be harmful to us. Two classical theories of desire are explained in order to arrive at a creative and contemporary understanding of it.

4.2.1 The stimulation of desire

Wants and needs   We desire many things that have little or nothing to do with sex. It will be helpful to distinguish between wants, or desires, and needs. The psychologist A.H. Maslow (1943) famously arranged these in a hierarchy shaped as a pyramid. At the base were physiological needs such as food and drink, followed by the need for safety and security (including health and well-being), the social need for love and belonging, and at the top of the pyramid, the need for respect or esteem. We want what we need, but we also want things that are not needs at all.

Needs and wants are different, but they shade into each other, and any demarcation line between them is likely to be blurred. Many readers will be wanting a good University education, and their parents will be wanting it for them. Peer popularity may be an unacknowledged want. Your choice of career may be swayed by the esteem you give to money, to success, to philanthropy, to God. It is hard not to want money, since money will buy most things, such as desirable properties in desirable neighborhoods and expensive holidays. Yet the author of 1 Timothy was right to observe "For the love of money is a root of all kinds of evil. Some people, eager for money, have wandered from the faith and pierced themselves with many griefs" (1 Tim. 6:10).

Wanting what is not yours   Gluttony and greed are also in the Church's catalogue of deadly sins. Wants too easily become needs. The last of the Ten Commandments is the command "You shall not covet your neighbor's house. You shall not covet your neighbor's wife, or his manservant or maidservant, his ox or donkey, or anything that belongs to your neighbor" (Exod. 20:17). Covetousness and greed are both states of excessive desire: if there is a difference between them, it is that coveting is desire directed to something already possessed by someone else, whereas greed may be a more general trait of character. King David and the judges *coveted* the wives of other men.

There are stark warnings in the Bible and the Christian tradition about excessive desire in its many forms. These warnings have a special and powerful relevance for millions of us living in an economic system that chases growth, endlessly stimulates desire, and persuades us to spend money, which, should we lack it, will be loaned to us with interest. At the time of writing this paragraph (January 2009), banks throughout the world have loaned so much money, so frivolously, that the world's entire banking system has collapsed. Desire is crucial to the entire enterprise of global capitalism, and relentless mass advertising with its brutally effective impact upon our fragile senses, incessantly stimulates our desire to acquire, to spend, to consume, to discard (Stivers, 1994). Baudrillard (1981) is not the first to link acquisitiveness to the personal and social prestige that consumer items confer upon their owners, much like the Porsche in the drive which is obviously more a statement about its owner than a means of getting around. Objects of consumption have become a "fetish."

> **Fetish:** Students of religion give the name "fetish" to an object that is believed to have supernatural powers. In the psychology of sex, fetishism is the devotion to a body part, commonly the foot, instead of devotion to the one whose body part it is. Social critics, beginning with Marx (1867/1992), have extended the notion of fetishism to include extreme mass purchasing behavior in "consumer societies."

The stimulation of desire through advertising and mass-production; the "fetishization" of shopping; and the availability of credit; these all contribute to unprecedented social conditions in the Rich World. While these conditions yield untold material benefits for us, they are perilous. The teaching of Jesus is unambiguous: "Watch out! Be on your guard against all kinds of greed; a man's life does not consist in the abundance of his possessions" (Luke 12:15). "You cannot serve both God and Money" (Matt. 6:24). The sheer extent of the stimulation of our desires might be an additional reason to "watch out" and to consider whether *sexual* greed might be included within the "kinds of greed" against which Jesus warned. The strength of our purchasing power can hurt us in several ways. It is not only that amassing debts cannot benefit us (or our countries) in the long term. We lose the sense that desiring something may entail *waiting* for it. Christians have taught from Paul onwards that patience is a "fruit of the Spirit" (Gal. 5:22). Waiting is a vital component of the virtue of chastity (see Section 11.3.3).

> *Activity:* In Section 4.1.1 above, a *continuum* was suggested between creative and destructive forms of sexual desire. In this section, two further suggestions have been made:
>
> 1. There is a similar continuum between creative and destructive forms of desire for food and drink (gluttony), for wealth (greed), and for the wealth of other people (covetousness).
> 2. Members of consumer societies are uniquely vulnerable to social forces which inflame their desires destructively.
>
> Say whether you strongly agree, agree, disagree, or strongly disagree with each of these suggestions.

4.2.2 Desire as a lack

The old idea that all desire is based on a lack, would seem to be confirmed by the practices of consumer economies. We need to get to the bottom of this idea in order to understand its deficiencies and to compare it with something better. That is the task of the present section.

In 360 BCE the Greek philosopher Plato wrote his dialogue *Symposium*. The teaching about the nature of *eròs* or desire in this dialogue has influenced Western theologians and thinkers ever since. It is still able to contribute to contemporary discussions about the meaning of love. It also enables a helpful contrast (often overstated) to be drawn between the *eròs* of Greek philosophy, and the self-giving love, or *agapè*, of the New Testament.

Being logical about love   At one place in the dialogue Plato establishes three logical points about *eròs*. Socrates is made to ask Agathon, a partner in the dialogue, a leading question – "Whether love is the love of something or of nothing?" (Plato, 360 BCE, *Symposium*, 199; see Jowett, 1953, p. 530). It turns out to be a logical or a "necessary" truth that love always has a direct object.

A logical truth: A statement that cannot help being a true one, like "A square has four sides."

You cannot argue whether a logical truth could be false – it has to be true! You *can* argue whether a statement *is* a logical truth, or whether it needs evidence to support it before it counts as true. A logical truth cannot help being true. Socrates gives an illustration of one. Love never exists as an abstract concept, but always as someone's love of something. Just as a person must necessarily have a son or daughter in order to be called a father or a mother, so love must always exist as the love of something. Desire has objects as certainly as parents have children.

The second logical point Socrates makes is that we must presently *lack* the objects of our desire, for if we had them we would not be desiring them. Agathon is forced to agree that "the inference that he who desires something is in want of something . . . is . . . absolutely and necessarily true" (Plato, *Symposium*, 200). Lack, then, is a condition of desire.

The third logical point is a refutation of Agathon's assumption (Plato, *Symposium*, 195–198) that Love is divine or a god. Since it is the nature of love to lack what it loves, it cannot be a god. A logical contradiction emerges. Love must desire what is beautiful and good for these things are thought to be desirable, as we would say, "in themselves." Yet if love desires these things, it must lack them. So its place in the Greek pantheon of gods is diminished. Why? Because it manifestly lacks the beautiful and the good. Love cannot be divine. Agathon's assumption that Love is a god, is refuted.

Activity: We have just noted three logical truths.

1. Desire always has an object.
2. Desire is based on a lack of what we desire.
3. Desire cannot be a property of the divine (because God or the gods lack nothing).

We can certainly argue *whether* these are logical truths or not. Consider each of them in turn and make up your mind whether you think they express logical truths or not.

Comment:

1. There is much to be said for the conclusion that the first statement just cannot help being true. It is possible to *speak* of love in the abstract. We do this whenever we ask what love is. But when we desire, do we not always desire *something* or *someone*?
2. The second is more doubtful. It seems logically true that we must lack what we desire. But can't we go on desiring something once we have it? We can decide to use the word "desire" so that it is always based on a lack, but there seems no good reason why we should do this.
3. The third presents real difficulties. Everyone knows that the English abstract noun "love" is overloaded with many meanings. When the word is used with reference to God, such as "God loves," or "God is love" (1 John 4:8, 17), another range of meanings may be indicated. Christian theologians have generally accepted that God is "self-sufficient," or lacks nothing. (This is the doctrine of *aseity*.) An argument to emerge later in the chapter is that God desires all that God has made; and that sexual desire can tell us something of that desire. Can *God*, then, be said to lack something (that is, the response of human love to God) after all?

4.2.3 Desire as union

Before we leave the *Symposium*, it is important to read on and note how Socrates proceeds to dig Agathon out of the logical hole he has dug for himself. This will give rise to a more satisfactory account of desire. He recounts a conversation about love with a wise woman, Diotima. He asked her

"What then is love? . . . Is he mortal?"

"No."

"What then?"

". . . he is neither mortal nor immortal, but in a mean between the two.'

"What is he then, Diotima?"

"He is a great spirit (*daimòn*), and like all spirits he is intermediate between the divine and the mortal."

"And what," I said, "is his power?"

"He interprets," she replied, "between gods and men, conveying to the gods the prayers and sacrifices of men, and to men the commands and replies of the gods; he is the mediator who spans the chasm which divides them, and in him all is bound together, and through him the arts of the prophet and the priest, their sacrifices and mysteries and charms and all prophecy and incantation, find their way. For God mingles not with man; but through Love all the intercourse and speech of God with man, whether awake or asleep, is carried on." (Plato, *Symposium*, 202–203)

This key conversation moves beyond the lack theory of desire, to suggest another, one that could be called the *union* theory. Costa (2006, pp. 39–46) notes that Diotima avoids arguing from polar opposites like divine/human, immortal/mortal. She is more focused on the relations between them. The French feminist philosopher Luce Irigaray (1993, pp. 20–33) suggests that it takes a woman (remember Diotima was one) to put opposites aside and go instead for *mediation* between opposed positions. Love is about promoting harmony between divine and human ("He interprets between gods and men"): but it is equally about bringing about understanding and cooperation between people and the gods. Love brings about union between them. Love operates between humans, between humans and the gods, and reciprocally, between the gods and humans.

It follows, says Costa, "that the relationship between the gods and humans is an erotic one" (2006, p. 41). The gods desire to have what he calls "erotic intercourse" with us. On this view, love is better defined not as a lack, but rather as what brings about relationship between separated subjects. Love, then, is better understood as an interactive process, *loving*, as the relationship between lovers.

Desire, then, is on this account more than the urge to possess an object, as in retail consumerism or commercial sex. And it is more than a lack, a void waiting to be temporarily filled. Rather,

> beautiful and good things are not acquisitions; ... Beautiful and good things could instead be viewed as gifts that animate desire, such that desire does not seek to fill a void or lack but rather seeks attachments to, or relationships with, those things that are beautiful and good. Happiness, too, then, is not a possession to be grasped, it "happens for someone" as a gift. (Costa, 2006, p. 43)

This is a very positive account of desire. Desire does not arise from a determination to possess what we lack. Rather, the world is already full of people, values, and things which, because they are good, draw us to themselves.

In the previous section we observed how desire fans greed and is easily and artificially stimulated in consumer societies. In this present section it was suggested that good things, because they are desirable, draw us to themselves, and it is good that they do.

4.3 Desiring God?

In this section desire is broadened still further. Drawing on the last two sections, it suggests how *God* might be desired.

4.3.1 Desire for God?

You may have just agreed with me that desire has an object. But that may pose another problem for you. Loving God is the aim of life of all theists. Remember the command of Jesus, "Love the Lord your God with all your heart and with all your soul and with all your mind and with all your strength" (Mark 12:30). But it is not at all clear how this aim is to be carried out. That is because God is not an object in the world of objects. So loving God must be a different sort of activity from loving your neighbor or your sexual partner or your favorite music group. God cannot be held, possessed, bought, or discarded. God is as much a "*no*-thing" as God is a "*some*-thing." How, then, can *God* be desired or loved? Plato's thought, before we leave it, might also help us solve this problem.

Platonic thought assumed that every particular thing in the world existed because it shared in one or more of the eternal Forms. There is not enough space to discuss these, except to note that among the forms there are supreme or ultimate forms, and these are Beauty Itself, Truth Itself, and the Form of the Good. So if you are drawn to, say, a beautiful picture, or you are pursuing the truth about something, or you are about to perform a good action, it turns out that you are attracted not by the beautiful object or the search for a particular truth, or the goodness your action achieves, but by the Forms that announce themselves in these particulars.

On a Platonic view, if you should think the body of a particular person is beautiful, you should end up appreciating the form of beauty that this beautiful body presents to you. Christians historically have found this theory agreeable. Since God is Spirit (John 4:24) and, according to Christian orthodoxy has no body (the doctrine of divine *impassibility*), the idea that beauty is abstract has generally appealed to the Church's theologians.

Question: Try to think of at least two difficulties with the view that beauty is essentially abstract.

Comment:
First, the view is likely to devalue the real world of objects and particulars. If a picture or a body is beautiful because of something that comes from beyond it, it is unlikely to be thought beautiful *in itself*. It is desirable because it reveals something about what is other than it, about what is "transcendent."

Second, it makes the desire for any particular object or body suspect, unless and until it is routed or directed towards the abstraction that it brings to our attention.

Third, the body is itself rendered suspect. Rather the fully real is always spiritual; the soul always superior to the body; the eternal Forms superior to compromising particulars, and so on.

Despite these misgivings, the theory of Forms remains useful for a contemporary account of how a human person might desire God. Plato thought that people naturally desired the gods. Augustine was speaking of what he deemed to be our essential nature when he famously cried "Thou awakest us to delight in Thy praise; for Thou madest us for Thyself, and our heart is restless, until it repose in Thee" (Augustine, 2009, p. I.1). While our desires are prone to distortion, the union theory of desire helps with the spiritual question of how God could be an object of desire at all.

A "no-thing" but not "nothing"   One answer is that God is a special sort of subject. God is a *grammatical* subject: that means God is the subject of predicates in sentences, so that it may be said "God is good," "God is love," and so on. (Of course, speaking of God does not establish that there *is* a God to speak of.) But, there is a good reason why God cannot be identified with anything in the created world, and that is because God is not created. God, for theists, is the reason why there is anything in the world. God is the Creator, and so God is a unique subject beyond comparison.

Theists say they *can* desire the God-who-is-no-thing through their desire for good things and the doing of good deeds. When they are attracted to the pursuit of truth, or goodness, or to the appreciation of beauty, they are already responding to the vestiges or the traces of the divine within them. These traces do not negate good or beautiful things.

Rather they point to the One who enables and wills them to be, and who is to an extent manifested through them. They carry the "imprint" or "vestige" of their Creator (see Section 4.4.2).

Here is one of those issues where Christians are right to appeal to one of their unique doctrines, that of incarnation. God became flesh in Jesus Christ (John 1:14). That doctrine shows that it is the nature of God to become manifest in what is other than God, and to encompass, to envelop, and to reconcile it back to God. The presence of God within the world does not *negate* the objects that comprise the world, but opens up that world to its depth of being. There are important differences between Platonism and Christianity here. However, there are also important insights held in common.

4.3.2 Desires and drives

An objection to union-based accounts of desire runs like this. Nature has seen to it that species reproduce. Embedded in our evolution there are mechanisms that bypass our conscious choices, our "wills." "There are ... autonomic sexual mechanisms that ignore the brain altogether. They underlie and contribute to the flooding of the body by desire" (Blackburn, 2004, p. 19). These mechanisms "drive" us. We may imagine a *feeling* of freedom in relation to these unconscious forces, but sexual desire will inevitably end in coitus.

Sigmund Freud (1856–1939) inherited the idea of a metaphysical power coursing through all things, largely indifferent to human choices. Atheists have often supposed that there is a cosmic force operating throughout nature. But it is blind, indifferent, impersonal. Arthur Schopenhauer (1788–1860) called it *Will*; Friedrich Nietzsche (1844–1900) the *Will to Power*; Richard Dawkins, the *Blind Watchmaker*. It is not necessary to be a Darwinian or a Freudian to believe in a cosmic force that ensures our species reproduction and overrules our lame attempts to redirect or refuse it.

In reply a certain realism may be granted to this view about the strength of our desires, and our difficulties in directing them. But that realism is no justification for the cosmic pessimism that accompanies such a view, nor the determinism that it assumes. Christians can benefit from an understanding of the power of desire. Ignorance of its power leads to its underestimation (as in some abstinence education programs or vows of celibacy too lightly made). Underestimation leads to unpreparedness and often to disaster.

Christians may have too little trust in sexual desire as part of the created order. It is right that desire should lead us out of ourselves and into the arms of others. An emphasis on "sinful desire" must not mask its basic goodness. Knowing our desires is essential to the command of Jesus to his disciples to love their neighbors *as themselves* (Mark 12:31). Christian faith is not opposed to self-knowledge – rather it requires it.

There has been an understandable suspicion of desire among the celibate clergy and theologians over the ages, whose own desires have been deeply problematic for them. "[E]ither man governs his passions and finds peace, or he lets himself be dominated by them and becomes unhappy" (*Catechism of the Catholic Church*, 1994, para. 2339). This advice acknowledges the power of desire and its possible consequences. But it uses the language of dominance and self-mastery as if there were no third way, and it does not acknowledge that governing one's passions may not lead to peace after all, but to further severe internal conflict and dangerous psychic turmoil.

Discipline, but not domination? However, there is a third way, that of being at peace with our desires, alert to them and their dangers, but also aware of them as part of the marvelous way we were made. Too much rigor in our control of them diminishes us as persons and impedes our achievements.

The titles of two recent books about desire suggest this third way. Tim Gorringe's *The Education of Desire* (2000) suggests that knowledge of our desires, rather than the subjugation of them, is essential to Christian discipleship. Desire needs to be *educated*. While the endless stimulation of our desires by capitalism turns out to be a mis-education of them, the tradition of *discipleship* (that is, learning a *discipline*) goes back to Jesus himself (Gorringe, 2000, p. 91).

Philip Sheldrake's *Befriending our Desires* assumes an internal hostility within many believers between spirit and flesh, between spirituality and sexuality. Sheldrake plausibly suggests that "the Christian mystical tradition" has attempted to transform "the sexual energy of *eros* into distinctively spiritual channels" (Sheldrake, 2002, p. 79). We will shortly note a key example of this – the biblical *Song of Songs*. While this transformation may be a specific calling for some people, the sad, unintended consequence of it for many more, observes Sheldrake, is "a complete separation between holiness and sexuality."

4.4 God Desiring Us?

In this section the *Song of Songs* is praised for its celebration of sexual love, and the work of three recent theologians on the idea of God's desire for us, is briefly affirmed.

4.4.1 Songs of desire

There is a book in the Bible which never ceases to amaze its students for its explicit treatment of sexual love – the *Song of Songs*, or *Song of Solomon*. The book is a "cycle of songs, of Hebrew love-poetry" (Gledhill, 1994, p. 26). It was

> sung as a celebration of love, beauty and intimacy . . . most probably . . . at local celebrations of the various harvest festivals, accompanied by dancing at a village wedding, sung as court entertainment at the royal palace in Jerusalem, or at happy family reunions or gatherings. (Gledhill, 1994, p. 14)

The history of the interpretation of this book shows how its reveling in carnal delight has been entirely redefined. Its fierce praise of passionate human love came to express instead the passionate longing of the individual's soul for God, or the spiritual love of Christ for His Church (see Section 6.3).

Originally these poems expressed praise for the delight of human physical love. Instead they came to praise the *denial* of physical love. Allegory came to replace metaphor, that is, the material, physical, human content of the songs came to represent something else. It had to have a superior abstract, spiritual meaning. The explicit sexual metaphors become instead allegories for a purely spiritual love, like the love for Plato's Forms (see Section 2.3.1), and the meanings of the poems are reversed and "de-materialized."

The surprise that is generated by an encounter with the erotic symbolism of the text indicates how successful this transformation has been. Fortunately, the wealth of available Hebrew scholarship, and a greater openness to sexual frankness, gives rise to new possibilities of interpretation.

I have chosen chapter seven in order to examine how the desire of the lovers for one another is expressed, and to point briefly to the theological vision behind it. Please read this slowly and carefully (text below).

Song of Songs 7

Lover

[1] How beautiful your sandaled feet, O prince's daughter!

Your graceful legs are like jewels, the work of a craftsman's hands.

[2] Your navel is a rounded goblet that never lacks blended wine.

Your waist is a mound of wheat encircled by lilies.

[3] Your breasts are like two fawns, twins of a gazelle.

[4] Your neck is like an ivory tower.

Your eyes are the pools of Heshbon by the gate of Bath Rabbim.

Your nose is like the tower of Lebanon looking toward Damascus.

[5] Your head crowns you like Mount Carmel.

Your hair is like royal tapestry; the king is held captive by its tresses.

[6] How beautiful you are and how pleasing, O love, with your delights!

[7] Your stature is like that of the palm, and your breasts like clusters of fruit.

[8] I said, "I will climb the palm tree; I will take hold of its fruit."

May your breasts be like the clusters of the vine, the fragrance of your breath like apples,

[9] and your mouth like the best wine.

Beloved

May the wine go straight to my lover, flowing gently over lips and teeth.

[10] I belong to my lover, and his desire is for me.

[11] Come, my lover, let us go to the countryside, let us spend the night in the henna bushes.

Activity:

1. Make a note of all the places where the young man (1–8) uses metaphors or similes to speak admiringly of his beloved's body.
2. Say how the young woman links their love-making to the place where it happens.
3. If you have time read more chapters of the *Song* from a modern translation, and note the metaphors the lovers use to describe each other and their love-making.

Desire and God   The chapter is clearly about fierce, insistent, desiring. The lovers clearly "turn each other on" (see Section 1.1), yet their longing for one another is also a longing for God.

Where does the passage say that? These two desires are not mutually exclusive (as they are in so much Christian preaching). Rather their desire *for God* intensifies their desire for each other, and conversely. How does that work? The connection is explained in the next few paragraphs.

His admiring gaze begins at her feet, and rapidly travels upwards. "Navel" in verse 2 is probably a euphemism for her "valley," situated a little lower down (Gledhill, 1994, p. 206; Brenner, 1993, p. 246). While he is still praising her hair and her mouth, she interrupts and rejoices in her lover's praise – "I belong to my lover, and his desire is for me" (verse 10).

When he admires "her graceful legs" ("the curves of your thighs" – Revised English Bible) (verse 1), he compares them with the finest jewelry of a master craftsman. But that word "craftsman" in the Hebrew is thought to point allusively but directly to *God*, the One who made all things well, the source of all beauty and desire.

The most direct reference to God in the *Song* is found at 8.6:

Stamp me as a seal upon your heart,

sear me upon your arm,

for love is as strong as death,

passion as hard as the grave.

Its sparks will spark a fire

An all-consuming blaze.

But where exactly? The last syllable of the Hebrew word for "blaze" or "flame" – *yah* – is "a shortened form of Israel's personal name for God, Yahweh" (Kearney, 2006, p. 308). It is explained that "the all-consuming flame is also the flame of Yah: divinity is the measure of the intensity of eros."

Sensuality and spirituality   As the male lover's gaze rises, he praises her beauty in ways that associate her body with the tastes and fruits and fecundity of nature. "Your waist [*or* belly] is a mound of wheat" (verse 2) is hardly a compliment a lover would be expected to accept. Yet think of an excellent harvest where all is safely gathered in and stacked together, and she is to him as the very culmination of nature.

Many verses of the *Song* celebrate the lovers' love by linking it with the world of nature in which it is set. Her shoulders and neck remind him of the top of Mount Carmel; her wild black hair of the trees and plants that grow there (verse 5). Close up, the contours of her nose link her with the steep ascent to Lebanon: her dark mysterious eyes link her in her lover's mind to the deep pools of Heshbon outside the dirt and dust of the city. When she stands up straight, no palm tree can compare with her: her lover returns repeatedly to the sight of her breasts (verses 3, 7, 8).

The male adulation of this young female body here is very far from the sleazy pics of tabloid "newspapers" and the pervasive genre of soft pornography. (When the Presbyterian Church of the United States published a report on pornography, they called it *Far From the Song of Songs*: PCUSA, 1988.) The allure of her breasts is not refused and reflected back into furtive auto-arousal. No, it is instead accepted and appreciation is extended by means of the references to the clusters of grapes and fruit, which are also alluring, visually pleasing, and luscious to the taste (verses 7, 8).

Love in the open air   In our time the environment is becoming wrecked and our unfettered desires are largely responsible. The *Song* gives a different vision of desire, while acknowledging and directing it. Deep sexual love and the honoring of the goodness, fruitfulness, beauty, and nurturance of God's creation are inextricably linked. Both of these together are the joint forms of our innate desire for the God who provides them. Conversely, environmental indifference and sexual immorality also belong together. Once the person, or creation, becomes an object for our exploitation, we have lost the sense of the divine in both, and in ourselves. We cease to be lovers and become plunderers instead.

The *Song* points to a better way of living with our desires, of having sex and even thinking about it, than the consumer-oriented constructions and expectations of immediate gratification which surround us in a fallen world. The lovers also practiced waiting. When she decides to give herself completely to him (verse 11), they decide it will be *al fresco*, among the blossoms, the henna bushes, the budding vines, the flowering pomegranates, and the perfume of the mandrakes or love-fruits (verses 11–13). They are all involved in the lovers' mutual ecstasy. With the lovers, the most sensual, beautiful and joy-giving fruits of creation join in a chorus of praise to the God whose love is expressed in human love and generously scattered throughout the natural world.

The *Song* is also remarkable for what we might call its "gender equality." It gives equal space to the woman's desire for her lover as it does the man's desire for the woman (if anything it gives more space to the woman). There are no power-plays in these narratives, no domination, no submission; no appeals to male "headship," to obedience, to procreation as a justification for making love. Rather "relationship in the Song of Songs . . . is defined by a sense of powerful connection which is not subordination" (Ostriker, 2000, p. 50). Ostriker is right to imagine "that God's love of us, and ours of God, might ideally be as tenderly ardent and as free of power-play as the love enacted in this Song."

4.4.2 Three defenders of God's *eròs*

Christian theology no longer has any reason to spiritualize this awkward and neglected biblical work. Indeed that God should have come among us as human flesh (John 1:14) could signal the acceptance and even celebration of many of the desires we find there. In this final section insights from three living, Christian theologians will conclude our reflections on the Christian belief that God desires us.

The body as the site and symbol of God's grace   In *God and Grace of Body*, David Brown (2007) meditates on the power of the body to express itself in gestures, signs, and movements. The upshot of this is that bodies are "open to the possibility of transcendence" (2007, p. 12). Brown agrees with those theologians who begin with the expressive character of the body and on that basis go on to speak of how, say, "sexual love points to a deeper heavenly love, or a gentle human touch to the healing power of divine grace." This is "a sacramental understanding of body," but he thinks it is not radical enough. They do nothing to scotch the assumption that God is normatively absent from bodily experience. They

> make the divine presence altogether too extraneous to our world, as though it has always to be searched for, rather than being already there, deeply embedded in our world in virtue of the fact that God is the creator of all that is.

The idea of the body as an "incarnating" or *icon* of God's grace underlines the emphases of this chapter. God is the Creator of the body and of all its delights. The name given to the presence of God within and among people is Spirit, or Holy Spirit, and this is a Person of God much neglected in sexual theology. Brown is correcting a popular understanding of God and our relationship to God which bypasses everything to do with the material, organic, physical world.

This is a defective understanding, thinks Brown, for "God's pre-eminent form of communication is seen to lie in a particular human body [that of Christ] and it is its interaction with other human bodies (including one's own) that constitutes humanity's way to salvation" (2007, p. 13). Once God is rightly relocated in the realm of the senses, "sexuality become[s] a natural image for divinity at work, it also becomes less a subject of embarrassment in other contexts . . . Sex is viewed as potentially rich in meaning because the divine is seen as already present within it, reaching sacramentally beyond its immediate meaning" (2007, p. 41).

Liberating our desires　Brown's attempt to reinstate desire as a creative power in human relations is supported by theologian Sebastian Moore's (2002) exposure of "The Crisis of an Ethic without Desire." He gives this disembodied ethic a sharp theological twist. He has in his sights that standard interpretation of the crucifixion of Christ that makes *His* sufferings *our* norm, in fact the "cross" that all disciples of Christ must expect to take up. The extinction of unruly desires then becomes a primary priority for all true followers of Christ seeking holiness.

Moore acknowledges that Jesus *did* exhort his disciples to take up their crosses (Matt. 10:38, 16:24; Luke 9:23). But he thinks a massive mistake is made when self-denial is thought to apply principally to the desires of the body. Christianity runs into deep trouble whenever "this ruinous identification of the crucifixion with the negation of desire" (Moore, 2002, p. 159), is made. The key distinction to be made is "the difference between liberation *from* desire (the latter equated with the insatiable self-promoting ego) and liberation *of* desire from the chains of my customary way of being myself" (2002, p. 159; emphases added).

Moore follows most New Testament scholars who do not interpret "the flesh" and its desires as primarily sexual. Rather "the flesh" means "our insatiable egoism that must utterly die if we are to come out of the half-life that goes for life in normal society" (2002, p. 159). Of course there can be a lot of sexual experience in this half-life and its egoism from which we need to be liberated. The real danger to our souls is selfishness and the desires that feed it. "Real desire is what the cross empowers, bringing us to the death that its liberation entails. The death is the death of our present ego, whose perpetuation is the work of egoism posing as desire" (Moore, 2002, p. 160).

These difficult contrasts are worth unraveling a bit further. Whenever I read someone talking about "real desire", or "true faith", or "authentic Christianity," and so on, I get suspicious. A contrast is being made between some state of affairs of which an author approves (the "real" bit), and some state of affairs of which s/he does not (the "less than real" bit). This move then begs the hidden question whether the approved state of affairs is "real" or just what the author advocates and no more.

But I cannot help thinking that here the contrast between "real desire" and the other kind (selfish desire) is perspicuous. These pain-metaphors about taking up a cross, and crucifying sinful desires clearly derive from the execution of Jesus, and the identification of the believer with it. Christ put first God's desire for us over everything else. The "self empowerment of the cross" is liberation from selfishness. Moore would approve of including in this process, liberation from the excesses of desire described earlier in this chapter (see Section 4.2.1). That makes "real desire" possible, untainted by the ego. This desire is not the elimination of passion, but rather its *intensification*, because it finds its prototype in God's passionate love for us revealed in God's incarnation, and of course, in Christ's Passion.

Seeing ourselves as desired   Rowan Williams powerfully conveys the confluence between divine desire for humanity and sexual desire for one another in "The Body's Grace" (2002). As the title of this popular article shows, he, like Brown, finds divine grace operative in human bodies and in their interaction with one another. The instance of this is a fictional character who is lovelessly seduced (2002, p. 311). Despite the distressing nature of the event and its consequences, she sees that "she had entered her body's grace." Williams explains this poetic phrase: "She has discovered that her body can be the cause of happiness to her and to another." This discovery is vital for a Christian understanding of the body. It "most clearly shows why we might want to talk about grace here. Grace, for the Christian believer, is a transformation that depends in large part on knowing yourself to be seen in a certain way: as significant, as wanted" (2002, p. 311).

Knowing that we are wanted, then, is both humanly significant for us, and also how we come to understand the *divine* love. Williams thinks that "The whole story of creation, incarnation, and our incorporation into the fellowship of Christ's body [the Church] tells us that God desires us, *as if we were God* (2002, p. 311; emphasis in original). Indeed the whole rationale of the Christian community is "the task of teaching us to so order our relations that human beings may see themselves as desired, as the occasion of joy" (2002, p. 312). These insights have the capacity to rejuvenate Christian understandings of sexuality and gender.

This chapter has explored sexual desire. A continuum between love and lust was suggested and illustrated. Desire was explored as a broader, social phenomenon, and a note of caution sounded against its constant stimulation and manipulation. The classical theory of *éros* was used to suggest the idea of desire as the *desire for union with what is desired.* The *Song of Songs* provided fine examples of how sexual desire may also be the desire for God, and we looked at the ways three contemporary theologians also found the presence of God in the body, in desiring, and in being desired.

Christians believe, or have believed, that only in marriage may the fullness of sexual desire be legitimately expressed. This belief makes an inquiry into what marriage is, an urgent one. The next two chapters are devoted to it.

References

Augustine (2009) *Confessions*, www.ccel.org/ccel/augustine/confess.ii.html (accessed November 4, 2010).

Baudrillard, J. (1981) *For a Critique of the Political Economy of the Sign*, Telos Press, St. Louis, MO.

Blackburn, S. (2004) *Lust*, Oxford University Press, Oxford/New York.

Brenner, A. (1993) "Come back, come back, the Shulammite" (Song of Songs 7:1–10): A Parody of the *wasf* Genre, in *A Feminist Companion to the Song of Songs* (ed. A. Brenner), Sheffield Academic Press, Sheffield, pp. 234–248.

Brown, D. (2007) *God and Grace of Body*, Oxford University Press, Oxford.

Catechism of the Catholic Church (1994) Geoffrey Chapman, London, www.vatican.va/archive/catechism/ccc_toc.htm (accessed November 4, 2010).

Costa, M. (2006) For the love of God: The death of desire and the gift of life, in *Toward a Theology of Eros – Transfiguring Passion at the Limits of Discipline* (eds. V. Burruss and C. Keller), Fordham University Press, New York, pp. 38–62.

Gledhill, T. (1994) *The Message of the Song of Songs*, Inter-Varsity Press, Leicester.

Gorringe, T.J. (2000) *The Education of Desire*, SCM, London.

Irigaray, L. (1993) Sorcerer love: a reading of Plato, *Symposium*, "Diotima's speech," in *An Ethics of Sexual Difference* (ed. L. Irigaray) (trans. C. Burke and G.C. Gill), Cornell University Press, Ithaca, NY, pp. 20–33.

Jowett, B. (1953) *The Dialogues of Plato, Volume 1*, Oxford University Press, Oxford.

Kearney, R. (2006) The Shulammite's song: divine eros, ascending and descending, in *Toward a Theology of Eros – Transfiguring Passion at the Limits of Discipline* (eds. V.

Burrus and C. Keller), Fordham University Press, New York, pp. 306–340.

Marx, K. (1867/1992) *Capital: Volume 1: A Critique of Political Economy*, Penguin, London.

Maslow, A.H. (1943) A theory of human motivation. *Psychological Review*, 50, 370–396.

Moore, S., OSB (2002) The crisis of an ethic without desire, in *Theology and Sexuality: Classic and Contemporary Readings* (ed. E.F. Rogers, Jr.), Blackwell, Malden, MA/Oxford.

Ostriker, A. (2000) A holy of holies: the Song of Songs as countertext, in *The Song of Songs. A Feminist Companion to the Bible* (eds. A. Brenner and C.R. Fontaine), Sheffield Academic Press, Sheffield, pp. 36–54.

PCUSA (Presbyterian Church of the United States of America) (1988) *Pornography: Far From the Song of Songs*, Presbyterian Distribution Services, Louisville, KY.

Pope Paul VI, (1968) *Humanae vitae*, www.vatican.va/holy_father/paul_vi/encyclicals/documents/hf_p-vi_enc_25071968_humanae-vitae_en.html (accessed November 12, 2010)

Plato (360 BCE) *Symposium*, available at http://classics.mit.edu/Plato/symposium.html (trans. B. Jowett) (accessed November 9, 2010).

Sartre, J.-P. (1969) *Being and Nothingness*, Methuen, London.

Stivers, R. (1994) *The Culture of Cynicism*, Blackwell, Malden, MA/Oxford.

Williams, R. (2002) The body's grace, in *Theology and Sexuality: Classic and Contemporary Readings* (ed. E.F. Rogers, Jr.), Blackwell, Malden, MA/Oxford, pp. 309–321.

5

Framing Sex

Must the Framework be Marriage?

Chapters 5 and 6 tackle an issue which for many Christians is the central feature of their sexual practice. Can marriage continue to provide the framework for all sexual relations among Christians? But that question requires answering another: what is marriage anyway? Tackling that question will reveal a rich theological heritage from which to draw, together with much disconcerting detail about the changes to marriage that have occurred in every period of Church history.

By the end of Chapter 6 our key question will be answered positively but broadly – yes, marriage can continue to provide the framework for sexual relations among Christians. There will be some reservations and qualifications too. The argument is for a marriage-shaped morality. Chapter 5 states the traditional framework (Section 5.1). Section 5.2 outlines a range of theological and sociological *critiques* of marriage. Section 5.3 outlines frameworks other than marriage for sexual relations, but remains unpersuaded by them. Section 5.4 provides a robust response to the critiques of marriage outlined in Section 5.2. Chapter 6 presents marriage in some contemporary Christian theology.

It has been necessary to separate questions about what marriage *is* from questions about when marriage *begins*, or how marriage is *entered*. These questions, which raise other questions about celibacy, virginity, and "sex before marriage," are dealt with in detail in Chapters 11–13.

5.1 The Traditional Framework: Celibacy or Marriage?

The traditional teaching of all the different branches of the Christian Church – Roman Catholic, Anglican, Protestant, and Orthodox is that you must not have sex unless or until you are married. Christian sexual morality has always been understood as a "marital morality" (Salzman and Lawler, 2008, pp. 162–191). The teaching assumes marriage is restricted to men and women, and for same-sex couples who are excluded from it, it is the classic "heterosexist" institution.

Heterosexism: A term that refers to a system of negative attitudes, bias, and discrimination in favor of opposite-sex sexuality and relationships. It can assume that opposite-sex attractions and relationships are the only norm and therefore superior.

The *Catechism* expresses well the traditional and official view. It says

> Those who are engaged to marry are called to live chastity in continence. They should see in this time of testing a discovery of mutual respect, an apprenticeship in fidelity and the hope of receiving one another from God. They should reserve for marriage the expressions of affection that belong to married love. (*Catechism of the Catholic Church*, 1994, para. 2350)

Few Christians uphold this teaching in practice. In 1991 some Anglican bishops candidly yet officially admitted the problem – they recognized that most people who marry are sexually experienced first, and they do not want to widen the gap between them, and the traditional Christian teaching. On the other hand, they want to support young Christians who sincerely believe that it is not simply better, but actually that it is the will of God (no less), that they should not have sex until they marry. That is why they say

> God's perfect will for married people is chastity before marriage, and then a lifelong relationship of fidelity and mutual sharing at all levels. We recognise that it is increasingly hard today for the unmarried generally, and for young people facing peer pressure in particular, to hold to this ideal, and therefore both the Church and its individual members need to be clearer and stronger in supporting those who are struggling against the tide of changing sexual standards. (House of Bishops of the Church of England, 1991, section 3.8)

This task is, however, very difficult. That is why the bishops go on to say

> we need to give this support in such a way that those who may eventually go with that tide will not feel that in the Church's eyes they are from then on simply failures for whom there is neither place nor love in the Christian community. (House of Bishops of the Church of England, 1991, section 3.8)

Activity: Why do you think that the churches' teaching about confining having sex within marriage is widely disregarded?

Comment: Perhaps the availability of cheap, reliable contraception was first on your list? For nearly 50 years, the contraceptive pill has separated the pleasure of sexual intercourse from a predictable consequence of it – babies. Whatever moral view is taken about contraceptives, they are not going to be "disinvented," so the temptation to use them will always be there.

Second, the comparatively late age of men and women at the time of their first marriages makes sexual experience before marriage practically inevitable. In Britain, the median age of women marrying for the first time, in 2007, was 28.7 years. For men it was

30.8 years (OFNAT, 2008). For most of Christian history it was permissible for young men to marry at 14, and young women at 12. (This is not to suggest that everyone did in fact get married at these early ages, especially the men.) Boys and girls could become betrothed or engaged as early as age seven. In these circumstances it was much easier to insist on virginity before a wedding.

One of the reasons for marrying late is the modern emphasis on education. Only in the nineteenth century did schooling become compulsory in developed countries. Nowadays, education followed by attendance at college, university, and further professional training is open to many more people and lasts longer. Graduates are in their twenties, sometimes their late twenties, before they are regarded as qualified for their first career or professional employment.

"Courting" and "chaperoning"   Third, the mixing of the sexes is a *fait accompli* unthinkable a century ago. Then, if you went out on a date and you belonged to the aristocratic, middle, or upper-middle class, a chaperone would have gone with you! "Courtship" would have been formally conducted under the wary eyes of parents or their representatives. Schools and colleges are now in the main "de-segregated." Men and women serve together in the armed services. Since most of the jobs formerly done only by men are now open to women, the workplace has become a primary space for romantic encounter. Single sex halls of residence in universities have been phased out in the past 30 years, and cars, mobile phones and cheap, effective electronic communication enable personal contacts to be continued whether between parts of the globe, or different corners of the same night club, and in and from shared public spaces such as trains, church services, and lecture halls. Almost all the barriers that impeded communication between the sexes, ingeniously erected by previous generations, have been dismantled.

Fourth, relative affluence and availability of consumer credit brings the purchase of cars, fashionable clothes, alcohol, entertainment, and expensive holidays within reach of many more people. These provide greater opportunities for leisure and for personal intimacy.

Fifth, the economic independence of women from men removes from them the necessity of seeking a husband for economic support, or ending up in uncertain spinsterhood. Young women no longer wait around for a man to take care of them, especially when up to a half of all marriages end in divorce. In Britain women now outnumber men as university students. This is a huge gain for women, and for the whole society.

Sixth, a good case can be made for accusing the churches of pastoral incompetence in relation to the sex lives of young adults. There is a real snag in the traditional teaching of the churches – one they have not really come to terms with at all. All churches teach that celibacy is a rare gift. So the churches repeat what they take to be "traditional" teaching, that marriages begin with weddings, and that you should not have sex until you are married. But they are also saying that you are very unlikely to have been granted the gift of celibacy to enable you to avoid having it. They are often embarrassed about talking about sex and so may lack basic communication skills in their ministries to a substantial section of the world's population. They may also be slow to recognize the impact of social changes on the beliefs and practices of their potential members.

5.2 The Case against Marriage

This section queries whether Scripture, Tradition, and Experience provide the endorsement of marriage that the churches generally want to claim. There is a response to these queries in Section 5.4.

Marriage remains a desirable state. Most people hope to marry, and all who do hope their marriages will last. Testimony to its enduring attraction can be found in the number of same-sex couples who hope to join its ranks. There are, however, also much greater reservations about marriage, based in part on growing awareness of the number of divorces and their impact on children, and a recoiling against the patriarchal structure of that institution.

Students of marriage need to know that contemporary readings of Bible, Tradition and Experience yield up a diversity of marital belief and practice, some of which is frankly bewildering and ambiguous. These are *internal* difficulties, belonging to Christian thought and practice. Theology has a serious obligation here – the requirement to tell the truth. The future of marriage will be better served by open discussion of these difficulties, than by defenses of it that seem merely to repeat familiar, exhausted readings of each.

It may come as a big surprise to entertain the possibility that *the New Testament is scarcely in favor of marriage at all.* There is a conundrum here that may be difficult to get our heads around. Did we not spend a whole chapter hearing how the churches base their beliefs and practices on Scripture, Tradition, Reason, and Experience? We now need to investigate the question whether marriage as it is presently practiced is in fact consistent with and authorized by these sources. If indeed the answer is ambiguous, then it is either the wrong answer or the churches are claiming too much for their sources.

5.2.1 Mixed messages from Scripture

Protestant Christians like myself were taught that marriage was pretty much inevitable. It was God's license for having sex. To this day, churches may emphasize marriage and families to the extent that unmarried people are made to wonder whether they are valued and what they are missing. Confident that our beliefs were based on biblical teaching, we never engaged with this saying of Jesus:

[27]Some of the Sadducees, who say there is no resurrection, came to Jesus with a question. [28]"Teacher," they said, "Moses wrote for us that if a man's brother dies and leaves a wife but no children, the man must marry the widow and have children for his brother. [29]Now there were seven brothers. The first one married a woman and died childless. [30]The second [31]and then the third married her, and in the same way the seven died, leaving no children. [32]Finally, the woman died too. [33]Now then, at the resurrection whose wife will she be, since the seven were married to her?"

[34]Jesus replied, "The people of this age marry and are given in marriage. [35]But those who are considered worthy of taking part in that age and in the resurrection from the dead will neither marry nor be given in marriage, [36]and they can no longer die; for they are like the angels. They are God's children, since they are children of the resurrection." (Luke 20:34–36)

> *Activity:* Why do you think this passage is hardly known? What view of marriage is found in it?

> *Comment:* Could it be that it contains a view of marriage that many churches have discarded and do not want to become known?

The brothers were all practicing Levirate marriage in accordance with the Law of Moses (Deut. 25:5–10). This incident is preserved in all the synoptic Gospels (Mark 12:18–27; Matt. 22:24–33) and because the answer Jesus gives in all three involves references to angels and to the resurrection of the dead (both beyond our experience) readers have been in some difficulty ever since. But Luke tidies the saying up and puts a different spin on it. Jesus, but only in Luke, *disparages* marriage (see also Luke 14:20, 26; 17:27; 18:29–30). Marriage is for "the people of this age." People who want to be not merely citizens of this age but also of the age to come, *avoid* marriage altogether.

Angels? Ancient beliefs about angels rendered them not subject to death. That detail exempts them from any imperative to reproduce themselves. On the other hand mortals, by reason of their mortality, *do* have an imperative to reproduce, and marriage was given for that purpose. As Martin explains, "Marriage, therefore, was completely implicated in the dreaded cycle of sex, birth, death, and decay, followed by more sex, birth, death, and decay" (2006, p. 105). Mortals can anticipate *now* that blessed state where there is no more death, and no more marriage, by refraining from sex and from marriage in this life. (For further textual details of Luke's anti-marriage stance, see Martin, 2006, pp. 106–109.) These verses in part explain why the Catholic Church still regards celibacy as a loftier state than marriage.

Singleness is better   The reservations of Paul regarding marriage are well known. Singleness is better. But if the unmarried and widows "cannot control themselves, they should marry, for it is better to marry than to burn with passion" (1 Cor. 7:9; 36b). The path of marriage leads to "many troubles" (1 Cor. 7:28b), and to "the affairs of this world" (1 Cor. 7:33a, 34d), and is best left untrodden. The imminent return of Christ renders it irrelevant in the last days (1 Cor. 7:29). The interests of husbands and wives are "divided" between their love for each other and their love of the Lord (1 Cor. 7:32–4). The single life is a better path, towards living "in a right way in undivided devotion to the Lord" (1 Cor. 7:35).

A later letter attributed to Paul adds to the ambiguity of the New Testament teaching about marriage. In 1 Corinthians marriage is discouraged: in Ephesians it is *endorsed*. A long section about the conduct of family life starts promisingly with the injunction "Submit to one another out of reverence for Christ" (Eph. 5:21). It is sometimes claimed that this verse may be a possible lingering echo of early marital equality. But it is the *kind* of marriage that this author assumes and commends, which is certain to trouble any serious reader of this passage.

While there are many positive features of the narrative to support a contemporary case for Christian marriage (see Section 6.3.2), there are also elements that grate against modern sensibilities. Three times husbands are told to love their wives (Eph. 5:25, 28, 33b) and three times wives are told to submit to their husbands (Eph. 5:22, 24b, 33c). There is an uncomfortable implication in this passage (and in parallel ones: Col. 3:18-22; 1 Pet. 2:11–3:6) that rarely surfaces in contemporary theological discussion. Marital love belongs to the husband only, as a function of his priority, or "headship," in the marriage. The husbands do the loving, and the wives do the submitting.

Unpalatable as this one-sided view of marital love may be to the taste of modern readers, including growing numbers of thoughtful evangelical Christians (Bartkowski, 1997, p. 406), it is embedded in the ancient worldview of the relations between the sexes, where the man is the active, and the woman the passive, subject (see Section 2.3). Osiek and Balch comment on the difficulty this ethic poses for those "many modern Christians," who "are responding to our recent experiences in social and political history by rejecting passive subjection to domestic and political hierarchical institutions" (1997, p. 47).

Dirty, stained, and wrinkled?   There is more to disturb us in this passage. Drawing from images from the prophet Ezekiel, the writer insists that the Church, the very Bride of Christ, must first be washed, sanctified and beautified.

> Christ loved the church and gave himself up for her to make her holy, cleansing her by the washing with water through the word, and to present her to himself as a radiant church, without stain or wrinkle or any other blemish, but holy and blameless. (Eph. 5:26–27)

Since Christ does all this, the process is a further example of male activity and female passivity.

And that is only part of the difficulty. There is a disturbing connection between pollution and the female body. Martin comments "Note how the gendering of dirt is introduced. The gender duality makes the male the active agent: the male brings holiness, cleanness, blamelessness, glory, and spotlessness to the profane, dirty, stained, wrinkled, guilty, *female* principle" (2006, p. 113; emphasis in original). When the New Testament is positive about marriage, it incorporates assumptions about the hierarchical relations between men and women, and about the inferiority and impurity of women's bodies. If there are good arguments for marriage, they must be based on different premises.

What then, is there, in the New Testament to encourage marriage? It is assumed, rather than commended. A bishop must be a "husband of one wife" (1 Tim. 3:2). A wedding feast at Cana is the place where Jesus performed "the first of his signs which revealed his glory" (John 2:11), but his presence at a wedding reception as a guest (and his supernatural generosity) does not justify assumptions about the meaning or value of marriage as an institution. When Jesus speaks of marriage it is in the context of then current disputes about divorce (Mark 10:1–12; Matt. 19:3–12). These disputes are more central to the Gospel writers' interests than Jesus' thoughts about marriage. Nevertheless, they indicate the importance of marriage at the time of Jesus, and Jesus heightens it by his opposition to divorce.

It can therefore be safely said that the New Testament provides support for marriage. But it discourages it too, and that remains a problem. There is ambiguity within and between the synoptic Gospels over marriage (and of course over divorce), and between Jesus' advocacy of lifelong marriage, Paul's view of marriage as a concession to desire, and Luke's dislike of it. These diverse views are hard to harmonize.

5.2.2 Mixed messages from Tradition

So there remains a *diversity* of teaching about marriage (and divorce) in the New Testament which deconstructs and qualifies modern assumptions that it commends marriage without qualification. The same ambiguity can be found in the churches' teaching about families. Any commendation of a particular family form must first accommodate the *anti*-family teaching of Jesus himself (Thatcher, 2007, pp. 25–63). Tradition is similarly ambiguous about marriage. Much that was once deemed essential to marriage has been quietly forgotten.

Traditional marriage: "A different institution altogether?"   For a brief foray into Tradition we will go to an early modern marriage service, "The Form of the Solemnization of Matrimony" of the 1662 Book of Common Prayer. All marriage services in Episcopalian or Anglican Churches derive from this classic text, and it remains a legal form of marriage in some of them. The priest says to the congregation,

> Dearly beloved, we are gathered together here in the sight of God, and in the face of this congregation, to join together this Man and this Woman in holy Matrimony; which is an honourable estate, instituted of God in the time of man's innocency, signifying unto us the mystical union that is betwixt Christ and his Church; which holy estate Christ adorned and beautified with his presence, and first miracle that he wrought, in Cana of Galilee; and is commended of Saint Paul to be honourable among all men: and therefore is not by any to be enterprised, nor taken in hand, unadvisedly, lightly, or wantonly, to satisfy men's carnal lusts and appetites, like brute beasts that have no understanding; but reverently, discreetly, advisedly, soberly, and in the fear of God; duly considering the causes for which Matrimony was ordained.
>
> First, It was ordained for the procreation of children, to be brought up in the fear and nurture of the Lord, and to the praise of his holy Name.
>
> Secondly, It was ordained for a remedy against sin, and to avoid fornication; that such persons as have not the gift of continency might marry, and keep themselves undefiled members of Christ's body.
>
> Thirdly, It was ordained for the mutual society, help, and comfort, that the one ought to have of the other, both in prosperity and adversity. Into which holy estate these two persons present come now to be joined.

The beauty of the archaic language lends itself to a deep sense that marriage is ancient, venerable, and time-resistant; that is why, just because it belongs to another age, some couples still choose it and reject more modern versions. But further scrutiny reveals an understanding of marriage that is unlikely to be shared any longer either by the couple or the church where the wedding takes place.

Activity: Please re-read the extract, and make a note of some of the clues the extract gives about its historical context.

Comment: There are various examples of archaic language that you will have spotted, and various ideas that look archaic too. We will now more closely identify some of these in order to indicate some of the differences between marriage then and now.

First, marriage is referred to as "holy Matrimony," an "honourable estate," a "holy estate," an ordinance, but not as a *sacrament*. Marriage was not designated a sacrament of the Church until the Council of Verona in 1184. Nearly 400 years later the new Protestant and Anglican churches "de-sacramentalized" marriage. So for 1,200 years marriage was not a sacrament. Then it became a sacrament. Now it is either a sacrament or not depending on the tradition or church to which you belong.

There are good reasons for calling marriage a sacrament, but these have to be better ones than the reasons originally given in the twelfth century, namely that the sacramental grace bestowed was literally a medicine, a *medicinum* for the sickness of sexual desire and the inevitability of physical pollution through having sex (yes, even in marriage). The medicine was "a divine help for keeping passion not only inside one's marriage, but even within it confined to the innocent and therefore permissible motive for having intercourse, which is to conceive a child" (Mackin, 1982, p. 32).

Second, as we have just seen, there must be some serious doubt whether Paul commended marriage "to be honourable among all men." Ephesians 5 endorses marriage, but 1 Corinthians only reluctantly permits it (above, 5.2.1).

Third, there may be no admission of sexual pleasure, even in marriage. Mark Jordan says "marriage shelters some sexual activity from an otherwise absolute critique of sexual pleasure" (Jordan, 2002, p. 107). Even this judgment may be too generous in the present context. The warning that marriage must not be entered "to satisfy men's carnal lusts and appetites," and the concession that it is "a remedy against sin," leave little room for enjoyment.

Fourth, the Latin word for "remedy," *remedium*, like *medicinum*, assumes that desire is a sickness, for which God has provided a strictly limited cure. Our difficulty with this teaching is likely to be that the permission it gives is almost wholly negative. There are better justifications for sex within marriage than avoiding having sex with someone else. Must there not be some doubt whether this is a moral justification for marrying at all?

Fifth, while marriage is open to "such persons as have not the gift of continency," is there not a valid inference to be drawn from this limitation that the gift of continency is better?

Sixth, children clearly belong, now as then, to the purposes of marriage. That is a crucial justification for marriage (see Section 5.4.2), but where are we going to find it in the Bible? The praises of sexual love in the *Song of Songs* do not mention procreation as any kind of justification for love making. There is no known teaching of Jesus that links being married to having children. The relation between husband and wife is examined by Ephesians 5, but children do not feature in it (apart from the requirement of their obedience – Eph. 6:1). Children may be among the "many troubles" that come with marriage and against which Paul warns (1 Cor. 7:28b). Children therefore can be a reason for *avoiding*, as well as for entering, holy matrimony.

There are further features of the broader ceremony itself that are unlikely to commend themselves to contemporary Christians, especially brides. The name of the service, the Form of the Solemnization of Matrimony, tells us something important about the beginning of marriage (see Sections 13.1 and 13.2). For most of Christian history, Christians followed the Greek, Roman, and Jewish practice of beginning marriage with betrothal. Mary and Joseph provide the best of several biblical examples (Matt. 1:18–25). The very name of the service assumes that *the marriage has already begun.* The service "solemnizes" the marriage that has *already been started* with a prior betrothal, by recognizing, formalizing, and blessing this marriage. Tradition indicates that the entry into marriage was a *process* over time, and not a single event (the "nuptials") (Thatcher, 2002). This fact alone sweeps away at least some anxieties about sex "*before* marriage," because "before" and "after" are differently located in a couple's history over time.

Or again, obedience, and the requirement of wifely submission is assumed by the ceremony. The wife must later answer "I will" to the question "Wilt thou obey him, and serve him. . .?" And the service also preserves the male guardianship of women. While unmarried women have *needed* the protection of men in every century (and are still not entirely safe from them), the bride, was, and often still is, "given away." The male minister inquires "Who giveth this woman to be married to this man?" A man, usually the bride's father if he is alive, responds. The great Anglican divine, Richard Hooker thought the giving away "putteth women in mind of a duty whereunto the very imbecility of their nature and sex doth bind them, namely, to be always directed, guided and ordered by others" (Cressy, 1997, p. 339).

Finally, only the bride received a wedding ring. Not only was this manifestly unequal, the symbolic meaning of the ring confirmed the patriarchal nature of the rite. While it may have been "a token of love and commitment," it "also served as a tag, a mark of ownership." The ring may even have "represented an ancient bride price, given by the man to the woman as a symbol of purchase as well as a token of commitment" (Cressy, 1997, p. 343).

Whatever the attractions and advantages of marriage may be today, it is judged to be a "different institution altogether" (Tolbert, 2006, p. 41) from the one practiced in the seventeenth, or the fifth or the first centuries CE. The *dis*continuities between the marital practices of earlier generations and our own do not amount to a case for rejecting marriage. But they *do* show that marriage has shown itself to be highly adaptable and developmental, and is clearly capable of changing further. (The arrival of easy divorce may have been the greatest change of all.) They also show that much early marital practice is no longer acceptable. That is why Martin accuses the churches of idolatry and hypocrisy in their bare-faced attempts to pass off current practices as an extension of traditional views. He writes

Not only is contemporary Christianity idolatrous in its focus on the family and marriage; it is also hypocritical. It either explicitly states or assumes that its current values are the obvious expression of Christian Scripture and tradition. Though most Christians assume that the current centrality of marriage and family represents a long tradition in Christianity, it is actually only about 150 years old. (Martin, 2006, p. 103)

And the ambiguities that a study of Scripture and Tradition reveals to us are intensified when we turn to Experience.

5.2.3 Mixed messages from Experience

We have spoken of internal difficulties within marriage as a Christian institution. There are of course *external* difficulties too. One is the impact of divorce on marital expectations. Generally only failed marriages come to public attention. The majority still remains intact. In Canada, in 2005, 38.3% of married couples were divorced by the time they reached, or would have reached, their thirtieth wedding anniversary, just over one in three (Ambert, 2009, p. 3). This compares with an estimated 44% in the United States. Nearly two in three remained intact after 30 years, and we can assume that many of these were happy. But the number of divorces greatly increased from the 1960s to the late 1980s in most developed countries, and this trend has had multiple effects.

One such effect is to make public just how bad some marriages actually are. Another is to make couples wary of entering marriage at all, since its fragility as an institution is all too obvious. Another is to change the nature of marriage fundamentally since everyone now knows that the vow to stay together until death can be readily revoked. Marriage continues to be blighted by domestic violence, yet for women it is safer than informal cohabitation, and much safer than living with an uncommitted boyfriend (Thatcher, 2003, 13–14; 2003a, pp. 13–14).

The *experience* of marriage has undergone remarkable changes. Perhaps the most significant change is the achievement of much greater equality for women (Browning, 2007; Witte, Green, and Wheeler, 2007; Tipton and Witte, 2005). Let us isolate three more of the many changes that might be listed: the influence of romantic love; the decline of patriarchy; and the changing pattern of work.

"What's love got to do with it?"   Did you note there was no mention of love in the extract from the Book of Common Prayer Marriage Service? The hope of "mutual society, help, and comfort" perhaps offers a solace akin to lasting love, but the idea of marrying for love was only being introduced to North America and Europe in the seventeenth century. Stephanie Coontz traces the history of marriage and shows that, for "thousands of years," marriage

> was not fundamentally about love. It was too vital an economic and political institution to be entered into solely on the basis of something as irrational as love. For thousands of years the theme song for most weddings could have been 'What's Love Got to Do with It?' (Coontz, 2005, p. 7)

Historians are agreed that "only in the seventeenth century did a series of political, economic, and cultural changes in Europe begin to erode the older functions of marriage, encouraging individuals to choose their mates on the basis of personal affection." Not until a further century had passed, "and then only in Western Europe and North America, did the notion of free choice and marriage for love triumph as a cultural ideal" (Coontz, 2005, p. 7).

Romantic love is probably grossly over-valued in present developed societies. It is readily confused with infatuation. It creates impossible expectations. It has suffered from the intense idealization that it gets in popular music and media. Yet people still marry "for love." However, there are now studies which warn against the destructive potential of romantic love. In the recent book *In the Name of Love*, romantic love is shown to have potentially violent, even murderous consequences. The authors interviewed 18 men, all of whom were convicted of *murder* or attempted murder of their female partner (Ben-Ze'ev and Goussinsky, 2008, p. xvi). They argue that thwarted romantic love is complicit in the actions of these men. Unrealistic expectations about love can lead to literally "lethal" disappointments (Ben-Ze'ev and Goussinsky, 2008, p. 23). Frustrated possessiveness leads to violence.

Activity: Think of some popular songs which peddle the myth of romantic love. Or, if you prefer, think of some popular songs that are a reaction against it.

Is marital conflict inevitable?   A sweeping survey of marriage and family throughout the world concludes that "Patriarchy, the law of the father, was the big loser of the twentieth century. Probably no other social institution has been forced to retreat as much" (Therborn, 2004, p. 73). Patriarchy was probably less securely lodged in Christendom than elsewhere, but the extent of its survival throughout the world remains disturbing. Therborn suggests the term "de-patriarchalization" for this process. We shall see that only a version of de-patriarchalized marriage is likely to interest people of marriageable age today. But even here, criticisms of the new "egalitarian marriage" are emerging.

A recent monograph on violence in marriage "depict[s] equality as the source of marital conflict, the problem rather than the solution" (Dolan, 2008, p. 20). The model of a couple becoming "one flesh" in marriage is thought to license the erasure of the weaker partner. The model of the man being the "head" of the woman in a marriage is a recipe for female submission; while the model of two equal partners is no less free from the possibility of violence than the other two models because it *leaves no room for resolving conflict*. Ben-Ze'ev and Goussinsky also find the "one flesh" model destructive, in fact "impossible in light of the physical separateness of the two lovers" (2008, p. 13). Rather *distance* in a close relationship is to be prized: "distance has a somewhat similar function to the cartilage in our bones: it protects the bones from rubbing against each other too much" (2008, p. 14).

The third change in the experience of marriage, after those of love and power, is work. Now that roughly two-thirds of mothers undertake paid work outside the home, the single most obvious improvement that must be made to marriage is reducing the "second shift" of domestic work for already working wives.

This means that the progress made by women in becoming family earners has to be matched by progress made by men in sharing the domestic and caring responsibilities. A decade ago, a study of the experience of the first five years of marriage in the United States showed that balancing paid work with family responsibilities was the major problem for couples. There was an extraordinary imbalance in the contribution of husbands and wives to doing household tasks. On average (Center for Marriage and Family, 2000), women then spent 18 hours per week, and men one hour, on these!

There can be no going back to fixed and dependent roles for wives. "New families are being formed, in which men and women share economic responsibilities as well as the domestic tasks that ensure that family members go to work or school clean, clothed, fed, and rested, and come home to a place where they provide for each other care and comfort" (Goldscheider and Waite, 1991, p. xiii). According to these authors the alternative to "new families" is not a return to "traditional families" but "no families" at all, as "women decide that the new marriage bargain – in which they hold a job and remain responsible for all child care and housework – is a bad deal, and as men decide that filling all the requirements of a traditional breadwinner but getting few of the traditional prerogatives or wifely supports is just as unattractive" (Waite and Gallagher, 2000, p. 171).

5.3 Alternative Frameworks: Justice and Friendship?

The criticisms of marriage that have just been aired are not fatal to marriage. Rather the defense of the "marital sexual morality" of the Christian faith must be an informed one, and these difficulties are genuine and require robust response (see Section 5.4). But the severity of these internal and external difficulties has led some Christian writers to seek alternative frameworks within which sexual relations might be set. Two of these are considered next.

5.3.1 Justice and sex

Perhaps the most convincing and attractive alternative framework is Margaret Farley's *Just Love*, in the book of that name. Farley has developed, carefully and sensitively, "a justice ethic for sexual activities and relationships based simply on a general understanding of justice" (2006, p. 178). Justice means "to render to each her or his due" (2006, p. 208). Within the context of sexual relations it appears as the "formal ethical principle" that "*Persons and groups of persons ought to be affirmed according to their concrete reality, actual and potential*" (Farley, 2006, p. 209; emphasis in original). Affirming persons requires granting them respect, and that includes respect for their autonomy, their relationality, and their well-being (2006, pp. 211–214, 231). That is the basis of a sexual justice ethic.

Seven norms of justice   The sexual justice ethic generates seven "norms." These norms "are not merely ideals; they are bottom-line requirements," but which nonetheless "admit of degrees" (Farley, 2006, p. 215). They are:

1.   do no unjust harm,
2.   free consent of partners,
3.   mutuality,
4.   equality,
5.   commitment,

6. fruitfulness, and
7. social justice (2006, p. 231).

If sexually active Christians were practicing just love there is no doubt that they would be better Christians, and probably better spouses and lovers! But Farley raises an important question that may already have occurred to you as you have read the last paragraph, "What is distinctive about a Christian sexual ethic" (2006, p. 240). The answer is "not that it offers something other than a justice ethic, but that it is contextualized differently and. . . it will no doubt give significance to additional norms." These are the norms that operate in Christian communities, and the examples given are "norms and ideals of faithfulness, loving kindness, forgiveness, patience, and hope" (2006, p. 241).

One looks in vain for marriage as a contributor to the basis of just love, or to the norms that just love generates, or to the additional norms that churches are able to provide. Rather practitioners of just love may turn to marriage as an institutional framework that can support them. Farley is far from hostile towards marriage, and well attuned to its historical and current ambiguities (2006, p. 254). She says, "For the sake of love and the ones we love, we commit ourselves to institutional frameworks that will hold us faithful to our love" (2006, p. 260). Marriage is one of these. Such frameworks "ought to be subject to norms of justice. If they are not, we challenge them or forsake them, or we shrivel up within them" (2006, pp. 260, 263). Marriage appears to be just one of the institutional frameworks for affirming our love. When marriage is commended as an optional institutional framework, it is subject to the prior norm of justice (2006, p. 265).

Justice-love and same-sex marriages   A justice-based sexual ethic can be an effective way of advocating same-sex marriages, but it is not clear that this is the best way. Marvin Ellison provides a good example. Justice "is the virtue of seeking abundant life for all" (Ellison, 2004, p. 36). Above all, "a justice ethic must address the use and misuse of power" (2004, p. 39). He holds that "marriage is an evolving institution whose meanings have been long contested" (2004, p. 39), so that "Once a patriarchal theory of male supremacy and female inferiority is discredited, and once marriage is valued primarily as a protective, stabilizing context for intimacy and ongoing care between partners, then justifications for excluding same-sex partners melt away" (2004, p. 74).

But marriage, he continues, is too discredited to monopolize sexual relations any longer. While Ellison thinks marriage should be available to lesbian and gay couples as a human right, he presses the question why they should conform to a heterosexual and heterosexist institution that has oppressed them and in any case is in deep trouble. The "single standard" for Christian sexual ethics is "justice-love" (2004, p. 142). Two of its "components" are "an affirmation of the goodness of sexuality and embodiment;" and "a genuine honoring of sexual difference and respect for sexual minorities."

Within this framework fidelity is commitment, not to one's partner "till death us do part," but "to honesty and fairness and an ongoing willingness to renegotiate the relationship to serve the needs of both parties." Marriage "should be de-centered" from its place in Christian sexual theology (2004, p. 143), and friendship preferred as "the most enduring basis on which to construct relationships of mutual respect, care, and abiding affection."

5.3.2 Friendship and sex

Several theologians now make the case for friendship over marriage as the basis of a Christian sexual ethic. Recently, Mary Ann Tolbert, alert to the biblical and historical reservations about marriage, some of which have been aired in this chapter, rightly says that the chief reasons for which marriage continues to be valued *now*, have never actually belonged to the marital tradition in the West.

> many of the values attributed to modern marriage, such as mutuality, fidelity, intimacy, companionship, and sexual pleasure, are in the main not found at all or not found in the same way in ancient constructions of marriage and are certainly not values associated with marriage in the Christian New Testament. (Tolbert, 2006, p. 41)

Elizabeth Stuart, a critic of marriage, acknowledges that "many heterosexual marriages do work," and *do* "manifest the presence of God within them" (Stuart, 1995, p. 117). But – now for the sting – she asks "if marriage as an institution does not automatically guarantee this kind of relationship, is there a relationship which is in operation among those couples who do have successful marriages?" Happy marriages are happy because the couple are *Just Good Friends* (the title of her book). Friendship is more valuable than marriage because friendship is what makes happy marriages happy.

Justice and friendship do not provide the only alternative sexual frameworks. Various theologians have offered *eròs*, trust, "right relationship," community, "pleasure, mutuality, embodiment, and spirituality," vulnerability, and so on, as the basis for alternative frameworks (Farley, 2006, p. 179). But it is high time to consider whether these alternatives are needed at all.

5.4 A New Case for Marriage?

The mixed messages that percolate through to us from Scripture, Tradition, and Experience need not be fatal to marriage. On the contrary they may provide an opportunity to commend marriage as a fundamental good for spouses, families, and societies. This section is a response to the objections and difficulties posed in Sections 5.2 and 5.3.

5.4.1 Mixed messages – robust responses

Marriage in the Gospels   It is true that the New Testament is ambivalent about marriage, but that tells us nothing about the importance of marriage now. One of Paul's reasons for refraining from marriage was his belief that the time was short before the Parousia or return of Christ (1 Cor. 7:29). Since the possibility of Christ's return does not stop us from training for careers and trades, and taking out mortgages, insurances, and pension plans, it should not stop us from marrying either.

Luke's Gospel depicts Jesus as against marriage. That may have been out of loyalty to a band of itinerant preachers who shunned family ties in order to devote themselves more successfully to proclaiming God's Reign (Theissen, 1978). But Jesus *accepts* marriage in

Mark's Gospel (Mark 10:2–12), and in Matthew's (19:2–12). Both Gospels have Jesus resist easy divorce (Thatcher, 1999, pp. 250–288). But why does Jesus do that?

If Jesus thought marriage was a corrosive or harmful institution, he might have advocated divorce, yet he adopts an opposite position, castigating both the men who divorced their wives for trivial reasons and those Pharisees who supplied the theological know-how to assist them. At the very least Jesus finds warrant for marriage in the creation narratives and sees it as an institution given by God in creation. Jesus in these Gospels endorses marriage. He sees it as an institution in which faithfulness, constancy, and care are encouraged and exercised.

Activity: Read Mark 10:2–12 and Matthew 19:2–12. Do you think the claim just made about faithfulness, constancy, and care can be justified from these verses?

Comment: Matthew uses Mark's Gospel when he writes his own, and his reshaping of Mark's narrative has given rise to many comparative studies. Our concern here is with something else – the character of marriage which Jesus, as presented by both Gospel writers, may have taught marriage to have. I think the claim just made is a valid one for three reasons:

First, Jesus teaches that divorce was permitted in the Hebrew Bible because of a lack of compassion ("hardness of heart").

Second, Jesus teaches that God joins people together in marriage, and that they should not be separated. This teaching supports constancy within marriage.

Third, Jesus teaches the closeness of husbands and wives within marriage, calling it a union. Within this context, care is intended (whether or not it is actually provided). (We will be looking more closely at Jesus' teaching recorded by Matthew; see Section 6.1.2.)

Marriage in the Tradition   If, and only if, the theology of marriage in Ephesians 5 is understood as a theology of marriage for all time, and not just for the time in which it was written, then, yes, it will be undoubtedly found to be hierarchical, sexist, and insulting to contemporary women. In fact several theologians think the exhortation to husbands to "love your wives, just as Christ loved the church and gave himself up for her" (Eph. 5:25) is the beginning of a Christian theology of marriage distinctively based on Christ's love (see Section 6.3). Others argue that it sets a "trajectory" towards the equal-regard marriage which is now advocated by liberal Christians (Thatcher, 2007, pp. 44–45). The passage is examined in detail in the next chapter (see Section 6.3.2).

Our single example of marriage from within Tradition, 450 years ago, exposed many assumptions that are not, and cannot be ours (see Section 5.2.2). But how many of *our* assumptions will be shared in 450 years time? Perhaps problems arise only when the sexism of another age is perpetuated in our own?

We have seen that Tradition provides examples of continuity and discontinuity between earlier times and now (see Section 3.3.2). A seventeenth century service provides one of many bridges that need to be crossed in order to retrieve how the Tradition that begins with the Bible has been handed on. The purposes of marriage that it describes (the birth and raising of children, a means of avoiding fornication, and "mutual society" – see

Section 5.2.2) have doubtless inspired millions of women and men to be caring parents, faithful partners, and lifelong companions. Marriage is still capable to helping and inspiring couples to attain these desirable goals. In this important sense it is not a "different institution altogether" from contemporary marriage, but an institution that contributes vitally to our own well-being and self-understanding.

Marriage and Experience   The mixed messages from Experience hardly count against the survival and commendation of marriage. The experiences of love, power, and work were clearly all variable, and their variability is a feature of marriage's strength and remarkable ability to adapt to new conditions and challenges. Late modern societies over-invest in romantic love, to their great detriment: but it is the over-investment in romantic love, rather than romantic love itself, that may be the problem.

The uncritical and total devotion to the loved other (which may be a form of delusion) is also capable of maturation, of critical development, of acquiring an increasing depth that strives towards reciprocity and mutual devotion. Jack Dominian, the renowned Christian psychiatrist, has investigated in several books what he calls "the process from falling in love to loving" (Dominian, 2001, p. 71). He has charted how couples over time are able to sustain, heal, and mutually empower each other. The over-emphasis on romantic love, and the murderous possessiveness that it appears to kindle in some psychopathically inclined individuals, are dangerous features of late modern cultures, but they should not be blamed on the institution of marriage and its advocates.

We have seen how pervasive personal and social power exudes from sexual relations (see Section 2.2.2), and it was evident, overtly and covertly, in the marriage ceremony just examined. Many critics of marriage are rightly critical of the exercise of patriarchal power within marriage, yet these criticisms generally resort to history in order to justify themselves. The issue as it affects marriage today is whether power is negotiated and fairly distributed within particular marriages. Judging marriages today on the basis of their history is like judging modern science on the basis of scores of abandoned scientific hypotheses, the memories of which may embarrass scientists today.

A similar response may be made to the objection that patriarchal marriage and egalitarian marriage are based on incompatible (and biblical) models, with the result that the institution suffers fatally from a structural flaw. Yet these models remain *models*, and our emphasis on each may vary. It does not follow from the growing acceptance of equality within a marriage that the means of resolving conflict (male authority) is removed. It follows that a *better* means of resolving conflict (negotiation) becomes necessary.

The *absence* of many of the effects of patriarchy within *contemporary* marriage services is evidence for the decline of patriarchal marriage, and the rise of a different egalitarian marriage that remains much less vulnerable to conventional feminist attack. The issue of the second shift remains a potent one; yet even here progress is being made.

Alternatives to marriage   Fourth, the alternative frameworks may not provide real alternatives to what marriage offers. The distinctiveness of a Christian sexual ethic might derive instead from what Christians believe about God, God's revelation through Christ and the Spirit, the Communion of Persons whom God is believed to be (see Section 6.2), and the Sacraments God has provided for our sustenance. Marriage requires unconditional commitments. The hope for marriage is not simply that it will be "subject to norms of justice," but that it will generate values of mutual, unswerving devotion and constancy as it becomes fully open to the spiritual resources that sustain it.

The common argument (which Farley does not herself make), that marriage is to be avoided because too many of them fail, is obviously bogus, for less formal norms (for example, of justice) are likely to fail too. Human beings are fallible, even in their aspirations to live according to norms. It helps to aspire to the best norms.

Similar difficulties attend the norm of friendship. Friendship is an elastic category with a wide span. Jesus "lay[s] down his life for his friends" (John 15:13). Liz Carmichael has written beautifully of how "The love of Christ on the cross is that of a friend who wills to draw all, through forgiveness and reconciliation, into friendship" (Carmichael, 2004, p. 6). Yet in New Testament times *amicitia* or friendship "carried a wide semantic field" (Osiek and Balch, 1997, p. 50), which also embraced relationships of trade and patronage. There is a similar wide range of meaning in today's use of friendship, ranging from lifelong devotion to a casual contact on a social network website. This wide range is also matched by a wide range of degrees of commitment.

Yet in marriage the commitments are unconditional and unreserved. The Anglican divine Jeremy Taylor (*d.* 1667) put this well. Marriage, he said, "is the queen of friendships" (Taylor, 1839, p. 308), yet he was equally clear that there were many different "kinds" of friendship and that marriage was "the measure of all the rest."

> *Activity:* This section offered "robust" responses to some of the criticisms leveled against marriage earlier. Were they too robust? Or not robust enough?

5.4.2 The "health paradigm" – marriage and children

The strongest argument for marriage is based on children. Children thrive best when they are brought up by their biological parents in a secure environment.

Children have been woefully neglected in theology. Why has this academic subject been, until recently, so prone to child neglect? Is it because so many theologians who write about sexuality and marriage are not parents, or have taken vows of celibacy, or are in same-sex relationships? A child-centered approach to family form cannot but conclude that children are more likely to thrive when brought up by the parents who conceived them. The evidence for this conclusion is overwhelming. In the United States it is summarized in the report *Why Marriage Matters: Twenty-One Conclusions from the Social Sciences* (Institute for American Values, 2002) and subsequently updated (Institute for American Values, 2006). (See Thatcher, 2007, pp. 120–134; Thatcher, 2010.)

The United States and Britain are the two countries that have the most to worry about with regard to the failure of children to thrive. In 2007 a UNICEF report undertook a comprehensive assessment of the lives and well-being of children and adolescents in the 20 economically advanced nations of the world and concluded that our two countries lag well behind the 18 others in all six measures of child well-being.

Europeans are unwilling even to reproduce their populations any longer, and in too many cases they do not care properly for the children they have. Philosopher Brenda

Almond has charted what she calls "the cherished 'idols' or dogmas of our day." These include

> The belief that, whatever the personal evidence of shattered lives, divorce or parting doesn't hurt; that deep attachments can be unilaterally shattered; that what adults in their personal lives do cannot seriously harm their children; that not making a commitment in the first place can solve the problem; that cohabitation is better than, or at least as good as, marrying; that genetic relationships don't matter; that genetic ancestry is available for sale or transfer. (Almond, 2008, p. 207)

Another secular inquiry, *The Good Childhood*, concluded "The most important act which two people ever perform is to bring another being into the world. This is an awesome responsibility and, when they have a child, the parents should [make] a *long-term commitment to each other* as well as to the welfare of the child." (Layard and Dunn, 2009, p. 155; emphasis in original)

Children provide, as they always have done, the best argument for marriage. But now there is also much empirical support for the view that they are more likely to thrive best in marriage than in alternative family forms. Theologian John Witte, Jr., calls this "the health paradigm of marriage" (Witte, 2002, p. 86), and it is why he says it is "both very new and very old." What is new is the

> wealth of recent statistical evidence demonstrating that, for most adult parties most of the time, married life is better than single life, marital cohabitation is better than nonmarital cohabitation, married parents do better than single parents in raising their children... [M]arried folks on average live longer, happier, and safer lives. They are more satisfied, prosperous, and efficient... Their children develop better emotional, social, and moral skills....

This then is what has been called in this section "the new argument for marriage." It easily outweighs the arguments of the marriage detractors. This is a conclusion that is taken forward to the next chapter where the *theological* framework for marriage can be analyzed and celebrated.

This chapter has commended marriage against the background of criticisms and alternatives. However, the case for marriage that is rooted in the core beliefs of Christian doctrine has yet to receive attention. That will happen in the next chapter.

References

Almond, B. (2008) *The Fragmenting Family*, Oxford University Press, Oxford.

Ambert, A.-M. (2009) *Divorce: Facts, Causes, and Consequences*, 3rd edn., Vanier Institute, http://30645.vws.magma.ca/node/80 (accessed November 12, 2020).

Bartkowski, J.P. (1997) Debating patriarchy: Discursive disputes over spousal authority among evangelical family commentators. *Journal for the Scientific Study of Religion*, 36(3), 393–410.

Ben-Ze'ev, A., and Goussinsky, R. (2008) *In the Name of Love: Romantic Ideology and its Victims*, Oxford University Press, Oxford.

Book of Common Prayer (1662) www.pemberley.com/janeinfo/compraym.html (accessed November 9, 2010).

Browning, D. (2007) *Equality and the Family: A Fundamental, Practical Theology of Children, Mothers, and Fathers in Modern Societies*, Eerdmans, Grand Rapids, Michigan/Cambridge, UK.

Carmichael, L. (2004) *Friendship: Interpreting Christian Love*, T&T Clark International, London/New York.

Catechism of the Catholic Church (1994) Geoffrey Chapman, London, www.vatican.va/archive/catechism/ccc_toc.htm (accessed November 3, 2010).

Center for Marriage and Family (2000) *Time, Sex, and Money: The First Five Years of Marriage*, Creighton University, Omaha.

Coontz, S. (2005) *Marriage, a History: from Obedience to Intimacy or How Love Conquered Marriage*, Viking Penguin, New York.

Cressy, D. (1997) *Birth, Marriage & Death: Ritual, Religion, and the Life-Cycle in Tudor and Stuart England*, Oxford University Press, Oxford.

Dolan, F.E. (2008) *Marriage and Violence: The Early Modern Legacy*, University of Pennsylvania Press, Philadelphia, PA.

Dominian, J. (2001) *Let's Make Love: The Meaning of Sexual Intercourse*, Darton, Longman & Todd, London.

Ellison, M.M. (2004) *Same-Sex Marriage? A Christian Ethical Analysis*, Pilgrim Press. Cleveland, OH.

Farley, M. (2006) *Just Love: A Framework for Christian Sexual Ethics*, Continuum, New York/London.

Goldscheider, F., and Waite, L.J. (1991) *New Families, No Families? The Transformation of the American Home*, University of California Press, Berkeley, CA.

House of Bishops of the Church of England (1991) *Issues in Human Sexuality: A Statement*, Church House Publishing, London.

Institute for American Values (2002) *Why Marriage Matters: Twenty-One Conclusions from the Social Sciences*, Institute for American Values, New York.

Institute for American Values (2006) *Why Marriage Matters: Twenty-Six Conclusions from the Social Sciences*, Institute for American Values, New York.

Jordan, M.D. (2002) *The Ethics of Sex*, Blackwell, Malden, MA/Oxford.

Layard, R., and Dunn, J. (2009) *A Good Childhood: Searching for Values in a Competitive Age (The Landmark Report)*, Penguin Books, London.

Mackin, T., SJ (1982) *What is Marriage?* Paulist Press, New York.

Martin, D.B. (2006) *Sex and the Single Savior*, Westminster John Knox Press, Louisville, KY.

OFNAT (Office for National Statistics) (2008) Marriages: Age at marriage by sex and previous marital status, 1991, 2001 and 2003–2005. Population Trends 127, http://www.statistics.gov.uk/STATBASE/ssdataset.asp?vlnk=9599 (accessed November 4, 2010).

Osiek, C., and Balch, D.L. (1997) *Families in the New Testament World: Households and House Churches*, Westminster John Knox Press, Louisville, KY.

Salzman, T.A., and Lawler, M.G. (2008) *The Sexual Person. Toward a Renewed Catholic Anthropology*, Georgetown University Press, Washington, DC.

Taylor, J. (1839) *A Discourse of the Nature, Offices, and Measures of Friendship: in Works XI*, Longmans, London.

Stuart, E. (1995) *Just Good Friends – Towards a Lesbian and Gay Theology of Relationships*, Mowbray, London/New York.

Thatcher, A. (1999) *Marriage After Modernity: Christian Marriage in Postmodern Times*, Sheffield Academic Press, Sheffield.

Thatcher, A. (2002) *Living Together and Christian Ethics*, Cambridge University Press, Cambridge, UK.

Thatcher, A. (2003) *The Daily Telegraph Guide to Christian Marriage and to Getting Married in Church*, Continuum, London/New York.

Thatcher, A. (2003a) *The Guide to Christian Marriage and to Getting Married in Church*, Continuum, London/New York.

Thatcher, A. (2007) *Theology and Families*, Blackwell, Malden, MA/Oxford.

Thatcher, A. (2010) Religion, family form and the question of happiness, in *The Practices of Happiness: Political Economy, Religion and Wellbeing* (eds. J. Atherton, E. Graham and I. Steedman), Routledge, London/New York, pp. 148–156.

Theissen, G. (1978) *The First Followers of Jesus*, SCM Press, London.

Therborn, G. (2004) *Between Sex and Power: Family in the World, 1900–2000*, Routledge, London/New York.

Tipton, S.M., and Witte, J., Jr. (eds.) (2005) *Family Transformed: Religion, Values and Society in American Life*, Georgetown University Press, Washington, DC.

Tolbert, M.A. (2006) Marriage and friendship in the Christian New Testament: Ancient resources for contemporary same-sex unions, in *Authorizing Marriage: Canon, Tradition, and Critique in the Blessing of Same-Sex Unions* (ed. M.D. Jordan), Princeton University Press, Princeton, NJ/Oxford, pp. 41–51.

Waite, L.J., and Gallagher, M. (2000) *The Case for Marriage: Why Married People Are Happier, Healthier, and Better Off Financially*, Doubleday, New York.

Witte, J., Jr. (2002) The goods and goals of marriage: The health paradigm in historical perspective, in *Marriage, Health and the Professions* (eds. J. Wall, D. Browning, W.J. Doherty and S. Post), Eerdmans, Grand Rapids, Michigan/Cambridge, UK, pp. 49–89.

Witte, J., Jr., Green, M.C., and Wheeler, A. (eds.) (2007) *The Equal-Regard Family and Its Friendly Critics: Don Browning and the Practical Theological Ethics of the Family*, Eerdmans, Grand Rapids, Michigan/Cambridge, UK.

6

Covenants and Covenant-Makers

Sexual partners should undoubtedly be practicing "just love" (see Section 5.3.1). They should undoubtedly be "good friends" (see Section 5.3.2). This chapter suggests that, in the quest for a theological framework that situates and gives meaning to sexual relationships, there are considerably deeper seams of Christian doctrine to be mined. These seams of doctrine support and commend *marriage* as a decisive Christian contribution to an understanding of the full meaning of sexuality. They will be mined in Sections 6.1–6.4.

A key doctrinal theme which blends together the relationship of God with the world, and the relationship of people with one another, is that of *covenant*, one of the subjects of this chapter. Marriage must begin "at the beginning" with God (Section 6.1). God is a Maker of Covenants (Section 6.2). Christ comes to found a New Covenant, which marriage is able to embody (Section 6.3). The New Covenant finds expression in the Eucharist – God's own way of making love (Section 6.4).

6.1 Beginning with God

6.1.1 Marriage: where to begin?

Any Christian *theological* understanding of marriage should begin with *theos* or God. This chapter will show how Christian beliefs about marriage derive directly from what Christians believe about *God*. Historical, anthropological, and social studies of marriage remain useful sources for theology, but beliefs about God are fundamental to, and mesh with, marital understanding, liturgy, and practice.

But there are other reasons why the theology of marriage should begin with God.

God, Sex, and Gender: An Introduction, First Edition. Adrian Thatcher.
© 2011 Adrian Thatcher. Published 2011 by Blackwell Publishing Ltd.

First, there may be a loss of understanding even among Christians of the theological meanings associated with marriage today. Yet a clear majority of adults still wish to marry. The churches, then, are presented with a remarkable teaching opportunity to tell Christian stories not just about marriage, but about the theological framework within which marriage is firmly set.

Second, there is a growing sense of ambivalence about marriage even within the churches, and certainly in the populations served by them. The links between the institution of marriage and core Christian doctrine need to be made more overt in the present century in order to dispel the doubts about, and criticisms of, marriage even *within the tradition itself* (some of which were examined in Section 5.2).

Third, when there was a ubiquitous expectation within Christendom that a large majority of people would marry, there was no need to *commend* marriage. Getting married was what people were expected to do. However, now there are many doubts about, and alternatives to, marriage. Since the churches remain committed to marriage, they need to commend marriage and its advantages more positively than ever before.

Activity: If you are not married, please ask yourself a highly personal question: whether you hope to marry someone some day? If yes, what draws you most to marriage?

Comment: You may have included in your answer terms such as the joy of sexual intimacy, love, companionship, mutual devotion, constancy, fidelity, a loving home for children, being devoted to your beloved, and so on. Later in the chapter these will be called "marital values." These values are human values (not necessarily Christian or religious), yet the Christian faith also proclaims, celebrates, and deepens them, and grounds them in the triune God. The rest of the chapter attempts to make good this claim.

6.1.2 Marriage: how to begin?

Beginning with God means, for Christians, beginning with Jesus. They believe that Jesus was the revelation of God. He was truly and completely divine. Beginning with His teachings about marriage is surely a promising start? Curiously when we look there, we find references to other beginnings. Jesus refers to the Book of Genesis ("The Beginning"), and when He does so, He assumes other beginnings as well – the beginning of time, and the beginning of the Reign of God. Matthew records,

[3]Some Pharisees came to him to test him. They asked, "Is it lawful for a man to divorce his wife for any and every reason?"

[4]"Haven't you read," he replied, "that at the beginning the Creator 'made them male and female,' [5]and said, 'For this reason a man will leave his father and mother and be united to his wife, and the two will become one flesh'? [6]So they are no longer two, but one. Therefore what God has joined together, let man not separate."

[7]"Why then," they asked, "did Moses command that a man give his wife a certificate of divorce and send her away?"

[8]Jesus replied, "Moses permitted you to divorce your wives because your hearts were hard. But it was not this way from the beginning. [9]I tell you that anyone who divorces his wife, except for marital unfaithfulness, and marries another woman commits adultery" (Matt. 19:3–9).

Matthew has slightly altered the version of this encounter he found in Mark's Gospel. In verse 3 he adds "for any and every reason." That small addendum enables his readers to locate the "test" within a controversy between two groups of Pharisees (followers of Shammai and Hillel). Both groups allowed divorce for the reason given in Deuteronomy 24:1 ("because he [a husband] finds something indecent about her, and he writes her a certificate of divorce") but they disagreed about what "something indecent" or "offensive" was. The Pharisees quote from this verse after Jesus has given his answer (Deut. 24:7).

Jesus knew his answer would land him in trouble with the Pharisees because the Mosaic Law (Deut. 24:1–4) allowed divorce whereas He did not (with one exception – "marital unfaithfulness"; Matt. 19:9). Whereas the passage is directly about divorce and only indirectly about marriage, it allows us to see into Matthew's understanding of the mind of Jesus.

6.1.3 Jesus on marriage

In this section, three vital insights into marriage, which obviously maintain their relevance for marriages in the present day, will be identified. They are:

1. about the way people are meant to be,
2. whether marriage is an arrangement for all peoples, at all times, and
3. how the image of God among women and men may be understood.

1 The way people are meant to be: First, Jesus appeals to a time "at" or "from the beginning" (it is the same phrase, *ap'archès*, in Greek). He goes behind the *time* of Moses (the point stands whether or not Moses is the author of Deuteronomy) to an earlier time before the law was given, indeed to the earliest time, to "the beginning." But this *chronological* point (about time) makes an *ontological* point (about *being*). It suggests that at the beginning, and before the catastrophe called "the Fall" (Gen. 3) there was no divorce, and indeed no need for it, since the couple were "no longer two but one" and unaffected by the havoc of divorce that was to come.

The later time is the time when divorce is permitted, when the "hard hearts" of husbands caused them to divorce their wives. This is the time that the Catechism calls "the regime of sin" (*Catechism of the Catholic Church*, 1994, paras. 1606–1608). In the Reign of God that begins with Jesus, there are no hard hearts. There is instead a peace between spouses that renders separation and divorce unnecessary.

While it is clear that Jesus talks here about divorce, what He says about it makes sense only in the light of these assumptions about marriage. Theological critics of marriage (see Section 5.2) leave these sayings well alone. Is that because it is uncongenial to their arguments that Jesus clearly honored and taught that the union between a man and woman was to be understood as lifelong and in principle, unbreakable?

2 Whether marriage is an arrangement for all peoples, at all times: Jesus refers in the passage to God as "the Creator," and quotes from the two creation stories that are found in

Genesis (1:1–2:4a and 2:4b–25). But now a new thought arises. Scriptural authority for marriage goes back to "the beginning," behind the law of Moses, to creation itself, and to the Creator who creates marriage along with the world. So, then, is marriage to be seen in the teaching of Jesus, as a *universal* institution, broader than Judaism, earlier than the Law of Moses, indeed preceding all religions, and belonging to the whole of humanity?

The Hebrew words for "man" and "woman" and "husband" and "wife" are the same, and there are obvious difficulties involved in regarding the mythical state of the first man and the first woman as a marriage. Jesus, however, *did* regard the relation of the first human pair as a marriage. His use of Genesis 2:24 (verse 7 in Section 6.1.2) supports the contention that human pair-bonding, universally and historically, is a fundamental "given" to the human species.

Leaving and cleaving   Alert readers will identify the suggestion that marriage may be a universal institution, as essentialist (see Section 2.1.1). The contrast between "conjugality" and "consanguinity" (Peachey, 2001, p. 5) will help to make clear what is at stake.

> **Conjugality:** The basic freedom of a person to marry.

On this view, consanguinity is *not* an ultimate relationship, whereas conjugality is. Rather, "The germ of society lies, not in kinship as biological descent, but in the

> **Consanguinity:** Being related to another by ties of blood.

leaving and clinging archetype that is the human *pair-bond*, the conjugal union" (Peachey, 2001, p. 5).

This archetype gets its name from Genesis 2:24 ("For this reason a man will leave his father and mother and be united to his wife, and the two will become one flesh.") that we have just read quoted by Jesus. The Authorized Version uses the rhyming terms "leave" and "cleave." "Leaving comes before cleaving" (Anderson and Fite, 1993, p. 13). Leaving and cleaving are the basic activities that help human societies to organize themselves.

The suggestion to be made is that there is a "universal proclivity" (which also allows for several exceptions) or a "propensity," for "a particular human male to bond permanently with a particular female. That propensity appears with our species. *We are made to so bond, and that bonding is archetypically foundational in the human story*" (Peachey, 2001, p. 5; emphasis in original).

The Vatican entertains a similar vision of the universality and divinely given nature of marriage: "Although the dignity of this institution is not transparent everywhere with the same clarity, some sense of the greatness of the matrimonial union exists in all cultures" (*Catechism of the Catholic Church*, 1994, para. 1603).

Language about bonding, archetypes, and foundations can sound forbidding to people unmarried and in sexual minorities, but it need not. Not everyone needs to bond permanently with someone else for children to thrive, and for societies to be organized.

3 How the image of God among women and men may be understood. Jesus' reference to the first human pair being made "male and female" draws directly on Genesis 1:27, "So God created man in his own image, in the image of God he created him; male and female he created them" (see Section 3.2.1). This text has been used in every century in order to establish the dignity or worth of all humanity over against everything else that God made.

"Man," it used to be said, is a "special creation." This is perhaps strange because the New Testament records that *Jesus Christ*, and not the first human pair, is the image of God (Col. 1:15).

Many different answers to the question just *how* the first pair image God have been given in Christian theology (Grenz, 2001), but the one which is deservedly common in Protestant and Catholic thought at present seems to be the *relational* one. In their relating to one another as male and female pairs, human beings image God. Marriage then becomes the paradigm or supreme example of loving relation. (The "essentialism" of this line of thinking and the easy complementarity it encourages has already been noted in Section 3.2.1.)

I just wrote "loving relation." If you thought "loving" was smuggled in, you are right! That relies on two more assumptions that Christian theology makes. The first is that "God is Love." That statement is found in a chapter of the New Testament (1 John 4:8, 17). The second assumption is that we can speak of God as three "Persons" who together are One in a community of love (see Section 6.2.3). The *Catechism* relies on both these assumptions in its handling of Genesis 1:27:

> God who created man out of love also calls him to love – the fundamental and innate vocation of every human being. For man is created in the image and likeness of God who is himself love. Since God created him man and woman, their mutual love becomes an image of the absolute and unfailing love with which God loves man. It is good, very good, in the Creator's eyes. (*Catechism of the Catholic Church*, 1994, para. 1604)

Once these assumptions are accepted, an ideal model of marriage emerges. In their love for one another, the spouses express something of the image of God, who is understood both as the Source of Love and as a Communion of (divine) Persons.

In summary, it is plausible to suggest from a reading of Jesus' teaching about marriage that He thought marriage at its best was able to symbolize the Reign of God, free from "hardness of heart." He thought it was a universal institution, given "at the beginning:" that it is to be practiced as a lifelong relation; and that it exemplifies supremely the relation in which the image of God is manifested.

We have at least begun the exploration of marriage with Jesus, even if the conclusions reached are tentative. Yet there is a stronger argument to be advanced. What has been claimed so far has been based on His *teaching*. But what if we consider His *work*, what Christians claim He came to do? And what was that? To establish a New Covenant. This is where the case for marriage gets stronger still (see Sections 6.2 and 6.3).

6.2 God the Father – Maker of Covenants

There are two suggestions in this section: that marriage is a covenant; and that it mirrors the divine covenant between God and God's people. In order to make these suggestions plausible, it will be necessary to disagree to some extent with the standard telling of marriage as a covenant and then to *re*tell it, paying close attention to how we use language when we make the attempt.

6.2.1 God the covenant maker

According to the standard view, God is a maker of covenants. God makes a covenant with Noah (Gen. 9:8–17), with Abraham (Gen. 15), and with Moses (Exod. 24). Christians call the Hebrew Scriptures the "Old Covenant" (Testament). Marriage too is a covenant. Hosea's marriage to his unfaithful wife, Gomer, indicates that marriage is a covenant. Her infidelity parallels Israel's infidelity to the covenant God. Israel is God's adulterous wife.

> **Covenant:** "[T]he normal translation in English of the Hebrew word *berit*, which in the Old Testament describes a wide variety of human relationships: for example Jonathan and David's solemn pledge of friendship (1 Sam. 20:1–11), treaties between states (1 Kgs. 5:12), and marriage (Mal. 2:14). Such covenants were often entered into with due legal formality and with religious rites such as sacrifice, with the gods of the contracting parties invoked as guarantors of the covenant (Gen. 31:44–54)" (Davidson, 2000, p. 141).

Isaiah (1:21–22; 54:5–8; 57:3–10; 61:10–11; 62:4–5), Jeremiah (2:2–3; 3:1–5, 6–25; 13:27; 23:10; 31:32), and Ezekiel (16:1–63: 23:1–49) all use the metaphor of marital unfaithfulness to illustrate the unfaithfulness (in their opinion) of Israel to their faithful God. Malachi thinks that a husband's divorce of his wife incurs divine displeasure. "'Why?' It is because the LORD is acting as the witness between you and the wife of your youth, because you have broken faith with her, though she is your partner, the wife of your marriage covenant" (Mal. 2:14).

> *Activity:* Look up "covenant" in a concordance. Discover how common the term is in the Hebrew Bible, and note some of its features.

The Hebrew Bible, then, is reckoned to teach that marriage is a human covenant that reflects the divine covenant between God and God's people. This view is thought to be confirmed by the New Testament where the covenant of marriage reflects Christ's covenant with the Church.

John Calvin, the Protestant reformer, confirmed the biblical view when he taught that marriage is "a covenant which God has consecrated" (Calvin, *Comm in Mal* 2:14; cited in Lawler, 2005, p. 79). He thought that "When a marriage takes place between a man and a woman, God presides and requires a mutual pledge from both. Therefore, Solomon in Proverbs 2:17 calls marriage the covenant of God ...." The Second Vatican Council taught that "The intimate partnership of married life and love has been established by the Creator and qualified by His laws, and is rooted in the *conjugal covenant* of irrevocable personal consent" (*Gaudium et spes*, 1965, section 48; emphasis added).

But this standard view of marriage as a covenant is not wholly accurate. The biblical God is undoubtedly a covenant-maker. But the Bible actually says little about marriage being a covenant. The Hebrew Scriptures use marriage metaphors in a variety of ways, but the idea of a single marriage metaphor, based on Yahweh's covenant with the people of God is "founded on a romantic and unsustainable ideal, unable to survive reality" (Moughtin-Mumby, 2008, p. 276). Malachi (and perhaps the author of Proverbs 2.17) *does* think of human marriage as a covenant. But there are no other direct references in the Hebrew Bible to marriage as a covenant, *and none at all in the New Testament.* Calvin is the first theologian to call marriage a covenant explicitly, and it does not finally appear in official Roman Catholic thought until the Second Vatican Council. This is strange indeed. Do you remember how everything the churches teach is supposed to be founded on Scripture and Tradition?

Metaphors and analogies   There is undoubtedly a sound theological case for thinking of marriages as covenants, but different grounds and arguments need to be employed which *develop* Tradition, not just repeat what is assumed to be there, or pretend it can be found (see Section 3.3). A promising start is to look at what is being done with language when marriage is described as a covenant. Since neither an invisible God nor a nation, nor the Church can be married in any straightforward sense, the language used must convey non-literal meanings. Analogy and metaphor provide two similar ways of doing this.

> **Metaphor:** "In metaphor a word or phrase ordinarily and primarily used of one thing is applied to another. The effect of a good metaphor is a shock of recognition for its appropriateness in spite of its unconventionality and inadequacy: 'all the world's a stage', 'a mighty fortress is our God', 'war is a chess game'" (McFague, 2000, p. 359).
>
> *Metaphora*, in Latin and Greek, means a transfer. In metaphor, meaning is transferred from one term to another.
>
> Metaphors may be substitutable or unsubstitutable. A substitutable metaphor is a figure of speech that can be swapped for another one. An unsubstitutable metaphor is used when what is described is necessarily described in an indirect way.

A description of the relationship between God and God's people as a marriage clearly involves a range of metaphors. It can be fairly said to "transfer" meaning from human marriages to God's relationship with God's people. In McFague's terms just quoted, it is "unconventional" and "inadequate," in fact downright odd. Is there however "a shock of recognition" for its "appropriateness?"

According to the prophets there is. They held in their minds certain features of human marriages, such as faithfulness, exclusiveness, and so on. Then they thought how their God was faithful and exclusively devoted to them, and they made a striking connection between one relationship and the other. Then they made another striking connection, but in reverse – between the faithfulness of a cuckolded husband whose wife was having affairs, and the faithfulness of their God whose people were messing with other gods.

Now an important question arises: is the marriage metaphor in this case substitutable or unsubstitutable? That difficult question is important because what lies behind it is an issue about the Israelites' *knowledge* of their God. It is a *cognitive* question. If their experience of God drove them to compare their relationship to God with the best features of human marriages; if they were searching for the least inadequate form of words to speak of the Holy One who had claimed the people of Israel as "His" own people, then the marriage metaphor is not merely "appropriate" but it is unsubstitutable too. There is something about being the people of God that the marriage metaphor expresses better than any other description.

So it makes real sense to speak, albeit metaphorically, of the relationship between God and the people of God as a marriage-covenant. A similar result awaits us when we turn to a similar type of language use – analogy.

> **Analogy:** An analogy is a type of reasoning where one thing is inferred to be similar to another thing in a certain respect, on the basis of the known similarity between the things in other respects. So analogies involve comparisons.
>
> An analogy of relation (or proportionality) is a type of reasoning where a relation between two things is inferred to be similar to a relation between two other things, on the basis of the known similarity between the relations in other respects.

Hosea compared his marriage to an adulterous wife, Gomer, with God's marriage to a faithless people (Hos. 1:2–3). That is an obvious analogy of relation. Analogy assumes there is a God and helps to explain how talk about God is possible. God's love, mercy, faithfulness, and so on transcend what we can know humanly about such qualities, but it nonetheless makes sense to ascribe such qualities to God truthfully. God has a covenant with God's people. To compare the marital covenant with the divine covenant is to use an analogy of relation. The crucial element in these claims is that they are not just optional figures of speech substitutable by other ones. They say something about God, and about God's own deep, committed interaction with humankind (see also Lawler, 2005, p. 74).

> *Activity:* Find some good examples of metaphor and analogy, not necessarily biblical ones, and perhaps discuss and compare them. (The point of the activity is not to get technical but to show how common they are, and how suggestive they can be in comparing meanings.)

6.2.2 The "matrimonial covenant"

The last section on "covenant" in the Bible and in theological language has shown, I hope, that to commend marriage as a covenant is to draw, positively and selectively, on Scripture and Tradition, to develop Tradition creatively, and to make good theological and practical sense. There are several other reasons why it is appropriate to think of marriage as a covenant.

First, there are positive resonances from contemporary colloquial English that support the use of covenant in connection with marriage. The term is often contrasted with "contract." "Covenant" eventually replaced "contract" in Catholic Canon Law (but not until 1983, when it was termed a *matrimoniale foedus* or "matrimonial covenant" (*Codex iuris canonici*, 1983, para. 1055.1).

Second, "covenant," as we have seen, has a rich theological heritage, whereas contract remains a legal term. In some parts of the United States, a "covenant marriage" is a legally distinct kind of marriage, in which the marrying couple agrees to obtain pre-marital counseling and accept more limited grounds for divorce. As Lawler notes,

> *Covenant* encompasses all that is legally and institutionally encompassed by *contract*, but it also insinuates more. It insinuates that the free, loving, mutual gifting and accepting that creates the community of marriage is not temporary and revocable, as it could be under contract, but permanent, irrevocable. (Lawler, 2005, p. 85)

Third, "covenant" expresses well what marriage requires. We know Jesus expected marriage to last for a life time because we know he was against divorce. A lifelong relationship requires much commitment, faithfulness and mutual devotion if it is to be achieved by non-coercive means. What would be an appropriate name for such an arrangement? Can you think of a better name than "covenant?"

Fourth, while covenant is an appropriate name for an arrangement that requires the making of solemn vows to one another in the presence of God and of witnesses, and which is intentionally lifelong, there is another, very theological, reason why the term "covenant" expresses the essence of marriage. Ultimately Christians think that God established a new covenant with the world through Jesus Christ (see Section 6.3). Christianity just *is* this new covenant, nothing more nor less. They proclaim this whenever they celebrate the Eucharist (see Section 6.4).

The wine symbolizes the blood of Christ, shed on the Cross, and Christ Himself when he instituted the Eucharist said "This is my blood of the covenant, which is poured out for many" (Mark 14:24). Jews naturally thought the biological basis of life lay in blood (Lev. 17:11) and Christians see the shedding of Christ's blood and His laying down of His life as the supreme act of divine love. Through His blood "the eternal covenant" is established (Heb. 13:20).

> **Icon:** From the Greek *eikòn*, "image," an icon is a sign or representation that stands for its object by virtue of a resemblance or analogy to it. In some Christian thought God or "the holy" is powerfully revealed by means of icons.

Fifth, the covenant of marriage is an *icon* or symbol of God's covenant with all that God has made. Marriage vows require the unconditional love of the spouses for one another. The vows offer the opportunity for spouses to say to one another that *they will love one another as God in Christ loves them both* (see Section 6.3). It is a *mimesis*, of the divine covenant, but also a *participation*, a mingling of the divine love with the mutual love of each partner for the other.

> **Mimesis:** From the Greek *mimeisthai*, "to imitate", and *mimos*, "imitator," mimesis is the strong representation or imitation of something else. ("Mime" and "mimicry" also come from this root.)

6.2.3 God: the communion of persons

There is another way for theological thought about marriage to begin with God. That is to follow the Roman Catholic advance in marital theology that begins with *Gaudium et spes* (1965), and continues through Pope John Paul II's *Familiaris consortio* (1981) and his *Letter to Families* (1994). Here, the basic statement that God is Love is explained by means of the Trinitarian understanding of the nature of God. God is a communion of Persons, a *communio personarum*.

Earlier, we noted how the idea of the image of God has been recently used to convey the thought that men and women image God in their relations with one another (see Section 6.1.2). The doctrine of the Trinity codifies what is meant by this. Men and women are made in the image of God. Jesus, we have noted, refers to this verse in his teaching about marriage and divorce. But God is the *triune* God. God is a single "communion of Persons": the Persons of Father, Son, and Spirit constitute the dynamic flow of Love that God is. Human persons too, are made for love and for communion, and they share this communion with friends and strangers, and if they are married, with their spouses and any children they have (Thatcher, 2009, p. 203).

Communion is essential for the fulfillment of men and women. Marriage, of course, is inessential for communion, but because it assumes the intimacy of love-making, it provides for the most intense form and experience of it. The *unio* or "one flesh union" of marriage symbolizes and enacts the union of the Persons within God, one in being yet distinct from each other, each an individual expression of the infinite love that God perfectly is.

These ideas are generally unfamiliar, even to theological students, not all of whom have learned the profundity of the doctrine of the Trinity. Any talk of God as a communion of three Persons seems to risk imagining three persons enjoying a more carnal communion in one bed. Bewilderment appears to arise due to unfamiliarity with any attempt to integrate human love between two persons with the divine Love between the three Persons.

The doctrine of the "social Trinity" (as it is called) may not arise *in* Scripture, but it arises *out of it*, and it is found in (parts of) the Tradition. The Church teaches that God is *communio personarum*; that we are made in God's image, and so on. There is another "analogy of relation" here. The comparison is made between the communion of persons, which is marriage and the communion of Persons, which is the triune God. The overlap or continuity between the two sets of relations is in the reciprocal, self-giving love found among each set of persons.

Identity, mutuality, and equality   Once the basic analogy is established between the relations of Persons within God and the relation of human persons within marriage, other powerful insights can be drawn that contribute greatly to the commendation of marriage today. Here are three.

First, there is genuine *difference* and *otherness* in God (see Sections 8.4.2 and 14.2.1). Historically, this was expressed by saying that while all three Persons are one in their divinity, they differ from each other in their separate identities and roles. The analogy to be drawn is with the distinct personalities of the partners in marriage. While they are too often assumed to be "one flesh," this analogy helps to separate and to safeguard the individualities of the spouses.

Second, the relations of the Persons within God are mutual and reciprocal. The analogy to be drawn is with the problem of power-relations in marriages. In God, there is no dominance of one Person over one another. There is just the *communio personarum*. What more effective insight could there be in countering the view that wives should submit to their husbands?

Third, there is no inequality in God. Historically, this was expressed by labeling as heresy the doctrine known as "subordinationism."

The analogy to be drawn is with the equality of the partners in marriage. Here is a view of equality in marriage that does not need to rely on the assumption that there are two sexes, which somehow are

> **Subordinationism:** This was the belief that God the Father was superior to the other Persons, who in turn were subordinate. It is a heresy because the Persons in the Trinity are co-equal.

"equal." Christians can get their understanding of co-equal Persons from their doctrine of God.

> *Question:* How convinced were you about the claims of the last three paragraphs?

> *Comment:* I am guessing you may have found the ideas quite strange, and so you may not have been much convinced by them. I think they derive very plausibly from basic Christian beliefs about God, and I hope they will in due course become better known among Christians.

6.3 Christ – The Bridegroom, Maker of a New Covenant

6.3.1 Christ: maker of the new covenant

It was suggested (see Section 6.2.1) that the covenant of marriage may be closely related to the new covenant between God and God's world established by the self-giving of Christ in his death. That very useful preposition "in" has just been used in the previous sentence, and is sometimes shorthand for "participating in." When Jesus says to His disciples, "I am the vine; you are the branches" (John 15:5), his relation to them is both intimate and mystical. There is overlap between the whole vine and its parts, the branches. He continues, "He that abideth in me, and I in him, the same bringeth forth much fruit: for without me ye can do nothing" (John 15:5, King James Version). There is a close mystical participation between the disciples and Christ Himself. The type of metaphor He uses is synecdoche.

Synecdoche: A figure of speech in which a part is used for the whole, or the whole for a part.

When Paul wrote "if anyone is in Christ, he is a new creation; the old has gone, the new has come!" (2 Cor. 5:17) he thought of the resurrected Christ continuing to be present in the world through the lives of Christians. They represent Him. The life of Christ, or the Spirit animates them: they are almost literally members of Christ's continuing body on earth, as parts of a body make up the whole.

This is halfway towards understanding how the human covenant of marriage might represent the divine covenant that is the Christian faith. A marriage takes two. The new covenant takes two, God and the world. Through it God overcomes everything that alienates people from God and from one another. "God was reconciling the world to himself in Christ, not counting men's sins against them" (2 Cor. 5:19). "God was pleased to have all his fullness dwell in him [Christ], and through him to reconcile to himself all things, whether things on earth or things in heaven, by making peace through his blood, shed on the cross (Col. 1:19–20). Notice how the "'in' of participation" occurs in both verses. The covenant is God's act of divine love and reconciliation, the making of peace or *shalom*.

There could hardly be a better model of marriage than this, for in marriage a couple also become one. They join together in love and share the peace of intimacy. However, that is not the whole story. There is also overlap here, and real, though mystical participation of the human covenant in the divine covenant. As a married couple come to form a covenant between them and any children they have; as commitment deepens and love matures; that covenant comes to stand for, to *participate in*, the divine covenant that is secured through the outpouring of the divine Love which is Jesus Christ. A marriage can actually be an *icon*, a lived embodiment of the greater covenant love that took Christ to His cross.

Another, but rather more technical, way of making the same point is to return to the idea of analogy (see Section 6.2.1). A human marital covenant might be compared with the new divine–human covenant and similarities noted. But the claim is a stronger one. The analogy is one of *relation*, where say, love, faithfulness, commitment, self-giving, and constancy in the human relation, is able (albeit finitely and imperfectly) to indicate what the (much greater) love, faithfulness, commitment, self-giving, and constancy is in the divine–human relation, which is the new covenant.

These relations can be close enough to warrant the use of the terms *icon* and *mimesis* (see Section 6.6.2). The human marital covenant can be an *icon* of the divine–human covenant sealed by Christ's blood. "Marriage is mimesis. It is an enactment of God's faithfulness and the unity of Christ and the church" (McCarthy, 2002, p. 201). Mimesis can be not simply part of a theological description of marriage, but a *reason* for marriage. A couple might want to give themselves over to one another as God gives Godself over to us in the gift of the Son, Jesus Christ. The strong imitation of that covenant of love in a marriage actually comes to resemble it.

6.3.2 Christ: the mystical bridegroom

Earlier (see Section 5.2.1), we noted how Ephesians 5 conveyed a mixed message about marriage. It conveys a mixed message about gender too. It is now time to draw attention to several of its *positive* features. Please read carefully the extract below. Five conclusions will be tentatively drawn from it, and then explained. They are:

1.   Marriage is about love.
2.   Christ's love for the Church is thought to shape what Christian marriage is.
3.   Christ's love for the Church is a marital love.
4.   The intimacy between husbands and wives resembles the intimacy between Christ and the Church.
5.   Marriage is a special kind of sacrament.

> [21]Submit to one another out of reverence for Christ. [22]Wives, submit to your husbands as to the Lord. [23]For the husband is the head of the wife as Christ is the head of the church, his body, of which he is the Savior. [24]Now as the church submits to Christ, so also wives should submit to their husbands in everything.
>
> [25]Husbands, love your wives, just as Christ loved the church and gave himself up for her [26]to make her holy, cleansing her by the washing with water through the word, [27]and to present her to himself as a radiant church, without stain or wrinkle or any other blemish, but holy and blameless. [28]In this same way, husbands ought to love their wives as their own bodies. He who loves his wife loves himself. [29]After all, no one ever hated his own body, but he feeds and cares for it, just as Christ does the church – [30]for we are members of his body. [31]"For this reason a man will leave his father and mother and be united to his wife, and the two will become one flesh." [32]This is a profound mystery – but I am talking about Christ and the church. [33]However, each one of you also must love his wife as he loves himself, and the wife must respect her husband. (Eph. 5:21–33)

Marriage is about love. Three times husbands are instructed to love their wives (5:25, 28, 33). Nowhere in the New Testament is marriage, or love-making within marriage, justified by its procreative purpose. Children are addressed in the next verse (6:1), but it is not assumed that having them constitutes the main reason for marrying. No, marriage is about love, and there is no doubt about the kind of love the author envisages – it is the kind of love shown by Jesus Christ who "loved the church and gave himself up for her" (5:25) (see Section 5.2.1). A husband must love his wife to the point of laying down his life for her, as Christ too laid down His life in establishing the

New Covenant between God and the world. This is remarkable, even "a stunning idea" (Browning et al., 1997, p. 145).

The modern emphasis on love as a reason for marrying is a recovery, a retrieval of an ancient and biblical insight. Of course the text makes unfortunate sexist assumptions about marital and gender relations. The analogy moves from the superior to the inferior items in several pairs:

Superior	Inferior
Christ	The Church
Husband	Wife
Love	Submission/respect
Activity	Passivity

But we do not need to replicate the gender relations of the first or any other century in order to learn from the text. Instead, it is helpful to see the author beginning a trajectory (Browning et al., 1997, p. 147; see Section 5.4.1) towards a real Christian theology of marriage, which for its completion needed further time. That time is now.

Why should a wife be subject to a husband? Jesus Himself had said "No one can serve two masters" (Matt. 6:24). That is exactly what Christian wives have been expected to do until recently. Why can husbands and wives not both be subject *to one another* and both of them jointly "submit to Christ?" That is a recipe for a genuine, egalitarian marriage which preserves the insight that marriage is about love and insists that marriage is a *mimesis* of Christ's love for us.

Christ's love for the Church is thought to shape what Christian marriage is. The writer rewrites relations within households and families, in the light of Christ's loving sacrifice of Himself for the Church. Christ's death as an outpouring of divine Love becomes the organizing principle, a new theological method, for thinking about and putting into practice human relationships that are now also "in Christ" or "in the Lord."

The re-thinking of household, marital, and family relations that Christian communities were undertaking had to be predetermined by Christ's sacrificial death, understood as the revelation of divine love. Being subject "to one another out of reverence for Christ" (Eph. 5:21) is starting to change everything (and is of course a source for the trajectory hypothesis).

The injunctions governing the conduct of fathers, slaves, and masters later in the Letter are similarly imprinted on their recipients by these relations being "in the Lord." Slavery is not yet expunged from Christian households, but slaves are enjoined to regard themselves instead "as slaves of the Lord rather than of men" (Eph. 6:7b). Masters are sternly reminded that they and their slaves "both have the same Master in heaven; there is no favouritism with him" (Eph. 6:9c). The death of Jesus changes everything.

Christ's love for the Church is a marital love. Based largely on this passage, the Church has confidently thought of itself as the Bride of Christ, the Bridegroom. In pressing the string of analogies between husbands and wives on the one hand, and Christ and the Church on the other, the strong inference has been drawn ever since that Christ is able to be presented as a Bridegroom to the Church who is His Bride.

This is how the argument unfolds in the text. First, the hierarchical relation between husbands and wives is compared with the hierarchical relation between Christ and the Church (Eph. 5:23–25).

Next married love is illustrated and represented by Christ's sacrificial love for the Church (Eph. 5:25).

Next, and generally overlooked, are the details (derived largely from Ezek. 16:8–14) that Christ prepares His Bride for their wedding by giving her a nuptial bathing. The Church is bathed in baptismal water and made clean.

Next Christ puts His Bride in her splendid wedding dress, so as to present her to Himself as gorgeous and "radiant." In her wedding finery, she shows no trace of "stain, or wrinkle or any other blemish" (Eph. 5:27). Christians are made holy and purged from the stains and blemishes of sin by Christ's sacrificial death.

It has already been conceded that there are elements of this argument that are deeply offensive. The author, to an uncomfortable degree, has replicated the then standard view of gender. Once the old gendered framework is removed, the love that couples have for one another in marriage can be reinvested with profound meaning.

The intimacy between husbands and wives resembles the intimacy between Christ and the Church. At 5:26 ("husbands ought to love their wives as their own bodies"), another analogy is generated by the flexible core term "body." Husbands are no longer exhorted to follow Christ's sacrificial example in giving themselves up in love for their wives. No, the appeal is made instead to a different idea, that of self-interest! A husband is to regard his wife's body as an extension of his own.

The influence on the writer here is Genesis 2:24, which comes to the surface and is quoted at Ephesians 5:31. A husband and wife "become one flesh." The argument is subtly different too. The writer thinks it natural and right that people should care for their bodies. In general they do. But the idea that a married pair constitute one flesh, central to the teaching of Jesus about marriage (and probably known to the writer) is used to extend the care of the self and its body to the husband's care of his wife's body.

We have already met the difficulty that "one flesh" metaphors have had the effect of erasing or subsuming wives, both in body and soul, as they become incorporated, legally and existentially, into the bodies of their husbands (see Section 5.2.3). But the text need not, and should not, be read as authorizing any longer the incorporation of wives into their husbands' bodies as extensions of them. The union of the bodies of husbands and wives is probably to be understood primarily as sexual love.

But it may also be understood as a partnership or *consortium* of the whole of life. Indeed that was a definition of marriage in the medieval period (Fellhauer, 1979; Thatcher, 2002, p. 222). Union or unity, need not stand for the absorption of the lesser partner into the greater one, but for them to be united in their common life while retaining and furthering their separate identities as man and woman. Marital union can suggest instead the shared intimacy of a common life.

This shared intimacy is authorized by the Ephesians text. Again using synecdoche the author depicts believers as the parts or members of the inclusive body of Christ ("for we are members of his body" – Eph. 5:30). The insight to be emphasized is about the importance of intimacy. Just as men and women care for their own bodies, so does Christ also care for His own body. After Christ's resurrection and ascension Christians are understood to be a principal means of His continued presence in the world – they are His "body." But a body consists of its parts and their integration in the whole. The relation is one of near identity. The marital relationship is potentially one of integration of the partners in their common life where their love is stronger than the disruptions set against it.

Marriage is a special kind of sacrament. The profound "mystery" (*musterion*) of Ephesians 5:32 was translated "sacrament" (*sacramentum*) by Jerome (347–420), so the text of the Latin Bible of the Western Church was thought later on to state plainly that marriage was a sacrament. It is helpful to distinguish between *formal* and *informal* uses of "sacrament." In its narrower and formal sense, "The seven sacraments are the signs and instruments by which the Holy Spirit spreads the grace of Christ the head throughout the Church which is his Body" (*Catechism of the Catholic Church*, 1994, para. 774). Marriage is one of the seven sacraments in Roman Catholic and Orthodox theology.

In its wider and *informal* sense it means any means by which the grace of God is communicated. Protestant Christians, insofar as they have a use for the term, can accept this informal meaning. The "profound mystery" of Ephesians 5:32 again looks back to the text from Genesis 2:24 which Jesus used: "the two will become one flesh." Yet the writer takes the text and gives it a new sense: "I am talking about Christ and the church." There are two profound mysteries: the first is the intimate union of a man and a woman in marriage. The second, the intimate union of Christ and the church, is modeled on the first. Insofar as sacramental grace is conveyed in a marriage, the channel through which it flows is the union of the couple. The more that channel is open to mutual self-giving love, the greater the experience of sacramental grace flowing through it.

Co-ministers of the sacrament of marriage   There is a controversial detail of Western thought about the marital sacrament that the East does not recognize. Marriage is the only sacrament that does not, or rather did not, need to be administered by a priest. It is also the only sacrament that requires the presence of a woman for it to happen. A couple is validly married (assuming no impediment) when they make vows to each other in the present tense before witnesses. The priest pronounces them married, and blesses them, but the blessing is not what makes the marriage. The Council of Trent (1549–1563) required the presence of a priest for the marriage to be valid, and both Catholics and Protestants reacted to the abuses of clandestine marriages by tightening their grip on the entry to marriage. The presence of the priest or minister at a wedding should not eclipse the ancient understanding *that the couple ministers the sacrament to each other.*

The contemporary relevance of this detail lies in the couple being co-ministers of the sacrament of marriage. They are co-equal in their mutual ministry. They marry each other. Two simple points may be tellingly made about this.

First, the joint ministry of the couple is a fine basis for equal regard and full mutuality over every detail of the marriage. Members of the couple are full and equal partners in the common enterprise. There is no suggestion that one loves while the other obeys.

Second, everything they do for one another is a ministry, an "ad*minister*ing" of the sacrament. One of the supplementary prayers in the Common Worship Marriage Service of the Anglican Communion comes near to saying this when the priest asks God to

Give them wisdom and devotion in ordering their common life,
that each may be to the other
a strength in need, a counsellor in perplexity,
a comfort in sorrow and a companion in joy.

Question: How convinced were you about the claims of the last three paragraphs?

Comment: Again, like the question at the end of Section 6.2.3, I'm guessing you may have found the ideas quite strange, and so you may not have been much convinced by them. Again, my comment is similar. They are grounded in Tradition, and provide another case where Tradition bursts into contemporary significance.

Activity: Read again Ephesians 5:21–33, noting the references to "body" or "bodies." Remembering what was said earlier in the chapter about analogy and metaphor, note the different meanings of the term. How many did you find?

Comment: I found four direct references, more if indirect ones are counted. First, it is a name for the Church that Christ leads as its "head." Second, it is what husbands care for when they care for themselves. Third, it is what husbands care for when they care for their wives, as a single body together. Fourth, it is the mystical body of Christ whose parts are believers.

6.4 The Eucharist – Sharing in the New Covenant

The language of covenant now takes us to the Gospel narrative of the Last Supper where Jesus makes God's New Covenant with all that God has made (see Section 6.2.1). If marriage is to be successfully commended as a covenant, the best justification for it lies in the New Covenant that Jesus names and inaugurates in the Last Supper meal with His disciples, and in His death. Basing the covenant of marriage directly on the New Covenant established at the Last Supper is not, it must be conceded, official Church teaching, but it is open to the churches to draw deeply on the spiritual and doctrinal resources that the Eucharist provides, and to develop their traditions in this direction. The increasing emphasis on marriage as a covenant leads inevitably to the Eternal Covenant established through Christ Himself.
Matthew (26:26–29) writes

> [26]While they were eating, Jesus took bread, gave thanks and broke it, and gave it to his disciples, saying, "Take and eat; this is my body."
> [27]Then he took the cup, gave thanks and offered it to them, saying, "Drink from it, all of you.
> [28]This is my blood of the covenant, which is poured out for many for the forgiveness of sins.
> [29]I tell you, I will not drink of this fruit of the vine from now on until that day when I drink it anew with you in my Father's kingdom."

Shared bodies   There is a different range of theological meanings associated here with Christ's "body." The activity we have just done revealed different senses accorded to human bodies, marital bodies, and the body of Christ as the Church. Now the linguistic landscape changes. At the Eucharist the Church thinks of the body of Christ in another form. The body of Christ is now the *bread*, which is taken, blessed, broken, given, and eaten, first in Jerusalem before His death and thereafter whenever that meal is eaten in His name. The red wine, poured out, taken, blessed, offered, and drunk, symbolizes the offering of His body, His life, in establishing the New Covenant.

The idea of the body of Christ as bread and wine is very different from the idea of the body of Christ as Church. Just as the intimacy between a man and a women in their joined, single flesh, becomes a symbol of the intimacy between Christ and the Church, so here Christ's body as bread offers intimate analogies of another kind.

The Eucharist proclaims the new covenant and does so by the giving and receiving of a body, the body of Christ "This is my body." There are many unexplored parallels to be made between the experience of receiving one's spouse's body in the intimacy of marriage, and receiving the body of Christ in the Eucharist. Both of these are life-sustaining, life-enhancing, life-creating activities. They engage all our senses, especially the less prominent ones of touch, taste, and smell. They are both intensely joyful celebrations, each deeply satisfying. Yet both may also be covenanted pledges of love, richly symbolic, festive, and liberating (Thatcher, 1993, p. 41).

The Eucharist is erotic principally because in it is enacted God's infinite desire for us. The sending of the Son and the breaking of His body are the measure of it. It is strong confirmation of the conviction that God infinitely desires us, and together with Christ's crucifixion, it is the principal ground for believing that God is Love. The crucifixion should be understood less as the death of desire, and more as the intensification of desire, God's desire, to become one with us (see Section 4.4.2).

6.4.1 God's way of making love

We have seen that God's desire for us is the proper starting point of a theology of desire. Begin here, and more unexplored analogies can then take shape. The Eucharist is aptly described as "God's way of making love." Christ is the very body of God, given in a supreme act of love. The lover's body is given and taken (albeit not broken) in the act of making love. "Whoever really loves his partner loves not only for what he receives, but loves that partner for the partner's own sake, content to be able to enrich the other with *the gift of himself*" (Pope Paul VI, 1968, section 9; emphasis added).

The abandonment of the self in the giving over of oneself to another, one of the many rich possibilities of love-making, is exceeded only by God's self-abandonment on a cross, the complete giving over of Godself in self-surrender. The Eucharist is a love-making in countless ways.

- It happens only after peace has been made and exchanged between the guests at the table.
- It increases the sum of love in the world.
- It inspires its recipients to give themselves as Christ gave Himself for us.
- It satisfies.

At the Eucharist, hospitality and generosity are rooted in the action of God.

These are only a few of the meanings that "transfer" across from the Eucharist to marital intimacy, that provide breathtaking analogies of relation that illuminate the sacrament of marriage.

One might even say the Eucharist encourages an understanding of sexuality that *encourages chastity*, inside and outside marriage, because it *expresses desire in covenant form*. It expresses a level of commitment that is total and unconditional. Christ's giving of His body is the operation and continuation of God's irrevocable covenant. When the erotic parallels between divine and human love are extended, the suggestion is allowed to arise that the sexual giving and receiving of bodies outside of covenanted love is fraught with risk, and especially the risks of mis-hearing the body language that is inevitably spoken. The tactile symbolics of love-making can be reduced to a pleasant but meaningless gratification.

> *Activity:* How convinced were you about the suggestions made in the last few paragraphs?
> Write down your initial responses to the ideas in this section. Is the link between the covenant of marriage and the New Covenant sound? The idea that the Eucharist is God's way of making love would be regarded by some Christians as scurrilous, even blasphemous. Perhaps it is. What do *you* think?

The centrality and possibilities for meaning-making of the central ideas of Christian faith in the context of marriage confirm my reservations about any de-valuing of marriage expressed earlier in Chapter 4. The doctrinal possibilities of Christian faith in relation to the commendation of marriage are huge. It is premature, unnecessary, and even harmful to write marriage off.

However, there remains a continuing problem. Marriage is not the only family form, and in some developed countries about half the population lives alone. How might the grace of marriage be extended to such people? Is it possible that the covenant of marriage might become more of an inclusive institution? Can there be marital values outside the formal, legal, and ecclesiastical institution of marriage which also radiate the blessing of God? These questions are explored in Parts IV and V. For the moment, the discussion of sex comes to a close with the closure of Part II. It resumes after we plunge into very deep waters in Part III, turning gender upside down.

References

Anderson, H., and Fite, R. C. (1993) *Becoming Married*, Westminster John Knox Press, Louisville, KY.

Browning, D.S., Miller-McLemore, B.J., Couture, P.D., et al. (1997) *From Culture Wars to Common Ground. Religion and the American Family Debate*, Westminster John Knox Press, Louisville, KY.

Catechism of the Catholic Church (1994) Geoffrey Chapman, London, www.vatican.va/archive/catechism/ccc_toc.htm (accessed November 3, 2010).

Codex iuris canonici (1983) http://www.intratext.com/IXT/LAT0010/_P3U.HTM (accessed November 4, 2010).

Davidson, R. (2000) Covenant, in *The Oxford Companion to Christian Thought* (eds. A. Hastings, A. Mason, and H. Pyper), Oxford University Press, Oxford, pp. 141–143.

Fellhauer, D. E. (1979) The *Consortium omnis vitae* as a Juridical Element of Marriage. *Studia Canonica*, 13.1.

Gaudium et spes (Pastoral Constitution on the Church in the Modern World) (1965) www.vatican.va/archive/hist_councils/ii_vatican_council/documents/vat-ii_cons_19651207_gaudium-et-spes_en.html (accessed November 4, 2010).

Grenz, S.J. (2001) *The Social God and the Relational Self: A Trinitarian Theology of the Imago Dei*, Westminster John Knox Press, Louisville, KY.

Lawler, M.G. (2005) Marriage as covenant in the Catholic tradition, in *Covenant Marriage in Comparative Perspective* (eds. J. Witte, Jr., and E. Ellison), Eerdmans, Grand Rapids, Michigan/Cambridge, UK, pp. 70–91.

McCarthy, D.M. (2002) The relationship of bodies: a nuptial hermeneutics of same-sex unions, in *Theology and Sexuality: Classic and Contemporary Readings* (ed. E.F. Rogers, Jr.), Blackwell, Malden, MA/Oxford.

McFague, S. (2000) Metaphor, in *The Oxford Companion to Christian Thought* (eds. A. Hastings, A. Mason, and H. Pyper), Oxford University Press, Oxford, pp. 359–361.

Moughtin-Mumby, S. (2008) *Sexual and Marital Metaphors in Hosea, Jeremiah, Isaiah, and Ezekiel*, Oxford University Press, Oxford.

Peachey, P. (2001) *Leaving and Clinging – The Human Significance of the Conjugal Union*, University Press of America, Lanham, MD.

Pope John Paul II (1981) *Familiaris consortio: On the Role of the Christian Family in the Modern World*, www.vatican.va/holy_father/john_paul_ii/apost_exhortations/documents/hf_jp-ii_exh_19811122_familiaris-consortio_en.html (accessed November 4, 2010).

Pope John Paul II (1994) *Letter to Families*, www.vatican.va/holy_father/john_paul_ii/letters/documents/hf_jp-ii_let_02021994_families_en.html (accessed November 4, 2010).

Pope Paul VI (1968) *Humanae vitae*, www.vatican.va/holy_father/paul_vi/encyclicals/documents/hf_p-vi_enc_25071968_humanae-vitae_en.html (accessed November 12, 2010).

Thatcher, A. (1993) *Liberating Sex: A Christian Sexual Theology*, SPCK, London.

Thatcher, A. (2002) *Living Together and Christian Ethics*, Cambridge University Press, Cambridge.

Thatcher, A. (2009) The virus and the Bible: how living with HIV helps the Church to read it, in *HIV Prevention: A Global Theological Conversation* (ed. G. Paterson), Ecumenical Advocacy Alliance, Geneva, pp. 100–112.

Part III

Being Theological about Gender

7

God

Beyond Male and Female

This chapter builds on the foundations laid in Chapter 2. Gender was defined there and linked to sex, power, and language, and to the power of institutions to convey gendered messages. The description of gender in the time of Jesus (see Section 2.3) will help to set the scene for the next two chapters, and to assist in suggesting a thoroughly Christian theory of gender in Chapter 8.

The book as a whole attempts to ground what Christians believe about sex and gender, and what they do with them, in the core doctrines of the faith. In Part III, as we move from sex to gender, the questions of the apparent masculinity of God, and its huge influence on Christian self-understanding, loom large. In this chapter, the assumptions that God the Father is masculine, and that God the Son is male, are confronted head-on. God is readily shown to be beyond the human male–female polarity, and so (it will be urged) is "suprasexual" (Section 7.1). God the Son, who became incarnate in the man Jesus of Nazareth, is suprasexual too (Section 7.2), and so is able to be represented by both men and women (Section 7.2.1).

Progressive Christians are likely to agree that gender should not, and need not, be an issue in the churches, but some Roman Catholic writers are finding in the figure of Mary a potent means of undermining the androcentric bias of that Tradition. We examine a recent, vibrant reinstatement of Mary as the Mother of God and the New Eve, Mother of all the Living (Section 7.3). There appear to be some historical difficulties in this approach to Mary (Section 7.4), but it is welcomed as an additional theological strand in overcoming the androcentric bias of the Christian tradition.

God, Sex, and Gender: An Introduction, First Edition. Adrian Thatcher.
© 2011 Adrian Thatcher. Published 2011 by Blackwell Publishing Ltd.

7.1 Does God Have [a] Sex?

The question whether God has a sex is an odd one. It must be pressed however, in order to undermine the widespread and idolatrous assumption, whether tacit or explicit, that God is male. According to this view, "He," the all-powerful Father, makes the world and sends the Son (John 3:16). The name "Son," like "Father," is male, and when the male Son becomes incarnate "He" does so necessarily in a man. The male Christ can therefore be represented liturgically only by a male priest. The male God creates and underwrites the sex–gender hierarchy, and the male priesthood is divinely authorized by Christ Himself who called 12 men, and no women, to be His disciples. The masculine language says it all. This view is of course a partial caricature, but unfortunately it resembles standard Christian teaching too closely, and it may be lodged deeply and unreflectively in believers' minds.

Linked to this caricature is another. God is a Person. As the Creator, "He" is active in relation to "His" passive creation. "He" has agency. Through faith we have a one-to-one relationship with "Him," and/or with "His" Son Jesus. Since God is a Person who is called Father, "He" must be a male Person.

God is "suprasexual"   There is a definite theological answer to the question of the sex of God. God is beyond the distinction between male and female. There are four possibilities regarding the sex of God (we will come to the use of metaphorical language about God in a moment).

1. God is male.
2. God is female.
3. God is male and female. S/he is androgynous.
4. God is neither male nor female.

Activity: Which of the four statements above do you think gets closest to being true?

Comment: Most Christians are likely to opt for (1). Almost no Christians will have opted for (2). The case for (3) might be based on Genesis 1:27: God is imaged in men and women alike, and so within God there must be male and female elements. In the next few paragraphs I'm going to argue that (4) gets closest to being true.

First, in all Christian thought there is a basic distinction between the Creator and what is created (creation, creatures). God's being is eternal, ours is temporal; God's being is absolute and necessary; ours is relative and contingent (it might not have been; it will cease to be). A basic characteristic of living beings is that they are capable of reproducing themselves. For this they need sex. Beings who reproduce need *to be sexed*. They will generally be recognizable as either male or female. But God does not need to reproduce. Being sexed is part of what it means to be *created*. God is *not* created. Instead God is the supreme creative power, and the reason why there exists anything at all that is capable of reproducing itself.

Second, it is often overlooked that the character of human language about God is metaphorical and analogical. To understand literally the names given to God in the Bible and in the Tradition is to risk identifying the name with the *bearer* of the name, and that comes perilously close to idolatry. In the unique case of the eternal God names are symbols which can express something of God's reality but do not ever reveal God's nature more than partially. That is why the Eastern theologian Gregory of Nyssa (*d*. 395) insisted that the term "Mother" may be applied to the Person of the Father, because, as he says, "Both terms mean the same, because the divine is neither male nor female" (Harrison, 1990, p. 441). He thought that being sexed was a temporary feature of humankind, a feature of the body but not the soul.

Third, to think of God as a Person, male or female, is to ignore or to contradict the doctrine of the Trinity, and to make a huge theological mistake. Christians believe God is *personal* because God was revealed in the Person of the Son, and that human persons are made in God's image. It is a mistake to think of God as *im*personal or *non*-personal. But Christians believe that God is Three Persons. God is One, but not one Person.

Fourth, the image of God is male and female (an argument for the truth of proposition 3 above). There are undoubtedly female images of God in the Bible. The authors of Deutero-Isaiah (Isaiah 40–66) liken God to a woman giving birth. God says "like a woman in childbirth, I cry out, I gasp and pant" (Isa. 42:14; see also Isa. 46:3). God tells the Jewish people "As a mother comforts her child, so will I comfort you; and you will be comforted over Jerusalem" (Isa. 66:13; see also Isa. 49:15). But these are weak similes, and while they appear to authorize feminine language to speak of God and God's action, they are rare in the Bible and in the Tradition.

The case for denying that God is exclusively male rests not on combing through the Bible to discover feminine images that counterbalance the more usual male ones, but on what deity in the Christian tradition must be. The much-cited verse from Genesis regarding the image of God in human beings ("So God created man in his own image, in the image of God he created him; male and female he created them" – Gen. 1:27) is clearly gender-inclusive. Two simple conclusions follow. First, God is beyond the distinction between male and female (proposition 4 above). God is im-aged by the male *and* the female. Second, any imaging of God which over-emphasizes one sex over the other is anthropomorphic. Even to think of God, then, as masculine is to make several mistakes.

> **Anthropomorphic:** From two Greek words (*anthròpos* [man] and *morphè* [form]), it means the attribution of human characteristics to what is not human. Here it means assigning to God a property, maleness, which derives from half of humanity.

We need an adjective which expresses that God is beyond the distinction between male and female, and is imaged by the male *and* the female. Indeed, God's image is also found in people who do not identify straightforwardly with either sex. An obvious word to use is "suprasexual." *Supra* in Latin has a range of meanings, including "beyond," "above," "more than," and "before." The word must be used with particular care, however, because the Roman Catholic theologian Hans Urs von Balthasar (1992) has used it extensively in his descrip-tions of the relations between Christ and the

> **Suprasexual:** When applied to God, the term means that God is more than, not less than, sexual. God is beyond the distinction between male and female. The image of God may be found in men and women alike. Since God is Love, it also follows that the suprasexual God may be found in the meaning of sexual love, while never being completely identified with it.

Church, between God the Son and His Mother, between the New Adam and his Bride, and so on. These descriptions have the effect of removing or negating human sexual love before it can be used of God and our relations with God (Beattie, 2006, p. 151). They can be criticized on several grounds. Nonetheless, I think it makes good sense to say "God is suprasexual" in the simple and preliminary way in which it has just been outlined. So:

Question: Why do you think Christians think of God more in masculine, than in feminine terms?

Comment: An obvious answer is the masculine language that is rooted in the doctrine of the Trinity. Another is the obvious biological maleness of Jesus. Perhaps you thought of the tendency of a Church governed by men to "anthropomorphize" a male God in *their* image, or the association made by men of women's bodies with temptation, uncleanness, and sin?

7.1.1 Is God the Father masculine?

The Christian God is "our Father." Human fathers are all male. How can the inference be avoided either that God is male, or that when we speak of God, masculine terms are more appropriate than feminine ones? Why *should* it be avoided when the example of Jesus in speaking of His "Father" is so plain? A direct answer is not difficult to find. We will need to think of "Father" in four ways: (1) as a name, (2) as a Person, (3) as a Relation, and (4) as the Cosmic Parent.

The name "Father"   First the term "Father" names God in Christian prayer. Jesus taught his disciples

> This, then, is how you should pray:
> "Our Father in heaven,
> hallowed be your name,
> your kingdom come,
> your will be done
> on earth as it is in heaven." (Matt. 6:9–10)

"Father" is a name for God, albeit one of many. The first petition in the prayer is that God's name be hallowed. God is to be named and addressed as Father in personal and intimate terms. The issue is not whether God is our Father but what we are doing with language when God is so named.

When we worked on covenants in the last chapter we needed to examine metaphors and analogies (see Section 6.2.1), and the conclusions reached there will help here. God cannot be *literally* our Father, so we arrive appropriately at metaphor. "Unless God has a penis, the language is metaphorical" (Young, 1999, p. 195). In terms of the earlier discussion, a similar question arises now whether the use of a particular metaphor is "substitutable" or "unsubstitutable." Is the metaphor "Father" substitutable or unsubstitutable when used directly of God?

I want to say, against some feminists, that it is unsubstitutable, that is, it is too important to our understanding of God simply to be substituted by another one (like Creator). No, God really is our Father. But in that case, what makes that name so indispensable? How does calling God "Father" evoke "a shock of recognition for its appropriateness in spite of its unconventionality and inadequacy?" (See Section 6.2.1.) What meanings are selected from the experience of earthly fathers and attached irreducibly to the heavenly Father?

It seems certain that a cluster of ideas has become historically attached to the metaphor of heavenly Father that has become counterproductive (Thatcher, 2007, pp. 167–178). That cluster consists of elements of male parenting like distance and detachment from the hands-on caring for children; the need for discipline and chastisement for wrong-doing; the presence of an unchallengeable authority-figure in the household, and so on. These then get transferred to the divine Father. While these important elements belong to shared human parenthood, and may often be undertaken by human fathers (when they are available), they should not be identified as having priority over other elements involving the intimate, costly care of offspring. Plenty of other positive possibilities emerge from the continuing application of the metaphor "Father" to God.

Here are some examples. The Lord's Prayer teaches us to ask the Father for daily bread (Matt. 6:11). This seems an odd petition because three verses earlier Jesus has said "your Father knows what you need before you ask him" (Matt. 6:8). So why ask? A good answer might be to learn that for the very gift of life itself, and the daily calories required to sustain it, God's name is to be praised. God's children depend on God's provision, as surely as children depend on their parents' provision.

Another example is the Parable of the Prodigal Son (Luke 15:11–24). Since "prodigal" means "reckless extravagance," the Parable could easily be renamed the Parable of the Prodigal *Father*, for the father's reckless extravagance in welcoming back his son, is at least as noteworthy as the recklessness of the son in squandering his inheritance. The Parable illustrates the virtues, or character traits, of a human father, which best resemble the actions of the heavenly Father.

Activity: Read this familiar parable, in Luke 15:11–24. What virtues does the father display? Are the virtues you identified, gendered?

Comment: I hope you included compassion, joy, forgiveness, and mercy in your list. The point of the second question was to suggest that these are *human* qualities, not gendered ones. Men do not have a monopoly on compassion! Undoubtedly the parable is about men – a father, two sons, and their servants – but the suggestion is that it does not matter which sex exemplifies them. And that conclusion holds for all the word-pictures in this section. They represent the ungendered divine nature by means of gendered terms, whose gendered properties are irrelevant to their function. Masculinity is not necessary for father-metaphors to work. It may actually impede them.

God the Father as a person　　Second, the name "Father" names God in at least two quite distinct ways. "Father" is a name for the One God, as Jesus clearly taught. But "Father" is also the name for one of the three Persons who are together the one God. The one God is a personal God, and the personal God comprises the three Persons of Father, Son, and Spirit.

In the first case when God is addressed as Father, the Godhead (what God is in the unity of Persons) is addressed. So the aspect of God that corresponds metaphorically to "Father" is not the single male individual that every human father is, but the community of Persons that comprise the One God. Since God is suprasexual, so is God the Father.

In the second case "Father" addresses a distinct Person of the Trinity. The three Persons are suprasexual too.

Father as a relation   There is a detail from Trinitarian theology that helps us to see what is unsubstitutable about God being Father. This involves us in using the device called a logical truth. When we discussed desire as a type of love (see Section 4.2.2), it was suggested that it was a logical truth that desire always had an object. You cannot desire something just in the abstract.

There is a logical truth about the Persons of the Trinity (and about human persons too). It is this: there cannot be Persons without Relations. Imagine that you are called "mother" or "father" yet, you have no children. (OK: you might be acting in a play, or be a priest.) It would sound peculiar, or even insulting, wouldn't it? The reason why it would sound peculiar is a logical one: having a child is a necessary condition for being a parent. It is a rule about the use of words that is everywhere observed.

Something similar is true in the divine case. No, God does not give birth to Jesus (Mary does that – see Section 7.2), but God is Father principally *in relation to the Son*. In this sense, without the Son, God the Father could not be Father. God the Son could only be Son in relation to the Father. That is why the names "Father" and "Son" do more than name particular Persons. They designate Relations.

How does the idea that God the Father is a Person-in-relation aid the case I am making that God is not masculine? It does so because it indicates that what is at stake in calling God "Father" in this sense is the insistence that God is intimately in-relation, in the first instance to Christ, but also to the world, and to ourselves: not that God is masculine at all.

God as the cosmic parent   Thinking of God as our cosmic Parent might generate the thought that all human beings are God's children, the ones God created and loves. They are created by God and they are sisters and brothers of Jesus. Just as parents seek to protect their children from harms, so the heavenly Father wills the Kingdom to come when everyone will benefit from the just distribution of material and spiritual goods due to them as God's co-equal daughters and sons. Or one might be reflecting upon the impact of the belief in God's parenthood upon our vision of, and for humanity, if all of us are God's children. The author of Ephesians had a similar thought when he was moved to exclaim "For this reason I kneel before the Father, from whom his whole family in heaven and on earth derives its name" (Eph. 3:14–15).

So none of the four ways of using the unsubstitutable metaphor "God the Father" just described – as a name, a Person, a Relation, and Cosmic Parent – requires maleness for their deeper meanings to come to the surface. For these reasons it is reasonable, is it not, to insist that God the Father is not masculine?

7.2 Is God the Son a Man?

No. God the Son is not male either. Perhaps you will think I have gone mad in denying this? All I can do is offer arguments, grounded (as I think) deep in Tradition.

Jesus Christ is God the Son. He is the second Person of the divine Trinity. Like the other two Persons, He shares in the single divine nature that God supremely is. Each of the Persons of God, and the divine nature of God in which they all share, is beyond the distinction between male and female and is suprasexual. This Person, according to the main creeds of the Christian Church, becomes incarnate as a male human being, Jesus of Nazareth. Suprasexual from all eternity to eternity, the Son assumes a human, male nature, for some 33, or perhaps up to 50, years for the duration of his incarnate life.

Human nature   The miracle of the incarnation of God the Son in Jesus of Nazareth is based in part on the teaching of the Fourth Gospel that "The Word became flesh and made his dwelling among us" (John 1:14). Becoming flesh is what "incarnation" means (Lat. *carnis* = meat, flesh). "Flesh" is not limited to male flesh, nor even to human flesh. When Apollinaris (*d.* 390) taught that the Word, in becoming flesh, replaced the human soul of Christ during his earthly life, the Church responded by insisting that Christ assumed human nature *in its entirety*. On this premise He must have possessed a full human mental, emotional, and spiritual life. The Word became not simply flesh. The Word became "man." And these dry and ancient terms, "man" and "nature," are able to contribute to contemporary conversations about gender.

> **Man:** In Greek, there are two words for "man." *Anèr, andros*, is an individual male human being. To be androcentric is to be "male-centered." *Anthròpos* is the collective name for "humanity," as in anthropological (the study of the human species).
>
> In Latin, there are also two words for "man." *Vir* is an individual male human being. To be virile is to be manly. *Homo* is the collective name for "humanity," as in *homo sapiens*.

Jesus of Nazareth was a man, an *anèr*, a *vir*. But remarkably *the creeds do not depict him just as a male human being.* It is the inclusive generic term that is used in both Greek and Latin versions of the creeds. He is "truly *anthròpos*," "truly *homo*." The Creeds of Nicaea (325) and of Constantinople (381) use the term *enanthròpèsanta* ("enmanned"), which needs to be translated "becoming human" (Leith, 1982, pp. 31, 33). It was important for the Church not to underline the maleness of Christ but to emphasize instead his humanness.

We may need to recall here that ancient peoples held that there was one sex, not two (see Sections 1.2 and 2.3), existing on a single continuum from male to female. It is sexist today to use the term "man" inclusively, for this suggests the erasure of half the human race. But within the thought forms of the ancient world, the inclusive use of "man" would not have been thought sexist. The exclusion of women from the generic "man" would have been unthinkable.

The ancient world considered that humanity had a single nature. Male and female are variants of this same nature. Christ is confessed as being made known in two natures. The Creed of Chalcedon affirms "we apprehend this one and only Christ . . . in two natures" (Leith, 1982, p. 36). Christ's two natures are divine and human, and His human nature is an inclusive one. His human person, or personality, is part of His divine nature. He still remains in His incarnate life the *divine* Person that He eternally was and is. The importance of this detail will be evident in the next section.

So Christ's human nature is not humanity in its male form, but humanity as such. The Council of Chalcedon also affirms that Christ's being or reality is identical with that of the Father (*homoousion tò patri*) and "of the same reality as we are ourselves (*homoousion hèmin*) as far as his human-ness is concerned; thus like us in all respects, sin only excepted." So when the ancient Christians speak of Jesus becoming flesh, or becoming man, or of his human nature, or of his being of the same reality as ourselves, they understood these terms inclusively.

This seems a meager conclusion to arrive at, since the masculine bias in the entire confessional theological language is obvious, and the men who have controlled theology for nearly two millennia have been quick to usurp the language of masculinity for shaping their understanding of God and of the Church. However, it is a start.

Word and Wisdom   God communicates to humankind through the Word, or *Logos*, the means or principle of divine self-communication. The Word is what becomes flesh in Jesus Christ.

> In the beginning was the Word, and the Word was with God, and the Word was God. He was with God in the beginning. Through him all things were made; without him nothing was made that has been made. (John 1:1–3)

It is usual for God's Word to be thought of as masculine. The word *logos* is masculine in the Greek language (where every noun is gendered masculine, feminine, or neuter), and Jesus was male. *Logos* is also associated with reason, with logic, with the study, or "*ologies*" of things. But that is not the end of the matter, for John ascribes to Jesus the Word that he previously found in the Hebrew Bible ascribed to *Sophia*, or Wisdom, and She is definitely female, both in linguistic gender and in her role in relation to God. She cries

> The LORD brought me forth as the first of his works,
> before his deeds of old;
> I was appointed from eternity,
> from the beginning, before the world began. (Prov. 8:22–23)

When the Lord created the world and "made earth's foundations firm,"

> Then I was at his side each day,
> his darling and delight,
> playing in his presence continually,
> playing over his whole world,
> while my delight was in mankind. (Prov. 8:29c–31, Revised English Bible)

Ecclesiasticus, or *The Wisdom of Jesus Son of Sirach* (inspired Scripture for Catholics, placed in the Apocrypha by Protestants) is replete with references to Wisdom. Consider, for example,

> Hear the praise of wisdom from her own mouth, ...
> "I am the word spoken by the Most High;
> it was I who covered the earth like a mist.
> My dwelling-place was in high heaven;
> my throne was in a pillar of cloud." (Eccles. 24:1a; 3–4)

What John does in his Prologue (opening chapter) is to take the figure of Wisdom from the Hebrew Bible and change Her into the Word. Paul, too, called Christ "the wisdom of God" (1 Cor. 1:24). Nevertheless, as Young says, "If Word and Wisdom are one, then the incarnation is not the incarnation of a literally male son from an all-male Godhead, but an incarnation of one who can be described in images of both Wisdom and Word" (1999, p. 196).

> *Activity:* If you are not familiar with references to Wisdom personified as a woman in the Hebrew Bible, you might like to look some of them up now, for they provide a remarkable antidote to loose assumptions about the maleness of God. Proverbs 8 is the clearest example in the Protestant Bible. Ecclesiasticus 24, Wisdom of Solomon 7:22b–8:1, and Baruch 3:9–4:4 should be read from a Roman Catholic Bible or from a modern translation of the Apocrypha such as the Revised Standard Version, or the Revised English Bible.

If the arguments in this section are sound, we can draw some conclusions about the sex of Christ which could be influential when we get to discussing what it means to be members of His Body, and so on, in the next chapter. My conclusions are as follows:

1. Jesus was a male human being.
2. Jesus had a human nature, not a male nature.
3. The humanity of Jesus was inclusive.
4. The divinity of Jesus Christ was suprasexual.

> *Activity:* I asked earlier whether readers thought me mad in denying that God the Son was male. Am I so daft after all? What do you think?

7.2.1 Can women represent Christ?

Of course they can. Our investigations into the sex of the Father and the maleness of the Son may have exploded a whole line of argument which concludes from sexist premises that women cannot be priests. Only one aspect of that fraught and suppressed conversation must be allowed to surface now – the alleged *inability of women to represent Christ*. We have noted that all social institutions whatsoever "are themselves *gendered* and are locations in which the *gendering* of individuals and relationships take place" (see Section 2.2). The exclusion of women from Christian priesthood is the outstanding example of gendering and genderedness to be found in the churches, and one of the arguments supporting female exclusion appears to be based on bad theology.

The Vatican's *Declaration On The Question Of Admission Of Women To The Ministerial Priesthood*, or *Inter Insigniores*, declares that a priest who celebrates the Eucharist "acts not only through the effective power conferred on him by Christ, but *in persona Christi*, taking the role of Christ, to the point of being his very image, when he pronounces the words of consecration" (Congregation for the Doctrine of the Faith, 2003, p. section 5). The priest is "a sign," which "must be perceptible and which the faithful must be able to recognize with ease." Following Aquinas' teaching that "Sacramental signs represent what they signify by natural resemblance," the Vatican concludes

> when Christ's role in the Eucharist is to be expressed sacramentally, there would not be this "natural resemblance" which must exist between Christ and his minister *if the role of Christ were not taken by a man: in such a case it would be difficult to see in the minister the image of Christ. For Christ himself was and remains a man.* (emphasis added)

The Vatican acknowledges, following Galatians 3:28, that "there are no more distinctions between Jew and Greek, slave and free, male and female, but all are one in Christ Jesus." However, distinctions between male and female clearly remain in its theology, for

> the incarnation of the Word took place according to the male sex: this is indeed a question of fact, and this fact, while not implying any alleged natural superiority of man over woman, cannot be disassociated from the economy of salvation.

Pope John Paul II, in 1994, confirmed the teaching of this unfortunate document, and declared "that the Church has no authority whatsoever to confer priestly ordination on women and that this judgment is to be definitively held by all the Church's faithful" (section 4).

Let's ask about the priest taking the role of Christ, being *in persona Christi*. But we have just seen that Christ's *persona* is *divine*, not human! It may come as a surprise to learn that in the ancient Christology of the Church Jesus has no human personality. His Personhood is divine; His *nature* is human. (The idea that Christ contained or was made known in two Persons, one divine and one human, was rejected as the Nestorian heresy.) Since the divine Person of Christ is suprasexual, beyond distinctions between male and female, it is unnecessarily and arbitrarily restrictive to confine the representation of that Person to a single human sex.

Not only *can* women represent the divine Person of the Son; given that Christian priests have historically all been men, it is urgently *necessary* for the imbalance to be rectified, and for Christians to recover and rejoice in the suprasexual divinity of the one God. Why must the faithful be able to "recognize with ease" the maleness of their priests, especially since they sometimes dress ambiguously as women? (If easy recognition was the main issue here, perhaps priests might consider exposing their genitals when celebrating the Eucharist to provide unambiguous evidence of their natural resemblance to Christ?) Genitals are irrelevant to who represents Christ, not least because, according to the New Testament, He represents a whole new humanity, and if He represents them, they can represent Him.

Nevertheless, "the incarnation of the Word took place according to the male sex," and "this is indeed a question of fact." No-one doubts the historical fact that Jesus of Nazareth was a man. But there are *theological* facts which are even more important. For to say that the incarnation of the Word took place according to the male sex is to draw attention to Christ's incarnation as *anèr*, not *anthròpos*; to his humanity as *vir*, not as *homo*. In order to advance a particular argument that keeps women out of the priesthood, the Vatican has had recourse to the maleness of Jesus, at the expense of His human-ness, and thus has appealed to a detail of incarnational doctrine that the creeds of the Church do not support.

> *Activity:* If you are a member of a Christian church, what is the policy of your church towards women becoming archbishops, bishops, priests, ministers, deacons, leaders? Do women take a full part in the conduct of worship? Whatever the practice of your church, try to find out what it is and explain the reasons for it.

7.3 Mary – Mother of All the Living

If the arguments in the last section are sound, women and men alike image God who exists beyond creaturely distinctions, including those of male and female. This understanding of God undermines male dominance in churches that acknowledge it. But perhaps you are unconvinced by these arguments? You may think that the names "Father" and "Son", together with their masculine bias, really do point to some heavenly masculinity. A further, sound reason why you may be unconvinced by the argument so far, is the absence of feminine names within God or the Godhead.

This obvious deficiency has been called "the erasure of the feminine." According to the influential Belgian feminist philosopher Luce Irigaray (1985a, 1985b) such an erasure extends far beyond the Christian doctrine of the Trinity. There is an utter lack of feminine divine representation in Western Christianity and this hiatus extends to the whole of Western culture. Furthermore, the lack of a historical sense of women as independent persons is linked to the lack of a historical sense of the Holy Spirit as a distinct Person of God within the Trinity. The roots of Irigaray's thought are complex, and for this author, the psychoanalytic tradition that she criticizes and in her own way corrects and extends, raises as many problems as it attempts to solve. However, her critique is clear and sharp, and her solution, ably summarized by Gavin D'Costa, is that

> It is only female divinity that can provide the imaginary, the symbolic order, whereby women can attain subjectivities, become persons, not "equal" to men – but different from them, and therefore in real relation to them, and to each other. (D'Costa, 2000, p. 5)

> The point she is making is that Jesus is finally male, and not until there is female divine embodiment and representation can there be Good News for women. (D'Costa, 2000, p. 6; see also Beattie, 2002, pp. 20–39)

A question that has been bravely taken up by several independent Roman Catholic scholars, and in particular by Gavin D'Costa and Tina Beattie, is whether Mary the mother of Jesus is able to restore the grave imbalance in the symbolic order. On the one hand, Beattie laments that in her tradition, masculinity is presently "a non-negotiable feature of God's fatherhood" (Beattie, 2002, p. 81). On the other hand she thinks "the symbols of maternal femininity invested in Mary are deeply embedded in Catholic consciousness," and that "there is no other symbolic resource for the construction of women's salvation within the Christian story" (p. 83). We will examine her case next.

7.3.1 Suspending the phallus?

An angel announces to Mary that the Holy Spirit will come upon her and that "the holy one to be born will be called the Son of God" (Luke 1:26). According to Beattie's reading of Pope John Paul II (1988) this encounter "between God and Mary in the annunciation is a unique and decisive moment for women in salvation history, when the mediation of God's covenant through patriarchal genealogies is ended, and woman becomes the medium of the new covenant" (Beattie, 2002, p. 74). So far, so good. But women still cannot represent Christ because Christ was a man. On the old understanding of humanity as a single sex with a gender gradient from greater to lesser degrees of perfection, women were unable to represent Christ because they were naturally defective. The charge is fairly made that while official thought now acknowledges the modern view of there being two sexes, the defectiveness of women is maintained by other means. They are no less perfect than men, but they belong to the sex that the male Jesus did not. They lack a penis:

> The Catholic Church has always been a patriarchal institution, based on descending hierarchies of male power starting with God the father, but this was in metaphors of relationality rather than metaphors of genitality. Now, however, it is not the patriarchal structure but the phallus itself that holds the symbolic system in place. (Beattie, 2002, pp. 80–81)

The phallus is now "the marker of sexual difference." The new beginnings, both of non-patriarchal institutions and of direct relations between women and God, signaled by the Annunciation, are strangled by the harsh insistence on sexual difference, phallically understood.

It is clear that far more is at stake regarding the miracle of Christ's birth than the belief in a supernatural intervention. The intervention is not merely the temporary suspension of the laws of human reproduction, but the permanent suspension of the phallocentric order. "The wonder of the incarnation lies not in its affirmation of but in its challenge to patriarchal concepts of generation" (Beattie, 2002, p. 93). Perhaps "Mary's virginal conception might signify an event outside the domain of the phallus, in a way that is not circumscribed within the values and laws of patriarchy" (Beattie, 2002, p. 125).

Kenosis: From Philippians 2:7, "he emptied himself . . .," kenosis is an emptying. There are perhaps two principal senses of kenosis. God the Son by relinquishing eternal power and glory, is emptied by becoming incarnate. Jesus Christ empties Himself in the self-abandonment that was His crucifixion. Both senses are understood as an outpouring of divine love.

Mary's self-giving   Christians often explain the meaning of the life and death of Jesus by means of the doctrine of *kenosis*.

A difficulty has arisen in some theological thought that kenosis has become sexualized. It has become caught up in ancient gender theories whereby men are active, women passive, and so on. The male God who sends the Son, the Son who expends His life, and the male priest who represents Him at the Eucharist, all convey the outpouring of divine, male life. In Balthasar's thought (as Beattie reads it), "the originating Word is a male ejaculation. It is the *kenosis* of God the Father, and the *kenosis* of Christ insofar as he is God" (2006, p. 159). The "kenotic self-giving of Christ" is compared with "the male orgasm" (2002, p. 108). But Mary's response to her calling subverts all this as well. Not only is this refutable, there is a *female* kenosis which Mary exemplifies. "The maternal is a more powerful kenotic symbol. The mother's body empties itself in the giving of life to another" (Beattie, 2002, p. 108).

7.3.2 Eve – mother of all the living

The role given to Mary in overcoming gender imbalance is given further credence by re-examining the writings of the Apologists of the second century CE, Justin Martyr, Irenaeus and Tertullian, all of whom spoke of Mary as "the new Eve." This is a good example of *typology*, so first we need to be clear what typological thinking is, and how it works.

The New Testament letters contain many examples of Hebrew figures prefiguring the revelation that was to come through Jesus Christ. Perhaps the best known is Adam's

> **Typology:** In common language, it means the classification of things according to their characteristics. In theology it is "The practice in the New Testament and the early church whereby a person or a series of events occurring in the Old Testament is interpreted as a type or foreshadowing of some person (almost invariably Christ) or feature in the Christian dispensation" (Hanson, 1993, pp. 783–784).

prefiguring of Christ – "Adam foreshadows the man who was to come" (Rom. 5:14 Revised English Bible). "For as in Adam all die, so in Christ all will be made alive" (1 Cor. 15:22).

In his work against heretics Irenaeus (*d.* 202) explicitly compares Eve's disobedience with Mary's obedience. Eve disobeys God in Eden (Gen. 3:6–7): Mary obeys God in Nazareth (Luke 1:38). Eve's disobedience prefigures Mary's obedience.

> For just as the former was led astray by the word of an angel, so that she fled from God when she had transgressed His word; so did the latter, by an angelic communication, receive the glad tidings that she should sustain (lit. carry) God, being obedient to His word. And if the former did disobey God, yet the latter was persuaded to be obedient to God, in order that the Virgin Mary might become the patroness (lit. Advocate – *advocata*) of the virgin Eve. And thus, as the human race fell into bondage to death by means of a virgin, so is it rescued by a virgin; virginal disobedience having been balanced in the opposite scale by virginal obedience. (Irenaeus, 1884, para. 19.1)

The argument is clear enough. Mary's obedience to God at the Annunciation cancels Eve's disobedience that leads to the Fall. Mary is Eve's "Advocate" (an official title accorded to her by the Vatican, see Pope Paul VI, 1994, section 62) and an advocate is one who speaks on behalf of another. The argument implies not so much a contrast between the wicked Eve and the righteous Mary, as a reinstatement of Eve, bringing to fulfillment an obedience of which she proved temporarily incapable.

Second, in the passage quoted the human race is rescued, not simply by Christ Himself, the One that Mary carries, *but by Mary as well* – "by a virgin; virginal disobedience having been balanced in the opposite scale by virginal obedience." When God punishes the serpent, God says "I will put enmity between thee and the woman, and between thy seed and her seed; it shall bruise thy head, and thou shalt bruise his heel" (Gen. 3:15AV). Mary derives from Eve, and Mary is the one who "bruises the serpent's head."

Beattie's quarrel with the Vatican differs from that of liberal Catholics and evangelical Protestants over Mary's lofty status in doctrine and in the Church. It is that when Eve and Mary are compared, the former is represented only as the foil for the latter, demonstrating her blessedness (Beattie, 2001, pp. 5, 12). But Eve is also *positively affirmed* in the damning narrative of Genesis 3: "Adam named his wife Eve, because she would become the mother of all the living" (Gen. 3:20). And this the Vatican forgets. The mother of all the living is recapitulated (repeated in a more complete form) in Mary.

> Mary is the culmination of Eve's becoming, in a way that affirms rather than negates the value of Eve's long journey through history from the gates of Eden to the gates of paradise. Mary is the shape of God's promise to Eve in Eden. (Beattie, 2002, p. 154)

The mother of all the living now finds her fulfillment in the Mother of God.

7.3.3 Mary – the new Eve

Tertullian (*d.* 220) also sees Mary as the culmination of Eve's becoming (Beattie, 2001, pp. 13–14; 2002, pp. 94–99). In his treatise *On the Soul* he discusses the phenomenon of human sleep and its many benefits. He then suggests how "the friendly power of slumber" helps us to think about the amiable meaning of our deaths. In that context two new typologies emerge. The first is between the sleep of Adam when the woman was made from one of his ribs, and the "sleep" of Christ upon the cross:

> For as Adam was a figure of Christ, Adam's sleep shadowed out the death of Christ, who was to sleep a mortal slumber, that from the wound inflicted on His side might, in like manner (as Eve was formed), be typified the church, the true mother of the living. (Tertullian, 2006, ch. 43)

Tertullian refers of course to the passage in Genesis from which Christians derive their understanding of marriage as a union of "one flesh." "So the LORD God caused the man to fall into a deep sleep; and while he was sleeping, he took one of the man's ribs and closed up the place with flesh" (Gen. 2:21). Adam's anaesthetized sleep was productive in that God took one of his ribs, and made the first woman out of it. Eve issues from Adam's side. The woman is brought to the man who recognizes her as "bone of my bones and flesh of my flesh" (Gen. 2:23).

The second typology is between the wound of Adam and the wound of Christ. Christ's *mortal* sleep was productive in that *the church issues directly from the wound in His side*: the direct allusion is to the detail in the Fourth Gospel that "one of the soldiers pierced Jesus' side with a spear, bringing a sudden flow of blood and water" (John 19:34). From earliest times the blood and water were thought to represent either the fluids present whenever there is a birth, and/or the sacraments of Eucharist and baptism that derive directly from Christ's crucified and sleeping body. Both Eve and the Church come miraculously not just from a sleep but *from a wound*. Eve remains "the mother of the living" but she prefigures not Mary but *the Church*, "the true mother of the living." Once the birth of the Church is described in this way, *Christ* of course becomes its mother. Christ is depicted as giving birth.

Yet Mary is not, and cannot be bypassed in this typology, for the flesh and blood of Christ come from Mary his Mother. The maternal role of the Church, as she who gives birth to, nurtures and nourishes her children, and which Tertullian and others emphasized, has been emphasized ever since. Eve, then, far from being the female symbol of rebellion, disobedience and sin, is renewed both in the figure of Mary and of the Church. Beattie explains why this is so:

> Mary is the new Eve because she is the mother of Christ and therefore the fulfillment of God's promise to Eve in Genesis. The church is the new Eve because she is created from the side of the new Adam, and because she is truly the mother of the living, a role foreshadowed and anticipated in the naming of Eve. (Beattie, 2001, p. 11)

Activity: The last few pages have worked with typology. Passages from the Hebrew Bible have been interpreted typologically. Adam is a type of Christ. Eve's disobedience is a type of Mary's obedience. The serpent's words to Eve are a type of the angel's words to Mary. Eve's issuing from the side of Adam is a type of the Church issuing from the side of Christ, and so on. This is a strange use of the Hebrew Bible. What, if anything, do you think we can learn from it?

Comment: For most of Christian history, it would *not* have been strange to interpret the Hebrew Bible in this way. Perhaps it occurred to you that typological thinking is no longer available to us in our present thought-world, dominated by science, technology, and critical reason? If so, typology can help us put our modern age in a different perspective. I think we are right to find typological readings "forced." But they may also challenge us to think more mystically and more symbolically about our own world, and to realize that the language of science and criticism cannot exhaust reality. Typology also shows us that the exegesis of the ancient Scriptures was very Christ-centered.

7.4 Womankind in God's Likeness?

How effective is this account of Mary in bypassing the patriarchal order? In providing an alternative understanding of God's actions and human responses in which women in particular may find themselves? Let us now answer the question posed at the beginning of the previous section: whether Mary the mother of Jesus is able to provide the female divine embodiment that would help to restore the fatal imbalance in the symbolic order.

7.4.1 Mary, mother of James, Joseph, Judas, and Simon

There is a problem regarding the lack of historical foundations on which theological narratives about Mary are built. Mark, Paul, and John do not appear to have knowledge of the idea even of the virgin birth of Jesus, though such occurrences were thought to be common enough in biblical times. But an argument from silence establishes nothing. However at times the New Testament itself seems to question this belief. The earliest Gospel records that an audience, amazed at Jesus' teaching, exclaim "Isn't this the carpenter? Isn't this Mary's son and the brother of James, Joseph, Judas and Simon? Aren't his sisters here with us?" (See Mark 6:3.) John's Gospel, written last, seems to repudiate any idea of virgin birth, for it twice refers to Jesus as the son of Joseph (John 1:45; 6:42).

Jesus' brothers and sisters pose a knotty problem for later traditions that Mary was *always* virginal, and the speculation that they are his stepbrothers and stepsisters is awkward and could be a fairly clear attempt to rewrite history in the light of theology. That, however, remains the Catholic view from Jerome (*d.* 420) onwards. Deep Catholic reflection on who Jesus was compelled the conclusion that Mary had no other child than Jesus.

Textual scholarship has uncovered further difficulties with this verse (Mark 6:3). The earliest version of Mark's Gospel, a third century manuscript called P^{45}, has the crowd ask, not "Isn't this the carpenter?" but "Is this not the *son* of the carpenter?" (Ehrman, 2005, p. 203). Matthew's version of this saying also makes Jesus the carpenter's son (Matt. 13:55). Accordingly, one of the two Gospels that records that Jesus was conceived through the Holy Spirit, also records that Jesus is the carpenter's son.

Perhaps Matthew allows the crowd some ironic misrepresentation of Jesus? May be he lets them get Jesus wrong. But this was his "hometown" (Matt. 13:53), where people might have been expected to know something of His origin. But Luke too assumes Christ's *human* origins. On the one hand Luke records the Annunciation. "The Holy Spirit will come upon you, and the power of the Most High will overshadow you. So the holy one to be born will be called the Son of God" (Luke 1:35). On the other hand, Luke's genealogy of Jesus begins with the detail "Now Jesus himself was about thirty years old when he began his ministry. He was *the son, so it was thought, of Joseph*" (Luke 3:23; emphasis added). Elsewhere in Luke it is assumed that Joseph is "the child's father" (Luke 2:33: see also Luke 2:48).

Matthew explains the virgin birth of Jesus as the fulfillment of a prophecy of Isaiah, "The virgin will be with child and will give birth to a son, and they will call him Immanuel" – which means, 'God with us'" (Matt. 1:23). Yet Matthew is ever eager to show the coming of Jesus is the fulfillment of messianic prophecy and the term he found in his Greek Bible for virgin, *parthenos*, may just mean a "young girl."

Then there is the question of the *character* of the two birth narratives, full of pictorial, supernatural detail, best appreciated when they are not approached literally but as material for the imagination to contemplate. They show, do they not, the conviction that miraculous divine intervention had occurred in the arrival into the world of Immanuel – "God with us" (Matt. 1:23)? They are uninterested in our demand for gynecological detail. On the one hand, a literalistic mind-set is capable of missing altogether the joy and wonder of the narratives, the interweaving of the supernatural and the natural, the marvelous divine initiative and the human response. On the other hand, the birth of the One who was son of Mary and Son of God was a real birth and required a real conception. But real conceptions *do* require literal understandings, and that is supernatural explanations lack conviction in the late modern world even where there remains a strong will to believe what the Tradition has bequeathed.

Beattie does not address these historical questions. Protestant Christians *do* take literally the belief that Jesus was born from a virgin, yet think that the belief in the perpetual virginity of Mary is not only *not* in Scripture; it controverts it. It is a case where Scripture and Tradition conflict. I take "born of the virgin Mary" to be a non-negotiable statement of Christian belief, which expresses the conviction that the birth of Jesus happened by sheer divine agency. But the historical foundations for her perpetual virginity and her enhanced role in the Christian symbolic order are lacking, and the growing assumption that she is ever-virgin may have been driven by other considerations, for example, the shame attached to women's bodies and to having sex.

Earlier we noted the two theories of conception that were accepted in the ancient world, those of Aristotle and Galen. According to Galen's theory, the sperms of both men and women are required for conception to occur. The representation of a virginal conception happening merely without male sperm would be inadequate since female sperm would also be required. It lacks explanatory power. Since people in the time of Jesus did not understand the process of natural conception, any modeling of a supernatural conception based on it is bound to collapse. Does that mean that honest Christians should abandon belief in the virginity of Mary? Not necessarily. Belief in the virginal conception of Jesus is best understood as pointing to the divine initiative in bringing it about, without insisting on how it took place.

In summary form, Christians may confidently say of Mary,

1. Through Mary God suspends male genealogies and the androcentric phallic order.
2. Mary too – and with her all mothers – has a kenosis. She empties herself, not by dying but by bringing about new life.
3. Mary fulfils God's promise to Eve that she should become Mother of all the Living.
4. Mary gives to Christ His body, His flesh, and blood. They do not come from heaven. They come from His mother. She is the Mother of God.
5. Mary, in giving birth to God by natural means shows her solidarity with all mothers.
6. Finally the typology that brings this portrait of Mary portrays Christ too as a Mother. He gives birth to the Church, and in this respect He too is feminine.

> *Activity:* You might like to look through this list, observing how each statement is arrived at from material in 7.3 above. Which of the statements do you think is the most valuable in helping to bring about a revaluation of the personhood of women before God?

Looking at this chapter as a whole I think that, strategically, priority should be given to the remodeling of the Christian God (see Sections 7.1 and 7.2). Gender imbalance in theology and Church is best addressed by retrieving and restoring the feminine elements of God within a suprasexual framework. That said, there remains in Mary what Beattie calls "a parousia in which woman's redeemed personhood is revealed as one who bears the image of God in a way that is different from but equal to the godlike personhood of man" (2002, p. 212). It is a compelling vision. The overcoming of androcentric theology and practice is best done from several perspectives. Protestant Christians may need to learn more of Mary as the new Eve, as the Mother of all the Living, and the Mother of God. Roman Catholic Christians may need to take their understanding of Mary to new and perhaps unfamiliar depths.

In the first section of this chapter we looked at the formal and doctrinal case for thinking God to be suprasexual. These considerations were *ontological*, about God's being. These now need to be supplemented by equal attention to God's *loving* and *doing*. That task will require an examination of Christ's own subversion of manliness and standard versions of masculinity in His incarnate life, and of the possibilities of life in a radical new community where there is "neither male nor female." This is attempted in Chapter 8.

References

Balthasar, H.U. von (1990 [1976]) *Theo-Drama: Theological Dramatic Theory, Vol. II: The Dramatis Personae: Man in God* (trans. G. Harrison), Ignatius Press, San Francisco.

Balthasar, H.U. von (1992 [1978]) *Theo-Drama III: The Dramatis Personae: The Person in Christ* (trans. G. Harrison), Ignatius Press, San Francisco.

Beattie, T. (2001) Mary, Eve and the Church. *Maria: A Journal of Marian Studies*, 1(2) (Feb.), 5–21.

Beattie, T. (2002) *God's Mother, Eve's Advocate*, Continuum, London/New York.

Beattie, T. (2006) *New Catholic Feminism – Theology and Theory*, Routledge, London/New York.

Congregation for the Doctrine of the Faith (2003) *Considerations Regarding Proposals to give Legal Recognition to Unions between Homosexual Persons*, www.vatican.va/roman_curia/congregations/cfaith/documents/rc_con_cfaith_doc_20030731_homosexual-unions_en.html (accessed November 4, 2010).

D'Costa, G. (2000) *Sexing the Trinity: Gender, Culture and the Divine*, SCM Press, London.

Ehrman, B.D. (2005) *Misquoting Jesus: The Story Behind Who Changed the Bible and Why*, HarperCollins, New York.

Hanson, A.T. (1993) Typology, in *The Oxford Companion to the Bible* (eds. B.M. Metzger and M.D. Coogan), Oxford University Press, New York, pp. 783–784.

Harrison, V.E.F. (1990) Male and female in Cappadocian theology. *Journal of Theological Studies*, 41(2) (Oct.), 441–471.

Irenaeus (1884) *Against the Heretics*, in *Ante-Nicene Fathers: Volume 1: The Apostolic Fathers, Justin Martyr* (eds. A. Roberts and J. Donaldson), Christian Classics Ethereal Library, www.ccel.org/ccel/schaff/anf01.ix.vii.xx.html (accessed November 4, 2010).

Irigaray, L. (1985a) *Speculum of the Other Woman* (trans. G. Gill), Cornell University Press, Ithaca, NY.

Irigaray, L. (1985b) *This Sex Which Is Not One* (trans. C. Porter and C. Burke), Cornell University Press, Ithaca, NY.

Leith, J.H. (ed.) (1982) *Creeds of the Churches*, 3rd edn., John Knox Press, Louisville, KY.

Pope John Paul II (1994) *Ordinatio Sacerdotalis – Letter to the Bishops of the Catholic Church on Reserving Priestly Ordination to Men Alone*, www.vatican.va/holy_father/john_paul_ii/apost_letters/documents/hf_jp-ii_apl_22051994_ordinatio-sacerdotalis_en.html (accessed November 12, 2010).

Pope Paul VI (1964) *Lumen Gentium – Dogmatic Constitution on the Church*, www.vatican.va/archive/hist_councils/ii_vatican_council/documents/vat-ii_const_19641121_lumen-gentium_en.html (accessed November 4, 2010).

Tertullian (2006) *A Treatise on the Soul*, in *Early Christian Writings*, in Tertullian (P. Kirby), www.earlychristianwritings.com/tertullian.html (accessed November 4, 2010).

Thatcher, A. (2007) *Theology and Families*, Blackwell, Malden, MA/Oxford.

Young, P.D. (1999) The fatherhood of God at the turn of another millennium. *Semeia*, 85, 195–203.

8

"In Christ there is neither Male nor Female"

This chapter continues the attempt, stated at the beginning of Part III, to think about gender by becoming immersed in the doctrines of Incarnation and Trinity and the practices of love that flow from them. According to Christians, God became incarnate not only in the flesh of Christ, but Christ lives or manifests himself in his body, the Church. In this chapter, the fluid notion of the body of Christ is brought more fully into the discussion. It is shown how, with regard to the performance both of sex and of gender, this vital notion has much to commend and suggest to contemporary readers. The title of the chapter (from Gal. 3:28) raises acutely the question of sexual difference within this body.

Being a member of the body of Christ directly affects with whom we have sex, and gives us reasons why (Section 8.1). The character of the body of Christ is allowed to shape how we perform our masculinity and femininity (Sections 8.2 and 8.3). The possibility of treating sexual difference differently in the body of Christ is the theme of Section 8.4.

8.1 Sex in the Body of Christ

8.1.1 Having sex in the body of Christ

We have already found that the metaphor "body of Christ" works in several different ways (see Sections 5.3.2 and 6.4). Christ's body is united with the Church: Christ's body *is* the Church: Christ's body is bread and wine given for us to eat and drink, and so on; and still that metaphor has other meanings to uncover. Another of them is to be found in the idea that Christians are *members* of Christ's body, so that whatever they *do*, Christ also does. Just as "I" act through the members of my body by using my tongue, raising my arm, kicking

God, Sex, and Gender: An Introduction, First Edition. Adrian Thatcher.
© 2011 Adrian Thatcher. Published 2011 by Blackwell Publishing Ltd.

a ball, so does Christ act through the members of *His* body, metaphorically understood as the limbs and organs of it.

One writer finds at least five meanings of the term "body of Christ" in Paul's letters:

1. Christ's *physical* body that suffered on the cross;
2. the *mystical* body into which Christians are incorporated;
3. the *sacramental* body given in bread and wine;
4. the *ecclesial* body, or Church; and
5. the *ethical* body, which is the mystical or ecclesial body as it performs Christ-like activities (Dinter, 1994).

Having sex with Christ?   Members of the body of Christ are thought to have an intimate relationship with Him. Some of them also have a very intimate relationship with each other. It is not often understood that, according to Paul, when members of Christ's body have sex with their partners, *Christ has sex with them as well!* This idea is of course shocking, even potentially blasphemous. But, according to Diana Swancutt, it is straightforwardly rooted in Pauline thought. Paul asks his readers

> [15]Do you not know that your bodies are members of Christ himself? Shall I then take the members of Christ and unite them with a prostitute? Never! [16]Do you not know that he who unites himself with a prostitute is one with her in body? For it is said, "The two will become one flesh."[17]But he who unites himself with the Lord is one with him in spirit.
>
> [18]Flee from sexual immorality. All other sins a man commits are outside his body, but he who sins sexually sins against his own body. [19]Do you not know that your body is a temple of the Holy Spirit, who is in you, whom you have received from God? You are not your own; [20]you were bought at a price. Therefore honor God with your body. (1 Cor. 6:15–20)

Paul's argument is clear enough. The bodies of Christians are part of the body of Christ. When the bodies of Christians are sexually joined with other bodies, the body of Christ is joined with them as well. The inference works by synecdoche – when a part does something, so does the whole (see Section 6.3.1). That is why he thinks the Christian men who have sex with prostitutes are behaving outrageously.

Once we think ourselves into the ancient physiology accompanying the argument, it becomes clearer still. According to Swancutt,

> Ancient doctors thought *pneuma* [spirit] collected most potently in the "seed" or *sperma*, which means that spirit could be ejaculated in intercourse. Since ancients thought men and women (as different embodiments of one basic human body) could *both* ejaculate *sperma*, and since Christ's spirit dwelt within believers' bodies, *when believers had sex (and ejaculated), they sent Christ's spirit out with their sperm.* (Swancutt, 2006, p. 94; emphases added)

We met some of these strange physiological ideas (that sperm contains spirit and that women ejaculate) earlier (see Section 1.2.2). So when married Christians have sex they share Christ with each other. Paul's understanding of the physiology of sex may be confirmed by his stance towards marital sex in mixed marriages (between believers and unbelievers). The issue was: was the unbelieving partner worthy to receive Christ's Spirit?

Paul answers "Yes," and gives his reason: "For the unbelieving husband has been sanctified through his wife, and the unbelieving wife has been sanctified through her believing husband. Otherwise your children would be unclean, but as it is, they are holy" (1 Cor. 7:14). A man who is a member of the body of Christ, and who has sex with a woman to whom he is not married who is not a member of the body of Christ, sends Christ's spirit into an unworthy and unholy receptacle. But if they are married, yet only one of them is a believer, their marriage sanctifies their relationship and the sexual exchanges within it.

Activity: How, if at all, do you think this passage could conceivably be a positive influence on the sexual behavior of Christians today?

Comment: The physiology may be fanciful, yet even here we might acknowledge elements of it that are not wholly inaccurate. True, women do not ejaculate sperm, but their eggs are potential carriers of life, just as sperms are. Might not your answer depend on whether you are prepared to see yourself as a member of the body of Christ, or not?

This is a belief that lies at the heart of Christian faith. As we have already noted, the metaphor "body of Christ" has several different uses (that is, it is *polysemic*) and these can sometimes confusingly overlap. If you believe that your body is part of Christ's body, and that Christ's body is in some way pure, perfect, or divine, then that belief will very likely influence what you do with your body. Such a belief would and should perhaps also influence other choices about what we take into our bodies. Drunkenness, gluttony, and the thrill-seeking exposure to excessive risks are all rendered theologically problematic by the belief that one's body is part of the body of Christ.

And could believers not advocate a similar position about the indwelling of the Holy Spirit in their bodies? Once the ancient physiology is unhooked from the deeper religious meaning, and the literal sense of an indwelling Spirit replaced by a creative metaphorical one, it becomes possible to think perhaps of the body as a possession of great beauty and worth, a gift of God to be treasured and honored. It is difficult to reconcile promiscuous behavior with the holding of these beliefs.

Of course it may be misleading to speak of the body as a "possession" at all, for that would at least imply that "I" am not my body, but I am related to it, as a thing or possession. Even here though, the idea of possession is a useful one. Paul uses it (1 Cor. 6:19–20) to convey the idea that believers do not belong to themselves. Rather they are *possessed by God.*

8.1.2 Is the body of Christ androgynous?

Yes. There is a simple argument, and a less simple one, that leads to this conclusion. After we have examined the arguments we will consider why this odd question is actually very important.

You will remember that an androgyne is someone who has both male and female characteristics and/or sexual organs (see Section 2.3.1). The simple argument runs like this.

Premise 1: Christian men and women are all members of the body of Christ.
Premise 2: The body of Christ is a single body, comprising its members.
Conclusion: Therefore the body of Christ is androgynous.

We know, and need to remember, that the expression "body of Christ" is a metaphor, so there will always be room for dispute about what meanings are legitimately drawn from it. However, can we not say, with some confidence, that Paul himself uses "body of Christ" as it has just been used in the argument above?

The second argument is based on the familiar bride/groom symbolism of Ephesians 5. A revisionary reading of that text has already been offered (see Sections 5.2.1 and 6.3.2). In a discussion of the work of Hans Urs von Balthasar, architect of contemporary Roman Catholic thinking on sexuality and gender, Tina Beattie writes of a

> tendency that has been present in the Catholic tradition from the beginning – for the man to attribute to himself qualities of divinity, transcendence, origination and initiative that he associates with masculinity, and to project onto the woman those rejected characteristics of his own humanity, immanence, receptivity and responsivity that he associates with femininity. (Beattie, 2006, p. 138)

Ephesians 5 is a classic text for buttressing up this kind of male dominance, but the suggestion is now to be made that that very passage is able to be plausibly employed to deliver a different account of the relation between the sexes in Christianity. The last part of it reads

> [29]After all, no one ever hated his own body, but he feeds and cares for it, just as Christ does the church – [30]for we are members of his body. [31]"For this reason a man will leave his father and mother and be united to his wife, and the two will become one flesh." This is a profound mystery – but I am talking about Christ and the church. (Eph. 5:29–31)

There are two distinct senses of "body" to be found even within these verses. Let us call them the *reflexive* use and the *marital* use. When I refer to myself as the subject of my actions ("I am thinking, shaving, day-dreaming," etc.) I am being reflexive. So when the author says "no one ever hated his own body" he is making a reflexive statement. He is assuming here that we *are* our bodies, and that (cases of self-harm excepted) we generally feed and care for them. In its *reflexive* use the "body of Christ" is, just is, the parts of the body that make it what it is. The figure of speech is again synecdoche. All Christians are the parts of the one, whole body of Christ. "We are members of his body" (meaning 4 – the ecclesial body – see Section 8.1.1).

In the *marital* use, there is not a single reflexive body, but two *pairs* of bodies, those of husband and wife, and Christ and the Church. The members of each pair, while distinct, become one, either sexually or mystically (meaning 2 – the mystical body – see Section 8.1.1). The marital use is intended in the earlier injunction, "Husbands, love your wives, just as Christ loved the church and gave himself up for her" (Eph. 5:25). In the reflexive sense there is one being, the self which includes its body: in the marital sense there are *two* beings, who become one in marriage.

The conclusion is that, according to the *reflexive* use of the term "body of Christ," that body just *is* its members. So it again follows that the members of Christ's body are male and female. The body of Christ is therefore male and female, and so androgynous. Why is that conclusion important?

There is a theological and ethical reason. First, it provides a further theological counterbalance to assertions that the Church can only be represented to God by a man, or that a man is required to represent Christ to the Church. Since the body of Christ is male and female, the exclusive male representation of it is not only unbalanced: it is a *mis*representation, for that body is *both* male *and* female. And that conclusion accords well with the demonstration in the previous chapter (see Section 7.1.2) that the divine, suprasexual Son of God is eternally above the creaturely distinctions of male and female, and so is capable of partial and finite representation by either of them.

Second, this conclusion also throws light on sexual activity between Christians. We have just seen that Paul condemned Christian men visiting prostitutes because when they did so, they made the body of Christ have sex with them also. This contention makes good sense once the premise is granted that the mystical body of Christ can be represented by a single member of that body. When a member of the body of Christ makes love, s/he represents the body of Christ! S/he has sex in the body of Christ. The body of Christ is having sex too. While Christians are unlikely to have these lofty thoughts in their minds at the time, they may well draw on them in their pre-coital and post-coital reflections.

8.2 Gender in the Body of Christ

8.2.1 Is the body of Christ "queer?"

If the body of Christ is both male and female, is that body "queer?" That question, like the question of androgyny will strike some people as blasphemous, associating the body of Christ directly with the practice of deviance. The question, however, runs much deeper, and draws for its answer on conventional biblical theology and doctrine. The answer to be developed in this section is that Christians have much to learn about how to "perform" gender by reflecting further on their membership of the body of Christ, not least because that body resists the application of all categories (even those of "queer" and "androgynous").

Until recently, "queer" was a term of abuse, used by people from the heterosexual majority, to refer disparagingly to sexual minorities or to assign inferior or deficient minority status to them (see Section 2.2.1). Such people collectively decided to take the sting out of the insult, to utilize the term as a kind of parody, and to reclaim it for themselves.

Queer theory: Queer theory is a set of ideas based around the idea that our sexual identities are not fixed and do not determine who we are. It suggests that it is meaningless to talk in general about "women" or any other group, as identities consist of so many elements that to assume that people can be seen collectively on the basis of one shared characteristic is wrong. It is associated in particular with the work of Michel Foucault and Judith Butler (see Sections 2.1.2 and 2.2.2).

Queer theology: This uses queer theory as a source. Queer theologians are a mixed bunch. Some come from lesbian and gay, liberationist, feminist and womanist traditions of theology; others are radically orthodox. Their intentions vary widely. Some want to deconstruct entirely the God they think presides over a system of "hetero-patriarchy" (Althaus-Reid, 2003; Althaus-Reid and Isherwood, 2004). Others want to reclaim the Christian tradition as itself queer, although it is not always clear what that involves. Some theologians turn the adjective "queer" into a verb, "queering," which means the activity of overcoming what they perceive to be heterosexual prejudice in religious language, doctrine, and practice (Althaus-Reid and Isherwood, 2004, pp. 1–15).

"Queer" as an adjective may just mean "odd," "strange," "non-normative." In this sense bothering with theology at all is queer. Gerard Loughlin thinks it is queer, but at the same commendable, for anyone in the modern West to be involved in theology at the start of a new century (Loughlin, 2007, p. 8). He thinks theology is queer because "it answers to the queerness of God, who is not other than strange and at odds with our 'fallen' world." His assertions show how elastic the term "queer" has become.

Marcella Althaus-Reid and Lisa Isherwood think the strangeness of some Christian doctrines, for example, the incarnation, make them queer.

Well, an androgynous body is certainly a queer body. I have already suggested that the human male, Jesus Christ, reveals the suprasexual divine Son of God who is neither male nor female (see Section 7.1.2). But is the historical Jesus himself, neither male nor female? We are next going to examine an influential argument that concludes that it is! If that argument is sound, then it can also be shown historically that the body of Christ is doubly queer. It contains male and female parts. And, it was never straightforwardly male in the first place.

Christ's physical body beyond gender?   The radical orthodox theologian Graham Ward has tried to show that the presentation of the body of Jesus in the Gospels indicates a "fluidity" about that body that enables it to be seen as *both male and female.* The argument is that the body of Christ is continually *displaced* in the Gospels and this "series of displacements or assumptions of Jesus's body continually refigures a masculine symbolics until the particularities of one sex give way to the particularities of bodies which are male and female" (Ward, 1999, p. 163).

Displacement: In physics, "displacement" means "the displacing in space of one mass by another," and in psychoanalysis it means "the transfer of an emotion from its original focus to another object or person."

Symbolics: The branch of theology dealing with the study of the history and meaning of church creeds and confessions. (Gr. *sumbolon* = creed) The term is used informally to mean the whole range of theological thought.

Put more simply, the body of Christ is depicted in the Gospels as strange, unlike any other male body. That process begins with his conception. "The XY chromosomal maleness of Jesus Christ issues from the XX chromosomal femaleness of his mother as miracle" (Ward, 1999, p. 164). There are "five scenes where these displacements are dramatically performed" (Ward, 1999, p. 166). The first scene is the Transfiguration of Jesus (Mark 9:2–8; Matt. 17:1–8; Luke 9:28–36) when "His face shone like the sun, and his clothes became as white as the light" (Matt. 17:2).

Ward finds this displacement "erotically charged" because the body of Jesus has the "power to attract." It is "not the physical body, as such, which is the source of the attraction but the glorification of the physical body made possible by viewing him through God as God." Christ's body becomes an icon of the beautiful and good, and the sheer physical attractiveness of Jesus "propels our desire towards what lies beyond and yet does so in and through this man's particular body."

The second scene is the Eucharist (1 Cor. 11:23–26; Mark 14:22–25; Matt. 26:26–29; Luke 22:15–20). Christ's body is now bread. It "can cross boundaries – gender boundaries, for example. Jesus' body as bread is no longer Christ as simply and biologically male" (Ward, 1999, p. 168). The third scene is the Crucifixion (Mark 14:43–15:41; Matt. 26:47–27:56; Luke 22:47–23:49; John 18:2–19:37). Ward notes how the two scenes of Christ being stripped naked bring "this vulnerable body to play in a field of violent power games" (Ward, 1999, p. 168). In these games "the actual maleness of the body of Jesus is forgotten" (Ward, 1999, p. 169). His body is now displaced as an object – "mere flesh, a consumable, a dead, unwanted, discardable thing, before Jesus breathes his last."

The fourth scene is the Resurrection (Mark 16:1–8; Matt. 28:1–10; Luke 24:1–15; John 20:1–18). Now the body can walk through walls, disappear and reappear, while at the same time it remains tangible and able to eat. Ward draws attention to the inability of the two disciples on the Emmaus road (Luke 24:13–35), of Mary at the tomb (John 20:11–18), and of the disciples out fishing (John 21:1–14) to *recognize* the resurrected body of Jesus as Jesus. The risen body is mysterious: it cannot be "an object to be grasped, catalogued, atomized, comprehended" (Ward, 1999, p. 175). That body "as a mystery, as a materiality which can never fully reveal, must always conceal, something of the profundity of its existence." The fifth scene is the Ascension. This is the "final displacement" when the body of the absent Christ becomes "the multi-gendered body of the Church" (p. 176).

Ward has attempted to show that these displacements of the body of Jesus really do demonstrate that "the particularities of one sex give way to the particularities of bodies which are male and female." If he is successful, he is also successful in dismantling a favorite question much discussed by feminist theologians during the past 25 years. In 1983 the famous feminist theologian Rosemary Radford Ruether threw down the question "Can a male Savior save women?" (Ruether, 1983, pp. 116–138). Ward has a clear riposte: the Savior is not exclusively male! While the incarnate Christ has a biologically male body, it incarnates a divine presence that cannot be identified with the male sex.

Question: Is Ward successful in his aim of refiguring a "masculine symbolics" until the particularities of one sex give way to the particularities of bodies which are male and female." Does he not struggle valiantly, but unsuccessfully, against the facts of Jesus' maleness?

Comment: Ward's hypothesis about the fluid body of Jesus is imaginative and thought-provoking. I doubt, though, whether he *is* successful. Nonetheless his analysis may provide some *empirical* support for the theological claim (see Section 7.1.2) that Jesus Christ reveals the suprasexual God who is unconfined by human gender. That said, there may remain several difficulties.

First, there may be a misleading conflation in the compound use of the terms "body" and "body of Christ." The body of Christ may refer variously to the humanity of Jesus, to the Church, to its collective members, to the eucharistic bread, to the post-Ascension presence of Christ in the world, and so on. We have seen that these terms are metaphors and that metaphors frequently rub up against each other and overlap. When metaphors collide they are best understood (following Wittgenstein's discussion of "language-games") as "a complicated network of similarities overlapping and criss-crossing: sometimes overall similarities, sometimes similarities of detail" (Wittgenstein, 1972, section 66). But Ward treats the body of Christ as a single entity with several displacements. The term "body of Christ" is treated differently in this book as producing a series of metaphors with similarities between them.

Second, there may be a worry that the body of Christ becomes *too* mysterious. The incarnate Christ had a *continuous* life. A very important creed declares the Christ to be "of the same reality as we are ourselves as far as his human-ness is concerned; thus like us in all respects, sin only excepted" (see Section 7.1.2). Is there a danger that the Christ of Ward's essay becomes a phantasm who drifts in and out of the Gospel narratives? "Displacement" is also a metaphor, and a body that is continually being displaced may cease to be like our own. But in reply Ward might retort that he has restored a much-needed emphasis on the mystery of Christ's being.

Third, there may be a danger that some of the detail of the five scenes may be over-sexualized. Even if "erotic" is understood very broadly (see Section 4.2.3) the attractiveness of Jesus at the Transfiguration may lie as much in the contrast with Moses the lawgiver and Elijah the prophet, with whom Jesus talked, as in Christ's desirability as God. There is an undoubted sexual element within the deliberate infliction of violence and torture on the flayed and crucified Christ. Perhaps the observation that "The actual male body of Jesus gets forgotten" in the onslaught against him, is to elevate gender to a position within the narrative that it does not hold? (For an alternative view, that the silence of Jesus in the face of his accusers and assailants may be better understood as an "exercise in self-mastery" of the kind ancient men were expected to make, see Moore, 2003, p. 11.)

Ward has successfully shown, I think, that the significance of Christ as a human being bursts out beyond his maleness, his belonging to a particular half of the human race. There is a stronger case for understanding the body of Christ as queer when that expression refers to the Church. We return to that case next.

8.2.2 Does the body of Christ have breasts?

The question raised in this section may seem needlessly coarse. I justify it by the need to know how far the female identity of the body of Christ as Church is to be pressed. Traditionally it has been pressed very far. The male priesthood needs a feminine body to act upon, and this emphasis on the femininity of the church lies at the root of the churches' problems about the ordination of women priests and bishops.

It was fairly common for breasts to be assigned metaphorically both to Christ and to the Church. The Church suckles her children as they grow in faith: Christ as Mother gently nourishes his disciples, especially women mystics whose devotion to Jesus was often expressed in a very physical language (Bynum, 1982). Our question is raised by the continuing resistance of most of Christendom to women priests and bishops, and the theological reasons that are dredged up in support of what is undoubtedly the traditional position. A key text (see Sections 5.2.1 and 6.3.2) is the extended analogy between Christ and the Church, and husbands and wives (Eph. 5:25–33). Let us return to that analogy for a final time.

According to a standard reading of this analogy, Christ and the Church are separate entities: so are husband and wife. Separate identities are the precondition of any subsequent union of them. Christ is male, so the Church must be female. Tradition then ascribes to each the gendered characteristics belonging to male and female in the ancient world. The male is the active, and the female the passive, partner: he the dominant, she the submissive. He is clean, she is to be cleansed (Eph. 5:26). He graciously purges her stains, removes her wrinkles, sundry "blemishes" (Eph. 5:27), and general feminine blameworthiness.

Once these gendered assumptions are allowed to determine patterns of ministry, not only are women excluded from it, men are also rendered sexually ambiguous. In Catholicism they must refrain from the taint of having sex. They alone represent the male Christ. They also represent the Church to Christ, and in order to do this they are part of the Church, and so they must be members of the *female* body of Christ understood as Church, as She stands before Her Bridegroom. But since the Church is female, they cannot be very good at doing what they are supposed to do. When male priests teach, preach, and administer the sacraments, they are active, representing Christ. To do this, they require a feminized body to which they minister: one that is receptive, submissive, obedient, unquestioning.

Men dressing up   This is already complicated enough. Men try to combine male and female roles. Clergy dress (itself a gendered word) invites analysis in terms of official ambiguity as men seek to exercise roles that are gendered masculine and feminine. There is a case for saying that clergy dressed up are transvestites, whatever their sex. They perform masculine *and* feminine roles, and the theological and psychological confusion becomes a sartorial and liturgical confusion as well. The clergy are cross-dressers! Once women are admitted to the priesthood the confusion doubles. Now there are women fulfilling male and female roles, as well as men! Too often the women are forced to become honorary men, whose honorific status continually undermines their ministry and legitimacy. No wonder the body of Christ is queer.

It need not be this way. If the confusion about masculine and feminine roles is removed, it cannot be doubled. And the confusion is easily removable. First, a careful and suitably reverent appropriation of meanings derivable from the core metaphor "body of Christ" allows us to say that that body is androgynous (see Section 8.1.2). It has male and female characteristics (hence the question about breasts) and so can be represented by men and women. And since Christ as God is not sexed, Christ actually requires male and female representation to the Church to avoid idolatry. But there is a stronger reason why the old churches, as well as some of the newer ones, need not be bound by ancient theories of gender (which arguably they confuse with the Gospel). Not only are ancient theories inappropriate for today's thinking about both sexuality and gender, the example of Jesus Himself suggests a different way of "doing" gender. We will explore this next.

8.3 Masculinity in the Body of Christ

8.3.1 Is there domination and submission in the body of Christ?

According to the New Testament, wives are to submit to their husbands. Husbands dominate them. *Dominus* is Latin for "Lord," and "Master." Domination requires "power-over" the submissive (see Section 2.2.2). Domination over others is also a definition of colonialism. Colonies were dominions. In many parts of the world domination is the default practice of relations between men and women. Some adults who play erotic games intensify the power-dynamics between them by reversing them, as when a partner acts out being the other's slave, or when a female partner dominates her partner and becomes a *dominatrix*.

There is a real possibility that Christian faith can initiate, ground, and encourage a reversal of domination/submission in relations between people. Indeed it may be seen to be re-enacted every time they celebrate the Eucharist. There are several passages about power-relations in the New Testament which are able to throw some transforming light on the conduct of gender-relations. Mark narrates how two disciples, James and John, ask Jesus directly for power and status "Let one of us sit at your right and the other at your left in your glory" (Mark 10:37). Jesus refuses to grant the request, but it leads to another episode:

> [41]When the ten heard about this, they became indignant with James and John. [42]Jesus called them together and said, "You know that those who are regarded as rulers of the Gentiles lord it over them, and their high officials exercise authority over them. [43]Not so with you. Instead, whoever wants to become great among you must be your servant, [44]and whoever wants to be first must be slave of all. [45]For even the Son of Man did not come to be served, but to serve, and to give his life as a ransom for many." (Mark 10:41–45; see also Matt. 20:24–28; Luke 22:24–30)

"Not so with you" suggests a strong contrast between the power-relations that are expected among the disciples in the Reign of God, and those that actually exist in the world. In the world people have to put up with other people bearing down on them. The people who are "regarded as rulers" may be petty officials but they enjoy their power and they dominate or "lord it over" (Vulgate *dominantur*) those they control. In the Reign of God, however, greatness is to be recognized in serving. Power is so radically reversed that in order to achieve greatness in the Reign of God one must become as a slave (a member of the lowest social class with no rights of one's own).

The teaching of Jesus about power is well known, but has perhaps yet to receive the importance it deserves. However it assumes additional importance in contemporary discussions of gender because of the recent work of some classical scholars which *locates an explicit gender reversal within it.* For example, Colleen Conway writes, "From the perspective of masculine identity in the ancient world, the implication of such teaching is that to be a disciple of Jesus means *to give up any claim to masculine status*" (2008, p. 98; emphasis added). While there are also plentiful rewards for faithful discipleship,

> those who want to be great must serve, and those who want to be first are to be slaves. Here then is the most open sign of resistance to . . . "the great ones" of the empire. The conduct that Jesus calls for in his own followers sounds like the language of submission, and of course, being servile was commonly associated with being effeminate. (Conway, 2008, p. 99)

Conway warns against seeing Jesus as a figure who turns the Roman gender hierarchy upside down. She finds examples of imperial rule where kingship and rule embody ideas of service (Conway, 2008, pp. 99–100). Nonetheless she concedes that the contrast between "the great ones" and the lowly crucified servant "can be an effective means of resistance to the dominant ruling powers" (Conway, 2008, p. 100).

Real men   Another classics scholar, Mathew Kuefler, shows how the followers of Jesus specifically undercut or subverted Roman masculinities, by redefining what it was for male Christians to be "real men." We will look at two obvious examples of this revaluation of values, and then assess whether a similar upheaval may be overdue in redefining masculinity in our own time.

The first case concerns the absence from the military of Christian soldiers. Christian men prior to the adoption of the Christian faith by the Roman Emperor Constantine, did not enlist as soldiers in the military. The clear teaching of Jesus about non-violence, non-retaliation, and love of enemies (Matt. 5:21–48) saw to that. Soldiers of Christ fought instead against sin and temptation. A biblical exhortation to "put on the full armor of God" (Eph. 6:10, 13; see 6:10–18) against "the devil's schemes" (Eph. 6:11) inspired them instead in a new battle. This was more than the substitute of a battle with an inner foe for a real, external, military enemy. Kuefler explains (within the context of the collapse of the city of Rome in 410):

> Christian men of late antiquity shared with their pagan counterparts a desire to see themselves as manly, a desire also threatened by the military crisis of the Roman Empire. They also worried about the unmanly stance of victimhood. Out of that desire and because of those worries, Christian men fashioned for themselves the image of the soldier of Christ. From the martyrs, who represented the best and bravest soldiers of Christ, the image grew to encompass all Christian men, whose daily struggles against sin and temptation – against the unmanliness of vice within themselves – were identified as warfare against evil. (Kuefler, 2001, p. 105)

A second and related case concerns what Kuefler calls "the manliness of sexual renunciation" (2001, p. 170).

> Christian leaders encouraged the code of male sexual restraint not only as a sign of Christian conviction but also as a sign of manliness. They did not rely on ancient medical beliefs in the dangers of sex to enforce the code but on Christian theological beliefs in sex as sin, and in this way they avoided the trap of unmanliness. They turned male sexual renunciation into a heroic act and created an intellectual environment in which men might abandon sex and its dangers without jeopardizing identity. (2001, p. 170)

In the last few paragraphs mention has been made of masculine identity, of real men, of manliness and unmanliness, all in the context of the classical and New Testament worlds. In the late modern world, and after the great achievements of feminism in bringing about the gradual acceptance of equal rights for women, pressing questions arise about these same concepts, and how men are to live them out in practical, relational terms. Our next task is to raise explicitly some of these pressing questions. Who is "a real man?" Does it even make sense to talk of manliness?

Activity: Do you think that the teaching of Jesus about the reversal of power-relations, and the teaching of early Christians about sexual renunciation can help men of all ages think positively about their masculinity now? If so, how? If not, why not?

Comment: With regard to *gender*, the example of Jesus as a servant who came to give himself to and for others, is hugely relevant for men and women alike. In the ancient world, the position of men over women was hegemonic.

   The dominance of men over women was taken for granted in the ancient and modern worlds alike, and it no longer is. At a time when "masculinism" is an attempt to reassert male hegemony, the Christian contribution to peaceful and whole gender relations is potentially huge. Following Christ, being "in Christ," or being a member of the "body of Christ," cannot entail relations of control, for all are conformed instead by the roles of service and self-giving. Men do not need to lose power: they need to share power, and in this they can be helped by the observation of Jesus that "whoever wants to save his life will lose it, but whoever loses his life for me and for the gospel will save it" (Mark 8:35).

In the Church and the world, there is a need for leadership to be exercised. While this is traditionally regarded in the Church as a vocation and as a gift, there is no need now (if there ever was) for men only to claim that gift as inherently theirs. Since women are more accustomed to the role of service, the argument may be put forward that they may be more prepared than men for the servant-leadership that the Church expects of its leaders. Men and women are learning to negotiate, to share, to cooperate with each other in the apportionment of the

Hegemonic: From the Greek *hègemòn*, "leader"; hegemony occurs when one group exercises control of another group.

Masculinism (or Masculism): The attempt to counterbalance feminism by reaffirming the rights of men: or, theories of masculinity that are thought to promote the interests of males.

tasks that they each have to do, in the home, or church, or workplace, and indeed even in law enforcement and the military. In the Church in particular it might be expected that the self-giving of Christ, the servant of all, should be continually re-embodied in the people who consciously call themselves members of Christ's body and reincarnate suffering love where hegemony is rife, and the "lording of gentiles" over one another is commonplace.

   More controversially, I would also hazard the suggestion that the ancient experience of sexual renunciation can also inform the late-modern sexual experience of women and men. There are huge differences between ancient and modern theories of gender, but also some similarities. Is it not the case that (among straight people) having sex is still too often something men do to women? Are not same-sex relations also susceptible to similar distortions? The coarse language used to describe having sex, and the pornographic depictions of having sex, make this clear, don't they? And the widespread provision of contraception, while it has brought undoubted gains for some women, has also created the expectation that their bodies will be more readily available to demanding men because the unwelcome possibility of pregnancy has been greatly reduced (see Section 12.1 and Thatcher, 2000).

The sexual renunciation that is celibacy is, frankly, extreme. That is why few people recognize it as a chosen vocation. Undoubtedly there are unhealthy motivations for the avoidance of sexual relations, such as misogynistic or misanthropic attitudes, or narcissistic tendencies which tempt us away from the intimacy of sexual relationship. Sexual desire has already been characterized as a good (see Section 4.2.3). But there is also a great need for sexual renunciation understood instead as *chastity* (see Section 11.3) as a positive means toward the maintenance of sexual health.

The renunciation of sexual contact that exploits or uses another for the indulgence of selfish pleasure is a prerequisite for sexual holiness. Sexual behavior which risks unwanted children, or the infection of a partner, is a serious failure of neighbor-love, whereas sexual love in the context of growing commitment can be a self-giving and self-receiving of inestimable personal and religious significance.

Is there not a strong case today for redefining manliness as boldly as the early Christians appear to have done? Manliness which is predatory, or macho, or promiscuous, and which creates among women the expectation of receptivity, availability, and conformity to a hegemonic culture, cannot be reconciled with any version of Christian faith.

8.3.2 Does the body of Christ have balls?

This very direct question addresses the role of eunuchs or "eunicism" in Christianity, the contribution eunuchs make to the body of Christ, and also the character of that body. Jesus says,

> For there are some eunuchs, which were so born from their mother's womb: and there are some eunuchs, which were made eunuchs of men: and there be eunuchs, which have made themselves eunuchs for the kingdom of heaven's sake. He that is able to receive it, let him receive it. (Matt. 19:12, Authorized Version)

How far does the sexual renunciation of Christians extend? Several writers have shed new light on this solitary reference in the New Testament to "eunicism," the deliberate removal of the testes. The sayings of Jesus about eunuchs refers fairly obviously to three classes of eunuch. The first class contains people who are born with ambiguous genitalia. The second class consists of men who have been castrated, whether forcibly or in order to secure employment as servants, generally to wealthy women, or in royal courts. (For the methods used, see Kuefler, 2001, p. 33.) The third class comprises *men who castrate themselves for the sake of God's Reign.* But who were these men?

The saying has remained baffling ever since Matthew wove it into his narrative. What is involved in making yourself a eunuch for the sake of the kingdom of heaven? Three types of answer are given to this question. The first is *literal.* Some early Christians (Origen is the noted example) castrated themselves. Kuefler thinks "it is at least possible that his words were intended literally" (Kuefler, 2001, p. 259). That interpretation would be hard to square with traditional Jewish sentiments. It was against Deuteronomic law and castrated Jews were disbarred from attending the Temple (Deut. 23:1).

The second type of answer is *metaphorical.* The translators of the New International Version are so confident that the metaphorical meaning is intended that they translate the phrase "made themselves eunuchs" as "have renounced marriage." That seems an unjustified inference from the text. Nonetheless, from the second century on, the verse was used as a foundation for the practice of clerical celibacy, and so a metaphorical meaning of the saying became assumed. Within the broader context of Jesus' teaching about marriage and the barring of divorce from God's Reign (Matt. 19:3–12), a metaphorical reading makes good sense.

The third type of answer is *hyperbolical* (exaggeration, deliberately heightened for effect). A.E. Harvey argues for this interpretation, comparing the saying with others in Matthew's Gospel that display a similar character, such as gouging out your eye or amputating your hand if either causes you to sin (Matt. 5:29–30). Harvey finds frequent cases of hyperbole in classical literature, which he calls "philosophical commonplaces", and he thinks "there is no evidence that those who attended to them often took them literally" (Harvey, 2007, p. 5).

Instead, what these teachers were trying to achieve was not self-mutilation but, by deploying lurid, aversive imagery, the "training of the will." The consequence of this type of answer is similar to the conclusion of the previous section. Yes, all Christians are called to a life of sexual restraint. But that requires renouncing some forms of sexual activity but not necessarily all of them. That too requires a training of the will.

Discipleship and gender-transgression   All three types of answer may miss some obvious points that Matthew's readers would not. The first is that eunuchs were common figures in the public world of the first century CE, and there are many references to them in the Hebrew Bible. They were of course, gender-ambiguous. They represented the feared slide from masculinity into femininity: they compromised the gender split between men and women (Kuefler, 2001, pp. 31–36, 96, 259–268; Conway, 2008, pp. 21, 40–41, 123–124). They were not "real men." They were often ridiculed, and frequently despised, not least because in their own bodies, all three types of *castrati* reminded men of the fragile difference between male and female bodies.

The second point, again likely to meet resistance among some contemporary readers, is that Matthew's Jesus models Christian discipleship upon "the ultimate ancient figure of sex-gender transgression" (Hester, 2005, p. 37). At a time when the modern two-sex theory is increasingly being called into question, the figure of the eunuch at last comes of age. J. David Hester thinks Jesus' saying about eunuchs shows "sex-gender transgression is a biblically sanctioned identity practice" (2005, p. 37).

That claim may entail making a difficult distinction between sexual identity and sexual practice, but the saying certainly reveals an ease with, and an acceptance of, people whose bodies do not fit neatly into binary male–female opposites. Harvey agrees. He argues the saying takes its origin from the knowledge that Jesus and the disciples had of local pagan priests who castrated themselves in the service of Cybele, the Great Earth Goddess (Hester, 2005, p. 10). Even these pagans display an admirable feat of will and prove their devotion! "even those who had deliberately castrated themselves for a pagan cult were to exchange the contempt and revulsion in which they were usually held for the dignity of full membership of the Kingdom of God" (Hester, 2005, p. 15). On the basis of the inclusion of eunuchs in the kingdom, Harvey cannot help expressing his sadness that there are still some Christians who still after twenty centuries of seeking to follow the teaching of Jesus, are capable of showing contempt and revulsion, or, more insidiously, some form of almost unconscious discrimination, towards those who, for no fault of their own, are of a particular race, colour, gender or sexual orientation. (Hester, 2005, p. 17)

Activity: In what ways, if any, might eunuchs provide a model for contemporary masculinity?

Comment: By combining together the metaphorical and hyperbolic interpretations of Jesus' saying, does not a construction of manliness appear where the supply of testosterone-fuelled energy to the male body is not dampened down or cut off? Quite the reverse. That energy is directed instead towards establishing the goals of God's Reign where the hungry are fed, justice is done, peace breaks out, and so on. The *performance* of divine love (I use Butler's term deliberately; see Section 2.1.2) need not entail emasculation either of the body or of the *psyche.* Indeed an intensification of the capacity to love is required.

Phallocentric behavior (and not necessarily sexual behavior) *is* dampened because raw energy is redirected in the service of self-giving love. I think there are two more senses in which the sayings of Jesus about eunuchs can inform our self-understanding.

First, the modeling of Christian discipleship by the example of an abnormal body speaks a strong word of affirmation to all men and women whose bodies are in some ways either abnormal, or considered so.

Second, the saying tells us more about the kind of body that the "body of Christ" is, and the kind of members who might wish to inhabit it. That body should not be reproducing hegemonic relations of gender, but rather enacting gentleness and kindness in the service of everyone.

8.4 ... Neither ... Male nor Female ...?

There is neither Jew nor Greek, slave nor free, male nor female, for you are all one in Christ Jesus. (Gal. 3:28)

8.4.1 Equal or one in the body of Christ?

The statement that there is no longer male nor female for those who are "in Christ" is one of the most disputed in the New Testament. Christians in favor of complete gender equality find their convictions authorized by this verse. If only matters were so simple! There are at least three reasons why the text may not give them quite the endorsement of contemporary equality between male and female that progressive Christians would like to find there.

First, there are plenty of other New Testament texts that continue to affirm the hierarchy of men over women. The weight of evidence overall is clearly against the egalitarian interpretation.

Second, there is little historical warrant for the liberal interpretation either (Kling, 2004, pp. 269–308). When the equality of the sexes was indeed conceded, as in some nineteenth century interpretations, what was given with one hand was soon taken away by the other. As Martin observes,

> Up until the 1970s, the majority of scholars insisted that the passage taught the equality of men and women "in Christ" ... But they then usually denied that this mandated or even allowed complete equality for women in society, the church, and the home. (Martin, 2006, p. 79)

What use is some ethereal, spiritual equality when material equalities are denied?

Third, the contention that Paul was preaching the equality of the sexes makes two awkward assumptions with which we have collided earlier: first, that in the ancient world there were understood to be two sexes; and second, that there was a concept of equality which was applicable to them (Elliott, 2002). The text is rather about the *unity* of believers in Christ. The statement "You are all one in Christ Jesus," "affirms the ethnic and social inclusiveness of the Jesus movement and the unity of all who are in Christ but says nothing about any equality of those included" (Elliott, 2003, p. 178).

Several interpreters, perhaps currently a majority, think Paul's reference to "neither ... male nor female" is a conscious reversal of Genesis 1:27, "male and female he created them." But Paul, unlike many conservative interpreters today, did not understand "male and female" to refer to two sexes. In 1974 Wayne Meeks argued that, at the time of Paul and subsequently, the creation of humanity in Genesis 1 and 2 was understood androgynously. (We will query this contention in a moment.) Martin explains

> The aboriginal human being had been a unified being, only later experiencing the fissures of ethnicity, status, and sex. The original Adam had been an androgyne, and the splitting of that androgynous being into male and female halves would be overcome in the salvation of the end time. (2006, p. 83; see Stuart, 2007, pp. 68, 71)

Several ancient Christian interpretations of the text support the androgynous reading (Martin, 2006, pp. 85–87). Galatians 3:28 was a formula used when Christians were baptized "in Christ Jesus." Christians on this view were baptized into a communal reality where the distinction between male and female had proleptically (by anticipation) been overcome in the resurrected life. Life in the Church now anticipated the end time when people would be like angels, neither marrying nor being given in marriage (Matt. 22:30; Mark 12:25; Luke 20:35).

More recent writers accept the androgynous reading of Galatians 3:28 but deny that it leads to the equality of the sexes. Rather, the state beyond male and female is assumed to be a state *where only the male exists*! Colleen Conway, for example, claims

> the passage draws on ancient ideas about an ideal state of unity or oneness in which there is "no male and female" *because there is only the masculine.* In the ancient world, androgyny was not the blending of female and male with an equal mix of the two. Instead, both Christian and non-Christian texts speak of a transformation to a higher state as a leaving behind of the female for the masculine. (2008, pp. 78–79; emphasis added)

Androgyny, on this view, does not imply equality, but the elevation of men and women into a restored form of masculinity where there is no longer a sexed existence of male and female.

Arguments about the adequacy of the androgyny interpretation are likely to continue for some time. Judith Gundry-Volf has put up a strong counter-argument, based on the broader themes that are treated in Galatians. The argument of that letter is specifically that the state of universal sinfulness jeopardizes the achievement of salvation through belonging to the Jewish race or conforming to the Jewish law. Despite this, salvation is open to Jews and Gentiles, because there is "no longer Jew and Greek." The higher unity of being in Christ unites people beyond the differences between races, classes ("slave nor free") and genders. The differences between people in the body of Christ have not been abolished. "Instead, these differences have been adiaphorized" (rendered inessential) (Gundry-Volf, 2003, p. 35).

Activity: Do you think any sense can be made today of the view that male and female Christians lose their sexual identity in a perfected maleness that leaves sexual differences behind?

Comment: I know the idea looks crazy, and insulting to women, but once we get behind it, it may be able to be rescued.

Perhaps we can say Christians looked towards a future when troublesome gender differences would be overcome in a new all male humanity. There is a genuine expression of Christian hope here, yet it is positioned in a notorious gender framework. Let us resist the easy temptation to throw out the hope along with the framework. What might be needed instead is the *nurture* of that hope, but within a framework that makes the nurture possible.

Can we not affirm the attempt to envision a new community where sexual difference is no longer troublesome, without affirming the ancient form (a single, male sex beyond both) in which that vision was expressed, and femininity eliminated. Masculinity beyond male and female is, for us, a nonsense for it remains masculine. The redeemed community in Christ, realized fully only in the afterlife, could be found realized partly in this life, where sexual difference is no longer the opportunity for hegemony, for power games, and for old dominances to appear in new guises. Such a view would be more consistent with Gundry-Volf's understanding of a new humanity where differences remain but no longer matter.

8.4.2 Is there sexual difference in the body of Christ?

Graham Ward thinks not. Ward has no time for the modern two-sex theory. In a provocatively titled essay, "There is no sexual difference," he refuses the obvious accounts of sexual difference which are based on physiology and on the two-sex theory. These "can be read off from bodies" (Ward, 2007, p. 76).

Instead he raises a new set of questions about difference, such as "Why is difference theologically significant? How is difference recognized?" His analysis of Mary's and Thomas' complex and particular encounters with the risen Christ (John 20:11–18, 20:24–28) lead him to two conclusions about sexual difference and sexual attraction in general.

First, there is no such thing as "pure difference" or difference in general (Ward, 2007, p. 81). Difference is always known in relation as one person becomes attracted to another when within his or her proximity.

Second,

> difference, to the extent that it concerns the bodies of other responsive beings, is always erotic and therefore sexually charged to a greater or a lesser degree. This is because it is only constituted in relation, and relations between responsive bodies become increasingly eroticised through proximity (Ward, 2007, p. 82).

The ingenuity of Ward's case rests both in his analysis of the encounters with Jesus (which there is no space here to describe), and in his overall thesis about sexual difference. He thinks "there is no difference as such, there is no sexual difference as such. Sexual difference is not a given, a fundament, a starting-point. It is always an 'achievement'," . . . something we become aware of only as it has already happened.

Ward's denial of sexual difference should probably be read as something else – the denial that the usual ways of thinking about it, or classifying it, have any point any longer. I think that is a more supportable thesis. We share a common humanity and we become most aware of sexual difference principally in the presence of others to whom we are attracted. That thesis reconfigures sexual difference but without eliminating it.

Sexual difference or divine difference?   Perhaps Miroslav Volf is on surer ground when he *affirms* sexual difference between men and women, but finds the significance of difference within *God*! There is difference in God because God is Three. *That* is the difference we should get to know if we want to understand better the differences between ourselves.

Volf's handling of the issue has much in common with the treatment of the idea of God beyond sex and gender, developed in the last chapter. Human beings have a sexed difference which they share with *animals*. But we cannot share these differences with God, for God is not a creature (see Section 7.1). God is beyond distinctions of sex. "Nothing in God is specifically feminine; nothing in God is specifically masculine . . . Men and women share maleness and femaleness not with God but with animals. They image God in their common humanity" (Volf, 2003, p. 161).

It follows, thinks Volf, that neither maleness nor femaleness directly represents God. Men do not represent God more adequately on account of God being "Father," any more than women can represent God, because they are "by nature more relational," or "closer to the divine as the power of connectedness and love." By a different route, Volf has arrived at a similar set of conclusions about the suprasexuality of God arrived at earlier (see Section 7.1.1).

Sexual differences, then, exist. They exist as they are actually found and manifested in societies, and they are socially and culturally produced. Volf finds this inevitable, unobjectionable, but also importantly *transformable*. He admits "The content of gender identity is underdetermined; anything seems to go" (Volf, 2003, p. 169). But he then wants to determine or perform sexual difference by embodying the difference that is found in the triune God. He proposes that we locate normativity in the formal features of identity as we encounter it in the identities and relations of divine persons. Instead of setting up ideals of femininity and masculinity, *we should root each in the sexed body and let the social construction of gender play itself out guided by the vision of the identity of and relations between divine persons.* (2003, p. 170; emphasis in original)

Here then is an admission of gender difference. There are many of them. But Christians take what is important about gender difference from the difference that is to be found, not in society or church, but at the heart of divine reality. There is difference in God certainly, for the three Persons are distinct. But in God the three Persons are also *equal*.

Taking our cue for handling difference from the differences that subsist in the life of God, he argues that "we must both affirm equality between men and women and seek to change social practices in which the inferiority of women is embodied and through which it is perpetuated" (Volf, 2003, p. 173).

So at the very heart of the Christian tradition, Volf finds resources for dealing with gender. The life of the Trinity is a communion or community where difference does not need to be overcome by elimination, domination, repression, or oppression, for each Person is already "in" the other, in the one Life that pours itself out in self-giving Love.

But though self-giving has no assurance of success, it does have the promise of eternity because it reflects the character of the divine Trinity. It is on account of self-giving that divine persons exist in a perfect community in which each is itself only by being inhabited by the others. And it is through the power of self-giving that a new community of men and women will emerge, in which distinct but dynamic gender identities that are "not without" the other will be fashioned and refashioned in peace. (Volf, 2003, p. 177)

Once again, we have arrived at God the Mystery of Personal Being (the title of Section 6.2.3). Within the Trinity difference will never be eliminated, for without difference none of the Persons could be known for how and who they are. Rather in the mystery of divine being difference is never allowed to become distorted so as to license hegemony, and silly gradations of greater or less, dominating and submissive. Indeed, divine difference is not mapped out onto sexual difference at all. Rather the Communion of Love that God is enables mutuality, equality, and reciprocity wherever it moves and flows.

This broad vision of God brings Part III to a close. This vision, together with our earlier conclusions about the performance of gender in both the ancient and modern worlds will help us to get theological about same-sex love, the theme of Part IV.

References

Althaus-Reid, M. (2003) *The Queer God*, Routledge, London/New York.

Althaus-Reid, M., and Isherwood, L. (eds.) (2004) *The Sexual Theologian: Essays on Sex, God, and Politics*, T&T Clark International, London/New York.

Beattie, T. (2006) *New Catholic Feminism – Theology and Theory*, Routledge, London/New York.

Bynum, C.W. (1982) *Jesus as Mother: Studies in the Spirituality of the High Middle Ages*, University of California Press, Berkeley/Los Angeles, CA.

Conway, C.M. (2008) *Behold the Man – Jesus and Greco-Roman Masculinity*, Oxford University Press, Oxford.

Dinter, P.E. (1994) Christ's body as male and female. *Cross Currents*, 44.

Elliott, J.H. (2002) Jesus was not an egalitarian: a critique of an anachronistic and idealist theory. *Biblical Theology Bulletin*, 32(2), 75–91.

Elliott, J.H. (2003) The Jesus movement was not egalitarian but family-oriented. *Biblical Interpretation*, 11(2), 173–211.

Gundry-Volf, J.M. (2003) Beyond difference? Paul's vision of a new humanity in Galatians, in *Gospel and Gender: A Trinitarian Engagement with being Male and Female in Christ* (ed. D.A. Campbell), T&T Clark International, London/New York, pp. 8–36.

Harvey, A.E. (2007) Eunuchs for the sake of the kingdom. *Heythrop Journal*, 48(1), 1–17.

Hester, J.D. (2005) Eunuchs and the postgender Jesus: Matthew 19.12 and transgressive sexualities. *Journal for the Study of the New Testament*, 28(1) (Sept.) 13–40.

Kling, D.W. (2004) *The Bible in History: How the Texts have Shaped the Times*, Oxford University Press, New York.

Kuefler, M. (2001) *The Manly Eunuch: Masculinity, Gender Ambiguity, and Christian Ideology in Late Antiquity*, University of Chicago Press, Chicago/London.

Loughlin, G. (ed.) (2007) *Queer Theology: Rethinking the Western Body*, Blackwell, Malden, MA/Oxford.

Martin, D.B. (2006) *Sex and the Single Savior*, Westminster John Knox Press, Louisville, KY.

Moore, S.D. (2003) "O man, who art thou . . .?": masculinity studies and New Testament studies, in *New Testament Masculinities* (eds. S.D. Moore and J.C. Anderson), Society of Biblical Literature, Atlanta, GA, pp. 1–22.

Ruether, R. (1983) *Sexism and God Talk: Towards a Feminist Theology*, Beacon Press, Boston.

Stuart, E. (2007) Sacramental flesh, in *Queer Theology: Rethinking the Western Body* (ed. G. Loughlin), Blackwell, Malden, MA/Oxford, pp. 65–75.

Swancutt, D. (2006) Sexing the Pauline body of Christ: Scriptural sex in the context of the American Christian culture war, in *Toward a Theology of Eros – Transfiguring Passion at the Limits of Discipline* (eds. V. Burrus and C. Keller), Fordham University Press, New York, pp. 65–98.

Thatcher, A. (2000) A strange convergence? Popes and feminists on contraception, in *The Good News of the Body: Sexual Theology and Feminism* (ed. L. Isherwood), Sheffield Academic Press, Sheffield, pp. 136–148.

Volf, M. (2003) The trinity and gender identity, *Gospel and Gender: A Trinitarian Engagement with being Male and Female in Christ* (ed. D.A. Campbell), T&T Clark International, London/New York, pp. 155–178.

Ward, G. (1999) BODIES – the displaced body of Jesus Christ, in *Radical Orthodoxy* (eds. J. Milbank, C. Pickstock and G. Ward), Routledge, London/New York, pp. 163–181.

Ward, G. (2007) There is no sexual difference, in *Queer Theology: Rethinking the Western Body* (ed. G. Loughlin), Blackwell, Malden, MA/Oxford, pp. 76–85.

Wittgenstein, L. (1972) *Philosophical Investigations*, 3rd edn., reprinted (trans. E. Anscombe), Blackwell, Oxford.

Part IV

Being Theological about Same-Sex Love

9

The Bible and Same-Sex Love

Chapter 9 traverses some territory with which some readers may be over familiar – the collection of passages from both Testaments that are thought to condemn homosexuality. The churches' reliance on the supposition that the Bible condemns homosexuality is noted (Section 9.1). Traditional and revisionary readings of these passages are compared (Sections 9.2 and 9.3). Attention is paid to how churches use these passages, and questions are raised about other, neglected, passages that may throw a different light on same-sex attraction (Section 9.4). Reasons are given for finding the traditional interpretation wanting (Section 9.5).

9.1 What the Churches Teach

The churches have long taught, and millions of Christians continue to think, that the Bible condemns homosexual practice. Only recently has a revisionary interpretation of biblical teaching "come out," and into the churches, where it is causing consternation. The insistence that the Bible condemns homosexuality will always require examination of the texts on which this claim is based. This has an unfortunate consequence. Those Christians who condemn, together with those who, under certain conditions approve, homosexual acts, can be seen to agree that the study of particular biblical passages is the key to the whole task. It would seem there is agreement around the proposition that the Bible is the churches' sexual guidebook: the obvious and vehement disagreement among Christians is about the rules to be found there, and how to apply them. We shall need to keep in mind continually that the "guidebook" view of the Bible is not the only one (see Section 3.3.2).

God, Sex, and Gender: An Introduction, First Edition. Adrian Thatcher.
© 2011 Adrian Thatcher. Published 2011 by Blackwell Publishing Ltd.

"Diligently studying the Scriptures"   A suggestive analogy may be made between the use of the Bible in relation to lesbian and gay sex and an incident recorded in John's Gospel. John compares Jesus' use of the Jewish Scriptures with the use of the Scriptures by some Jews with whom Jesus is in conflict. Jesus says to them "You diligently study the Scriptures because you think that by them you possess eternal life. These are the Scriptures that testify about me, [40]yet you refuse to come to me to have life" (John 5:39–40).

The incident about the Scriptures contrasts Jesus' understanding of them as *witnessing about him*, with the Jews' understanding of the Scriptures as *witnessing about them*. In the first case, the Scriptures are rightly used because they witness to Christ (their use is "Christocentric"): in the second case, they are wrongly used, because they do not. We may have reason to think that the proof-texts showing that homosexuality is wrong, illustrate this "non-Christocentric" position only too well.

That many churches oppose homosexual practice on the ground that the Bible forbids it, can be found by a cursory look at some of the official statements issued by the churches themselves. Here are a few:

1. For according to the objective moral order, homosexual relations are acts which lack an essential and indispensable finality. *In Sacred Scripture they are condemned as a serious depravity and even presented as the sad consequence of rejecting God.* (Sacred Congregation for the Doctrine of the Faith, 1975, section 8; emphasis added)
2. There is nevertheless *a clear consistency within the Scriptures themselves on the moral issue of homosexual behavior.* The Church's doctrine regarding this issue is thus based, not on isolated phrases for facile theological argument, but on the *solid foundation of a constant Biblical testimony.* (Sacred Congregation for the Doctrine of the Faith, 1976, para. 5; emphases added)
3. *Basing itself on Sacred Scripture, which presents homosexual acts as acts of grave depravity,* Tradition has always declared that "homosexual acts are intrinsically disordered." (*Catechism of the Catholic Church,* 1994, para. 2357; emphasis added)
4. This Conference ... *while rejecting homosexual practice as incompatible with Scripture,* calls on all our people to minister pastorally and sensitively to all irrespective of sexual orientation and to condemn irrational fear of homosexuals. (Lambeth Conference, 1998, Resolution 1.10d; emphasis added)
5. We affirm God's plan for marriage and sexual intimacy – one man, and one woman, for life. Homosexuality is not a "valid alternative lifestyle. "*The Bible condemns it as sin.* It is not, however, unforgivable sin. The same redemption available to all sinners is available to homosexuals. They, too, may become new creations in Christ. (Southern Baptist Convention, n.d.; emphasis added)

The first three of these proscriptions are Roman Catholic: the fourth is Anglican; the fifth Baptist. In all of them there is an appeal to "Sacred Scripture," "the Scriptures themselves," "Scripture," "the Bible." In all of them, the teaching of the Bible is clear and constant, and its judgment grave. Given that the term "homosexuality" is found nowhere in the Bible, the confidence that homosexuality is referred to is impressive. What precisely is being condemned? It has various names – "homosexual relations," "homosexual behavior," "homosexual practice," or just plain "homosexuality." We shall inquire next how the Scriptures give rise to these unambiguous teachings and judgments.

9.2 Same-Sex Relations in the Hebrew Bible

The second quotation above is from an influential document, *Homosexualitatis Problema*, the Letter to the Bishops of the Catholic Church on the Pastoral Care of Homosexual Persons, issued by Pope Benedict XVI when, in 1986, he was Cardinal Joseph Ratzinger. The "solid foundation of biblical testimony" is said to include Genesis 19:1–11, and Leviticus 18:22 and 20:13. These verses need to be quoted in full.

Angels dropping by

> The two angels arrived at Sodom in the evening, and Lot was sitting in the gateway of the city. When he saw them, he got up to meet them and bowed down with his face to the ground. [2]"My lords," he said, "please turn aside to your servant's house. You can wash your feet and spend the night and then go on your way early in the morning." "No," they answered, "we will spend the night in the square."
>
> [3]But he insisted so strongly that they did go with him and entered his house. He prepared a meal for them, baking bread without yeast, and they ate. [4]Before they had gone to bed, all the men from every part of the city of Sodom – both young and old – surrounded the house. [5]They called to Lot, "Where are the men who came to you tonight? Bring them out to us so that we can have sex with them."
>
> [6]Lot went outside to meet them and shut the door behind him [7]and said, "No, my friends. Don't do this wicked thing. [8]Look, I have two daughters who have never slept with a man. Let me bring them out to you, and you can do what you like with them. But don't do anything to these men, for they have come under the protection of my roof."
>
> [9]"Get out of our way," they replied. And they said, "This fellow came here as an alien, and now he wants to play the judge! We'll treat you worse than them." They kept bringing pressure on Lot and moved forward to break down the door.
>
> [10]But the men inside reached out and pulled Lot back into the house and shut the door. [11]Then they struck the men who were at the door of the house, young and old, with blindness so that they could not find the door. (Gen. 19:1–11)

Lot, himself a stranger in the land of Israel, entertains two men who, unknown to the men of the town, are angels. The men of the town want to have sex with the strangers. Lot offers his two virgin daughters to them instead! The angels not only cause their attackers to become blind, they say they are sent by the Lord to destroy it (Gen. 19:13). After Lot and his family make their escape, "The LORD rained down burning sulfur on Sodom and Gomorrah" (Gen. 19:24).

According to a standard view of the passage, the wickedness of Sodom is homosexuality, a fact indicated by the invention of the words "sodomy" and "Sodomite." According to Roman Catholic official teaching, their wickedness is an intensification of the wickedness demonstrated at the Fall of Adam and Eve. Ratzinger comments on the story – "Thus, in Genesis 19:1–11, the deterioration due to sin continues in the story of the men of Sodom.

There can be no doubt of the moral judgment made there against homosexual relations" (1986, para. 6).

There are two further apparent references to homosexuality in the Hebrew Bible. These occur in the Holiness Code, a part of Leviticus (chs. 17–26) whose provisions are aimed at maintaining the ritual purity of the people.

> Do not lie with a man as one lies with a woman; that is detestable. (Lev. 18:22)

> If a man lies with a man as one lies with a woman, both of them have done what is detestable. They must be put to death; their blood will be on their own heads. (Lev. 20:13)

Men having sex with men as they would with women, is an "abomination." It is detestable, punishable by death. The prohibitions reinforce the horror of homosexuality, for which the cities of Sodom and Gomorrah were destroyed.

Activity: Re-read Genesis 19:1–11. The traditional interpretation of the story is that God punishes homosexuality. Can you think of some reasons why this interpretation might no longer be sound?

Comment: I know that question is difficult to answer without some more specialist knowledge. But, first, you might have thought, with good reason, that the narrative is *morally repellent as it stands*, so no moral conclusion at all can be drawn from a story where two young girls can be surrendered to an angry mob by their father, for sexual abuse. Other details, such as the visiting angels or the punitive character of the God who destroys, might make us wary of assuming too much continuity between the religious milieu of the story and our own.

Second, there is good evidence from within the Bible itself that the wickedness of Sodom lay, not in homosexual acts, but in the failure of the citizens to take Israel's hospitality laws seriously, and offer respect and protection to the strangers. That interpretation would account for Lot's plaintive cry, "don't do anything to these men, for they have come under the protection of my roof" (Gen. 19:8). Lot appeals "not to the sinfulness of (male) homosexuality, but to the fact that the men are his guests. Hospitality demands that the visitors be treated with honor, in fact as superiors" (Moore, 2003, p. 71).

The example of Sodom occurs in several subsequent biblical passages, notably Ezekiel 16, "where Sodom is described as being guilty of pride, excess of food, and prosperous ease and not helping the poor and needy" (Groves, Holder, and Gooder, 2008, p. 118). Failure of hospitality is the clear meaning of Jesus' references to Sodom (Matt. 10:15; Luke 10:12), for the issue at stake there is the hospitality that his disciples may or not receive from the towns to which they are sent on their mission.

Buggery or rape?

Third, it may be assuming too much to infer that the sin of the citizens of Sodom is homosexuality. The sin is intended gang rape. Moore (2003, p. 71) comments:

The visitors themselves are to be reduced to a state of passivity. They are not asked to come out; Lot is to bring them out. That is, they are not even humanized by being addressed directly, they are treated as a commodity to be handed from Lot to the citizens. They are not invited to get acquainted; they are to be known. Their wishes are not consulted; they are to be treated as mere objects for the pleasure of the citizens.

But the intention was *homosexual* gang-rape, was it not? (The rape of Lot's daughters would not have been considered to be rape, because their father and owner had consented to their abuse.) Yes, the citizens intended to violate hospitality laws by the homosexual violation of the visitors. But the narrative does not license a blanket condemnation of consensual homosexual practices (whatever these may be). It condemns the intention to rape strangers in violation of the laws of God. Is it not principally the violation of strangers that makes the intention wicked?

The two commands in Leviticus clearly proscribe anal sex between men. Such a practice would be "detestable" and unholy. Refraining from anal penetration is one way of remaining within the bounds of acceptable behavior.

Activity: Can you think of any reason why this passage might *not* be applied to sexual behavior today?

Comment: I think the most obvious reason is that there are many laws in the Holiness Code and elsewhere in the Hebrew Bible that Christians do not regard as binding upon them.

The Code begins with instructions about bringing slaughtered animals to the Tent of Meeting (Lev. 17:1–7) – hardly to be heeded now. There are still commentators who think "that the rules about sexual behavior in the Old Testament are not simply a product of their culture and era: they are absolute" (Brandon, 2009, p. 213). But this seems bizarre, not least because Jesus himself contradicted the law on divorce. Later in the Code men must not have sex with women during menstruation because they make themselves unclean (Lev. 18:19, 24). Oh. Having sex with slave-girls is fine, though (Lev. 19:20). Problems arise only when they belong to someone else (Lev. 19:20–24). This is hardly an absolute rule, transcending time.

This is the milieu where anal sex between men is condemned. The milieu is one governed by consideration of male ownership of women (property) and the avoidance of uncleanness (purity). Neither consideration is relevant to contemporary Christian sexual morality today, except that it helpfully and usefully shows us how culturally and socially relative our own modern assumptions about sex actually are (Countryman, 1988, p. 237).

The mixing of kinds   The Levitical laws, *do*, however, condemn men having anal sex with men. We may be in a better position than previous generations to understand why this is so. The frequent references in this book to ancient theories of gender create a picture where *gender* difference is what principally divides men from women; where men are active, leading, hard, and penetrative. Women conversely are passive, led, soft, and penetrated. The sin of homosexuality, on this view, is that of transgressing a noted gender divide. Penetrative, anal sex is wrong because a man is feminized. He acts like a woman in consenting to being penetrated. It is this that is disgraceful.

A recent writer, Daniel Boyarin, shows how, in Jewish thought too, a similar gender continuum is in evidence, but here the language used is that of "kinds." Men and women constitute a "kind." He argues that the prohibition of male–male anal sex in "biblical culture" is based on

P: This stands for the Priestly Source, a strand of the Pentateuch (the first five books of the Bible) that includes Genesis 1. It was the latest of the four principal sources, probably written by priests around 500 BCE when the Jews were in exile in Babylon.

the much broader series of prohibitions about the mixing of kinds. The source of the prohibition of mixing kinds is the P tradition which includes Genesis 1.

In this account of creation God is repeatedly said to make plants and animals according to their kind (Gen. 1:11, 12, 21, 24, 25). Boyarin reminds us that the Torah forbids *hybrids* (cross-breedings, or mixings of say, plants and animals of different types): "one may not hybridize or even plant two species together, mate a horse to a donkey, weave linen and wool into linsey-woolsey, etc. God-given categories must be kept separate" (Boyarin, 2007, p. 135). Boyarin argues that the Hebrew word *tebhel*, usually mistranslated as "abomination" or "perversion," means a "mixing" of what should be kept separate. A man having penetrative sex with another man, like a man penetrating an animal, or an animal penetrating a woman (Lev. 18:23) is a similar mixing of kinds.

Cross-dressing as a mixing of kinds   Cross-dressing is also forbidden in the Torah. "A woman must not wear men's clothing, nor a man wear women's clothing, for the LORD your God detests anyone who does this" (Deut. 22:5). This too is a mixing of kinds. No self-respecting man would ever appear in public as a woman. Boyarin finds a strong parallelism in the Hebrew of this verse and Leviticus 18:22, which strengthens his thesis that the wrongness of men having anal sex with men has nothing at all to do with a particular type of sin, homosexual sin, and everything to do with the mixing of kinds that the Torah forbids. So,

> The Torah's language is very explicit; it is the "use" of a male as a female that is "*to eba,*" the crossing of a body from one God-given category to another, analogous to the wearing of clothes that belong to the other sex, by nature as it were. Moving a male body across the border into "female" metaphysical space transgresses the categories in the same way as putting on a female garment, for both parties, since both participate (presumably willingly) in the transgressive act. (Boyarin, 2007, p. 136)

Boyarin comes to a controversial conclusion, on which we do not need to adjudicate. While acknowledging that anal sex between men is prohibited by the Holiness Code, he goes on to observe that it is the only homosexual act that *is* condemned. Going behind the invention of homosexuality, a homoerotic culture may have flourished "precisely because biblical and Talmudic cultures did not have, according to my reading, a category of the homosexual, they therefore allowed for much greater normative possibilities for the homoerotic" (2007, p. 142). Saul Olyan, again using a detailed exegesis of the Hebrew texts and the social background, comes to a similar conclusion (1994, pp. 179–206; 2006, p. 15).

Our study of these Hebrew texts shows that the traditional reading is neither the only, nor the most plausible, of those available. A study which deliberately sets out to enable discussion between Christians divided over homosexuality, offers as a conclusion acceptable to both sides, "It is clear that male homosexual activity is prohibited in the Holiness code" (Groves, Holder, and Gooder, 2008, p. 126). While this is offered as a genial conclusion acceptable to all participants in the bitter argument over homosexuality, it claims too much. The claim has two defects.

First, the Holiness Code does not condemn "male homosexual activity." It may do no more than condemn the practice of men being penetrated by men because that is womanish and a mixing of kinds. In a similar way the Sodom story does not condemn "homosexual relations" or "homosexual practices" considered as a class. Within the context of caring for strangers it condemns same-sex *rape*.

The second defect is more common. The assumption is made that there is a historically continuous sexual phenomenon, *homosexuality*, which can be found in the Hebrew Bible, so that what we find there is also what we are talking about when we talk of same-sex relations now. That is to ignore the severe gender inequality that gave rise to the abhorrence of men acting like women, and to project onto the Bible categories that are alien to it. We will meet this difficulty again in the next section.

> *Activity:* In order to place in historical context the prohibitions we have just discussed, read the whole of Leviticus chapters 18–20, noting where the prohibitions appear, and the reference in 19:19 prohibiting the mixing of kinds. You may want to jot down which of the laws may still be helpfully applicable today, and which are not.

9.3 Same-Sex Relations in the New Testament

There are three New Testament passages that appear to condemn homosexuality. The most detailed and influential is Romans 1:18–2:3, at the heart of which is thought to be an explicit condemnation of lesbian and gay sex acts. It will be necessary to examine the full argument of the passage in some detail. It is difficult to follow; key terms are hard to translate; the secondary literature is vast; and interpretations vary immensely.

9.3.1 Reading Romans 1

Shameful lusts and indecent acts   In what follows I break down the argument into six steps, and try to describe it dispassionately. Paul says what he is doing in Romans 1. He is commending the Gospel to "Greeks and non-Greeks" (1:14). That Gospel is "first for the Jew, then for the Gentile" (1:16). In 1:18—23, he argues that the Greeks (or Gentiles) are both sinful and without excuse for their sins. That is why they need to hear the Gospel that Paul wants to proclaim to them. Now for the six steps:

First, Paul holds that belief in the one, true God is actually obvious to the Gentiles. It is obvious:

> since what may be known about God is plain to them, because God has made it plain to them. For since the creation of the world God's invisible qualities – his eternal power and divine nature – have been clearly seen, being understood from what has been made, [or, visible to the eye of reason – Revised English Bible] so that men are without excuse. (1:19–20)

Second, Paul accuses the Gentiles of turning away from God and committing the basic sin of idolatry. Using an argument that would have been familiar to any reader of Wisdom 11–15, he observes

> For although they knew God, they neither glorified him as God nor gave thanks to him, but their thinking became futile and their foolish hearts were darkened. Although they claimed to be wise, they became fools and exchanged the glory of the immortal God for images made to look like mortal man and birds and animals and reptiles. (Rom. 1:21–23)

"The wrath of God" (1:18) is against the Gentiles, and God delivers it not by actively intervening to punish them directly, but by leaving them in their sinful state to make an ungodly mess of their lives.

Third, a blatant example of their degraded and dissolute state is their sexual immorality.

> Therefore God gave them over in the sinful desires of their hearts to sexual impurity for the degrading of their bodies with one another. They exchanged the truth of God for a lie, and worshiped and served created things rather than the Creator – who is forever praised. Amen. (Rom. 1:24–25)

The sin of the Gentiles is clearly idolatry. Gentile nations and civilizations are all idolatrous, and the sexual immorality among them follows from their idolatry.

Fourth, Paul further elaborates what kind of immorality is being practiced. The next two verses appear to refer straightforwardly to sexual practices between women and women, and between men and men.

> Because of this, God gave them over to shameful lusts. Even their women exchanged natural relations for unnatural ones. In the same way the men also abandoned natural relations with women and were inflamed with lust for one another. Men committed indecent acts with other men, and received in themselves the due penalty for their perversion. (Rom. 1:26–27)

Fifth, the Gentiles' rejection of God has further grave consequences. Paul observes how, in addition to sexual immorality,

> They have become filled with every kind of wickedness, evil, greed and depravity. They are full of envy, murder, strife, deceit and malice. They are gossips, slanderers, God-haters, insolent, arrogant and boastful; they invent ways of doing evil; they disobey their parents; they are senseless, faithless, heartless, ruthless. (Rom. 1:29–31)

Finally, there is a "rhetorical sting operation" (Hays, 1986) in the tail of the argument. Jewish, or rather Jewish Christian readers, familiar with the depiction of Gentiles as godless, and themselves as a holy people, find the argument turned against them. Having made a series of negative judgments against Gentile culture, those from a Jewish background are told that they too are as much sinners as the Gentiles!

> You, therefore, have no excuse, you who pass judgment on someone else, for at whatever point you judge the other, you are condemning yourself, because you who pass judgment do the same things. Now we know that God's judgment against those who do such things is based on truth. So when you, a mere man, pass judgment on them and yet do the same things, do you think you will escape God's judgment? (Rom. 2:1–3)

The Anglican bishops are convinced, on the basis of standard treatments of this passage by New Testament theologians that "there is ... general agreement that St Paul sees homosexuality as a manifestation of that rebellion against God that we have seen to be the theme of Romans 1" (House of Bishops' Group on *Issues in Human Sexuality*, 2003, paras. 4.3.13 and 4.3.23). Evidence is found in the writings of C.K. Barrett (1971), Joseph Fitzmeyer (1996), J.D.G. Dunn (1988), and the polemical anti-gay Robert Gagnon (2001) for this conclusion, which is doubtless shared by hundreds more theologians and a big majority of lay readers of Romans. But their case is far from certain.

9.3.2 Re-reading Romans 1

There are several good reasons for doubting the dependability of the traditional reading. Here are five.

First, it is a legitimate question to ask whether Paul's overall argument, outlined above at some length, can be thought sound for us today. He rehearses the familiar contrasts between Jews and non-Jews as a first century Jew might have outlined them. In the course of this rehearsal there are some assumptions about Gentile civilization that may not hold.

Is the existence of God really so obvious that to deny it is not merely an honest intellectual mistake, but an act of moral rebellion against this God, deserving ruin?

Or again, our understanding of the history of religions (including of course the Jewish religion) is that there was no transition from an original monotheism to a disgraceful polytheism where "images made to look like mortal man and birds and animals and reptiles" were worshiped instead. It is the other way round. The transition is from polytheism to monotheism. The turn to polytheism was no act of global Gentile apostasy. It never happened. Some standard features of Jewish apologetics current then, do not convince now.

Second, there are questions about the role of the references to unnatural sex in the course of this argument. The argument is not directed against homosexuality. It is directed against idolatry. It is idolatry that is punished. The "unnatural" same-sex relations are not punished either. That some women, like some men, were "inflamed with lust for one another," is not punished. Their lust is rather a consequence of a broader, general act of apostasy in turning away from God. Unnatural sex for Paul is perverse, but it is not why Gentiles are punished. Unnatural sex is a consequence of idolatry.

Third, Paul's view of "sinful desires" (Rom. 1:24) may not correspond with traditional, or indeed with very modern, assumptions. In this verse, the example of unnatural sex has not yet arisen (Rom. 1:26). As a result of "the sinful desires of their hearts" God gave them over . . . to sexual impurity for the degrading of their bodies with one another." The impurity here could include homosexual sex but is not confined to it. It is about any sex that is degrading or dishonoring to the body.

More importantly, the point often missed is that Paul, when he speaks of sexual desire, is *against all expressions of it, even the desire for straight sex within marriage.* Dale Martin shows both by an analysis of Paul's use of "desire," and by comparing it with both classical medical opinion and Stoic teaching, that, in Paul's view, all sexual desire is sinful (2006, pp. 65–76). *Burning* with passion (1 Cor. 7:9), or being in*flamed* with lust (Rom. 1:27) are sinful states, not just incendiary ones.

An illustration of this point may be found in Paul's advice to the unmarried and to widows: "if they cannot control themselves, they should marry, for it is better to marry than to burn with passion" (1 Cor. 7:9). His meaning is not that sexual desire is acceptable within marriage. Rather, marriage is the means towards the extirpation of desire, the way of bringing desire to an end. The way to avoid "the pollution" of sinful desire "is for men to possess and control their 'vessels' (their wives) as safe receptacles for their sexual overflow. But the idea that passion could be a part of that process is not entertained; in fact, it is excluded" (Martin, 2006, p. 67). If Paul is to be our guide in sexual morality we will need to deal with all desires of a sexual nature, not just homosexual ones.

What were the women up to?   Fourth, were the women in Romans 1:26 lesbians? The verse is thought to be the only, but very direct, reference to women having sex with each other. "Even their women exchanged natural relations for unnatural ones." The King James Version has the more familiar (and more literal) "even their women did change the natural use into that which is against nature." There is good reason to doubt that Paul had lesbian sex in mind at all. Whatever are "unnatural relations?" Who were the women having them with?

The reference to "*their* women" draws attention to the men in the background. These women would be subject to men, and passive in relation to them. "Unnatural" might mean "non-coital" (Miller, 1995, p. 1). Taking the lead, appearing too keen, having oral or anal sex, having sex sitting on top of their male partners, might all have counted as unnatural.

Unnatural sex in the case of women, thinks Moore, "involves acts such as oral and anal intercourse with men – forsaking their 'natural' sexual instrument" (2003, p. 99). That too was the view of Clement of Alexandria and of Augustine (Allison, 2006, pp. 124–125). On this interpretation the women having unnatural sex were not lesbians at all.

Fifth, what exactly is the problem with sex that is "contrary to," or "against" nature (*para phusin*)? The men are having sex with men; it is unnatural; they are "inflamed with lust for one another;" they commit "indecent acts;" what they do is "perversion." That much is plain. Are they perverse because they are having homosexual sex? Or is the sex they are having, indecent and perverse for some other reason?

Perhaps so. *Para* also means "in excess of" or "beyond" (as in "*para*normal"). Later in the letter Paul uses the phrase to describe God's gracious act in bringing the Gentiles to salvation (Rom. 11:24). Rogers thinks "in excess of nature" is the right meaning in both cases. Men having sex with men is due to excessive passion: God saving the Gentiles is due to God's excessive generosity. Both are "*para physin.*"

"Excess" is used in different ways in these two places, but Rogers sees another "rhetorical sting" in the argument. Paul deliberately repeats the phrase he has already used to describe Gentiles having excessive sex, in the context of God bringing Gentiles to salvation. "The sting is this: saving the Gentiles, God shows solidarity with something of their nature, the very feature that had led the Jew Paul to distinguish himself from them: their excessive sexuality" (Rogers, 1999, p. 65).

The argument here may not convince. The meaning may be that sexual desire is sinful: the desire of men for men is excessively sinful, contrary to nature. God's grace is also contrary to nature. Isn't that a bit like saying that if you drink excessively and I work excessively we have a solidarity between us, our excess. What would that be worth?

> *Activity:* In this long section the traditional case against homosexuality has been outlined, together with a case against it. You may find it useful to discuss which of the two points of view you find most convincing, and why? Whatever your answer, you may find it helpful to pick out from the list of the five difficulties which the traditional case was thought to present, the ones you found the most, and perhaps the least, plausible.

9.3.3 Why is unnatural sex perverse?

But there is another way of accounting for the excessive vehemence that Paul reserves for men having sex with men, and that has to do less with sex than with gender. The question to be addressed is why did Paul consider unnatural sex perverse? Throughout the book I have found it essential to refer to classical assumptions about gender; to the "one-sex theory;" to assumptions about the fixed social and sexual roles of men and women in relation to each other; even to the feared slide whereby men, through effeminate behavior, would effectively *be* women. They would become "womanized." To be male is to be more perfect, and more like God, than to be female.

This material is certainly queer (in the sense of its being strange and unfamiliar to most of us). Equally queer in the construction of early Christian sexuality is Paul's understanding of sex in the body of Christ (see Section 8.1.1). Modern assumptions about there being two sexes, together with the concealment of, and medical interventions upon, intersex people, has contributed to our (wrong) assumption that there have always been two sexes. These details from the ancient understanding of gender may well assist us in getting to the bottom of what unnatural sex was.

Girly men   The indecent acts which men committed with other men are likely to have exposed the passive partner to "the disease of effemination" (Swancutt, 2006, p. 76; and see Swancutt, 2003). This term could also have been used with regard to the prohibitions of Leviticus 18 and 20 (see Section 9.2). The troublesome sin was "gender transgression that led to somatic change" (2006, p. 76). Since "sex acts impacted one's standing in the one-body gender hierarchy of human nature," a man being penetrated, at all, feminized him. Since masculinity was an achieved state (2006, p. 78), not a somatic or biological one, *any* effeminate act willfully undermined a man's masculinity. So even men "who habitually engaged in over-passionate acts – whether in the form of gluttony, anger, strife, cowardice, or effeminate (passive sex) – ran the risk of morphing, contrary to nature, into *cinaedi* ('androgynous girly-men')." The price to be paid for a man who failed to achieve self-mastery and who succumbed to taking the passive role in sex was to traverse the gender continuum and destroy his "hard-won maleness" (Stowers, 1994, pp. 45–46).

Images of God in ancient thought are overwhelmingly male (but remember Section 8.4.1 for a re-reading of them), so to be masculine is to be more like God than to be feminine. The masculinity of God was hotly denied (see Section 7.1), but I cannot deny that, in Paul's time as in ours, God is assumed, superficially and pre-critically, to be male. On this view, if a man consents to be penetrated he forsakes an important part of the God-likeness in him. He willfully allows his own body to be treated as if it were the body of a woman. The mysterious link between passive male sex and idolatry now becomes explicable. A man abandons his God-likeness if he is buggered by another man. His giving in to shameful lusts threatens the very characteristic of masculinity that males share with the divine.

Being unmasculine   Paul's claim that the Gentiles "exchanged the glory of the immortal God for images made to look like mortal man" (Rom. 1:23) is said to give further support to this interpretation. "Glory" (*doxa*) means "appearance" (as in 1 Cor. 15:38–41). There is a bodily appearance or *doxa* of God among men. This is not "exchanged" as the NIV translates. Rather it is "*changed*." The danger is that God's appearance in masculinity is changed by this very unmasculine behavior. In other words the Gentiles "damaged the appearance (*doxa*) of His divinity, degrading His masculinity as Creator to the status of created things" (Swancutt, 2006, p. 81).

Once again the understanding of gender provides the key to unlocking Paul's disgust at (at least some) same-sex relations. Having natural sex in the ancient world involves a man penetrating a woman. If a man is penetrated, he compromises his masculinity. It is unnatural for a man to want or to consent to this. Presumably, if they have non-penetrative sex, then the masculinity of both of them is compromised, because neither of them is a penetrator.

Paul thought all sexual desire sinful. He thought same-sex desire excessively sinful. He thought it sinful, not because it was homosexual, but because it involved the forsaking of gender roles he considered natural. He thought that it involved the most serious sin of idolatry because he thought that if a man forsook his God-given masculinity, he forsook part of his favored likeness to God. It represented a turning away from God into depravity.

9.4 What Else Does the Bible "Say" about Same-Sex Relations?

A traditional reading of the New Testament finds two further references to homosexuality:

[9]Do you not know that the wicked will not inherit the kingdom of God? Do not be deceived: Neither the sexually immoral nor idolaters nor adulterers nor male prostitutes nor homosexual

offenders [10]nor thieves nor the greedy nor drunkards nor slanderers nor swindlers will inherit the kingdom of God. (1 Cor. 6:9–10)

law is made not for the righteous but for lawbreakers and rebels, the ungodly and sinful, the unholy and irreligious; for those who kill their fathers or mothers, for murderers, [10]for adulterers and perverts, for slave traders and liars and perjurers. (1 Tim. 1:9–10)

There are two troublesome words in these passages, generating much argument. The "male prostitutes" and "homosexual offenders" of 1 Corinthians 6:9 are *malakoi* and *arsenokoitai,* and they are troublesome because no one quite knows how to translate them. The second one crops up again in 1 Timothy 1:10. The Anglican study, *Some Issues in Human Sexuality,* is confident that "most scholars have continued to maintain that the traditional interpretation is correct" (House of Bishops' Group on *Issues in Human Sexuality,* 2003, para. 4.3.53). You may have spotted that this interpretation is followed by the translators of the New International Version. Hays says *malakoi* is Greek slang for the passive partner in homosexual sex (1996, pp. 384–385). The second term, *arsenokoitai,* seems to have been invented by Paul (there is no earlier use), but its closeness to the Greek text of Leviticus 20:13 may suggest a direct allusion to men lying with men as if they were lying with women.

Martin, another influential New Testament theologian, dismisses these interpretations entirely. He accuses the traditionalists of finding in these texts only what they wish to find, and thinks they "have been driven more by ideological interests in marginalizing gay and lesbian people than by the general strictures of historical criticism" (Martin, 2006, p. 38). He finds *malakoi* easy to translate:

> *Malakos* can refer to many things: the softness of expensive clothes, the richness and delicacy of gourmet food, the gentleness of light winds and breezes. When used as a term of moral condemnation, the word still refers to something perceived as "soft": laziness, degeneracy, decadence, lack of courage, or, to sum up all these vices in one ancient category, the feminine. (Martin, 2006, p. 44)

The *malakoi* are effeminate men. Some of them may have had sex with other men, but there was a narrower term for that activity, *kinaedoi* (see Section 2.3.1). Martin's extensive trawl of uses of *arsenokoitès* leads him to conclude that it is found, not among lists of sexual sins, "but among vices related to economic injustice or exploitation" (Martin, 2006, p. 40). He lists "rape or sex by economic coercion, prostitution, pimping, or something of the sort" (2006, p. 41). While not denying that Paul may have had homosexual sex in mind, the detailed evidence he has collected should allow no one "to get away with claiming that 'of course' the term refers to 'men who have sex with other men'" (2006, p. 43). The meaning is much more open, and translators and exegetes may be reading there only what they expect to find.

How gay-friendly is the Bible?   Before the claims the churches make about the Bible condemning homosexual sex are evaluated, it may be helpful to draw attention to another set of references in the Bible that suggest that it may be seen to be a more gay-friendly book than it is in the hands of many Christians. The passages examined are the ones that feature in the conservative case. What about others that may provide evidence of a different view, for example those which describe the relationship between Jesus and someone called "the beloved disciple"?

> Now there was leaning on Jesus' bosom one of his disciples, whom Jesus loved. (John 13:23, Authorized Version)

> Then Peter, turning about, seeth the disciple whom Jesus loved following; which also leaned on his breast at supper, and said, Lord, which is he that betrayeth thee? (John 21:20, Authorized Version)

There are four references in the Gospel of John to the disciple whom Jesus loved (13:22–25; 19:26–27; 21:7; 21:20–23). Jesus loved all his disciples, so why was there a particular disciple for whom Jesus had a particular love? What was this love? One detailed examination of these texts yields the conclusion that

> The singling out of one who is loved by Jesus makes clear that some kind of love is at stake other than the love that unites Jesus to the rest of his disciples. The text itself suggests that we should recognize here some form of love that certainly does not contradict the more general love of Jesus for all, but which does set it apart from this general love. A reasonable conclusion is that this difference points us to a different sphere or dimension of love: love characterized by erotic desire or sexual attraction. (Jennings, 2003, p. 22)

Nor are these references the only ones which may suggest a more gay-friendly reading of the Bible. In the garden of Gethsemane as Jesus was being arrested, Mark's Gospel records "A young man, wearing nothing but a linen garment, was following Jesus. When they seized him, he fled naked, leaving his garment behind (Mark 14:51–52). It is plausibly suggested that

> we are left with an apparent allusion to the typical recipient of homoerotic attention (the nude youth) in Hellenistic pederastic culture at a decisive moment in the passion of Jesus, and with the suggestion of a particularly close relationship between Jesus and this youth. (Jennings, 2003, p. 113)

Jesus, we may speculate, was just the sort of company with whom a sexually exploited young man could relax and feel accepted.

The Gospels of Matthew and Luke both record that Jesus healed the servant of a Roman centurion (Matt. 8:5–13; Luke 7:1–10). But Matthew's version uses the term *pais*, or boy, not *doulos* (servant) at 8:13, giving rise to the suggestion that the relation between the centurion and his boy may have included another dimension not normally considered (Jennings, 2003, pp. 131–140). These are suggestions, nothing more, but they may indicate that the New Testament, and in particular Jesus himself, may be more gay-friendly than conventional readings have been able to acknowledge. Moralists who think the Bible is unambiguous in its condemnation of homosexuality may not be taking the whole Bible seriously enough.

David and Jonathan   That is true for the Hebrew Bible too. The long narratives describing the relations between David and Jonathan in 1 and 2 Samuel make little sense unless they were lovers (Jennings, 2005, pp. 3–80). Imagine a male candidate for ordination today confiding to his bishop that his love for another man was "wonderful, more wonderful than that of women" (2 Sam. 1:26). And if he is an honest Roman Catholic ordinand he will certainly be deemed to "present deep-seated homosexual tendencies" which will "gravely hinder" him "from relating correctly to men and women" (Congregation for Catholic Education, 2005, section 2).

Another detailed study concludes that the Ruth–Naomi stories (Ruth 1–4), together with the David–Jonathan stories,

> both deal with persons of the same gender loving one another. Because of the passionate romance that characterizes the relationships depicted, and the deep feeling and undying loyalty of the love narrated, these two stories have regularly served as models not only of same-sex but also of cross-sex friendship and lifelong loyalty. (Jennings, 2005, p. 227)

The question whether these relationships were "homosexual" might be to make a similar mistake as those theologians who keep on finding homosexuality in the earlier texts just considered. A more positive way of reading these different texts might be to see in them evidence for a more homosocial or "homophilic" social environment where same-sex desire was actually taken for granted, and allowed some expression.

9.5 Finding What We Want to Find? Evaluating Official Teaching

It seems then, that the traditional case for saying that homosexual acts are inconsistent with biblical teaching can be unraveled quite easily. But that conclusion, whether it is right or not, is not the conclusion of most churches. The conventional interpretation of the biblical passages remains a possible one. But the claim that it is the right one seriously exceeds the biblical evidence available. The churches should be more honest in admitting the difficulties of the traditional case. In this final section, we will consider a very recent conclusion and ask some further questions about it.

A very recent document for Christians, sub-titled "A resource to enable listening and dialogue," comes to a conclusion about the attitudes of New Testament theologians to homosexuality. It says:

1. By far the majority is the view that the New Testament condemns homosexual practice.
2. Another group of scholars accept that the New Testament is opposed to homosexual practice but would argue that this is due to cultural attitudes that no longer hold sway. These scholars would point to the gap between first and twenty-first century culture as the reason for not condemning homosexual practice today.
3. Yet another group of scholars would deny that the New Testament opposes homosexual practice on the grounds that the texts use words that are hard to translate or that they are referring to pederasty or temple prostitution and not to homosexual practice between mutually loving partners. (Groves, Holder, and Gooder, 2008, p. 150)

The authors say they put forward their conclusion as "only one step in the ongoing process of mutual listening" and "as a resource to facilitate further discussions on the subject." In the spirit of respectful dialogue with them, here are some reservations about their conclusions that might generate further discussion:

First, the Bible does not refer at all to "homosexual practice" (whatever these unspecified activities are). Paul's argument at Romans 1:26–27 refers fairly unambiguously to men having anal sex. A similar problem was discovered in relation to the Sodom story of Genesis 19. Do they not make a simple but unfortunate, *logical* mistake in confusing "some" with "all?" Yet all three groups of scholars are presented as agreeing that the New Testament condemns "homosexual practice," while disagreeing over what to do about it.

This reads as an *overbelief* – a philosophical term for a belief adopted that needs more evidence than is actually available. The troublesome term "homosexuality," invented (according to Diana Swancutt 2006, p. 70) as recently as 1892, is deployed as if all the biblical writers were familiar with it, and mean the same thing by it.

Second, we might ask what follows from the truthful finding that a sizeable majority of New Testament scholars agree that the New Testament condemns homosexuality. The issue is not one to decide democratically. Majorities of biblical scholars have in the past agreed on various positions, which have been shown, over time, in the light of new knowledge and experience, and perhaps through the promptings of the God the Holy Spirit, to be indefensible.

Then there is, of course, the question of *competency*. New Testament scholars are generally a humble bunch of people, not given to generalizations or over-beliefs. They are likely to say they benefit from the wider context that recent classical scholarship brings to their deliberations. Many of them are rightly reluctant to accept that the New Testament does not respond well to modern questions that are thrown at it by anxious interrogators impatient for authoritative answers.

Third, should not the possibility be more seriously considered, that these scholars are not immune from the temptation to find what they expect to find? The assumptions of centuries are not necessarily the ones to continue to govern our thinking.

Fourth, has the effort to discover what the Bible "says" about homosexuality perhaps led to a marked neglect of the biblical world within which, and only within which, the discussion of same-sex relations makes sense? Perhaps Paul's astringent remarks have effeminacy, not homosexuality as their target? In the effort to elicit a biblical view of homosexuality, has there not been a reluctance, especially in the choice of authors and authorities, to address the bigger picture?

Fifth, if Paul is to be our guide in our Christian understanding of sex, and so to have the last word about same-sex relations, then should he not have the last word about opposite-sex relations too? That would, at least on some views of the matter, require Christians to desist from marriage at least when they are able to, and to attempt to suppress all sexual desire, not just same-sex desire, in the attempt at self-mastery.

Yet more worries   Does not an awareness of the bigger picture cause us to have other reservations about the traditional case?

For example we do not think that early Gentiles were monotheists, so we do not see their idolatry as a fall from a pristine belief in the one God.

We do not see homosexual desire as an excess of heterosexual desire. People of different sexes and orientations have different levels of *libido*. There must be plenty of straight people who are randier than some gays.

Crucially, and against the wisdom of the ancients, we need not think God is ultra-masculine and so we do not think that men compromise the image of God when they do things that women do. Since God is (in the view outlined in Sections 7.1 and 7.2) imaged by women as much as by men, what is so perverse about men being like women? What matters is that both men and women reflect the divine image in them more fully.

Finally, the conclusion should not necessarily be seen as an endorsement of anal sex between men. If the analysis undertaken in this chapter passes scrutiny, it shows that Paul *did* condemn it, but for reasons that need not convince anyone any more.

> *Question:* Several times in this chapter reference is made to the possibility that traditional interpreters merely find what they want to, or expect to, find, in the Bible. Is that true of this author as well? If so, is it important?

This chapter has examined the traditional view, that the Bible condemns homosexuality, once unassailable, and found that it is no longer sustainable; indeed that it should be abandoned. That remains a minority position. But there is a weaker conclusion that ought to command more widespread assent. Given the obvious disagreement between scholars of all kinds, the proposition that the Bible condemns homosexuality cannot be sufficient ground for condemning it. There just is insufficient assent. The legitimate diversity of interpretation does not permit the calm certainty that the advocates of the traditional position assume.

This conclusion has been reached apart from broader arguments about what the Bible is, how it should be used, and what weight should be placed on this single leg of the four-legged stool (see Section 3.1). Chapter 3 set the scene for those discussions, and the other legs (Tradition, Reason, and Experience) form the subject of Chapter 10.

References

Allison, J. (2006) *Undergoing God: Dispatches from the Scene of a Break-In*, Continuum, London.

Barrett, C.K. (1971) *The Epistle to the Romans*, A&C Black, London.

Boyarin, D. (2007) Against rabbinic sexuality: textual reasoning and the Jewish theology of sex, in *Queer Theology: Rethinking the Western Body* (ed. G. Loughlin), Blackwell, Malden, MA/Oxford, pp. 131–146.

Brandon, G. (2009) *Just Sex – Is It Ever Just Sex?* Inter-Varsity Press, Nottingham, UK.

Catechism of the Catholic Church (1994) Geoffrey Chapman, London, www.vatican.va/archive/catechism/ccc_toc.htm (accessed November 3, 1010).

Congregation for Catholic Education (2005) *Instruction Concerning the Criteria for the Discernment of Vocations with regard to Persons with Homosexual Tendencies in view of their Admission to the Seminary and to Holy Orders*, www.vatican.va/roman_curia/congregations/ccatheduc/documents/rc_con_ccatheduc_doc_20051104_istruzione_en.html (accessed November 4, 2010).

Countryman, L.W. (1988) *Dirt, Greed and Sex*, SCM Press, London.

Dunn, J.D.G. (1988) *Romans 1–8, Word Biblical Commentary 38a, Vol. 1*, Thomas Nelson, Nashville, TN.

Fitzmeyer, J.A. (1996) *Romans*, Doubleday, New York.

Gagnon, R.A.J. (2001) *The Bible and Homosexual Practice: Texts and Hermeneutics*, Abingdon Press, Nashville, TN.

Groves, P., Holder, J., and Gooder, P. (2008) The witness of scripture, in *The Anglican Communion and Homosexuality* (ed. P. Groves), SPCK, London, pp. 81–154.

Hays, R. (1986) Relations natural and unnatural: a response to John Boswell's exegesis of Romans 1. *Journal of Religious Ethics*, 14, 184–215.

Hays, R. (1996) *The Moral Vision of the New Testament*, T&T Clark, Edinburgh.

House of Bishops' Group on *Issues in Human Sexuality* (2003) *Some Issues in Human Sexuality – A Guide to the Debate*, Church House Publishing, London.

Jennings, T.W., Jr. (2003) *The Man Jesus Loved: Homoerotic Narratives from the New Testament*, Pilgrim Press, Cleveland, OH.

Jennings, T.W., Jr. (2005) *Jacob's Wound: Homoerotic Narrative in the Literature of Ancient Israel*, Continuum, New York/London.

Lambeth Conference (1998) Resolutions from 1998. *Resolution 1, 10: Human Sexuality*, www.lambethconference.org/resolutions/1998/1998-1-10.cfm (accessed November 4, 2010).

Martin, D.B. (2006) *Sex and the Single Savior*, Westminster John Knox Press, Louisville, KY.

Miller, J.E. (1995) The practices of Romans 1:26: Homosexual or heterosexual? *Novum Testamentum*, 37.

Moore, G., OP (2003) *A Question of Truth: Christianity and Homosexuality*, Continuum, London/New York.

Olyan, S.M. (1994) "And with a male you shall not lie the lying down of a woman": On the meaning and significance of Leviticus 18:22 and 20:13. *Journal of the History of Sexuality*, 5, 179–206.

Olyan, S.M. (2006) "Surpassing the love of women": Another look at 2 Samuel 1:26 and the relationship of David and Jonathan, in *Authorizing Marriage: Canon,* *Tradition, and Critique in the Blessing of Same-Sex Unions* (ed. M.D. Jordan), Princeton University Press, Princeton/Oxford, pp. 7–17.

Rogers, E.F. (1999) *Sexuality and the Christian Body*, Blackwell, Malden, MA/Oxford.

Sacred Congregation for the Doctrine of the Faith (1975) *Persona Humana: Declaration on Certain Questions Concerning Sexual Ethics*, www.vatican.va/roman_curia/congregations/cfaith/documents/rc_con_cfaith_doc_19751229_persona-humana_en.html (accessed November 4, 2010).

Sacred Congregation for the Doctrine of the Faith (1976) *Inter Insigniores: Declaration on The Question Of Admission Of Women To The Ministerial Priesthood*, www.papalencyclicals.net/Paul06/p6interi.htm (accessed November 4, 2010).

Southern Baptist Convention (n.d.) *Position Statement: Sexuality*, www.sbc.net/aboutus/pssexuality.asp (accessed November 10, 2010).

Stowers, S.K. (1994) *A Rereading of Romans*, Yale University Press, New Haven, CT.

Swancutt, D. (2003) 'The disease of effemination:' The charge of effeminacy and the verdict of God (Romans 1:18–26), in *New Testament Masculinities* (eds. S.D. Moore and J.C. Anderson), Society of Biblical Literature, Atlanta, GA, pp. 193–234.

Swancutt, D. (2006) Sexing the Pauline body of Christ: Scriptural sex in the context of the American Christian culture war, in *Toward a Theology of Eros – Transfiguring Passion at the Limits of Discipline* (eds. V. Burrus and C. Keller), Fordham University Press, New York, pp. 65–98.

10

Tradition, Reason, and Same-Sex Love

Chapter 9 considered the testimony of the Bible with regard to its alleged proscription of homosexuality. It offered arguments why it could not be fairly claimed that the Bible condemns homosexual experience. Chapter 10 adopts a similar strategy with regard to the other sources of Theology – Tradition (Section 10.1), Reason and Natural Law (Section 10.2), and, briefly, Experience (Section 10.4). The growing influence of complementarity requires a separate section (Section 10.3).

10.1 Tradition and Same-Sex Love

We have discovered, have we not, that the blanket proposition that the Bible condemns homosexuality is hard to sustain? That, of course, was not the traditional view. Our conclusion, if indeed it turns out to be right, might act as an example of how the Christian Tradition is capable of change – an example of how change might actually work. But Tradition is a recognized source for thinking about doctrine and ethical practice, and it was evaluated positively (see Sections 3.1.2 and 3.2.2). The witness of Tradition against homosexuality is an important constituent in the conservative case, and could sway the argument decisively. In this section the following questions are answered: *Can* Tradition change? What changes are called for? How could Christians know that these changes were consistent with the Tradition they profess?

God, Sex, and Gender: An Introduction, First Edition. Adrian Thatcher.
© 2011 Adrian Thatcher. Published 2011 by Blackwell Publishing Ltd.

10.1.1 Can Tradition change?

The answer to this question is, for once, simple: yes, it can.

The reason for asking the question at all is because it is often suggested that Tradition has maintained a consistency or constancy about a belief or a practice, so that to change it now would be inconsistent or inconstant with the past. This appears to be the position of the Roman Catholic Church, at least with regard to homosexuality, in its *Catechism*:

> Basing itself on Sacred Scripture, which presents homosexual acts as acts of grave depravity, *Tradition has always declared* that "homosexual acts are intrinsically disordered." (*Catechism of the Catholic Church*, 1994, para. 2357; emphasis added)

There are related reasons why it is claimed that Tradition cannot change. For instance, it might be argued that Gospel values are eternal, or that God cannot change God's mind. The idea of relativism might be invoked in order to suggest, damagingly, that Christian truth is required to bend itself to every cultural context in which it finds itself. A "slippery-slope argument" might be mounted: If the Church changes its mind about *a*, it will then have to change its mind about *b*, and so on.

Some people embrace Christian faith just because it provides a bulwark against change. Aware of the ephemerality ("lasting-for-a-day-ness") of much of their surrounding culture, they rightly discern in Christian faith deeper, more permanent, spiritual realities. And the admission that change is needed also requires the acknowledgement that the Church got some things wrong.

Development or distortion?   The argument from the constancy of Tradition is used in Catholicism against suggestions that there may be room for some revision of historical proscriptions on contraception and divorce. However at other times the Catholic Church admits, even *advocates*, change. And on some moral issues, it has reversed its earlier teaching. The present Pope, when Cardinal Ratzinger, admitted:

> Not everything that exists in the Church must for that reason be also a legitimate tradition; in other words, not every tradition that arises in the Church is a true celebration and keeping present of the mystery of Christ. There is a distorting, as well as legitimate, tradition, . . . [and] . . . consequently tradition must not be considered only affirmatively but also critically. (Ratzinger, 1969, p. 185; see also Salzman and Lawler, 2008, p. 214)

The warfare of ideas   Earlier, Aquinas' teaching about the evil of fornication was used as an example of how tradition could be used today, in Ratzinger's terms, "affirmatively but also critically" (see Section 3.2.2). Theologians have long abandoned the question *whether* Tradition changes, and have moved on to the question *how* it does so. John Henry Newman led the way in 1845 with his *Essay on the Development of Doctrine*. He said the development of an idea

> is not like investigation worked out on paper, in which each successive advance is a pure evolution from a foregoing, but it is carried on through and by means of communities of men and their leaders and guides; and it employs their minds as its instruments and depends upon

them while it uses them … It is the warfare of ideas under their varying aspects striving for the mastery. (Newman, 1949, p. 74)

Is there not an engaging realism about this reflection? Development is never smooth or predictable. It comes from beyond the communities of people that it affects in a process that is uncomfortable and difficult, and that inevitably causes conflict. That could well be a description of the turmoil within the churches about homosexuality at the present time.

The best essay on the development of *sexual ethics* in Christianity in recent times is probably Joseph Monti's *Arguing about Sex.* He wants all Christians to be faithful to Tradition, but notes that there is more required in that task than merely repeating it. If faithful repetition only were required, there would be no need to construct a sexual ethic at all, only to hand one down hoping it would be gratefully received by individuals and congregations from one generation to the next. He thinks:

> The denominations are forgetting how the obligation of fidelity must be dialectically engaged with the equal obligation of contemporaneity – how Christian life must make sense in its own time, must be truthful and right-making, and promote the good in whatever world we find ourselves. (Monti, 1995, p. 5)

Monti explains what faithfulness to Tradition amounts to. For the sake of people whose lives are not touched by any of the churches, faithfulness to Tradition includes the serious obligation to share it with people who know nothing of it, and this faithful activity requires linking the "internal story" that Christians tell about themselves, with the "external stories" of others who are marginalized by the Church's teachings or who understand themselves in a quite different way. Relevance is not simply a requirement in accounts of Christian faith. It requires a creative weaving of past and present, of internal and external stories, and this process inevitably brings about change in doctrine and ethics.

How to transcend time   Monti also handles well the contention that the Church's beliefs and values must transcend time. He does this by introducing the idea of a "cosmological world" (1995, p. 31), that is, the self-understanding of any particular group of people at a particular time, in a particular place. Just because the Church *is* a trans-historical body, it spans more than one cosmological world: indeed, it spans all of them. Now, for the Church to span all historical or cosmological worlds, it cannot *identify* its teaching with any one of them! While there are foundations to be found in the Bible, even the language and ideas found there are not eternal. As for our own cosmological worlds, they are certain to be partial, and defective in important ways. But we live within them, and only within them does the possibility of faith arise. Church teaching successfully transcends time to the extent that it resists the temptation to cling to any particular set of thought forms.

Since God is eternal, and everything else is temporal, all our understanding, even our understanding of the eternal God, is going to be temporal too. Since Jesus Christ is "the truth" (John 14:6), both about God and about ourselves, it follows that no other belief or truth-claim can be elevated to the same ultimacy as Christ Himself. How the Truth of Christ is understood and expressed across time and place will be varied. Christ is well able to call people to Himself at different times and in different ways.

The "slippery-slope argument" is more of a slur than an argument. It has been said, for example, that if the Church sanctioned same-sex unions, it would undermine marriage or encourage something called the "homosexual lifestyle." Suggestions like these may be actually slanderous, for marriage is undermined by straight people divorcing too readily, not by same-sex couples desiring to enter into it. The point of blessing same-sex unions is not to encourage promiscuity, but to stand against it by affirming the religious virtue of lifelong commitment to one's partner.

> *Question:* The Tradition of the Church *can* and *does* change. Can you think of any limits to any changes that might be proposed?

> *Comment:* If the Church were to contradict any of its doctrines contained in its creeds, that would be unacceptable, wouldn't it? If Christian people loved their neighbors *less* in their practice, or became less just, that too could never be acceptable either, could it?

10.1.2 What changes are called for?

So far we have thought about the *possibility* of moral change in the Church's teaching, and about change as an abstract principle. What real changes do lesbian and gay Christians want? In the first instance they want the freedom to be open about their sexuality. Many more who are "in the closet," would "come out" if they belonged to churches who accepted them. But do they want marriage? Or an institution that is not marriage, but strongly analogous to it?

There is real disagreement about this. Some advise against the advocacy of marriage for same-sex partners. They see it as a failing heterosexual institution that lesbigay couples would be crazy to adopt. They may resist fiercely the pattern of domination/submission that they think still belongs to traditional marriage. And they are advised by Jordan not to "sign on to efforts at propping up failing models of relationship" (Jordan, 2005, p. 194). On the other hand, any legal framework that is not marriage, such as a civil partnership, may signify a social inferiority or second-class status in relation to marriage.

While there may be different answers to the question what gay couples want from the churches, the line we took in Chapters 5 and 6 was that Christian sexual morality was a *marital* morality, and the best prospects for the incorporation of lesbian and gay partnerships within Christian morality was an extension of the institution of marriage towards them. That, of course, is not the only way. It is, however, a way that would accommodate with least difficulty the vexed problem of there being "out" lesbian and gay people in stable relationships which have no status in the eyes of the churches because they are not marriages.

10.1.3 How change happens

If a development in Christian doctrine or practice is to command acceptance, it will need to be tested. But how? One way of answering that question is to take past examples of change and to analyze why and how they happened. John Noonan (2003) shows how the Roman Catholic Church changed its moral teachings towards usury, marriage, slavery, and religious freedom. Marciano Vidal points to a whole raft of recent changes including freedom of conscience, the moral reappraisal of war, the acceptance of human rights, the Church's adoption of "the preferential option of the poor," and so on (Vidal, 2003, pp. 327–328). (This last idea is the belief that the physical and spiritual welfare of the poor is always to be a priority for Christians.) Why did these, and other comparable changes, happen?

These authors agree that part of the answer is to be found in the Church's deeper insight into, and a deeper, more "profound understanding of the mystery of Christ and its meaning to explain and orient the mystery of the human person" (Vidal, 2003, p. 329). This understanding expressed itself in a deeper awareness of the solidarity of Christ with the suffering and marginalized human being. It was seen as increasingly untenable and un-Christian to deny people their freedom of conscience, or to be unmoved by the dehumanizing and degrading effects of poverty. If the modern notion of human rights was a means, by secular language, to protect individual people and to assert their worth and inviolability, then the Church was able to support it.

However, they also agree that this is only part of the story. Being drawn into a greater appreciation of the significance of Jesus is not confined to the "internal story" that the Church unhurriedly discerns. Often the world is ahead of the Church in legislating to protect individuals or to enhance their lives. Any new knowledge of Christ may also be prompted by the "external stories" of others that sometimes impinge and impact themselves on the assumptions and answers of yesterday. Newman understood this well. He understood that conflict was to be expected, in the world and in the Church, as new ideas entered the heads of their advocates and sought to replace other ideas that were no longer adequate.

Blessings or marriages?   It would seem then that any proposal to extend *marriage* to same-sex couples constitutes a development within the Tradition of the churches, which the churches are capable of making.

The *blessing* of same-sex unions is, and is not, within this category. Blessings are not marriages (even though the Orthodox Churches regard the blessing of the marrying couple as the priestly act that makes them married). A blessed relationship that is not a marriage introduces a new category of relationship, which may cause the churches difficulty. These relationships are "quasi-marriages" (*quasi* is Latin for "as if"). Yet, from an existential perspective, they are *real* marriages. They bind couples in covenants that are made before God, and that are endowed with religious, moral, and spiritual meaning.

If the Church were to extend the sacrament or rite of marriage to same-sex couples, these are some of the criteria that the development would need to pass:

First, the Church would need to recognize that this was, in Ratzinger's words, a "legitimate" development. Conversely, the exclusion of same-sex couples from these rites would come to be seen in a different light as "distorting" the Gospel values on which all Christian Tradition rests.

Second, does this development arise out of a more profound understanding of the mystery of Christ? Is there a solidarity between Christ and lesbian and gay people comparable to that solidarity of Christ with other marginalized people that the Church also has discerned in its recent past? It has already been suggested (see Sections 6.2–6.4) that the covenant of love between two people of the same sex could become an embodiment of the covenant love of God for the world, and of Christ for the Church. The sources of Reason and Experience will also be helpful here.

Third, does new knowledge about sexuality, coupled with a deeper awareness of God's love for all people, compel a change in the churches' attitude to same-sex love? Advances in theological understanding coupled with new knowledge are able to transform the attitude of majorities to minorities. Christians commonly thought that black people were black because they were the children of Canaan whom God had cursed; that sick people were sick because God was punishing them for sin; that poor people were poor because God had ordered societies in a hierarchical way; that unbaptized babies were destined for eternal hell, and so on. New knowledge, coupled with a deeper understanding of God's love for all people led to an abandonment of these terrible ideas.

Out lesbigay people have until recently been part of the "external story" told by people outside the Christian faith. As the "internal story" continues to be told, would this story be enriched as it hears and embraces the external story told by others who ask to be admitted? Newman understood well how conflict surrounded doctrinal and moral development, but he did not shy away from it, or argue that proposals for change could be dismissed by assertion, threat, or failure to engage. There are good reasons for supposing that Tradition could accommodate this change, especially since the old arguments from Scripture increasingly fail to convince.

> *Questions:* Do you have any reservations about the assumption that the Church can change its mind? How strong do you think the case for the recognition of same-sex marriages is?

10.2 Reason, Natural Law, and Same-Sex Love

10.2.1 The contribution of Reason

The different and confusing senses given to "Reason" have already been noted (see Section 3.1.3), and it was suggested that Reason in theology is "principally that gift of God which enables us to understand the world and ourselves within it." We noted "It is the faculty we press into service in the divinely given task of loving God 'with all your mind'" (Mark 12:30). A consequence was that a "green light is then given to the explorations of the sciences and the social sciences, and to have some confidence in what they say."

There are three components to a basic Christian doctrine of Reason. First God has given us minds to understand the world. Second, God has given us a world, outside ourselves yet including ourselves. And third, God has allowed for the possibility of human knowledge by creating a structure of intelligibility. There is a correspondence between the inquiring mind and what the mind inquires into, so that real knowledge becomes possible. That knowledge will always be partial and relative. In the domain of morals, it is likely also to be affected by human fallibility, or sin. This basic structure of the world has been widely accepted by Christians. They do not, or need not, fear the conclusions of science and philosophy, since scientists and philosophers are using their minds as God intended.

10.2.2 Natural Law

In Catholicism, the emphasis on reason has become a developed doctrine of Natural Law. Protestants have been generally suspicious of this doctrine. They have been unable to find it in the Bible (which is not to say it cannot be found there). And they tend to think that human sinfulness fatally impairs any natural knowledge of God. But arguments based on Natural Law form a large part of the case against homosexuality. In this section, Natural Law is briefly described, and the use of it in the condemnation of homosexuality is assessed.

Natural Law has attracted much discussion recently. It provides a unique framework for a universal morality, which is theistic on the one hand and objective on the other. Since it deals with the first principles of law, it is possible to see it as the basis both of civil law, and of various universal precepts such as "natural" or "human rights." It is an expression of human reason, which for Christians is itself given by God. It is an extremely important tradition, and criticism in the paragraphs that follow is directed not at the tradition of Natural Law itself, but at the attempt to enlist it in the catalogue of arguments proscribing homosexuality.

Here are some features of Natural Law found in the *Catechism*:

> The natural law expresses the original moral sense which enables man to discern by reason the good and the evil, the truth and the lie
>
> The natural law is written and engraved in the soul of each and every man, because it is human reason ordaining him to do good and forbidding him to sin
>
> [It] shows man the way to follow so as to practise the good and attain his end. The natural law states the first and essential precepts which govern the moral life . . .
>
> The natural law is nothing other than the light of understanding placed in us by God; through it we know what we must do and what we must avoid. God has given this light or law at the creation.
>
> The natural law . . . is universal in its precepts and its authority extends to all men. It expresses the dignity of the person and determines the basis for his fundamental rights and duties: in the diversity of cultures, the natural law remains as a rule that binds men among themselves and imposes on them, beyond the inevitable differences, common principles.
>
> The natural law provides revealed law and grace with a foundation prepared by God and in accordance with the work of the Spirit. (*Catechism of the Catholic Church*, 1994, paras. 1954–1960)

These are positive features of Natural Law. But considerations based on Natural Law are shaped into an important strand of argument against homosexuality. For the Catholic Church,

> God has wisely ordered *laws of nature* and the incidence of fertility in such a way that successive births are already naturally spaced through the inherent operation of these laws. (Pope Paul VI, 1968, section 11; emphasis added – for Natural Law and contraception, see Chapter 12)

> Tradition has always declared that "homosexual acts are intrinsically disordered." They are *contrary to the Natural Law.* They close the sexual act to the gift of life. They do not proceed

from a genuine affective and sexual complementarity. Under no circumstances can they be approved. (*Catechism of the Catholic Church*, 1994, para. 2357; emphasis added)

10.2.3 Why Natural Law arguments are weak

The overall argument that homosexual sex is condemned by the Natural Law has to survive a basic difficulty. Jean Porter has written extensively and persuasively on Natural Law (1994, 1999, 2005). She shows how the Natural Law tradition developed during the scholastic period, and how it is capable of further development in such a way that some same-sex relations *can* be seen to conform to it. Her striking insight is that the scholastic "interpretation of the purposes of sexuality," which seems to us "uncritical or arbitrary, is in fact a theological judgment, formulated and defended in the face of serious doctrinal challenges to Christian orthodoxy" (1999, p. 189). She claims that a "reappropriation of the natural law that preserves the central scholastic insights into the human and theological significance of sexuality" is possible, "while allowing for subsequent developments in our understanding" (1999, p. 190).

A standard interpretation of Natural Law in the case of all sexual acts is that the purposes of these acts can be read off from the sexual organs. On this interpretation, which Aquinas taught, the sexual organs are for procreation only. Nature teaches this. Aquinas had in view marital sex but the teaching of nature is applicable more widely. Immediately it follows that masturbation and anal penetration, because they are clearly non-procreative, are contrary to the Natural Law.

But Porter (1999, p. 197) has shown that Aquinas and the scholastics

do not typically argue in this way. Rather, they focus on the proper purposes of sexuality and marriage as these are revealed through theological reflection, and then they judge particular kinds of acts to be unnatural because they are not in accordance with those overall purposes.

Porter is here discussing arguments offered against contraception in *Humanae vitae*, but she intends her conclusions to apply in the area of homosexuality as well. The kind of judgment that the scholastics came to make can be observed by examining the (notorious) contention that pleasure cannot be a purpose of having sex. The scholastics understood the tension between, on the one hand, "the good of nature, with its implication that any expression of a natural inclination is *prima facie* good" (1999, pp. 190–191) and, on the other hand, the observation that sexual sins are the result of natural inclinations. Their pessimism about sexual pleasure is explicable partly by their attempts to preserve Christian doctrine against errors represented by the dualists and Cathars (among others) who were opposed to all sexual acts absolutely. Eventually they were led "through their moral reflections to modify their understanding of human nature, in a way that finally acknowledges the goodness of sexual desire." There was a tendency "to move away from the claim that sexual pleasure is wrong in itself, toward a view according to which heterosexual sexual sins involve a misdirected or excessive exercise of sexual function" (1999, p. 194).

We can see, then, how the realization of the goodness of at least some sexual pleasure dissipates the cloud of pessimism over it. "Once we let go of the view that sexual pleasure is itself morally problematic, we can consider the possibility that sexual activity has other purposes besides procreation" (1999, p.199). Porter considers this possibility positively, arguing that while Catholic sexual morality will always stress the priority of marriage, family and children, it may also hold "that other purposes, in particular the fostering of interpersonal love, are also theologically valid aims for a sexual relationship" (1999, p. 222).

Doing what comes naturally   We may conclude with Porter that the particular *reading* of the Natural Law found in current official documents constitutes the continuing problem, not the Natural Law tradition itself. Even if she were found to be mistaken about this it would not follow that the Natural Law *does* after all condemn homosexual sin, masturbation, and contraception. All that would follow is the reversion to the assumption that nature teaches that these practices are wrong.

And that assumption cannot hold, for several fairly obvious reasons. The idea that nature tells us that homosexuality is wrong can hardly be reconciled with an obvious fact – "Homosexual sexual acts are 'natural' for people with a homosexual orientation, just as heterosexual sexual acts are 'natural' with a heterosexual orientation" (Salzman and Lawler, 2008, p. 227). Or again, Salzman and Lawler remind us that nature is "always an interpreted category. Notions of the natural are socially controlled. We construct what is natural. We cannot pretend that the concept of nature has a fixed meaning" (2008, p. 226).

> **Naturalistic fallacy:** The fallacy of supposing that it is possible to argue from a claim that something is natural to the claim that it is right or good. A main criticism of it often takes the form, "You can't derive an ought from an is."

Finally, if nature can teach us how to behave, it is difficult to see how we could avoid the "naturalistic fallacy."

There is much in nature that should *not* be imitated, and countless human interventions in nature that are beneficial, such as the attempt to eliminate malaria or the human-immunodeficiency virus that leads to AIDS. The conclusion seems plain. Natural Law arguments against homosexual acts are weak. They contribute little to a moral assessment of them. It might seem surprising that certain theologians go on using them.

> *Question:* Do you think some heterosexual people think homosexual acts are unnatural because, at root, they are *disgusted* by them?

> *Comment:* If you said "Yes" I think you are right. But in that case do you agree that private disgust is not morally reliable? Vegetarians may be disgusted at the practice of feeding on the cooked flesh of dead animals, but they will need good arguments, not just disgust if they are ever to convince the carnivorous majority.

10.2.4 The sin of wasting semen

The adjustments made to, and in accordance with, Natural Law just described can also apply to the near-universal practice of masturbation. These adjustments were (1) acceptance of a developing understanding of human nature that remains reasonable; (2) an acknowledgement that not all sexual acts need be procreative; and (3) a concession that some sexual pleasure is both natural and good. Aquinas' view of the wrongness of masturbation remains the teaching of the *Catechism*. The Congregation for the Doctrine of the Faith warns, "Both the Magisterium of the Church, in the course of a constant tradition, and the moral sense of the faithful have been in no doubt and have firmly maintained that masturbation is an intrinsically and gravely disordered action" (1975, para. 9: see *Catechism of the Catholic Church*, 1994, para. 2352).

Having explained that the human body discharges excrement, urine, and sweat for the good of the body and for no other purpose, the discharge of semen is very different. The good of the body

> is not the object in the emission of the semen, but rather the profit of generation, to which the union of the sexes is directed. But in vain would be the generation of man unless due nurture followed, without which the offspring generated could not endure. The emission of the semen then ought to be so directed as that both the proper generation may ensue and the education of the offspring be secured.
>
> Hence it is clear that every emission of the semen is contrary to the good of man, which takes place in a way whereby generation is impossible; and if this is done on purpose, it must be a sin. I mean a way in which generation is impossible in itself as is the case in every emission of the semen without the natural union of male and female: wherefore such sins are called 'sins against nature.' But if it is by accident that generation cannot follow from the emission of the semen, the act is not against nature on that account, nor is it sinful; the case of the woman being barren would be a case in point. (Aquinas, 1905, section 3.122)

The suppositions are easy to detect. The act lacks procreative purpose, and the pleasure it provides is also wrong. But once the goodness of at least some sexual pleasure is allowed and the procreative purpose of sexual acts is suspended, the grounds for calling masturbation wrong are called into question (although there may be other reasons for qualifying approval of the practice). Other accounts of masturbation according to which it is harmlessly pleasurable, or an appropriate release of sexual tension may be found to be reasonable and so cause no offence to the Natural Law.

If we are impatient with the Natural Law denunciation of masturbation, it may be appropriate not to blame Aquinas for his restrictive remarks about it, but rather to direct our impatience towards modern versions of Natural Law, which, when applied to sex acts do not incorporate reasonable changes into it.

The topic provides another interesting example of a difference between Catholic and Protestant approaches to the body and to sexuality. Masturbation is historically a sin among Protestants as well, but they do not appeal to Natural Law. Protestants appeal directly to the Bible whenever possible. But in the cases of masturbation and contraception there was a problem. Convinced that these practices were sins, where exactly could biblical condemnation of them be found?

The narrative surrounding Onan was pressed into service:

> [8]Then Judah said to Onan, "Lie with your brother's wife and fulfill your duty to her as a brother-in-law to produce offspring for your brother." [9] But Onan knew that the offspring would not be his; so whenever he lay with his brother's wife, he spilled his semen on the ground to keep from producing offspring for his brother. [10] What he did was wicked in the LORD's sight; so he put him to death also. (Gen. 38:8–10)

Onan's capital offense, of course, was his failure to perform his duty, under the law of Levirate marriage (Deut. 25:5–10), to provide children for his dead brother and his dead brother's wife. He was practicing the earliest known form of contraception. But John Calvin taught in his *Commentary on Genesis* that Onan deserved to die for the crime of the unreproductive discharge of semen. "The voluntary spilling of semen outside of intercourse between a man and a woman is a monstrous thing. Deliberately to withdraw from coitus in order that semen may fall on the ground is doubly monstrous" (Provan, 1989, p. 15).

Both attempts to find masturbation sinful fail. It may be compatible with the Natural Law, while the appeal to the story of Onan is a fanciful application of Scripture to what was once an anxiety-generating moral problem.

10.3 Complementarity and Same-Sex Love

We met "complementarity" earlier (see Sections 3.2.1 and 6.1.3). We need to collide with it once more because in the past 30 years or so it has become an important strand in the conservative case against homosexuality. Perhaps aware that the usual biblical arguments against same-sex love lack the objectivity that they are supposed to deliver, attention is turned instead to the "natural" pairing of man and woman found in Genesis 1. This strand of thinking is particularly appealing to Protestants because two well-known biblical texts (Gen. 1:26–28, 2:24) are used to support it. For a Catholic constituency, the use of complementarity to proscribe same-sex relations has much in common with the Natural Law tradition since it is based on the created order of nature, and so is thought to state the plan of God for human sexual relations. It could form part of either Section 10.1 or Section 10.2 above. I have given it a separate section because of its growing appearance in official church literature.

A man needs a woman?   This unusual term first appeared in official Roman Catholic teaching in 1981 when Pope John Paul II spoke of "the natural complementarity that exists between man and woman" (1981, section 39). It is something that contributes to full "conjugal communion" between the sexes. However, in a more recent official document, *Considerations Regarding Proposals to give Legal Recognition to Unions between Homosexual Persons* (Congregation for the Doctrine of the Faith, 2003), the term has a different use. It is invoked to establish, by an alternative route, that same-sex love is disordered and depraved:

> The Church's teaching on marriage and on the complementarity of the sexes reiterates a truth that is evident to right reason and recognized as such by all the major cultures of the world ... No ideology can erase from the human spirit the certainty that marriage exists solely between a man and a woman

> In the first place, man, the image of God, was created "male and female" (Gen. 1:27). Men and women are equal as persons and complementary as male and female

> God has willed to give the union of man and woman a special participation in his work of creation. Thus, he blessed the man and the woman with the words "Be fruitful and multiply"

(Gen. 1:28). Therefore, in the Creator's plan, sexual complementarity and fruitfulness belong to the very nature of marriage

There are absolutely no grounds for considering homosexual unions to be in any way similar or even remotely analogous to God's plan for marriage and family. Marriage is holy, while homosexual acts go against the natural moral law. (Congregation for the Doctrine of the Faith, 2003, section 1:2–4)

The exclusionary nature of these remarks is fairly obvious. Although complementarity only recently appeared, the Church is represented as having an established teaching on the subject, even though its meaning is only implied and not defined. *Reason* (and even global culture) is invoked to support it. The voice of *nature* speaks its truth. The full equality of the two sexes is effortlessly discovered in the first chapter of the Bible. Complementarity is inseparably linked to having children. Any alteration to the combined witness of Scripture, Reason, Nature, and culture constitutes mere unwarranted "ideology." The language of absolutes is invoked against same-sex love. Even analogies that involve comparisons between the love of same-sex partners and the love of married partners for each other, are not to be entertained.

Anglicans have also invested heavily in complementarity, and for similar reasons. We were surprised to be told by the influential discussion document of 2003, that we have "five core beliefs" (House of Bishops' Group on *Issues in Human Sexuality*, 2003, section 1.2.25). We were more surprised still that one of these core beliefs was complementarity:

The second [core] belief, based on the teaching of Genesis 1.26–27 and 2.18–24, is that the division of humankind into two distinct but complementary sexes is not something accidental or evil but is, on the contrary, something good established by God himself when he first created the human race. By complementarity what is meant is that the differences between men and women were intended for the mutual good of each. (House of Bishops' Group on *Issues in Human Sexuality*, 2003, section 1.2.9)

The statement of complementarity in this document is less exclusionary than in Catholic documents, but its use is similar. God has planned and ordained heterosexual marriage as the sole framework for legitimate, holy, sexual relations. Any deviation from these God-given norms constitutes a break with Tradition that these Anglicans are not yet, if ever, able to make.

Activity: The criticisms of complementarity made in Section 3.2.1 above are all applicable here. Please re-read them now.

More problems with complementarity   It is surprising that these churches have continued to deploy this notion in their effort to retain their "traditional" positions about homosexuality. Rowan Williams has called it a "problematic and non-scriptural theory" (Williams, 2002, p. 320). In particular it seems very odd that the churches continue to insist, not simply that "the differences between men and women were intended for the mutual good of each," but that the text authorizes its own interpretation as a divinely appointed rule that permits absolutely no exceptions. In addition to the criticisms made of complementarity in Section 3.2.1 (where the insertion of modern sexual theory into ancient texts was being noted) some further observations about the use of complementarity in delegitimizing same-sex relations are pertinent.

First, it is simply not true that the Bible and Tradition assert the equality or the complementarity of the sexes. As Andrew Mein (2007, p. 27) observes, "The traditional Christian interpretation of Genesis 1–2 is that it portrays not equality between men and women but a relationship of power and subordination." That is how the New Testament, Augustine, and Aquinas, and most theologians up to the second half of the twentieth century have understood the relationship. It is ironic that many traditionalists adopt unconsciously revisionist positions about sexual equality. Convinced on other grounds that women are "equal" to or with men, they then look for the equality of the sexes in the Bible, and claim that complementarity represents the Church's traditional teaching.

Second, complementarity is a notion probably imported into theology from physics. It does not sit well in its new home. In the early twentieth century, scientists were baffled by the behavior of light. Depending on the experimental conditions of its observation, light sometimes appeared as corpuscles, and at other times as waves. There was no doubt that light was a single phenomenon. The logical innovation was that apparently contradictory observations of the single phenomenon could turn out to be not contradictory after all, but, under certain experimental conditions, complementary.

It took another 50 years for theologians to latch on to complementarity, and in the process they changed its meaning. The parallels between its uses in science and theology are poor. Light is a single phenomenon in physics giving rise to complementary descriptions, but men and women are, in this kind of theology, *two* phenomena, in fact two complementary sexes (in a relationship of equality with each other!). The use of the term in theology is another example of the subject's uncritical assimilation of scientific terminology into its discourse.

Third, assuming that complementarity remains a notion that theologians and churches can work with, it can easily be used to support different conclusions. Salzman and Lawler note that there are two basic *types* of complementarity in Catholic teaching, *biological* and *personal* (Salzman and Lawler, 2008, p. 141). There is *biological* complementarity, which is "heterogenital" and "reproductive," and *personal* complementarity which consists (in part) of "communion complementarity" and "affective complementarity." Both types are confined to heterosexual marriage.

Without further defining these terms, the essential point is not difficult to detect. Salzman and Lawler shrewdly note that biology drives the theory, and want to know how the Magisterium knows that homosexual acts "do not proceed from a genuine affective and sexual complementarity." It is assumed in advance, and without argument, that biological complementarity is a necessary precondition for personal complementarity. However "affective complementarity" may be defined, why assume that among same-sex couples it cannot be "genuine?" If Experience is to count for anything at all, the accounts lesbian and gay couples give of their unions may tell a different story.

Fourth, the references in Genesis to relationships between the sexes may give rise to different interpretations. For example, Gareth Moore takes different details from Genesis

2:15–24 in order to suggest biblical support for the view that God wants people to have the sexual partners they want to have! The narrative, of course, recounts how "The LORD God said, 'It is not good for the man to be alone. I will make a helper suitable for him.'" Many different creatures were brought to the man "but no suitable helper was found." A woman is made from one of the man's ribs. God brings her to the man for his approval (Gen. 2:22).

Moore's take on this narrative is unusual, to say the least. He concludes

> God seeks for each of us, not the partner that pleases God, but the partner that pleases us, for it is only thus that he can fulfil us as the needy creatures he has made us, and only thus that he can succeed in his own project of providing us with a companion. (Moore, 2003, p. 142)

This is perhaps an unorthodox interpretation of this text, finding more within it than one is entitled to find. But that is the problem with the more standard interpretations as well.

Question: Salzman and Lawler work with the notion of complementarity but see no reason why it cannot be applied to same-sex couples as well. Biologically these couples cannot be complementary, but on the *personal* level, complementarity between them is possible. What do you think about this claim? Is it sound?

Comment: I think it is sound. There is a pretty obvious fit between penises and vaginas that might be deemed natural, but there is clearly more to complementarity than its "heterogenital" dimension. Same-sex couples report deep, lasting, and mutually satisfying relationships, just as opposite-sex couples do. For these relationships the language of complementarity in its communal and affective dimensions is clearly appropriate. The Vatican's conclusion may even be defamatory.

10.4 Experience and Same-Sex Love

Experience was claimed as a fourth source for thinking theologically about sex (see Sections 3.1.4 and 3.2.3). It fairly obviously makes a contribution to a revaluation of the churches' dilemma of whether to bless same-sex unions.

We have just seen how people's experience of injustice, persecution, cruelty, and so on, has proved decisive in several cases where the Church has changed and deepened its moral teaching (see Section 10.1.3). Noonan's weighty analysis of how change comes about in the Church's moral thinking emphasizes the *positive* power of *negative* experience in inspiring a change in Christian attitudes. He cites as an example the "experience of the evil of religious persecution in Europe" in the sixteenth to eighteenth centuries as the catalyst for bringing about belief in religious freedom.

Slavery is another example: the "centuries-old experience of slavery ... led to the conclusion that slavery was destructive both for the slaves and for the masters" (Noonan, 2003, p. 298). A similar case may be made for the recognition of human rights or for the experience of the pain of broken marriages in the case made by Protestant churches to recognize divorce and offer opportunities for further marriage.

The contribution of the experience of lesbians and gays, out but in the churches, offers a strong analogy with other occasions of the experience of injustice. Hearing their stories and empathizing with them in their exclusion and stigmatization can contribute much to their full habilitation in the churches. Listening to their experience is essential to the dismantling of stereotypes about them, often religiously spun and perpetuated.

For example, it is not true, as the Vatican insists, that gays make bad adoptive parents "whose absence of sexual complementarity . . . creates obstacles in the normal development of children" and actually means "doing violence" to them (Congregation for the Doctrine of the Faith, 2003, section 7). Research on gay parenting over 20 years shows

> There is no evidence to suggest that lesbians and gay men are unfit to be parents or that psychoscial [including sexual] development among children of gay men or lesbians is compromised in any respect relative to that among offspring of heterosexual parents. (Patterson, 1995; in Salzman and Lawler, 2008, p. 229)

Chapters 9 and 10 have provided an extensive analysis of the sources of Theology as they are brought to bear on same-sex couples. If lesbian and gay couples are to continue to be denied full recognition by the churches, there is a need for better arguments to be found.

This chapter also brings Part IV to a close. Theologies of sex, of gender, and now of same-sex love have been undertaken, and in the final part, the attempt will be made to integrate them in a single coherent theology of sexual love.

References

Aquinas, T. (1905) *Summa contra Gentiles* (trans. J. Rickaby), www.2.nd.edu/Departments/Maritain/etext/gc.htm (accessed November 4, 2010).

Catechism of the Catholic Church (1994) Geoffrey Chapman, London, www.vatican.va/archive/catechism/ccc_toc.htm (accessed November 3, 2010).

Congregation for the Doctrine of the Faith (2003) *Considerations Regarding Proposals to give Legal Recognition to Unions between Homosexual Persons*, www.vatican.va/roman_curia/congregations/cfaith/documents/rc_con_cfaith_doc_20030731_homosexual-unions_en.html (accessed November 4, 2010).

House of Bishops' Group on *Issues in Human Sexuality* (2003) *Some Issues in Human Sexuality – A Guide to the Debate*, Church House Publishing, London.

Jordan, M. (2005) *Blessing Same-Sex Unions: the Perils of Queer Romance and the Confusions of Christian Marriage*, University of Chicago Press, Chicago/London.

Mein, A. (2007) Threat and promise: The Old Testament on sexuality, in *An Acceptable Sacrifice? Homosexuality and the Church* (eds. D. Dormor and J. Morris), SPCK, London, pp. 22–32.

Monti, J. (1995) *Arguing about Sex: The Rhetoric of Christian Sexual Morality*, State University of New York Press, New York.

Moore, G., OP (2003) *A Question of Truth: Christianity and Homosexuality*, Continuum, London/New York.

Newman, J.H. (1949) *An Essay on the Development of Christian Doctrine*, Longman, New York.

Noonan, J.T., Jr. (2003) Development in moral doctrine, in *Change in Official Catholic Moral Teachings: Readings in Moral Theology, No. 13* (ed. C.E. Curran), Paulist Press, New York, pp. 287–305.

Pope John Paul II (1981) *Familiaris consortio: On the Role of the Christian Family in the Modern World*, www.vatican.va/holy_father/john_paul_ii/apost_exhortations/documents/hf_jp-ii_exh_19811122_familiaris-consortio_en.html (accessed November 4, 2010).

Pope Paul VI (1968) *Humanae vitae*, www.vatican.va/holy_father/paul_vi/encyclicals/documents/hf_p-vi_enc_25071968_humanae-vitae_en.html (accessed November 12, 2010).

Porter, J. (1994) *The Recovery of Virtue: The Relevance of Aquinas for Christian Ethics*, SPCK, London.

Porter, J. (1999) *Natural and Divine Law: Reclaiming the Tradition for Christian Ethics*, Eerdmans, Grand Rapids, MI/Cambridge, UK.

Porter, J. (2005) *Nature as Reason: A Thomistic Theory of the Natural Law*, Eerdmans, Grand Rapids, MI/Cambridge, UK.

Provan, C.D. (1989) *The Bible and Birth Control*, Zimmer Printing, Monongahela, PA.

Salzman, T.A., and Lawler, M.G. (2008) *The Sexual Person. Toward a Renewed Catholic Anthropology*, Georgetown University Press, Washington, DC.

Vidal, M. (2003) Progress in the moral tradition, in *Change in Official Catholic Moral Teachings: Readings in Moral Theology, No. 13* (ed. C.E. Curran), Paulist Press, New York, pp. 319–334.

Williams, R. (2002) The body's grace, in *Theology and Sexuality: Classic and Contemporary Readings* (ed. E.F. Rogers, Jr.), Blackwell, Malden, MA/Oxford, pp. 309–321.

Part V

Learning to Love

11

Virginity, Celibacy, Chastity

This chapter asks why Christianity values virginity (Section 11.1). It examines a particular form of virginity, "virginity for the sake of the Kingdom." While the conventional arguments for this state may no longer convince, better and more contemporary theological reasons are suggested. Surprising help from a secular source commending virginity, is gratefully utilized (Section 11.2). A similar approach is taken to celibacy, in which unconvincing and more convincing reasons are laid out and compared (Section 11.3). Then chastity is defined, enlarged and further commended in Section 11.4.

> *Activity:* The chapter assumes and builds on the initial discussion of celibacy (see Section 5.1). You may want to glance over this section again.

11.1 Valuing Virginity?

In this chapter we will be thinking about virginity, celibacy, and chastity. There are subtle differences and shadings of meanings between these terms, so here are some definitions:

One could say there appear to be two ways virginity comes to matter in contemporary Christian sexual thought. First, since

> **Virginity:** A virgin is a man or a woman who has not had full penetrative sex. (What counts as having sex was discussed in Section 1.3.)
>
> **Virginity "for the sake of the Kingdom":** Someone who is a virgin for the sake of the Kingdom will have taken a vow of celibacy, or chastity, and entered the priesthood or the religious life. Roman Catholic priests, and monks and nuns take this vow.

there is officially no having sex before marriage, virginity remains the ideal from which Christians enter marriage. Second, virginity is a state of devotion to God and to the service

---

God, Sex, and Gender: An Introduction, First Edition. Adrian Thatcher.
© 2011 Adrian Thatcher. Published 2011 by Blackwell Publishing Ltd.

Celibacy: This is a gift of God which enables Christians to concentrate fully on God's work. It is that state of being a virgin for the sake of the Kingdom. Ordained Catholic priests, "Called to consecrate themselves with undivided hearts to the Lord and to 'the affairs of the Lord,' . . . give themselves entirely to God and to men." Celibacy is "a sign of this new life to the service of which the Church's minister is consecrated; accepted with a joyous heart celibacy radiantly proclaims the Reign of God." (*Catechism of the Catholic Church*, 1994, para. 1579)

Chastity: Despite its association with virginity, it is not the same. Chastity is broader. It is the virtue of sexual restraint, not necessarily sexual abstinence. There is a large difference between the two. (Chastity is described in greater detail in Section 11.4.1.)

of God free from the distractions of devotion to a spouse. This is "virginity for the sake of the Kingdom."

It seems that celibacy and virginity for the sake of the Kingdom are the same thing. According to this definition celibacy is a lifelong state of the person. It is recognized as a divine gift rather than a mere human life-choice, and it is undertaken for the deepest of religious reasons, a vocation from God.

Losing one's virginity　　Deeply rooted in vernacular discussion about having sex for the first time, is the phrase "losing one's virginity." It does not take much thought to realize that that phrase belongs to an age when a woman's virginity was more highly prized, so that its loss was potentially ruinous for a woman's reputation. Terms like "slag" and "slut" still become attached to sexually experienced young women, however unfairly, and these terms indicate the survival of a double standard. No such opprobrium attends the first sexual experience of a man, whose "conquest" would be likely to form the subject of banter and boasting. But losing one's virginity may no longer carry the same sense of loss that it did until recently, and this loss of meaning of the loss of virginity may itself be a grave social, as well as personal, loss. If indeed that is so, it is important to say why, and that involves weighing up various beliefs and assumptions about virginity.

Like angels?　　There is little doubt that the ancient world expected the great majority of women to reproduce, and to start the dangerous business of bringing children into the world as soon as they were physically able. Some Christians however were more concerned with anticipating the world to come, when they would be as angels (see Section 5.2.1). Virginity was better, not least because it guaranteed release from the endless cycle of birth, sex, child-rearing, and death, and, when it was preserved it earned respect from a surprised populace. But that was not its only reward. As Peter Brown explains,

> It was left to Christian treatises on virginity to speak in public on the physical state of the married woman – on their danger in childbirth, on the pain in their breasts during suckling, on their exposure to children's infections, on the terrible shame of infertility, and on the humiliation of being replaced by servants in their husbands' affections (Brown, 1988, p. 25).

Over centuries the contrast between virginity and marriage was explained by means of the physical, spiritual, and theological superiority of the former. Darker justifications for remaining virginal became central within Christian doctrine (Ranke-Heinemann, 1992, pp. 119–135; Wiesner-Hanks, 2000, pp. 28–34). A late letter of the New Testament blames Eve for bringing sin into the world adding that women may be saved through childbearing (1 Tim. 2:14–15). That indeed was the lot of the many, while for a few the path to salvation lay not in childbearing, but in the renunciation of all sexual activity. The identification of Eve as a temptress, and the association of all sexual activities with sin, led too easily to a male suspicion of women that in turn sometimes led to outright misogyny.

"Clogged up" virgins   Here then are two theological reasons for valuing virginity that are not generally to be heard on the lips of contemporary advocates of that state: that by refraining from having sex one is anticipating the next life; or that one is avoiding the inevitable religious contamination that is caught in sexual contact.

While Christians, for different reasons, valued virginity, the classical medical profession, through to the eighteenth century, took a more negative view of it. Anke Bernau (2007, p. 12) explains, "As a female virgin did not experience intercourse and orgasm, her unspilled 'seed' built up in her body, with harmful consequences." Doctors at least from the early modern period to the 1930s believed that the lack of sexual experience in young women caused the disease of chlorosis, or "greensickness" (King, 2004). Early marriage was advised, not simply to avoid extra-marital pregnancy, but to avoid the state of "the clogged-up virgin" (Bernau, 2007, p. 18).

Vigorous rubbing   The Christian saint and Doctor of the Church Albertus Magnus (*d.* 1280), was aware of this problem, and that a vigorous rubbing was a practical way of dealing with it:

> Certain girls around fourteen years old cannot be satisfied by intercourse. And then, if they do not have a man, they feel in their minds intercourse with a man and often imagine men's private parts, and often rub themselves strongly with their fingers or with other instruments until, the vessels having been relaxed through the heat of rubbing and coitus, the spermatic humour exits, with which the heat exits, and then their groins are rendered temperate and then become more chaste. (Cadden, 1996; in Bernau, 2007, p. 18)

It is easy to imagine a clash between religious reasons for remaining a virgin as long as possible and medical reasons for not remaining a virgin for long.

Young women in many cultures have long been accustomed to huge social pressures to prove their virginity by having an intact hymen prior to their wedding night. Scandalously, in some religious groups and societies, this pressure shows little sign of receding. An Internet search under, say "hymen restoration," "hymenoplasty," or "hymen repair" reveals scores of agencies prepared to carry out the required work at a price. Apparently the provision of fake or "reconstructed hymens" or cosmetic vaginal surgery is meeting a growing social need (Bernau, 2007, pp. 25–29).

Protestant mainline Churches generally teach that sex before marriage is wrong, but the language they use is generally equivocal, and there is often an absence of theological reasons in support of their teaching. For example, the Book of Discipline of the United Methodist Church of the USA teaches that "Although all persons are sexual beings whether or not they are married, sexual relations are only clearly affirmed in the marriage bond" (United Methodist Church, 2004).

There then follows a condemnation of "exploitative, abusive, or promiscuous" behavior, inside and outside marriage, but it is not said whether consensual sexual relations outside the marriage bond can also be affirmed, albeit less "clearly" than sexual relations within it. There is almost deliberate and open ambiguity about the matter which doubtless reflects the diverse practices of its younger members.

There are two issues to consider here aside from the understandable ambiguity of these statements. Is virginity valued only as an important prelude to the normative state of marriage? If so what are the theological reasons for this, especially since desire for the angelic life or the idea that the taint of sin attaches to sexual contact, are not obviously Methodist themes? Or can virginity be valued and "clearly affirmed" as an alternative style of Christian life and service? In order to find *theological* reasons for valuing virginity it is necessary to examine virginity "for the sake of the Kingdom."

Discussion: If you are a member of a Christian denomination, or have knowledge of one, share the understanding of virginity that that denomination has given you.

11.2 Virginity "for the Sake of the Kingdom"

Perhaps only in the Roman Catholic and Orthodox Churches is there much of any remaining sense of the overt religious value of virginity. Here it is still able to symbolize mastery over the body and its passions in the service of God, or anticipation of that heavenly state where there is no longer any marriage. The Orthodox Church in America calls the monastic life "the angelic way," and says it is "to be defended, protected and promoted in witness to life in God's coming kingdom where all holy men and women will be 'like angels in heaven' (Matthew 22:30)" (OCA, n.d.). In these cases, virginity belongs to a special vocation, which the great majority of Christians do not receive. For such people, the Catholic *Catechism* explains

> From the very beginning of the Church there have been men and women who have renounced the great good of marriage to follow the Lamb wherever he goes, to be intent on the things of the Lord, to seek to please him, and to go out to meet the Bridegroom who is coming. (*Catechism of the Catholic Church*, 1994, para. 1618)

> Virginity for the sake of the Kingdom of heaven is an unfolding of baptismal grace, a powerful sign of the supremacy of the bond with Christ and of the ardent expectation of his return, a sign which also recalls that marriage is a reality of this present age which is passing away. (*Catechism of the Catholic Church*, 1994, para. 1619)

Activity: This activity is in two parts. First, how do you think virginity in this passage is a possible sign of God's future?

Comment: I think there are three ways the passage makes connections between the sexless life and the life to come.

Defiling themselves with women?   First, the vision of heaven in Revelation 22 (to which this passage refers) describes 144,000 *men* (not men and women) and identifies them as "those who did not defile themselves with women, for they kept themselves pure. They follow the Lamb wherever he goes. They were purchased from among men and offered as first fruits to God and the Lamb" (Rev. 22:4). The Catholic Church clearly associates virginity for the sake of the Kingdom with the vanguard of élite male Christians in heaven.

Second, Matthew's Gospel records a parable of Jesus known as "The Parable of the Ten Virgins." They were waiting for a bridegroom who "was a long time in coming" (Matt. 25:5). "At midnight the cry rang out: 'Here's the bridegroom! Come out to meet him!'" (Matt. 25:6). The Vatican links Christians who renounce sex and devote themselves to God with those who are regarded as betrothed instead to Christ, the spiritual Bridegroom who will come again and whom consecrated virgins eagerly await. Again in Revelation, "the new Jerusalem" is "prepared as a bride beautifully dressed for her husband," Jesus Christ (Rev. 21:2).

Third, the comparison of virginity with marriage makes clear that while marriage is an earthly institution, which is passing away, the virginal state is eternal.

Activity: The second part of the activity is to assess the theological reasons given for valuing virginity for the sake of the Kingdom. How effective are they as a rationale for remaining without sexual experience today?

Comment: Were you disinclined to think that *any* of them is effective? Perhaps if you thought you were called by God to do exacting, lifelong, fulltime, Christian work you would think differently?

There seem to be several difficulties with the rationale for celibacy given above.

11.2.1 Four bad reasons for being a virgin

First, the detail that the privileged males in heaven are rewarded because they "did not defile themselves with women," and "kept themselves pure," expresses the ancient and derogatory, gendered, male view of women. Surely it has no place in contemporary Christianity, does it? The view that contact with women contaminates the male person in soul and body is sexist, if not misogynist. And of course it is about *male* virginity only.

Second, the Parable of the Ten Virgins awaiting a Bridegroom does not appear to be about either virginity or marriage. It is about *waiting*, about the Disciples of Christ being prepared and alert, for the return of the Messiah, personified as One who is already spiritually betrothed to His followers who are collectively His bride. The ideas of virginity and marriage are used to signify something else. The virgins are in any case *bridesmaids, not brides.*

Third, there are a growing number of married Christian couples who, *together*, consecrate themselves "for the sake of the Kingdom" (Stanton, 2002). That total dedication of the whole person to the work of God does not preclude married couples *together* dedicating themselves to that work.

Fourth, the thought that being a virgin is a reminder that the state of marriage is "passing away" sounds pessimistic. Attention is not drawn to the contrasting differences between the two states, but to the eternal value of one, and to the temporal value of the other. One wonders whether these judgments about virginity for the sake of the Kingdom, and about marriage, actually correspond with the real judgments of virginal and married people?

This pessimism with regard to marriage also lies uneasily at variance with the doctrine that marriage is "a very great good" and a *sacrament*. Every thought we entertain about the next life has to be by means of pictures drawn from this life. While our lives might anticipate the next life in some way, we do not know what that life will be like. Paul clearly acknowledges this (1 Cor. 2:9). Does Catholic teaching mean that husbands and wives will no longer be, or recognize, themselves as husbands and wives in the life to come?

That is the Catholic teaching, which sits oddly with the teaching of Jesus about the "one flesh" of marriage. That teaching is based on a reply of Jesus to a trick question about the resurrection of the dead. He says "When the dead rise, they will neither marry nor be given in marriage; they will be like the angels in heaven" (Mark 12:25). But the teaching does not follow from Christ's saying, and the Orthodox Churches do not understand it in this way. The saying may indicate only that *the practice of marrying* will not take place in the hereafter; not that the married in this life will be unmarried in the next.

While there are difficulties associated with the value placed on virginity for the sake of the Kingdom, credit must surely be given for offering theological reasons, *at all*. Perhaps *better* theological reasons can be found than those in the *Catechism* for being and remaining a virgin, whether or not for the sake of the Kingdom? Perhaps virginity can be positively celebrated, and commended to people who have not received the vocation to fulltime Christian work? In order to explore this possibility, we will first examine a purely *secular* account of virginity; then a theological account from a religious Sister; then draw some conclusions for ourselves.

11.2.2 The cult of the born-again virgin

People of faith may be encouraged to see that within the secular world there is a backlash against the normative expectation of teens and twenties having lots of sex, whatever the consequences. An example of the genre is Wendy Keller's *The Cult of the Born-Again Virgin* (1999). This author, neither born-again nor a virgin, loads the title of her book with religious overtones because she advocates a transforming personal conversion from having frequent sexual relationships to an alternative state in which women refrain from sexual contact that turns out to be unfulfilling and harmful. Women testify to getting off "the hamster wheel of dating and sex and relationships," and rejoicing in their "readmission to virginity" (1999, p. xxiii). There are lists, running to five pages, of benefits accruing to women who become Born Again Virgins, "BAVs." Here are just a few. Under the heading, "Personal Growth", the reasons for becoming a BAV (even for a short time!) include:

> To nurture yourself
> To restore a sense of dignity and elegance

To breathe deeply and learn new ways of interacting
To cultivate more power over your thoughts
To stand up for yourself . . .
To cultivate a sense of personal dignity
To enhance self-control
To enhance self-esteem . . .
To re-establish your identity in the world . . . (pp. 11–12)

Under the heading "Relationships", the reasons for and benefits from becoming a BAV include:

To be peacefully single
To attract and marry the "right" man
To grieve lost loves
To heal from divorce
To repair a broken heart
To break the bonds of dependency on men
To develop relationships with women friends
To develop closer bonds with your child(ren)
To care for an aging parent
To get off the dating fast track
To prepare for your next relationship
To stop playing games. (pp. 12–13)

Finally, why do all this?

One of the primary benefits women experience when reclaiming their sexual natures appears to be the accompanying sense of self-love and self-esteem. Self-love is critical before we can love others, and reclaiming our sexuality is for some women a way of increasing their own sense of self-control and self-respect.

One of the remarkable benefits and transcendent qualities for women so inclined is the development of purer attitudes of service and dedication to loftier goals. Some women find themselves coming into alignment with higher spiritual values as a result of their decision not to have sex (Keller, 1999, p. 116).

Activity: Remembering that these are extracts from a popular secular book, please re-read them and notice which reasons and benefits are also *religious*.

Comment: I am struck by the common ground between theological and secular reasons for embracing virginity; between, in the first case as a way of living a holy, healthy life that is pleasing to God and a sign of rejection of a decadent culture; and in the second case as a way of living a prudent, self-affirming lifestyle that is critical of the sexual and gendered roles we are invited to assume. The confluence of emphases on self-love and self-esteem are particularly interesting.

Christians have better reasons for affirming virginity. Not only are their reasons for temperate sexual behavior rooted in faith and doctrine, their understanding of self-love is always balanced by love of neighbor, and this requirement does not admit of either use or abuse of another person as an object.

The Born-Again Virgin has little to teach sexual minorities, for it addresses only standard heterosexual arrangements for meeting up (now that the practice of courtship has virtually ceased). While it appears as a feminist book, feminists are likely to find it wanting in analysis of the historical and social conditions that have given rise to a veritable sexual anarchy.

The value of the book for Christian ethics is to indicate to Christians, that, *outside* Christian morality, a strong case can be made for sexual restraint, from which Christians can learn. The serviceable reasons solemnly listed for being a BAV can be grounded in deeper, time-honored ways of honoring God by honoring the body. In this way, the practice of virginity really is a *sign*, an embodied way of living that points to alternative performances of sexuality.

11.3 In Praise of Restraint

We have already noted (see Section 4.2.1) how sexual desire, a gift of God, is easily intensified into lust and endlessly stimulated by social and cultural pressures on us. Desire is artificially stimulated. Our culture includes, for example, the popular musical styles of the day; fashionable clothes; discos; night clubs; lap-dancing clubs; erotic entertainment; TV soaps; the cult of celebrity; the ubiquitous presence of porn on the internet; the use of stereotypical (= "sexy") female bodies and muscular male hunks in advertising, and so on.

A terrifying consequence of immersion in this cultural atmosphere is the temptation of many young women and men to internalize, to slide uncritically into, and to adopt the roles of sex marauder and sex object respectively. It becomes too easy to opt into the socially approved roles of predator and predated, where (at least in straight dating arrangements) men are interested more in screwing women than loving them, and women present themselves as they think men want them. The latest fashion is just another way of concealing, while at the same time enabling, their public presence as sex objects worthy of male attention.

The love commandments   Once these pressures are recognized and unmasked, the possibility of being a non-conformist in relation to them becomes positively attractive, and celibacy is a positive way of non-conformity. Having a faith becomes an essential aid in the forging of a lifestyle that, like that of the first Christians, is consciously counter-cultural. Looking back over earlier themes in this book, perhaps the first ingredient of an alternative sexual culture is to be found embedded in the foundation of all Christian morality, the commandments of Jesus to all His disciples, to "Love the Lord your God with all your heart and with all your soul and with all your mind and with all your strength," and to "Love your neighbor as yourself" (Mark 12:29–31).

This second of the Great Commandments makes clear that the foundation of all morality, including sexual morality, is love. Any sexual partner we ever have is also, in Christian faith, a neighbor whom we are to love as we love ourselves.

This second commandment is the more intelligible when we have a very high estimation of ourselves and of our great worth as persons. Christians have not always been good at saying this. The emphasis on sin has too readily led to a loss of self-esteem and self-regard which makes self-love difficult, if not impossible. But self-love can express itself in strong positive self-regard, which differs much from an attitude of selfishness, or of disregard of the needs and interests of others, or of narcissism, which becomes a preoccupation of oneself with one's life, one's body, one's career, one's success, almost at any price. These considerations about basic attitudes to ourselves and to our partners should by themselves be sufficient, not to justify never having sex, but to justify never having sex without many conditions first being satisfied.

One of these is self-respect. While this is a secular value in its own right, in Christian thought it is rooted in appropriate self-love. Another belief that constrains casual sex is the identification of the body of a Christian with the Body of Christ (see Section 8.1.1). While we will not be convinced by the ancient physiology of what happens when we have sex, the self-understanding of believers as parts of the mystical Body of Christ is surely illuminating.

A Christian understanding of children ranks high in the determination of Christians to confine the possibility of conceiving children to a permanent relationship between parents, which embraces any children they have. When we looked at Aquinas' teaching on the evil of fornication (see Section 3.2.2), I strongly suggested he was right to emphasize the wrongness of fornication as a sin against any children conceived by it (though I also thought his condemnation of all sexual pleasure was daft). Children deserve to be permanently loved by both their parents. All churches teach that children are "gifts of God." Their conception should be an occasion of joy, not regret, and especially not regret leading to the termination of a pregnancy.

The past few paragraphs counsel sexual restraint, but not celibacy. But they are preparing the way. Celibacy may also be wisely counseled, and Sr. Janette Gray's advocacy of it (1997) will be examined next.

11.3.1 The four phases of celibacy

Gray convincingly describes four historical phases in the theology of celibacy. The first of these is a kind of martyrdom, where the celibate replicates "the bodily sacrifice of the saviour" (1997, p. 145).

Pelvic anxiety   Celibacy is influenced by movements such as Gnosticism and Manichaeism that rejected sex. Avoiding sex led to its devaluation, to a "virulent strain of pelvic anxiety," which produced "common misery" for scores of saintly Christians. "At the core of this negativity is disbelief in the humanness of sex and the sexuality of being human, despite the central Christian doctrine of creation – that what God creates is good". This kind of theology "rejects the body and sexuality [and] sees the material as inferior to the spiritual, and negatively associates woman, matter, earth, nature and sexuality" (Gray, 1997, p. 146; see also Ruether, 1983, p. 80).

A second historical phase in her construction of celibacy is its social form, monasticism. In monasteries and convents "a corporate identity was envisaged transcending the individual limitations of human nature and abandoning the corporeality and sinfulness of the personal body for the spiritually enhanced communal body."

A third phase is the rational/intellectual phase – "the privileging of the reasoning self and imagination over and against the body, the seat of sensory illusion" (Gray, 1997, p. 147). Mind and body are at war. The battlefield is the interior soul. This phase of celibacy reshaped "the suspicion of the body ... through the ascendancy of the spiritual over the body and the employment of the reflective intellect in the turn to God away from the flesh and worldly distractions."

Being sexual, being celibate   Gray is well aware of the destructive legacy of all these historical phases of celibacy. So why defend celibacy at all? Well, there is a fourth, "embodied" and still experimental phase, "still taking form, being consciously embodied within the ranks of the body-denying theologies and the carnage and hatred they have engendered" (Gray, 1997, p. 149). This is "the search for union with God, mediated in human relationships other than sexual partnership. It happens *through* being sexual, not by imagining that sexuality can be abandoned as a zone of sin beyond God's saving action" (Gray, 1997, pp. 149–150; emphasis in original).

This form of celibacy is "a way of being sexual. It recognizes the body as constitutive of our being, not merely as a vessel for the spirit." Celibate living that positively values sexuality "finds that sexual attraction, warmth, and energy permeate all human relationships." The erotic is allowed to diffuse itself throughout the body instead of remaining focused in the genitals.

Embodied celibacy provides emancipation from the "negative concept of woman as sensual, temptress, and 'other'," which still inhabits too many male celibate minds (Gray, 1997, p. 151). No, God does not have "a particular concern to keep women's bodies under sexual control" (Gray, 1997, p. 152). Speaking for women who refuse to be male-defined in negative ways she says "Women need to redress the powerlessness of definition by others and to find new ways of integrating their embodiment with an identity of their own" (1997, p. 153). This kind of celibacy can be subversive. Not only is it "a deviation from the usual role of being a sexual partner." It also "challenges the male-mirroring of itself in woman as 'other'" (p. 154). It subverts "the male definition of woman as sexual object."

The insight that the expression of our sexuality need not catapult us into a sexual relationship or into even looking for one may be welcomed by many lay people for whom celibacy is not a lifelong project but just a state they happen to be in. A recent report from the Evangelical Lutheran Church in America helpfully develops this theme, counseling that:

> One does not need to be in a relationship to experience one's sexuality. Bodies do not suddenly become sexual at puberty and do not cease to be sexual when, for example, there are physical or developmental limitations, menopause, erectile dysfunction, or the absence of a sexual partner. This means that throughout our lives we need to find life-enhancing and appropriate ways of giving expression to this complicated dimension of ourselves. (ELCA, 2009, p. 25)

In the last two sections we have thought about the traditional state of virginity "for the sake of the Kingdom;" about an entirely *secular* recommendation of virginity; and about good and bad contemporary theological arguments of celibacy. These thoughts will help us to enlarge and commend chastity. Chastity will be defined, criticized, refined and commended.

11.4 Commending Chastity

The examination of virginity and celibacy has enabled us to think theologically about good reasons for not having sex when we might otherwise want to. Virginity is a bodily state we keep until it is surrendered. Sometimes it is referred to as a temporary state to opt into before opting out again. Virginity "for the sake of the Kingdom" clearly starts out as a lifelong endeavor, the vocation of a few people. For most of us, most of the time, the virtue of chastity is what we may find we need.

Chastity was compared earlier with celibacy and virginity (see Section 11.1). We will proceed as we did with virginity "for the sake of the Kingdom" in the last section: first, the account will be described, then analyzed, and then its relevance assessed.

11.4.1 Defining chastity

> *Activity:* The quotations above give only a flavor of the Catholic account of chastity. You may want to read the more complete account in the *Catechism*, paragraphs 2337–2359, easily available online.

There are four features of this account that need to be emphasized.

First, chastity on this account is not a characteristic of relationships, however holy they may be, but a particular attention paid to the individual's self-preservation before God. "The chaste person maintains the integrity of the powers of life and love placed in him. This ensures the unity of the person."

Whatever unity the person may have is with himself or herself. Chastity is about refusing to allow the disturbance to the equilibrium of body and spirit that sexual desire constantly threatens. The powers of life and love, the very God-given forces that drive us into relation with others are to be held within the fragile unity of the chaste self.

Chastity: "[T]he successful integration of sexuality within the person and thus the unity of man [*sic*] in his [*sic*] bodily and spiritual being" (*Catechism of the Catholic Church*, para. 2337).

"The chaste person maintains the integrity of the powers of life and love placed in him. [*sic*] This integrity ensures the unity of the person; it is opposed to any behavior that would impair it" (para. 2338).

"Chastity includes an *apprenticeship in self-mastery* which is a training in human freedom. The alternative is clear: either man [*sic*] governs his [*sic*] passions and finds peace, or he [*sic*] lets himself [*sic*] be dominated by them and becomes unhappy" (para. 2339; emphasis in original).

"The virtue of chastity comes under the cardinal virtue of *temperance*, which seeks to permeate the passions and appetites of the senses with reason" (para. 2341).

"People should cultivate [chastity] in the way that is suited to their state of life ... Married people are called to live conjugal chastity; others practise chastity in continence" (para. 2349).

Second, hierarchical language is deliberately deployed in the description of how chastity is to be obtained. People must rid themselves "of all slavery to the passions" (para. 2339).

"Master" and "slave," with the corresponding states of domination and subjugation, feature prominently. Drawn originally from concrete historical relationships between real masters and real slaves, those relationships are relocated reflexively in the inner struggle where the person experiences himself or herself as both master and slave in the heart of their divided being.

Third, the old dualism between reason and passion survives unamended in the *Catechism*. References to slavery suggest that Chastity belongs to "the cardinal virtue of *temperance*, which seeks to permeate the passions and appetites of the senses with reason." Priority is clearly given to reason over passion in the anthropology that informs the analysis, since passions are only to be controlled, and reason provides the means.

Fourth, a final observation concerns the requirement of chastity binding on people before marriage. It is unsparing in the injunction that having sex is unavailable to them, whatever their circumstances or degree of commitment to each other. Particular efforts at self-mastery are required at certain times, especially during childhood and adolescence (para. 2342). "Those who are *engaged to marry* are called to live chastity in continence" (para. 2350). If this should prove difficult, it is to be received as a "time of testing." Engaged couples "should reserve for marriage the expressions of affection that belong to married love."

> *Question:* Do you find any similarities between the *Catechism*'s teaching on chastity, and Gray's account of the phases of celibacy in the previous section?

> *Comment:* I expect you found several. Did you note the common theme of the need to control? The dualism between mind and body, and between reason and passion? The use of reason as a means of control? Negativity about the body and desire?

11.4.2 Five principles for enlarging chastity

Chastity and church   Christians need an account of chastity that is not overly shaped by the experience of male celibate theologians whose own struggles present difficulties of their own, difficulties that should not be projected onto everyone else. I once suggested that the meaning that people give to sexual activity can be helpfully, but not exclusively, described by reference to one or more of these four concepts: exploration, recreation, expression, procreation (Thatcher, 1997, p. 131).

Children and young people will want to explore their bodies, and as desire grows, the bodies of others. *Exploration* is a name appropriately given to these activities, which contribute to self-knowledge and are a consequence of the way God made us. The desire to explore desirable bodies is as natural as any alleged requirement of the Natural Law, isn't it? This is a legitimate meaning of sexual activity. The idea of sex as *recreation* conveys a sense of playfulness, of pleasure, of continual re-creating of a relationship.

Since we belong to a species that makes symbolic gestures and actions, it is almost obvious to remark that sexual behavior is *expressive*, and can express a range of meanings from a loving, mutual self-surrender to misogyny and humiliation. Any Christian theology of sex assumes this. Finally, the principal meaning given to having sex by the church for most of its history, is *procreation*. Christian women and men are not immune from any of these processes.

Chastity and the growth of sexual experience   There is a detail from the definition of chastity just considered that will come to our aid shortly. It is the injunction that "People should cultivate [chastity] in the way that is suited to their state of life." The idea of a "state of life" in accordance with which appropriate sexual behavior is a virtuous response, will soon be shown to be a fruitful one.

It is obvious that chastity is more likely to be acquired when it is encouraged and practiced by parents, in families, among peers, and certainly within church communities. Local churches do not always provide this encouragement positively. The churches need to *understand adolescence better.*

Older Christians and Church leaders should understand better the exploration that adolescents need to undertake in order to experience, enjoy, express and control their sexuality, and the intense pleasure that can accompany sexual activity. The adolescent period can also be emotionally painful and disturbing, and experimentation prior to the onset of domestic and career responsibilities is to be expected. There has never been such a lengthy period between puberty and marriage. Christian sexual ethics has to deal with this unique situation at a time when secularity is advanced, and openness to revision of traditional teachings is generally discouraged.

Whatever our age there is always room for further maturity, emotionally, intellectually, personally, sexually, and spiritually. Exploration and experimentation are going to happen and will not be deterred by parental or ecclesiastical embarrassment. Rather a loving, sympathetic, and honest environment both at home, and at church or chaplaincy, is more likely to enable young people to negotiate their explorations on their way to growing sexual maturity. A positive theology of sexuality within which the body, desire, and intimate relationships can be located, and the practice of learning to love can be encouraged, will have vastly more influence than any display of clerical anxiety, and uncomfortable exhortations to be abstinent.

I suggest the following five principles that might help in the reclamation of chastity in a permissive age. They are:

1. The principle of positive waiting.
2. The principle of proportion.
3. The principle of loving commitment.
4. The principle of exclusion.
5. The principle of honoring states of life.

The principle of positive waiting   For people of faith the principle of positive waiting for something can be enriching, and it can be applied to the onset of sexual partnerships. A convincing, and counter-cultural reason for *delaying* having sex lies in the unashamed benefits of waiting for something. People who live in affluent societies are accustomed to getting what they want without having to wait for it, whether it is fast food, express delivery, instant gratification, or instant response to an e-mail. How can waiting be a virtue? Waiting for a late flight, or for snow to melt, or for full recovery from illness is hardly virtuous, but there are several advantages in waiting for sex.

First, there are *prudential* advantages. We save ourselves lots of bother by not getting emotionally involved with potential sexual partners until we can handle it. If we try to get sexually involved without getting emotionally involved, a consequence of this may the separation of the body of the person from his or her totality as a physical/emotional/spiritual being.

Waiting is a means of acquiring patience, and patience is itself a trait of character essential to the success of a long-term relationship.

Waiting may also be a means of avoiding regret. Several studies show that over half of young women who were asked about their first experience of having sex, said they were disappointed (or worse) with it, and wished that they had *waited* until they were older.

But there is a *spiritual* dimension to waiting, and that is because waiting is central to the practice of Christian faith and life (see Section 4.2.1). Waiting is more than a prudential policy, an unattractive but necessary means for acquiring virtue. Waiting is one of the things all Christians do!

Yes, one may speak, following the argument of Paul in Romans 8:14–30, of a "theology of waiting." Christians currently in a state of suffering are said to be waiting for future glory (8:17–18) and, indeed, even "the whole creation" is "groaning as in the pains of childbirth" (8:22), awaiting its liberation. In a deep sense all Christian people are expectant, waiting, longing, not for sex but for Christ's second coming, and for the restoration of all things that will happen in that time beyond time called "the end of time," or "the end of the age."

Precisely in these circumstances of waiting, the virtue of hope is acquired, eager anticipation is enjoyed, and in the experience of impatience "the Spirit helps us in our weakness" (8:26). Here is a way of expressing strong *sexual* desire. It is not disowned or denied. It is recognized and affirmed. But it is linked to the deepest desires Christians have, and which they believe God has – for the triumph of good over evil, love over hate, reconciliation over enmity. That link can turn waiting into a profound prayer for all God wants for the world, and a determination to play one's part in reaching it. Waiting for what one most desires can have profound spiritual implications.

The principle of proportion   In 1991 some Anglican bishops wrote

> one basic principle is very definitely implicit in Christian thinking about sexual relations. It may be put this way: *the greater the degree of personal intimacy, the greater should be the degree of personal commitment* ... Often it is only because a relationship has advanced to a point of deep trust, valuing and commitment that inhibitions and privateness are surrendered, and intercourse becomes a possibility. For Christian tradition this has been, as it were, codified in the principle that full sexual intercourse requires total commitment. (House of Bishops of the Church of England, 1991, para. 3.2; emphasis added)

The bishops did not use the term "proportion" but it is directly implied in their treatment of the relation between the degrees of intimacy and of commitment. The more intimacy negotiated, the greater must be the commitment to match it. Their advice, far from being moralistic, is intended to show that the bottom line in any theology of sexuality is God's love for all God's people. In this case the sheer vulnerability of people in sexual relationships is assumed, recognized, and honored. The potentiality for hurt, regret, and emotional trauma is so great that time, above all, is needed to develop a mutual trust within which our personal privacies are respected, and our physical and emotional space revered.

The principle of loving commitment   The bishops commend what I have called the principle of proportion, and in doing this another principle is suggested – the principle of loving commitment.

The meaning of sex as an expression of love is far from obvious, either in the church or in secular societies. We noted earlier that marrying for love is an alarmingly modern idea (see Section 5.2.3). As two secular commentators observe: "In the absence of notions like commitment and responsibility, horniness can look an awful lot like 'love'" (Coles and Stokes, 1985, p. 85). Christians have worried more about whether having sex was lawful than whether it was loving. The view that sex and love are related is found in the *Song of Songs* (see Section 4.4.1). For long periods sex had nothing to do with love, only with procreation and the avoidance of sin. Chapter 6 showed how human love is able to mingle with the divine love, and how sexual love may also be a means of giving and receiving God's love for us. But the position taken there is far from obvious, and needs argument to establish it.

To be fair to the bishops, they say full sex requires full commitment, and they understand this requirement to be one of the positive meanings of Christian marriage. But the idea that *loving* someone is a sufficient reason for having sex with them is a common one.

Activity: Can you foresee any difficulties with the idea that "loving commitment" is a good enough reason for having sex?

Comment: I suspect there are several difficulties with it.

If there are *degrees* of commitment, how does one measure them?

How does one *know* when one is ready?

Then there is the horrible problem of self-deception: when we most want to trust our feelings (as well as our partner's), these may deceive us, not least because they are overwhelming, and can swamp our more guarded intuitions.

Romantic love is known to be unreliable and to play tricks of self-deception on us. The principle needs all the others if it is to be useful. But neither is the principle worthless. Our discussions of desire (see especially Sections 4.3 and 4.4) and of covenant love (see Sections 6.3 and 6.4) have indicated and assumed the presence of divine love within at least some expressions of human love.

The principle of exclusion   The principle of exclusion is a principle related to intimacy. It excludes a penis from a vagina unless certain conditions are satisfied. For conservative Christians that condition is nothing less than marriage. It is possible to derive this principle from some insights of Paul, and especially the distinction he makes in the course of a long argument, between sins which are "outside" the body and sins which are "against" the body:

> [18]Flee from sexual immorality. All other sins a man commits are outside his body, but he who sins sexually sins against his own body. (1 Cor. 6:18)

At Corinth, some Christians were celebrating their freedom in Christ by regarding themselves as free from all sexual constraints whatever. Against them Paul introduced a very positive appraisal of the human body that precluded its casual sexual use. Central to his argument is the claim: "The body is not meant for sexual immorality, but for the Lord, and the Lord for the body" (1 Cor. 6:13).

We have already encountered a reading of Paul's argument (see Section 8.1.1) to the effect that Christ is present wherever the members of His body are, and whatever the members of His body do. It was suggested that once the ancient physiology associated with Paul's thought is laid aside, a valuation of the body comes into view that has powerful ethical implications.

The suggestion made now may take a touch too literally the distinction Paul makes between sins committed "outside" the body, and "against" the body, but it may still be helpful. (It is not clear that *all* sins other than sexual sins are committed outside the body: gluttony would be a good counter-example.) The principle of exclusion draws attention to two details of Paul's characterization of sexual sins as being *inside* and *against* the body.

It could hardly be more obvious that penetrative sex is an act committed "inside the body." The question is whether the act is also "against" the body. In many cases the answer must be "yes," and sexual partners themselves acknowledge this by taking steps to protect themselves against consequences that directly affect their health. The principle might also be regarded as an expression of the Pauline teaching that the honoring of God with the body and its mutual recognition as incarnate Spirit be regulative for at least some sexual relations involving Christians.

The principle of honoring states of life   But individuals and couples are not going to wait forever. The four principles listed above may serve them well – but only for a while. When waiting gives out, the principle of honoring states of life comes a valuable one. What exactly is it?

At the beginning of the chapter, the *Catechism* was cited: "People should cultivate [chastity] in the way that is suited to their state of life . . . Married people are called to live conjugal chastity; others practise chastity in continence" (para. 2349). Mention of "states of life" also occurs in the preceding paragraph of the *Catechism*:

> All the baptized are called to chastity. The Christian has "put on Christ", the model for all chastity. All Christ's faithful are called to lead a chaste life *in keeping with their states of life*. At the moment of his Baptism, the Christian is pledged to lead his affective life in chastity. (para. 2348; emphasis added)

There are three interesting features of this account of chastity, and they invite a further proposal.

First, the recognition of states of life itself introduces a welcome sense of relativity, of change, of growth, in the circumstances of people. There are states of life which people reach, and pass.

Second, chastity is not the same as celibacy, or virginity, and is very different from abstinence from sex. If chastity was the same thing as virginity, then married people would not be exhorted to live "conjugal chastity." They are not expected to abstain from sex. They are expected to abstain from sex with anyone else.

Third, the number of states of life is limited to two, "married people" and "others" (though the state of widowhood is also mentioned). People who are engaged are ranked among the "others," "called to live chastity in continence" (para. 2350). ("Continence" is an appalling choice of word. An incontinent person is one who cannot control his or her urinary or faecal discharges. There is no doubt what continence means here: no orgasms.)

A new "state of life"   My proposal is simple: there is a third, intermediate state of life between singleness and marriage. In this state of life straight people on their way to marriage may be free to have contracepted sex. There are two broad reasons for proposing this:

First, the interval between puberty and marriage has never been greater. It is unprecedented. Healthy individuals cannot be expected to wait until around 30 years of age for their first experience of full sex. It is pastorally insensitive, as well as unrealistic, to expect them to do so.

Second, there is a name for this intermediate state. It has been around longer than Christianity. It is betrothal. A third state of life is not a new invention: it is the recovery of an old one. I shall propose (Chapter 13), in line with the need to *develop* Tradition, not merely to repeat it, that having sex in this state of life is fully compatible with the Christian call to chastity.

This chapter has attempted to make contemporary sense of virginity, of celibacy, and of chastity. The proposal just stated requires considerable theological discussion about contraception and its uses; indeed for many Christians whether contraception may be used at all even with marriage. This is attempted in Chapter 12. It also requires an effort of retrieval, which will show that the entry into Christian marriage did not begin with weddings (Chapter 13).

References

Bernau, A. (2007) *Virgins: A Cultural History*, Granta Books, London.

Brown, P. (1988) *The Body and Society: Men, Women and Sexual Renunciation in Early Christianity*, Faber & Faber, London/Boston.

Cadden, J. (1996) Western medicine and natural philosophy, in *Handbook of Medieval Sexuality* (eds. V.L. Bullough and J.A. Brundage), Garland, New York.

Catechism of the Catholic Church (1994) Geoffrey Chapman, London, www.vatican.va/archive/ catechism/ccc_toc.htm (accessed November 3, 2010).

Coles, R., and Stokes, G. (1985) *Sex and the American Teenager*, Harper & Row, New York.

ELCA (Evangelical Lutheran Church of America) (2009) *Human Sexuality: Gift and Trust*, www.elca.org/What-We-Believe/Social-Issues/Social-Statements/JTF-Human-Sexuality.aspx (accessed November 4, 2010).

Gray, J., RSM (1997) Celibacy these days, in *Sex These Days: Essays on Theology, Sexuality and Society* (eds. J. Davies and G. Loughlin), Sheffield Academic Press, Sheffield, pp. 141–183.

House of Bishops of the Church of England (1991) *Issues in Human Sexuality: A Statement*, Church House Publishing, London.

Keller, W. (1999) *The Cult of the Born-Again Virgin*, Health Communications, Deerfield Beach, FL.

King, H. (2004) *Disease of Virgins; Green Sickness, Chlorosis and the Problems of Puberty*, Routledge, London.

OCA (Orthodox Church in America) (n.d.) *Celibacy and Virginity*, www.oca.org/DOCmarriage.asp?SID=12&ID=21 (accessed November 11, 2010).

Ranke-Heinemann, U. (1992) *Eunuchs for the Kingdom of Heaven: the Catholic Church and Sexuality*, Penguin, Harmondsworth, UK.

Ruether, R. (1983) *Sexism and God Talk: Towards a Feminist Theology*, Beacon Press, Boston, MA.

Stanton, H. (2002) Obligation or option? Marriage, voluntary childlessness and the Church, in *Celebrating Christian Marriage* (ed. A. Thatcher), Continuum, London, pp. 223–239.

Thatcher, A. (1997) Postmodernity and chastity, in *Sex These Days: Essays on Theology, Sexuality and Society* (eds. J. Davies and G. Loughlin), Sheffield Academic Press, Sheffield, pp. 122–140.

United Methodist Church (2004) *Book of Discipline*, http://archives.umc.org/interior.asp?mid=1728 (accessed November 4, 2010).

Wiesner-Hanks, M.E. (2000) *Christianity and the Regulation of Sexuality in the Early Modern World: Regulating Desire, Reforming Practice*, Routledge, London/New York.

12

"Condilemmas"

Sex and Contraception in the Time of HIV/AIDS

The chapter begins with a preamble about why continued theological reflection on contraception is necessary. It then contributes to that reflection. It records some details about
earlier, pre-modern sexual practices, and laments both the growth in penetrative sexual
activity from the eighteenth century onwards and in contraceptive use which normalizes
and encourages penetrative sex as the principal act of intimacy between straight couples
(Section 12.1).

   Theological considerations about contraception are visited by means of the showdown
between Roman Catholics and Anglicans in 1930 about that topic, and which deepened
later in that century (Section 12.2). Three types of argument against the use of contraception, *even within marriage*, are analyzed and criticized, but also assessed for their positive
elements (Sections 12.3–12.5). The use of condoms as a defense against infection is commended, and the religious teaching that forbids it is deplored (Section 12.6).

12.1 Contraception, Still a Theological Issue

Contraception is a fact of late-modern life, yet the largest Church in the world is trenchantly
and officially opposed to contraception, outside marriage, inside marriage, and even as
potentially life-saving protection from HIV. In the final part of the book I take it for granted
that Christians, including a majority of Roman Catholics, will at some time in their lives
use contraception.

   The issue of contraception may seem to have arisen very late in the book. There are sound
reasons for this. Contraception plays an important part in the process of "Learning to Love"
that is the final part of the book. Yet, on the one hand, there is strident opposition to it from
the Vatican; while, on the other hand, the Protestant churches appear to have little to say

God, Sex, and Gender: An Introduction, First Edition. Adrian Thatcher.
© 2011 Adrian Thatcher. Published 2011 by Blackwell Publishing Ltd.

about it, whether from embarrassment; or from the lack of an appropriate pastoral language; or from theological neglect; or from a resigned acceptance of its widespread use (or some or all of these).

This situation is clearly unsatisfactory. Catholic intransigence leads to a loss of respect for that Church outside itself, and a deserved loss of authority for its Magisterium inside the Church. One consequence of this is that many of its deep insights into the theological meanings of sexuality are largely unknown and entirely unsought. The Protestant situation is little better.

In the secular world meantime (or at least in the Protestant countries of the United States and Britain) Sex Education is politicized and contested. The tragic problem of teenage pregnancy leads to divergent approaches from Church and State. While the Church side tries to convince itself that the problem is one of voluntary restraint, the State side suspends moral judgments about whether and when young people have sex and provides them with the knowledge, and the means, to avoid pregnancy.

The social and pastoral consequences of this situation are gravely disappointing. Some laypeople and Church leaders vociferously oppose Sex Education in schools, claiming that it encourages promiscuity. The voice of the Church, insofar as anyone listens, is then heard to be condemnatory. Protestants and Catholics alike adhere to the fiction that young people continue to marry at puberty (or shortly afterwards) without regard to the real ages at which, if they marry, they actually do. The pastoral neglect of the real needs of young Christians between puberty and marriage is almost, with a few exceptions, scandalous.

The persistence of opposition to the use of condoms in the face of a 25-year epidemic of HIV can scarcely be believed.

I take for granted that all readers, with the exception of one or two saints, and one or two liars, will have had sex before they marry (if they do, and if they are straight). They will need contraception. So the uses of contraception must continue to be a matter of lively theological reflection. But where is this reflection?

12.1.1 Before condoms

The term "contraception" can be "applied to any behavior that prevents conception" (Noonan, 1986, p. 1). An introduction to contraception before condoms were invented is provided by the discussion of a love memoir of John Cannon, a literate farm laborer in the English countryside, written about his relationship with his uncle's servant Mary in 1705, which lasted for 12 years. Commenting on the memoir, historian Tim Hitchcock writes,

> John and Mary ... never had full penetrative sex, and throughout his memoir Cannon congratulates himself on his studious avoidance of the sins of fornication and adultery. But, he, Mary, and the two other young women John courted at the same time, did have very active sex lives. Mutual masturbation, long drawn-out sessions of kissing and fondling, and sincere promises of future marriage characterised all these relationships. None of the three women involved became pregnant, and each was, by Cannon's account at least, considered a virgin on marriage. While unusual in being recorded, there is nothing to suggest that the experiences of these people were other than typical of popular sexual activity at the turn of the eighteenth century. (Hitchcock, 1996, p. 73)

Sexual outercourse   It will be at once apparent that what John and Mary were practicing was what from the 1980s was called "safe sex," and that it was a version of safe sex that did not require condoms, which were yet to be manufactured. A good name for this is "sexual *outer*course." It did not involve the insertion of a penis in a vagina and its withdrawal before the male orgasm (*coitus interruptus*). Hitchcock thinks that in the eighteenth century "sex changed. At the beginning of the century it was an activity characterized by mutual masturbation, much kissing and fondling, and long hours spent in mutual touching, but very little penile/vaginal penetration – at least before marriage." But

> by the end of the century sex had become increasingly phallo-centric. Putting a penis in a vagina became the dominant sexual activity – all other forms of sex becoming literally fore-play. Indeed, it is little wonder that use of the word "play" without its prefix, died out in our period. But, more significantly, it was the penis that became the active member. What the eighteenth century saw was the development of an obsession with the penis, and of an assumption that there was only one thing to do with it. (Hitchcock, 1996, p. 79)

Hitchcock thinks that young men and women had plenty of sex in the eighteenth century but what they did with each other at the beginning of that century was quite different from the normative expectation of penile penetration that dominates straight sexual rela-tions today. He links this to other social changes, such as the movement of men into fac-tories and cities, their growing independence from home and home life, and the financial independence, higher factory wages, and the increasing sense of esteem that went with them. Trends in pornography at the time which depict penetration provide further support for his thesis.

Male interests   An increase in penetrative sex in this period also

> fits well the story of change in gender relations and the development of separate spheres [between men and women] . . . Forms of sexual activity which dramatically increased the risk of pregnancy generally reflected the interest of men over those of women. Mutual masturbation and anti-natal forms of sex reflected instead a set of gender relations in which women's interests were more likely to be taken into account, and in which negotiation between partners was more equal. (Hitchcock, 1996, p. 80)

Young people in this period still held to the double ejaculation theory that the sperm of both sexes was needed to mingle for conception to take place (see Section 1.2.2). Later in the century women's orgasms were known to be unnecessary for conception, and the lack of necessity of orgasm led to a diminution in the valuing of women's pleasure in enjoying them. Inconsiderate phallocentric practice made them more difficult to come by.

There was much anti-masturbatory propaganda around in that century, and this also helped to normalize penetrative sex which "became increasingly the only form of sexual activity which could be countenanced" (Hitchcock, 1996, p. 82). Sexually active Christians today should want to relate to each other in *other*-centric, not phallocentric ways. In this respect they may have much to learn from pre-modern, pre-secular ways.

Modern contraception   Sexually active couples today have no fewer than 15 methods to choose from (NHS, 2009). These include the progestin implant (Implanon) and the IUS device inserted into the uterus which also releases progestin, which thickens cervical mucus to act as a barrier to sperm. Both of these are 99.8% effective. There is the IUD or coil, the contraceptive injection (Depo-Provera), the vaginal ring, contraceptive patch, the mini-pill (progestin only), the combined pill, the male condom, and the diaphragm. Condom use is recommended *in addition* to the chosen method as protection against sexually transmitted infections (STIs), which include chlamydia, genital herpes, genital warts, gonorrhea, HIV, and syphilis. And there is Natural Family Planning (NFP) (see Section 12.3). Vasectomy and female sterilization also provide effective contraception. But they involve surgical procedures and should be considered irreversible.

The responsibility for all these methods (except the condom and vasectomy) is born by women, together with possible negative effects on women's health. A consequence of the availability of these contraceptives is that young males, scarcely pubescent, expect penetrative sex, and young women are under great social pressure to provide it. Contraception normalizes the expectation. Modern sexual mores provide a strong argument for women's celibacy (see Sections 11.2 and 11.3). In 1993, Sally Cline wrote "A big disadvantage of reliable contraception was that women no longer had a justifiable excuse to refuse unwanted sexual advances. The removal of the threat of pregnancy meant coercive sex became more frequent" (p. 27). Now that progestin is almost completely effective, the element of pregnancy risk reduces almost to zero, and with it a reason for refusing sex disappears.

Activity: Think about the kind of intimacy that John and Mary enjoyed. Think of some of the benefits they enjoyed in the pre-condom era. What can they teach us about beginning sexual intimacy today?

Comment: Provided that seminal fluid goes nowhere near the vagina, isn't the chief benefit that sexual intimacy can happen without fear of pregnancy, and without use of any of the panoply of available contraceptives? However, there has to be a clear agreement about boundaries, and *mutual* control exercised about remaining within them.

Also, might they not remind us that intimacy develops over time and that the rush into having full sex is untimely, unnecessary, and perhaps the regrettable product of an affluent consumer culture?

12.2 Lambeth against Rome

In 1958 the Anglican Communion reaffirmed its earlier decision made in 1930 to support the use of contraception, under appropriate criteria, within marriage (Lambeth Conference, 1958: Resolution 115). Nearly all Protestant Churches tacitly, if not explicitly, agreed with this. The expectation that the Roman Catholic Church would come to a similar conclusion a decade later was dashed when Pope Paul VI declined the advice of the papal commission he had set up and in 1968 published *Humanae vitae* instead.

12.2.1 Anglicans say "yes, but . . ."

In 1930 the Lambeth Conference representing Anglican churches throughout the world, approved of the use of contraception, that is of the use of condoms, in particular circumstances. It was the first statement of approval of contraception of any major Christian church, and it included "Christian principles" governing their use. Resolution 15 stated:

> Where there is clearly felt moral obligation to limit or avoid parenthood, the method must be decided on Christian principles. The primary and obvious method is complete abstinence from intercourse (as far as may be necessary) in a life of discipline and self-control lived in the power of the Holy Spirit. Nevertheless in those cases where there is such a clearly felt moral obligation to limit or avoid parenthood, and where there is a morally sound reason for avoiding complete abstinence, the Conference agrees that other methods may be used, provided that this is done in the light of the same Christian principles. The Conference records its strong condemnation of the use of any methods of conception control from motives of selfishness, luxury, or mere convenience.

More than 80 years have passed since this resolution was passed. There are at least five guiding principles embedded in the resolution, all of which indicate how differently contraception is practiced today.

Contraceptive principles First, couples must be married. Any extension of the use of contraception outside marriage would have been unthinkable.

Second, couples must be under "a felt moral obligation to limit or avoid parenthood." It was not enough merely to wish to have few or no children or to postpone their arrival. Moral obligations are stronger, verifiable reasons, such as belief in parental inability to provide for children, or for further children; or risk to the health of the mother, or likelihood of a child seriously deformed being born.

Third, the Conference uses strong language to exclude "motives of selfishness, luxury, or mere convenience." Couples may not use contraception because they wish to separate procreation from pleasure; or because children are likely to lower their parents' standard of living, or (again unthinkably) because married women might wish to pursue a career.

Fourth, abstinence from full sex is better than having contracepted sex. Couples under an obligation to limit or avoid births have the choice between the preferred method of abstinence from sex and "other methods." The rhythm method of contraception was insufficiently well known in 1930 for the Conference to take it into account. The influence of St. Paul (1 Cor. 7:5) is obvious here. Paul approved of abstinence from sex *for short periods*, but was aware of the dangers of abstinence for longer ones. His "concession" (1 Cor. 7:6) becomes the chief unspoken reason why other methods than abstinence are permitted. The Conference is clear that abstinence is better than indulgence, and the former is an appropriate expectation within an ordered and disciplined Christian life.

Fifth, there must be a "morally sound reason" why complete abstinence is impossible. This presumably is the honest admission that managing without sex is too difficult or unnecessarily demanding (Paul would have been happy with these reasons).

The Lambeth bishops in 1930 affirmed sex outside marriage to be a "grievous sin," noted an increasing use of contraceptives among the unmarried, and resolved to press for legislation "forbidding the exposure for sale and the unrestricted advertisement of contraceptives, and placing definite restriction upon their purchase" (Resolution 18). They would be astonished and dismayed at the widespread use of contraception now, inside and outside marriage, just because it does not conform to their statement of principles.

> *Activity:* I have not come across any comparable statement of Christian principles for the use of contraception. Do you think Christians can continue to affirm these principles, or should they be modified or supplemented in some way?

12.2.2 Catholics say "no . . . never"

The response of the Vatican was swift and robust. Pope Pius XI's rebuttal was published on the last day of 1930 in *On Chaste Marriage* (*Casti connubii*). Here contraception was depicted as the first of the "vices opposed to Christian marriage," and a "criminal abuse" (section 53). The Pope's principal argument was that nothing which is "intrinsically against nature may become conformable to nature and morally good." Contraception was "shameful and intrinsically vicious" (section 54). With specific reference to the Lambeth decision, the Pope declared,

> Since, therefore, openly departing from the uninterrupted Christian tradition some recently have judged it possible solemnly to declare another doctrine regarding this question, the Catholic Church, to whom God has entrusted the defense of the integrity and purity of morals, standing erect in the midst of the moral ruin which surrounds her, in order that she may preserve the chastity of the nuptial union from being defiled by this foul stain, raises her voice in token of her divine ambassadorship and through Our mouth proclaims anew: *any use whatsoever of matrimony exercised in such a way that the act is deliberately frustrated in its natural power to generate life is an offense against the law of God and of nature, and those who indulge in such are branded with the guilt of a grave sin.* (Pope Pius XI, 1930, section 56; emphasis added)

While contraception of any kind was absolutely proscribed, the use of infertile periods (about which little was still known) for having sex was a permitted exception. There were Catholics "who in the married state use their right [to having sex] in the proper manner although on account of natural reasons *either of time or of certain defects*, new life cannot be brought forth" (section 59; emphasis added). They are not to be "considered as acting against nature."

Both Lambeth and Pius XI accepted that there was a "primary" end of marriage, procreation, and also secondary ends such as mutual help and love. These secondary ends were used to establish what became known as the "rhythm method" for the spacing of births, and in allowing this practice, the Pope directly affirmed, for the first time, the value of mutual love between the spouses:

> For in matrimony as well as in the use of the matrimonial rights there are also secondary ends, such as mutual aid, *the cultivating of mutual love*, and the quieting of concupiscence which husband and wife are not forbidden to consider so long as they are subordinated to the primary end and so long as the intrinsic nature of the act is preserved. (Pope Pius XI, 1930, section 59; emphasis added)

12.3 Contraception and Natural Law

A principal argument against adopting the Anglican position in 1930 was based on Natural Law. (For an examination of the technical and controversial "New Natural Law Theory", see Bamforth and Richards, 2008; Salzman and Lawler, 2008, pp. 48–92.) The quotation above makes that very clear. It played a large part in Pope Paul VI's encyclical *Humanae vitae* in 1968 which continued to forbid all Catholic Christians to use contraception, while allowing married couples to make love during infertile periods (Natural Family Planning, or NFP). We will look at this encyclical next.

The "sin against nature"   Paul VI discerned that "God has wisely ordered laws of nature and the incidence of fertility in such a way that successive births are already naturally spaced through the inherent operation of these laws" (1968, section 11). The monthly cycle of women was not fully understood in 1930, but by 1968 the Church was able not simply to accept the new understanding but to affirm that this cycle is itself a product of the Natural Law which Catholics must obey.

God has seen to it that women are infertile most of the time, and does not forbid having sex during those times. However, during fertile times the Natural Law teaches that, apart from abstinence from sex, fertility is not to be suppressed.

> The Church, nevertheless, in urging men to the observance of the precepts of the natural law, which it interprets by its constant doctrine, teaches that each and every marital act must of necessity retain its intrinsic relationship to the procreation of human life.

"Today," says the Pontifical Council for the Family, writing in 1996, "the scientific basis of the natural methods for the regulation of fertility are recognized" (section 35), and abstinence from sex during fertile periods is to be "inserted into the pedagogy and process of the growth of love," thereby leading spouses to "practice periodic continence." This language requires some unpacking.

Refraining from sex in fertile periods becomes a discipline of withholding which fosters self-control, and self-control is thought to enhance the couple's relationship and so increase the growth of love. (Does it also rekindle exhausted passions?) Church and society both require "responsible parenthood." This is "rooted in the objective moral order established by God – and only an upright conscience can be a true interpreter of this order."

Conscience, however, cannot be the only arbiter of decisions about abstinence from sex in fertile periods, for

> in regard to the mission of transmitting human life, it is not right for spouses to act in accord with their own arbitrary judgment, as if it were permissible for them to define together subjectively and wilfully what is right for them to do. (Pope Paul VI, 1968, section 10)

Activity: You may find it helpful to re-read Section 10.2.2, on Natural Law, its uses in Catholic teaching forbidding homosexual practice, and the difficulties associated with its use. We are about to find some difficulties regarding the use of Natural Law in relation to contraception, and then to compare these with the difficulties discovered in relation to homosexuality.

12.3.1 Yet more difficulties with Natural Law

There appear to be various difficulties in the advocacy of Natural Family Planning as the only allowable method of contraception.

First, there seems to be a good argument, used by Anglican bishops in 1958, that human beings are not bound by anything called "Natural Law" at all. That is because they are not wholly embedded in nature, but are also above it, and so are able to act decisively upon it and improve it. In the language of their time they concluded that "man" is "at once a child of nature, and a spirit standing outside nature" (Lambeth Conference Study Guide, 1958, p. 145). Human sexuality is "demonstrably supranatural," and "the fact that man in his freedom stands above nature" leads the writers to conclude that "contraception is morally right in certain circumstances."

With an eye on Roman teaching they even doubted whether there was any such activity as *natural* sex, holding it to be "pertinent, therefore, to ask whether 'natural' *coitus* . . . is not simply an arbitrary *a priori* concept to which there is no correspondence in reality." They preferred the Church to act as a "spiritual adviser" to married couples, helping them to reach their own decisions about sex, while refraining from telling them what to do.

Second, contraception *may* be used for the good of the spouses and their family. Another way of putting the claim that man is a child of nature and a spirit above nature is to evoke language about persons. Persons belong to nature yet are able to transcend it at the same time. So, then, Christian morality is about whole persons and their flourishing, not simply about "acts." An early critic of *Humanae vitae*, Bernard Häring, argued that the "biological functions must be subordinated to the good of the whole person and marriage itself" (1969a, p. 61; see Häring, 1969b, pp. 176–192). He held that contraceptives forbidden by the Vatican, but used to ensure stability within marriage and the best means of responsible parenthood, fell "in the same category as insulin injections for diabetics, hearing aids, false teeth, organ transplants, plastic surgery, blood transfusions, or any other intrusion or frustration of nature for the good of the total organism and community life." In other words, contraceptives may belong to the class of medical interventions that are able to improve on the state of nature and to increase the sense of the wholeness of the person.

Third, as Catholic writers have pointed out, the Vatican position that Natural Law does not allow contraception, may be damagingly compared with other assertions that are clearly absurd. Suppose the Natural Law can be expressed this way: "We may not use contraceptives, since God made man without such aids." Next, compare that assertion with these daft assertions:

1. Since God has created only black and white sheep, we should not dye woollen clothes blue and red.
2. Since God sends rain, we should not open an umbrella.
3. Since God created day and night, we should not use artificial light to illuminate the night. (Steininger, 1969, pp. 125–126)

Contraception by another name?   Fourth, couples who deliberately abstain from love-making during fertile periods but who make love at other times, *do* appear to be practicing contraception by another name. This is because not having sex at certain times is not just not doing anything, and so not doing anything wrong. As Gareth Moore points out, "They do not just not have intercourse; they actively avoid intercourse, as part of their plan to avoid children" (2001, p. 165). Their intentions are clear.

While the practice began to be allowed in 1930, it seems to be at odds with that encyclical's portentous condemnation of "any use whatsoever of matrimony exercised in such a way that the act is deliberately frustrated in its natural power to generate life." If the term "contraception" can "be applied to any behavior that prevents conception" (Noonan, 1986, p. 1), then these couples are practicing contraception. They intend not to have children and to separate love-making from baby-making.

Fifth, the physiological knowledge on which NFP is based sits poorly with the older tradition of Natural Law which, by modern standards, knew nothing about the processes of human fertilization, ovulation, and conception. Full knowledge of all of these has been available only for the last two-thirds of the twentieth century (Thatcher, 1999, p. 183). The difficulty is not that the theological teaching relies on recent medical knowledge, or that this knowledge has shown earlier versions of "the rhythm method" (which wrongly dated infertile periods) to have been useless and counterproductive. The conclusion is hard to avoid that NFP, medically verified and understood only from the 1930s on, is seized on and commended in the 1950s and 1960s, and subsequently, in order to shore up antiquated understandings of how nature works. It may also act as a concession to the millions of fertile couples who are officially forbidden to use contraceptive methods that the Vatican considers unnatural.

Sixth, there is a difficulty surrounding "responsible parenthood" as Paul VI understands it. Responsible parents are "required to recognize their duties toward God, toward them-selves, toward the family, and toward human society." When they follow this requirement, they may do so in tacit or pre-conscious ways. But a consequence of the official Catholic understanding may actually be *irresponsibility*.

In fulfilling these responsibilities they are *not* free to decide for themselves, for as we have just seen, they must be obedient to formal Catholic teaching and may not use "their own arbitrary judgment." Their exercise of responsibility is cramped. The obligation seems to require a theological erudition few mothers and fathers can match, and it may compare poorly with the Anglican way of leaving the matter to the consciences of married people while confining the role of the church to be spiritual advisor.

> *Activity:* We have looked at Natural Law arguments in relation to homosexual acts (Section 10.2.2), and now in relation to heterosexual marriage acts. Are there any difficulties in Natural Law arguments that apply in both cases?

> *Comment:* I think the second, third, and fifth difficulties at Section 10.2.2 also apply here. The difficulty that the appeal to nature always requires someone to interpret or construct it is relevant here, isn't it (because we might have problems with the construction the Vatican offers)? Both analyses commit the "naturalistic fallacy." And the insistence that procreation should always be a purpose of having sex looks dubious in both cases.

We have just considered the idea that persons stand to some extent outside nature (because they are also spiritual beings). That is a consideration that also makes sense when considering same-sex relationships.

12.3.2 Learning from "nature"

Natural Law arguments, then, should convince no one. But that does not mean that every appeal to nature, however constructed, is worthless. Yes, there are elements of Natural Law that are more than just salvageable. The world is created by God, and all Christians agree in finding, to different degrees, the mind of the Creator in the creation.

First, any appeal to nature or Natural Law encourages us to look for basic considerations that are fundamental to being human, discoverable by human reason, and logically prior to historical change or social construction. One such consideration is that heterosexual sexuality cannot be finally separated from reproductive capacity and so from prospective parenthood.

Second, NFP actually works. There are good reasons for commending it. Natural methods make a couple more aware of their fertility. They provide a self-knowledge that comes about through heightened body-awareness, through listening, observing, touching, sensing. They can be used to plan pregnancies as well as prevent them.

> *Activity:* Might you like to find out more about Natural Family Planning? It is not the first choice for straight couples having sex, and there remains widespread ignorance about it. Most Anglophone countries provide information about it on official websites. For example, in the United States, the American Academy of Family Physicians has a website (http://familydoctor.org). In the United Kingdom, the National Health Service is a reliable source of information (www.nhs.uk/Livewell/Contraception/Pages/Naturalfamilyplanning.aspx). The United States Conference of Catholic Bishops provides a good official Catholic source (www.usccb.org/prolife/issues/nfp/intronfp091211.shtml). All the websites stress the importance of receiving tuition in NFP before practicing it.

Third, there are several connections between "natural" and "pre-modern" contraception (see Section 12.1.1). The basic difference, of course, is that the pre-modern contraception described earlier in the chapter was non-penetrative, while NFP clearly is. Natural methods proclaim that none of the modern paraphernalia of chemicals, hormones, implants, injections, bits of copper, plastic or rubber, and so on, are needed to enjoy sex without becoming pregnant. These methods apply whether couples are married or not, but they have particular relevance for couples who are initiating intimacy or just beginning the journey into marriage. Chastity (see Section 11.4) may be the means whereby the standard assumptions about phallocentric behavior, the normativity of penetration as standard sexual activity, and the continuous availability of women's bodies are deliberately subverted in the name of a mutual tenderness and joint responsibility.

Popes and feminists agree!   Fourth, there is a remarkable congruence between the refusal of contraception by the Vatican and the objections to it posed by early twentieth century feminism. It is well known that feminists were much in favor of condom use, because it allowed them greater control over their fertility. It is not at all well known that, a century ago, other feminists opposed contraception using similar arguments to those adopted by Pope Paul VI in 1968. This is indeed a strange convergence (Thatcher, 2000).

Lucy Re-Bartlett and other feminists, with no idea that they were proclaiming long-standing Christian teaching, held that "Sex union in the human being should be limited strictly to the actual needs of creation" (Jeffreys, 1987, p. 51). Re-Bartlett could see that the condom, by greatly reducing the risk of pregnancy, removed the main reason for not having sex. She argued that "frigidity" was invented in this period. Women who refused sex after condoms were readily available were deemed to be pathologically odd. They were "frigid." While Marie Stopes and everyone else in the birth control movement thought they were restoring to women control over their fertility and sexuality, an alternative interpretation of their achievements held that they were "in many respects undermining the sexual autonomy of women even further" (Jackson, 1994, p. 173).

The coital imperative   Margaret Jackson strikingly summed up twentieth century sexology as an affirmation of what she called, by a striking phrase, "the coital imperative," which contraception encouraged and enforced. The coital imperative, she argued, legitimized "male sexual violence and exploitation and undermined both the campaign for an equal moral standard and the construction of a feminist model of sexuality." In her damning judgment, contraception helped to promote "a form of heterosexuality and sexual pleasure which eroticized male dominance and female submission, and pathologized all manifestations of female sexual autonomy or resistance, including spinsterhood, lesbianism and 'frigidity'" (Jackson, 1994, p. 183).

12.4 Sex and Love: An "Unbreakable Connection"?

Humanae vitae insisted on there being two meanings of marital sex, the personal or "unitive" meaning, and the reproductive or "procreative" meaning. According to the new fledgling orthodoxy of that document, there is an "inseparable connection, established by God, which man on his own initiative may not break, between the unitive significance and the procreative significance which are both inherent to the marriage act" (Pope Paul VI, 1968, section 12). Artificial contraception is wrong because it breaks the connection.

There is a principal reason given for the unbreakable connection (which alert readers will recognize as "essentialist" – see Section 2.1.1). The "marriage act" has a "fundamental nature," which

> while uniting husband and wife in the closest intimacy, also renders them capable of generating new life – and this as a result of laws written into the actual nature of man and of woman. And if each of these essential qualities, the unitive and the procreative, is preserved, the use of marriage fully retains its sense of true mutual love and its ordination to the supreme responsibility of parenthood to which man is called.

There is an obvious corollary: if the link is broken the marriage loses its sense of true mutual love.

The gift of self   The unbreakable connection was many times reiterated by Pope John Paul II, and quickly became settled moral doctrine. In 1995 he even depicted it as "the constant teaching of the church" (section 12). He warned that a couple breaking the connection by using contraception "degrade human sexuality and with it themselves and their married partner by altering its value of 'total' self-giving" (1981, section 32).

The "sincere gift of self" has its own "logic." Any holding back from reproductive opportunity is also a holding back of the self, and so cannot be a whole-hearted self-giving. The unitive and procreative dimensions of marriage "cannot be artificially separated without damaging the deepest truth of the conjugal act itself (1995, section 10). As a consequence even contraceptive practice that avoids penetration altogether is also forbidden. It cannot be an expression of love because a true expression of love has to be capable of producing life.

> There must be a rejection of all acts that attempt to impede procreation, both those chosen as means to an end and those chosen as ends. This includes acts that precede intercourse, acts that accompany intercourse, and acts that are directed to the natural consequences of intercourse. (Pope Paul VI, 1968, section 14)

12.4.1 Breaking with the unbreakable connection

These are dark, opaque warnings, which appear to be unable to name the very activities that remain forbidden. Is there not a fear of all forms of sexual intimacy except the one which conforms to God's reproductive plan? Again, there are difficulties. The claim that the procreative and unitive meanings of marriage cannot be broken is recent, and if it is successful it would provide a new argument against contraception. Here are some reasons why it may *not* succeed.

First, there is a suspicious ring about the centrality of love in the doctrine of marriage. The use of contraceptives is said to impair the spouses' mutual love. However welcome the emphasis on mutual love, it is a very late development in Catholic thought. It is none the worse for that, of course, but it sits uncomfortably alongside Natural Law considerations and traditional discussions of contraception.

Second, we might ask *why* it is that the link between procreation and union cannot be broken. To write the unbreakable connection into the "marriage act" and to insist that the act has a fundamental nature, tells us nothing about what married people actually do. Married people may wish, as an *expression* of mutual love, to separate union from procreation, something "nature" in any case may be said to achieve for them most of the time. Why should they believe that this cannot validly be done or that it is contrary to God's laws?

Whether an act of love represents total self-giving is presumably better assessed by the spouses themselves, rather than by essentialist considerations about what must necessarily be the case for all marriages. Put another way, self-giving is better assessed on *existential*, not *metaphysical* grounds.

Every time?   Third, why should we assume *all* love-making, every marriage act must be potentially open to new life? Why could the couple not cooperate with God in the mission of procreation by being open to new life just *sometimes*? That every act of love-making be subjected to these stringent criteria of marriage is said by one positive Catholic theologian to combine "a preposterous ... harmful and even oppressive suggestion" with "an unreal idealization of sex acts" which "can demean married persons' positive experience of sexuality" (Cahill, 1996, p. 204). The Anglican position, and that of the overwhelming majority of theologians advising the Pope, is that a marriage as a totality should be open to new life, not that all sex within marriage ought to be (Hogan, 1993).

So it is fair to conclude that the unbreakable connection is readily breakable, and that as a new argument forbidding contraception it fails. Noonan's long-concealed impatience with the teaching of *Humanae vitae* finally surfaces at the end of his long book:

> That intercourse must be only for a procreation purpose, that intercourse in menstruation is mortal sin, that intercourse in pregnancy is forbidden, that intercourse has a natural position – all these were once common opinions of the theologians and are so no more. Was the commitment to an absolute prohibition of contraception more conscious, more universal, more complete, than to these now obsolete rules? (1968, section 532)

Question: The last few paragraphs have criticized the alleged unbreakable connection between the two basic meanings of marital sex. Do you think these criticisms are over-hasty? Is there an abiding truth in the Catholic insistence on this connection?

Comment: Perhaps the criticisms *do* proceed a little too quickly? It takes only a moment's thought to admit that any genital contact between straight couples involves organs which are also reproductive. Sometimes it is necessary to state something obvious. It is necessary to state this because contracepted sex can become so routine that the reproductive purpose of sex can get forgotten, and with it part of its meaning.

12.5 Moral Deficit Arguments

We are still not quite finished with Catholic arguments against contraception. A third type of argument is based on the "moral deficits" and the "sinful mentalities" associated with their use. They contribute to a culture of death or are already a consequence of such a culture. Pope Paul VI held contraception "could open wide the way for marital infidelity and a general lowering of moral standards" (1968, section 17). The young in particular, he warned, "who are so exposed to temptation – need incentives to keep the moral law, and it is an evil thing to make it easy for them to break that law." Contraception is a further disincentive.

Another effect that gave cause for papal alarm was that

> a man who grows accustomed to the use of contraceptive methods may forget the reverence due to a woman, and, disregarding her physical and emotional equilibrium, reduce her to being a mere instrument for the satisfaction of his own desires, no longer considering her as his partner whom he should surround with care and affection. (1968, section 17)

"Public authorities" and "governments" who "care little for the precepts of the moral law" may pursue policies of birth limitation, using the very means that the Vatican finds deeply objectionable (1968, section 17). Finally, contraceptive users will mistakenly think they have unlimited power over their bodies, whereas "there are certain limits, beyond which it is wrong to go, to the power of man over his own body and its natural functions." These are limits "which no one, whether as a private individual or as a public authority, can lawfully exceed." Since all these predictions are said to have come true, Paul VI has been declared a prophet (Smith, 1993, pp. 499–518).

12.5.1 Four sinful mentalities

The four "sinful mentalities"

- The contraceptive mentality
- The hedonistic mentality
- The consumer mentality
- The anti-life mentality

In the thought of John Paul II the "contraceptive mentality" was associated with three other mentalities, "hedonistic," "consumer," and "anti-life."

The "contraceptive mentality," was associated with

> a corruption of the idea and the experience of freedom, conceived not as a capacity for realizing the truth of God's plan for marriage and the family, but as an autonomous power of self-affirmation, often against others, for one's own selfish well-being." (Pope John Paul II, 1981, section 6)

Contraception, then, is direct evidence of selfishness. By 1995 the tone becomes more strident, the objects of the Pope's opprobrium more specific. In *Evangelium vitae* contraception and abortion are linked with a "culture of death," a "conspiracy against life," and another negative mentality, hedonism.

> It is true that in many cases contraception and even abortion are practised under the pressure of real-life difficulties, which nonetheless can never exonerate from striving to observe God's law fully. Still, in very many other instances such practices are rooted in a hedonistic mentality unwilling to accept responsibility in matters of sexuality, and they imply a self-centered concept of freedom, which regards procreation as an obstacle to personal fulfilment. The life which could result from a sexual encounter thus becomes an enemy to be avoided at all costs, and abortion becomes the only possible decisive response to failed contraception. (Pope John Paul II, 1981, section 13; see also Pontifical Council for the Family, 1996, section 49)

Investment in both contraception and abortion is evidence of a "veritable structure of sin." The "'moral conscience'" of societies "tolerates or fosters behavior contrary to life," and "encourages the 'culture of death,' creating and consolidating actual 'structures of sin' which go against life."

Alternatively contraception is associated with *consumer* and *anti-life* mentalities. Couples "imprisoned in a consumer mentality" value money more than babies. Their "sole concern is to bring about a continual growth of material goods," and they end up "by ceasing to understand ... the spiritual riches of a new human life." Pope John Paul II concludes "The ultimate reason for these mentalities is the absence in people's hearts of God, whose love alone is stronger than all the world's fears and can conquer them." An "anti-life mentality" is born, and this is reflected in panic about population growth. There are two cultures, the "culture of life" and the "culture of death" (1995, sections 21, 24).

12.5.2 Criticisms of moral deficit arguments

These arguments combine deeply held convictions held by almost all Christians with contentious claims, which detract from the extent of agreement that may already exist. Several questions are raised by moral deficit arguments. Here are some of them:

First, would it not be more effective (and less strident) to seek to *modify* the use of contraceptives instead of forbidding them completely? They cannot be uninvented, but their use is able to be modified. Analogous cases might be provided by the use of the motor car or the consumption of alcohol. Cars have become an environmental nuisance but fewer journeys in smaller vehicles seem preferable to the elimination of them all. In a similar way the appropriate modification of the sale of alcohol seems preferable to the banning of its sale altogether.

Second, might not the moral deficit arguments actually encourage the *loss* of responsibility and respect, two personal qualities they aim to protect? Couples having sex in relationships, which do not have the approval of the churches, may nonetheless be exercising responsibility in safeguarding against pregnancy. While promiscuous sex may well lead to a loss of respect for the body of one's partner (as well as one's own), it is not at all obviously true that in marriages where there has been no contraception, husbands' respect for their wives was always maintained.

Limits to population growth?   Third, does not the projected rise in global population make unpopular birth-limitation policies inevitable? World population is expected to grow from 6.1 billion in 2000 to 8.9 billion in 2050, increasing by 47% (United Nations, 2004, p. 4). A principled argument exists that in at least some countries it would be better for fewer children to be born. It is possible to be broadly "pro-life" while arguing also for population limitation.

Fourth, there are few signs that the "culture of life" which the Church unwaveringly supports is being extended to, say, experimentation on animals, or the factory-farming of chickens or veal calves, or the killing of migrating birds or wild animals for sport. "Serving life" might carry more conviction if it were environmentally as well as fetally worked out.

Fifth, isn't it difficult to see how the temporary suspension of fertility contributes to an unwholesome transgression of the body's natural limits? Couples who postpone the advent of children in order to establish careers, or to pay off their university or college tuition fees, or afford the down payment on a house and subsequent mortgage, may be offended by the suggestion that consumerism drives and ultimately corrupts their intentions.

> *Question:* This question is similar to the last one. The last few paragraphs have raised some questions about papal teaching about the moral deficiencies of contraceptive use. Do you think these criticisms are over-hasty? Is there an abiding truth in the papal analysis of sinful mentalities?

> *Comment:* Again, perhaps the criticisms *do* proceed too quickly. If you are a Christian or a Roman Catholic prepared to be both appreciative but also critical of papal teaching, you will have a problem. You are likely to think this teaching combines fundamental theological insights about sex, love, and marriage, with conclusions drawn from these that are difficult to establish. I think the analysis of the sinful mentalities is both valuable and true if it is understood as a commentary on promiscuity and on the social conditions that encourage it. When the analysis is taken into marriage itself or to couples preparing for marriage, at that point I switch off.

12.6 Condoms in the Time of HIV/AIDS

In recent years a terrifying pandemic has fallen upon the human race, the arrival of the human immunodeficiency virus (HIV), which leads to full-blown AIDS (acquired immunodeficiency syndrome). From its discovery in 1981 to 2006, AIDS has killed more than 25 million people. A particular contraceptive, the condom, is highly effective in preventing the transmission of the virus. That is, its use may primarily be for the purpose of protection from infection. In this case it is a *prophylactic*, that is a medication or a treatment designed and used to prevent a disease from occurring.

Arguments about contraception acquire a different dimension altogether in the context of HIV/AIDS. Condoms were originally used as a prophylactic in the mid-nineteenth century so that the military could avoid syphilis when having sex with prostitutes. In relation to the virus that causes AIDS, the failure to use condoms, still forbidden even in these circumstances by the Catholic Church, may result not simply in failing to avoid becoming pregnant, but in failing to prevent one's own untimely death.

HIV: the epidemic   There is some good news about the global HIV/AIDS epidemic (UNAIDS, 2008, p. 5). The global percentage of people living with HIV has stabilized since 2000, but the overall number of people living with HIV has increased as a result both of the ongoing number of new infections each year and the beneficial effects of more widely available antiretroviral therapy, which keeps larger numbers of infected people alive.

Sub-Saharan Africa remains most heavily affected by HIV, accounting for 67% of all people living with HIV and for 72% of AIDS deaths in 2007. The global epidemic is stabilizing but at an unacceptably high level. There were an estimated 33 million people living with HIV in 2007. The annual number of new HIV infections declined from 3.0 million in 2001 to 2.7 million in 2007. In sub-Saharan Africa, most national epidemics have stabilized or begun to decline. However, in Kenya and in other countries outside Africa, infections are on the rise.

Increasing condom use is one of the most important elements of a global HIV-prevention strategy. UNAIDS advised in 2009 that "the male latex condom is the single, most efficient, available technology to reduce the sexual transmission of HIV and other sexually transmitted infections." This is an evidence-based judgment. This should be preferred to the misinformation on various religious websites that it offers poor protection or that the HI virus is small enough to leak through it.

Other factors mentioned in prevention were "delay of sexual initiation, abstinence, being safer by being faithful to one's partner when both partners are uninfected and consistently faithful, reducing the number of sexual partners, correct and consistent use of condoms, and male circumcision."

There is unanimity among Christians in the belief that casual, promiscuous sex is morally wrong and harmful to those involved. Most Protestant Christians are likely to think that while having illicit sex is wrong, it is not wrong, if one is having illicit sex, to protect oneself from infection. But that is not the official position of the Roman Catholic Church, and many Catholic theologians, doctors, and medical staff of Catholic hospitals and missions have great difficulty with it. We have found the case for opposition to contraception within marriage very weak. We may soon conclude that opposition to condoms as a prophylactic is not only very weak but self-defeating for a Church that condemns the culture of death and frequently proclaims itself to be pro-life.

12.6.1 Principles, prophylactics, and prevention

Early on in the epidemic Catholic moral theologians had used principles from the Catholic tradition that had seemed at the time to justify a change to the official ban in the context of HIV. While these principles may seem cerebral and distant from concrete cases, they successfully and dispassionately overcome the apparently rational case for condom prohibition. There are at least four principles:

Four moral principles relevant to the prophylactic use of condoms

- The principle of toleration
- The principle of cooperation
- The principle of double effect
- The principle of epikeia

The principle of toleration   Thomas Aquinas stated this principle (1947, sections I–II, Q. 96, A. 2). According to the principle of toleration,

> those who govern ... society ... may at times – where prudence dictates – tolerate the evil actions of others (including some intrinsic evils), if two criteria are met: 1) if a greater good or set of goods would be lost if the evil action were not tolerated; or, 2) if *greater* evils would occur were the original evil not tolerated. (Ascension Health, 2009)

The United States Catholic Conference Administrative Board adopted this principle in the fight against HIV/AIDS as early as 1987. The Conference made plain:

> They were opposed to the promotion or advocacy of condoms, but when faced with a person who could further spread the disease and whose conduct would not be altered, they *tolerated* the advice that the patient should use a condom to prevent the spread of the disease. This position allowed the bishops both to resolve the new case and to protect the material principle that sex is illicit outside of marriage. (Fuller and Keenan, 2005, p. 22; emphasis added)

The principle of cooperation   The principle of cooperation is similar. There are occasions in our morally messy world when it is impossible for an individual to do good in the world, without being involved to some extent in evil (Ascension Health, 2009). In the case of condom distribution, appearing to condone sex outside marriage would be an evil, but cooperating with institutions that aim to promote the common good of HIV prevention, would itself be a good that would outweigh the evil of the action (Keenan, 1988; Kelly, 1991; Rotter, 1992; McDonagh, 1994).

The principle of double effect   When Aquinas discussed the morality of self-defense, he introduced what came to be known as the principle of double effect (1947, sections IIa–IIae Q. 64, art. 7). He wrote "Nothing hinders one act from having two effects, only one of which is intended, while the other is beside the intention." A moral act must be judged by its principal intention, and not by what may accidentally occur "beside" it. "Accordingly the act of self-defense may have two effects, one is the saving of one's life, the other is the slaying of the aggressor." Saving one's life is a right intention: killing the attacker in self-defense is accidental.

The principle may be successfully applied to prophylactic condom use. In the case of a married couple where one partner is infected, the principle is surely effective: condom use is licit. There is no illicit sex being had. In the case of governments or agencies seeking to slow down the spread of the virus, and in the case of individuals having extra-marital sex, but seeking to protect themselves from a potentially fatal disease, the question is a little different. The agencies and individuals suspend moral judgment about the activity of extra-marital sex in favor of preventing infection and saving lives.

The principle of epikeia   The term derives from a Greek adjective meaning "reasonable." Aquinas found the term in Aristotle and developed it into a Christian virtue. He argued that law-makers could not foresee future cases where their laws did not apply – "it was not possible to lay down rules of law that would apply to every single case." Aquinas clearly states that "if the law be applied to certain cases it will frustrate the equality of justice and be injurious to the common good, which the law has in view" (1947, section II–II. Qn. 120). There are even cases where "it is bad to follow the law, and it is good to set aside the letter of the law and to follow the dictates of justice and the common good." *Epikeia* is what enables us to distinguish such cases. In some cases, "To follow the letter of the law when it ought not to be followed is sinful."

The principle of *epikeia* seems effective in overturning versions of Natural Law which do not allow condom use on the ground that any version formulated before the onset of HIV would have been unable to take the virus into account. According to the principle, the dictates of justice and the common good *are* served by the prophylactic use of condoms, and advocates of condom use at least as a prophylactic may therefore be praised for exercising a Christian virtue.

All four principles have been tragically set aside by the Roman Magisterium, even in the death-dealing context of HIV. In a well-known letter Cardinal Ratzinger (1988) almost immediately rebutted the use of the principle of tolerance in the case of the prophylactic use of condoms. While claiming that condoms were "insufficiently reliable," he insisted the main reason for rejection was that

> Such a proposal for "safe" or at least "safer" sex – as they say – ignores the real cause of the problem, namely, the permissiveness which, in the area of sex as in that related to other abuses, corrodes the moral fiber of the people.

In a sad attempt to achieve closure of any speculation about a change to the Vatican line by means of the principle of tolerance, he ruled,

> In the case here under discussion, it hardly seems pertinent to appeal to the *classical principle of tolerance of the lesser evil* on the part of those who exercise responsibility for the temporal good of society. In fact, even when the issue has to do with educational programs promoted by the civil government, one would not be dealing simply with a form of passive toleration but rather with a kind of behavior which would result in at least the facilitation of evil. (emphasis added)

Non-Catholic Christians are generally aghast that purity of moral doctrine matters more than HIV-prevention. These principles cry out for application in the context of HIV, and the failure to apply them is itself arguably an instance of a lack of the very *epikeia* that the Catholic tradition advocates. They could have helped to bring about the doctrinal and moral development that is clearly needed.

12.6.2 From ABC to SAVE

A standard mantra used in HIV-prevention programs was ABC, **A**bstinence; **B**eing faithful to one partner for life; Using **C**ondoms. There was a "descending order of acceptability" about this advice, with abstinence remaining the ideal solution, while condoms were recommended only for people who could not control themselves (Paterson, 2009, p. 70). But there were huge problems with this approach to prevention.

Not as easy as ABC   First, as a principle of prevention it "focused exclusively upon sexual behavior and takes no account of mother to child transmission, transmission through injecting drug use, or transmission in healthcare settings" (Paterson, 2009, p. 47).

Second, the ABC approach led people into a false sense of security by encouraging women particularly to think that as long as they were in a monogamous relationship they were safe from the virus. In fact being a wife is high-risk: in Uganda 42% of new infections are contracted within marriage (Paterson, 2009, p. 71). Only 15% of people infected with HIV know that they are (at least initially, and the stigma associated with it is a major disincentive to being tested, even when testing facilities are available).

Third, the problem of gender loomed large. ABC implied "that people who enter into sexual relationships are always in a position to make choices about how, where and with whom they are conducted" (Paterson, 2009, p. 49). This was "manifestly not the case for the majority of the world's women, for young people or for other vulnerable groups." Congolese theologian Ka Mana Kangudie reports that

> The ABC message is not only useless to women, but also to men who believe that abstinence reduces virility, "being faithful" reduces male power and vital force and condoms block body tubes and the flow of vital juices and thus masculinity. (in Paterson, 2009, p. 49)

SAVE   On the other hand, SAVE embraces a more comprehensive prevention policy: **S**afer practice, **A**vailable medical interventions, **V**oluntary counseling and testing, and **E**mpowerment (Heath, 2009, pp. 71–72). SAVE is more about public prevention policy, whereas ABC was about individuals' self-protection. Each category itself contains a list of factors. For example, "Safer practice" includes abstinence, the delay of sexual début, mutual fidelity within a committed relationship; the use of vaginal microbiocides; needle exchange; use of condoms, and sterile implements in surgery. The use of condoms becomes just one item in a long list of safer practices. But it remains a key, effective item.

12.6.3 Transforming gender as a preventive measure

In 2003 UNAIDS established a theological workshop that had on its agenda the identification of "those aspects of Christian theology that endorse or foster stigmatizing attitudes and behavior towards people living with HIV and AIDS and those around them"

(UNAIDS, 2005, p. 11). It noted that women's risk of infection is hugely increased by "extensive theoretical and practical gender inequalities ... unequal power-relations give women a subordinate position and make them submissive to men" (Kelly, 2006, pp. xiv, 26–31). How did we ever get this way?

Women's donkey work   A report on religious women in Malawi concluded that "religious groups do little to nothing to change socially structured gender inequalities." Religious institutions "do little to support women" or lighten their "multiple burdens." Indeed, "Women's 'donkey work,' as countenanced and indirectly supported by religious attitudes, beliefs, and practices regarding sexual activity, results in at-risk sexual behavior, primarily sex work, as a means of sheer survival" (Rankin et al., 2005, pp. 13–14). That judgment could be made in many other countries. The very firmness of the churches' teaching about abstinence from pre-marital sex and fidelity in marriage, it is claimed, has underlined the false assumption that HIV infection is God's punishment for disobedience to God's law, irrespective of how the virus was contracted (Scarborough, 2001).

The African theologian Teresa Okure compares the HI virus with two other, meta-phorical viruses which she thinks are even more dangerous (assuming that to be possible): one "assigns women an inferior status to men in society": the other is "global economic injustice" (quoted in Foster, 2005, p. 160). The churches are unanimous (and in my view right) in commending marriage, but marriage "is also the centre of patriarchy, which constructs the subordinate position of African women" (Phiri, 2004, p. 425).

Gender and HIV   Where testing for HIV is available, it is an imperative that everyone in doubt about their HIV-status receives reliable information about it. To infect someone is very far from loving him or her as one loves oneself!

Most of the themes of Chapter 8 apply to defeating the second virus of drastic gender inequality. For example,

1. Christians are invited to think of each other as members of the Body of Christ (see Section 8.1). The bodies of our sexual partners are members of that Body or should be treated as such. That belief generates deep and profound respect for the bodies of any people with whom we share our own.
2. As men and women we *perform* our genders (Section 8.2.1). Knowing this, we can perform our genders more "knowingly," choosing to screen our actions and behavior for signs of misuse of power, of exploitation, deception, and so on.
3. In ancient gender codes, domination and submission in male/female relationships dominates (see Section 8.3). The problem is that, to differing extents, they still do. Christians have a *Dominus*, a Master or Lord, whose teaching and example has the power to reverse notions of domination and identify instead with the dominated.
4. We noted that the Christian tradition has at times associated manliness with sexual renunciation (see Section 8.3.1). The time of HIV is a time for *safer sex*. The renunciation of sex for most of us is impossible, but the renunciation of *unsafe* sex is both possible and urgently necessary. For Christian men and women it is an absolute requirement.

5. We noted in Section 8.3.2 how the eunuch was able to be a model of discipleship. At a time when seminal fluid may carry a deadly virus, there are alternative ways for men to demonstrate their virility. They can measure their prowess instead by the extent of their care and respect. Instead of hegemonic relations of gender, the Body of Christ can be presented as enacting instead relations of gentleness and kindness in the service of everyone. In these and scores of other ways, Christian faith can inform, equip and inspire a generation that has had to face HIV.

This chapter owes much to Catholic thought. It states the issues in its own uncompromising way. It provides materials for all Christians with which to engage. I have engaged with them critically, but not without some appreciation also. While heeding warnings from different Popes, I assume that contraception will play a large part in the account of sexual love to be developed in the next chapter.

References

Aquinas, T. (1947) *Summa Theologica*, Benziger Bros. edn., www.assumption.edu/users/gcolvert/summa/SS/SS154.html#SSQ154A2THEP1 (accessed November 5, 2010).

Ascension Health (2009) *Key Ethical Principles*, www.ascensionhealth.org/index.php?option=com_content&view=article&id=91:principle-of-toleration&Itemid=171 (accessed November 5, 2010).

Bamforth, N.C., and Richards, D.A.J. (2008) *Patriarchal Religion, Sexuality, and Gender: A Critique of New Natural Law*, Cambridge University Press, Cambridge.

Cahill, L.S. (1996) *Sex, Gender and Christian Ethics*, Cambridge University Press, Cambridge.

Cline, S. (1993) *Women, Celibacy and Passion*, André Deutsch, London.

Foster, C. (2005) Disease, suffering, and sin: one Anglican's perspective. *Christian Bioethics*, 12, 157–163.

Fuller, J.D., SJ, and Keenan, J.F., SJ (2005) Introduction: at the end of the first generation of HIV prevention, in *Catholic Ethicists on HIV/AIDS Prevention* (ed. J.F. Keenan SJ with J.D. Fuller, L. Cahill, and K. Kelly), Continuum, New York/London pp. 21–38.

Häring, B. (1969a) The encyclical crisis, in *The Catholic Case for Contraception* (ed. D. Callaghan), Arlington Books, London, pp. 30–41.

Häring, B. (1969b) The inseparability of the unitive–procreative functions of the marital act, in *Contraception, Authority and Dissent* (ed. C.E. Curran), Burns & Oates, London, pp. 176–192.

Heath, J.P. (2009) The need for comprehensive, multi-faceted interventions, in *HIV Prevention: A Global Theological Conversation* (ed. G. Paterson), Ecumenical Advocacy Alliance, Geneva, pp. 69–77.

Hitchcock, T. (1996) Redefining sex in eighteenth century England. *History Workshop Journal*, 41, 73–90.

Hogan, M.M. (1993) *Finality in Marriage*, Marquette University Press, Marquette, WI.

Jackson, M. (1994) *The Real Facts of Life: Feminism and the Politics of Sexuality c.1850–1940*, Taylor & Francis, London.

Jeffreys, S. (1987) *The Spinster and Her Enemies: Feminism and Sexuality*, Pandora, London.

Keenan, J. (1988) Prophylactics, toleration, and cooperation: Contemporary problems and traditional principles. *International Philosophical Quarterly*, 28, 201–220.

Kelly, D. (1991) *Critical Care Ethics*, Sheed & Ward, Kansas City.

Kelly, M.J., SJ (2006) *HIV and AIDS: A Justice Perspective*, Jesuit Centre for Theological Reflection, Lusaka, Zambia.

Lambeth Conference Official Website (1958) Resolutions from 1958. *Resolution 115: The Family in Contemporary Society – Marriage*, www.lambethconference.org/resolutions/1958/1958-115.cfm

Lambeth Conference Study Guide (1958) www.lambethconference.org/lc2008/resources/index.cfm (accessed November 5, 2010).

McDonagh, E. (1994) Theology in a time of AIDS. *Irish Theological Quarterly*, 60, 81–99.

Moore, G., OP (2001) *The Body in Context: Sex and Catholicism*, Continuum, London/New York.

NHS (National Health Service) (2009) *Guide to Contraception*, www.nhs.uk/Livewell/Contraception/Pages/Guidetocontraception.aspx (accessed November 5, 2010).

Noonan, J.T., Jr. (1986) *Contraception: A History of its Treatment by the Catholic Theologians and Canonists*, Harvard University Press, Cambridge, MA.

Paterson, G. (ed.) (2009) *HIV Prevention: A Global Theological Conversation*, Ecumenical Advocacy Alliance, Geneva.

Phiri, I.A. (2004) HIV/AIDS: an African theological response in mission. *Ecumenical Review*, 56.4 422–431.

Pontifical Council for the Family (1996) *Preparation for the Sacrament of Marriage*, www.vatican.va/roman_curia/pontifical_councils/family/documents/rc_pc_family_doc_13051996_preparation-for-marriage-en.html (accessed November 5, 2010).

Pope John Paul II (1981) *Familiaris consortio: On the Role of the Christian Family in the Modern World*, www.vatican.va/holy_father/john_paul_ii/apost_exhortations/documents/hf_jp-ii_exh_19811122_familiaris-consortio_ en.html (accessed November 5, 2010).

Pope John Paul II (1995) *Evangelium vitae*, www.vatican.va/holy_father/john_paul_ii/encyclicals/documents/hf_jp-ii_enc_25031995_evangelium-vitae_en.html (accessed November 5, 2010).

Pope Paul VI (1968) *Humanae vitae*, www.vatican.va/holy_father/paul_vi/encyclicals/documents/hf_p-vi_enc_25071968_humanae-vitae_en.html (accessed November 12, 2010).

Pope Pius XI (1930) *On Chaste Marriage* (*Casti connubii*), www.ourladyswarriors.org/teach/castconn.htm (accessed November 11, 2010).

Rankin, S.H., Lindgren, T., Rankin, W.W., and Ng'oma, J. (2005) Donkey work: women, religion, and HIV/AIDS in Malawi. *Health Care for Women International*, 26, 4–16.

Ratzinger, Cardinal J. (1988) On "the many faces of aids." Letter to Archbishop Pio Laghi. May 29, www.catholic.

org/featured/headline.php?ID=2249 (accessed November 11, 2010).

Rotter, H. (1992) AIDS: some theological and pastoral considerations. *Theology Digest*, 39, 235–239.

Salzman, T.A., and Lawler, M.G. (2008) *The Sexual Person. Toward a Renewed Catholic Anthropology*, Georgetown University Press, Washington, DC.

Scarborough, D. (2001) HIV/AIDS: the response of the Church. *Journal of Constructive Theology*, 7(1) (July), 3–16.

Smith, J.E. (1993) *Humanae vitae* at twenty, in *Why Humanae vitae was Right: A Reader* (ed. J.E. Smith), Ignatius Press, San Francisco, pp. 499–518.

Steininger, V. (1969) *Divorce: Arguments for a Change in the Church's Discipline*, Sheed & Ward, London.

Thatcher, A. (1999) *Marriage after Modernity: Christian Marriage in Postmodern Times*, Sheffield Academic Press, Sheffield.

Thatcher, A. (2000) A strange convergence? Popes and feminists on contraception, in *The Good News of the Body: Sexual Theology and Feminism* (ed. L. Isherwood), Sheffield Academic Press, Sheffield, pp. 136–148.

UNAIDS (2005) *A report of a theological workshop focusing on HIV- and AIDS-related stigma*, December 8–11, Windhoek, Namibia.

UNAIDS (2008) *Report on the Global AIDS Epidemic 2008*, http://data.unaids.org/pub/GlobalReport/2008/JC1511_GR08_ ExecutiveSummary_en.pdf (accessed November 5, 2010).

United Nations Department of Economic and Social Affairs/Population Division (2004) *World Population to 2300*, New York, www.un.org/esa/population/publications/longrange2/ WorldPop2300final.pdf (accessed November 5, 2010).

13

Marriage and the "States of Life"

The conclusions of the last two chapters are put to further use in the present one. The examination of betrothal in the Bible reveals a forgotten understanding of when a marriage begins (Section 13.1). It will be shown that the forgotten practice will prove valuable in thinking about the acquisition of sexual experience and the development of sexual maturity now (Section 13.2). Marriages do not begin with weddings. Weddings solemnize or ratify marriages. It is then shown that many couples who are not yet formally married are nonetheless exercising chastity in their sexual relations (Section 13.3).

13.1 Betrothal in the Bible

In Chapters 5 and 6, the position was taken that Christian sexual morality is a *marital* morality. Alternatives to marriage, such as those based on *justice* and on *friendship*, were found to sidestep the opportunities for developing a renewed marital theology (see Section 5.3). The practice of chastity was strongly defended in Chapter 11. It was suggested there that a new "state of life" be introduced into Christian sexual theology (see Section 11.4.2). However, the proposal of a new "in-between" state of life turns out hardly to be new. Rather it is an old practice, thoroughly rooted in Christian tradition, which awaits retrieval and full recovery. This chapter "excavates" that practice, grounded in Bible and Tradition, called betrothal, or "processual" marriage. If a marital sexual morality is to continue to be preferred to its alternatives, the case for this state of life as a marital one, must be successfully made. Ancient and pre-modern marital practices will turn out to make good sense of this uniform social trend.

God, Sex, and Gender: An Introduction, First Edition. Adrian Thatcher.
© 2011 Adrian Thatcher. Published 2011 by Blackwell Publishing Ltd.

13.1.1 Why betrothal?

I have commended the ancient practice of betrothal elsewhere (Thatcher, 1997, 1998, 1999, 2000, 2001). There is also an extended monograph about it, *Living Together and Christian Ethics* (Thatcher, 2002). I am sanguine about the possibility of reintroducing the ancient betrothal rite to the store of official church liturgies. However, betrothal services happen, and when they do, they constitute admirable practice (Harcus, 2001).

There are three main reasons for commending betrothal. First, we shall shortly see that it is a thoroughly biblical practice. Churches who say they base their practices on the Bible (see Section 3.1.2) are obliged to take betrothal seriously.

Second, betrothal is deeply rooted in the Christian Tradition. For 18 centuries it was continuously practiced. Recalling the fuss made about conformity to Scripture and Tradition as sources for theological thinking about sex (see Sections 3.1 and 3.2), it is remarkable that the churches no longer practice betrothal, and have not reintroduced it, or at least something like it. It was rooted in Tradition and practiced until the eighteenth century.

Third, it provides churches and thoughtful Christian couples, with resources and with precedents, for thinking about living together "before" marriage. It is highly relevant to couples who marry much later than did previous generations. A task of this chapter is to indicate how it can be a state of life within which the virtue of chastity may be acquired and practiced.

The basic distinction: Pre-nuptial and non-nuptial cohabitation   "Pre-nuptial" co-habitors live together before they wed – before they proceed to their *nuptials*. Non-nuptial cohabitors do not intend to marry. They may be avoiding marriage. Between 1960 and 2008 the number of unmarried couples in the United States increased more than twelvefold. Well over half of all first marriages are now preceded by living together, compared to virtually none 50 years ago (Institute for American Values, 2009). In the United Kingdom over three-quarters of marrying couples live together first. Statistics kept over nine years of marriage preparation in the Roman Catholic Archdiocese of Southwark in London reveal the startling conclusion that "couples who do not cohabit are only about 1% of those seeking marriage preparation" (Ball, 2009, p. 33). (The latest figures for cohabitation, and details of the latest research about it in the United States, are available at the Institute for American Values, and the National Marriage Project websites.)

Overall more couples who live together informally, split up and become single than go on to marry. A small minority continues to live together as if permanently married. Non-nuptial cohabitation cannot be commended. Commitment levels, especially those of men, are generally lower. A high proportion of single mothers conceive a child during cohabitation, and the partnership proves transient, leaving them alone. Cohabitors with children are more likely than married couples to split up. (For the likely personal and statistical consequences of non-nuptial cohabitation, see Thatcher, 2002, pp. 3–38.) However, there is also good news about cohabitation. Those couples who intend to marry and live together first, enjoy relationship quality equal to married couples who were formally non-cohabitors. Their marriages last as long. This chapter is about pre-nuptial cohabitors only.

Armed with the important distinction between pre-nuptial and non-nuptial cohabitation it is possible to see how the abandoned practice of betrothal would restore a sense of order and direction to living together before marriage. It provides an alternative account of when marriages begin. The rite of betrothal is retained in the churches of the East (where it is combined with marriage in a single lengthy rite). It was deprived of legal recognition by the Council of Trent in 1563 and in England and Wales only in 1753. It has been written out of the churches' marital scripts for a couple of centuries or more. Even astute theologians barely refer to it and thereby unwittingly confirm its demise.

13.1.2 Jesus chatted up

There are four cases of couples becoming married in the Hebrew Bible which provide insights into early biblical marriage practice. They are Rebecca and Isaac (Gen. 24:1–66), Rachel and Jacob (Gen. 29:1–35), Zipporah and Moses (Exod. 2:15–22), and Sarah and Tobias (Tobit 6–7). (For a full discussion, see Thatcher, 2002, pp. 124–130.) The marriage of Mary and Joseph (Matt. 1:18–25) illustrates well the practice of betrothal.

Activity: If you have time, read one or more of the Hebrew narratives now. The next few paragraphs draw on them.

Betrothal is the assumed means of entry into marriage in the Bible, and in Greek and Roman custom. It is also assumed in the marital imagery of the New Testament. St. Paul compares the Corinthian church to a bride betrothed but not yet presented to Christ her "true and only husband" (2 Cor. 11:2–3). The accounts of the Hebrew marriages just listed contain many similarities. These similarities have prompted the suggestion of a "biblical betrothal type-scene." They include "the encounter of the prospective groom and bride by a well, the act of drawing water, the swift communication of the encounter to the bride's family, followed by a festive meal and a betrothal agreement" (Fuchs, 1993, p. 274).

There is much to discover here about ancient betrothal practice (and also little to emulate, since all four of the betrothed women are treated as chattels at the disposal of men and given no say in the decision to give them away.) However the task is not to berate the narratives because, by our standards, they are sexist (and worse). It is to understand better the theological account of the betrothal of Jesus Christ Himself to His followers in John's Gospel. This will show how central betrothal is to New Testament theology. This centrality is important to grasp; more important than the fascinating details. The narrative assumes the familiarity of its readers with the practice, and it is able to make good theological use of it in commending Jesus as the Messiah to Jews and non-Jews alike.

This is how another New Testament theologian describes the conventions. They include these details:

1. The hero travels to a foreign land far away.
2. The hero stops at a well.
3. A maiden comes to the well.
4. The hero does something for the maiden, showing superhuman strength or ability.
5. The maiden hurries home and reports what has occurred.

6. The stranger is invited into the household of the maiden.
7. The hero marries the maiden-at-the-well. (He will eventually take her back to his native land.) (Williams, 1980, p. 109)

Jesus too, travels to a foreign land, Samaria. He too stops at a well, Jacob's well. A woman comes to the well. Unlike Rebecca and Rachel whose striking physical and virginal attributes are remarked on by the narrators, the Samaritan woman has had five husbands and currently has a live-in lover. Jesus, like Abraham's servant, asks her for a drink. Abraham's servant gives gifts to Rebecca (Gen. 24:22) and her family (24:53). Jesus has "living water" to offer the woman (John 4:10). It is His "superhuman gift."

And the parallels mount up. Just as Rebecca "ran and told her mother's household about these things" (Gen. 24:28), just as Rachel "ran and told her father" (Gen. 29.12), and just as the seven daughters of Reuel returned to him (Exod. 2:18), so, "leaving her water jar, the woman went back to the town and said to the people, 'Come, see a man who told me everything I ever did. Could this be the Christ?'" (John 4:28–29). Jesus stays two days in the woman's town (4:40).

There are other parallels which cannot detain us. In this narrative it is Jesus, not the woman, who has water to offer, and even Samaritans are welcome to drink it. Even the final convention, that of marriage, is not neglected, just adjusted. Jesus does not marry the woman but union with him is possible, even for a Samaritan woman with a chaotic love-life. The use of "We know" (*oidamen*: "we know that this man really is the Savior of the world") at 4:42 can bear the suggestion of a sexual, marital union, along with the more cognitive sense of being "convinced."

Betrothed love   The more important point is that the very gift of salvation is to be understood in the narrative as the self-gift involved in a marriage. It assumes a theology of betrothal in which God takes the initiative of self-giving to all humanity in a relationship of infinite love that is finitely lived out in the loving commitments that make marriage what it is. Christ is again the bridegroom (see Section 6.3.2). There are no worries about virginal status here. The woman who appears in the guise of his betrothed at the well is immoral and aware that Jews regard her racial origin as inferior (John 4:9). Unlike the brides of Ezekiel and Ephesians (see Section 5.2.1) who have to be prepared by the beautician in order to be made ready for the nuptial ceremonies, this woman does not conform to type.

Such is the depth of the love of God for humanity that no one is excluded from its embrace on grounds of religion, sex, or race. Christ in offering them "living water" to drink offers himself. Like all the other encounters that began at a well and led to betrothal and the union of marriage, the encounter with Christ the bridegroom leads to a union of faith and knowledge that has its counterparts in betrothed love. An adequate understanding of the narrative becomes achievable once forgotten betrothal practice is recovered and built into it.

13.2 Betrothal and Tradition

The twelfth century Western church developed two rival theories of what made a marriage. Lombard and the Parisians held that consent alone made the marriage. Gratian and the

Italians held to a two-stage theory of initiation and consummation. The exchange of consent was the first phase; the first time a betrothed couple had sex was the consummation (Brooke, 1989, pp. 126–139; Brundage, 1993, pp. 407–411). This view combined the emphasis in Roman law on marriage being defined by mutual consent, together with the biblical emphasis on marriage as a "one flesh" union of partners.

Consent could be made in either the present tense (*de praesenti*) or the future tense (*de futuro*). Consent in the present tense was marriage. Consent in the future tense was not marriage, but betrothal, the beginning of marriage (*sponsalia*). Betrothal "was dissoluble by mutual agreement or unilaterally for good cause."

13.2.1 The betrothal of Mary and Joseph

There was a strong belief, unquestioned from the fifth century onwards, that the marriage of Mary the mother of Jesus, was never physically consummated. She remained the Virgin, *virgo perpetua*. If it was consent that made a marriage valid, Mary could be seen to have both remained a virgin and still been validly married. Matthew's narrative leaves several questions unanswered:

> [18]This is how the birth of Jesus Christ came about: His mother Mary was pledged to be married to Joseph, but before they came together, she was found to be with child through the Holy Spirit. [19]Because Joseph her husband was a righteous man and did not want to expose her to public disgrace, he had in mind to divorce her quietly.
> [20]But after he had considered this, an angel of the Lord appeared to him in a dream and said, "Joseph son of David, do not be afraid to take Mary home as your wife, because what is conceived in her is from the Holy Spirit." (Matt. 1:18–20)

> [24]When Joseph woke up, he did what the angel of the Lord had commanded him and took Mary home as his wife. [25]But he had no union with her until she gave birth to a son. And he gave him the name Jesus. (Matt. 1:24–25)

Question: Do you think Mary and Joseph were married? If they were not married, why did Joseph have it in mind to divorce her?

Comment: It all depends on when you think marriage begins. The NIV makes a hash of "pledged to be married" (see verse 18 above). It assumes readers will not know what being "betrothed" means. But the King James Version rightly, has "betrothed." Why would he need to "divorce" her if he was only "pledged" to marry her? Whether intentionally or not, the text assumes that betrothal is a *real beginning of marriage*.

If betrothal is not the beginning of marriage, then Mary and Joseph were not married at the time of the conception and birth of Jesus. Whether they were married depends upon a prior view of when marriage begins. This is a forgotten question, of continuing importance. Aquinas and his contemporaries could not have allowed that the Mother of God had undergone the inevitable impurities involved in having sex, even with her husband. Matthew, of course, had no such worries. He merely remarks that Joseph hung on "until she gave birth to a son" (Matt. 1:25). However, the adoption of the consent theory of marriage allowed Mary and Joseph to be considered married, since having sex was thought to be inessential to the marriage.

The "marriage" of Mary and Joseph was a major influence on the consent theory. It is a remarkable historical fact that throughout Christianity today, marriage is thought to rest on the exchange of consent because the sexless marriage of Mary and Joseph had to be regarded as nonetheless a real marriage.

Aquinas dealt with the problem by contending that a marriage was "true" if it conformed to its true purpose of producing and training children (Aquinas, 1920, section 2a2ae.154.2). Carefully side-stepping how in this case the children were produced, he concluded that the sexless marriage of Mary and Joseph was therefore a true marriage.

Question: In Christian teaching marriage is *consummated* the first time the couple have sex. Does anything strike you as odd about this teaching?

Comment: Perhaps the separation of consent and consummation strikes you as odd? The Canadian Catholic André Guindon launched a successful attack on the idea that consummation of a marriage happened the first time a married couple had sex. He asked "What kind of symbolism, what kind of sign-value does a single act of copulation actualize?" (1977, p. 156). He thought the unintended consequence of saying that having sex consummated a marriage was that it made consummation a trivial matter: a single act can bring it about. Neither does the act have to express the couple's total commitment to each other. Mechanical intravaginal ejaculation will suffice.

It is odd that a single act of having sex has the power to achieve a crucial transformation in the relationship in the sight of God. That is, it becomes impossible to undo. Guindon thought that deepening love, tried and tested, was a better solution. (For more on consummation, see Thatcher, 2002, pp. 226–236.)

13.2.2 The Reformation and the reform of marriage

The importance of the distinction between betrothal as a real *beginning* of marriage, and a wedding as the *ratification* of a marriage, can hardly be overestimated. The distinction continued until well after the Reformation (Macfarlane, 1987, p. 291). Up to the sixteenth century, the spousal or spousals "probably constituted the main part of the contract." A child could be betrothed at seven years old. A girl could be married at 12, a boy at 14. Children born to couples conceived during betrothal would be regarded as legitimate, provided that they married.

According to Macfarlane,

> It was really only in the middle of the 16th century that the betrothal, which constituted the "real" marriage, was joined to the nuptials or celebration of that marriage. Consequently, during the Middle Ages and up to the 18th century it was widely held that sexual cohabitation was permitted after the betrothal.

In France sexual relations regularly began with betrothal, at least until the sixteenth century when the Counter-Reformation Church moved against it. "Previously the engagement or betrothal carried great weight" (Rémy, 1979, p. 9).

In Great Britain, until well into the eighteenth century, the engaged lovers before the nuptials were held to be legally husband and wife. It was common for them to begin living together immediately after the betrothal ceremony (Macfarlane, 1987, p. 374). Social historian John Gillis confirms that while "the church officially frowned on couples taking themselves as 'man and wife' before it had ratified their vows, it had to acknowledge that vows 'done rite' were the equivalent of a church wedding" (Gillis, 1985, p. 20).

Processual marriage   The term "processual marriage" is sometimes used to describe these arrangements, that is, "where the formation of marriage was regarded as a *process* rather than a clearly defined rite of passage" (Parker, 1990, p. 19). Social historian Geoffrey Quaife notes that at least

> for the peasant community there was very little pre-marital sex. Most of the acts seen as such by Church and State were interpreted by the village as activities within marriage – a marriage begun with the promise and irreversibly confirmed by pregnancy. (1979, p. 61)

The promise to marry "was often *presumed* by local opinion so as to avoid illegitimacy and any consequent charge on the rates" (Parker, 1990, p. 19). There had long been a name for this – *matrimonium presumptum*. Far from this practice being seen as promiscuous or immoral, it was actually approved and enforced by the community. It was "located in a general belief in the ability of public opinion to command obedience to community values." It was very common in the seventeenth and eighteenth centuries.

Pregnant and "unmarried"? So what?   It has also been forgotten that about half of all brides in Great Britain and North America were pregnant at their weddings in the eighteenth century. Social historian Lawrence Stone says that "tells us more about sexual customs than about passionate attachments: sex began at the moment of engagement, and marriage in church came later, often triggered by the pregnancy" (1993, p. 176). He concludes that "among the English and American plebs in the last half of the 18th century, almost all brides below the social elite had experienced sexual intercourse with their future husbands before marriage" (Stone, 1979, p. 609).

This is a remarkable statistic. We citizens of the twenty-first century may have been taught that widespread pre-marital sex began in the 1960s. If so, we need to think again. After the Reformation the churches may have temporarily succeeded in reducing pre-nuptial pregnancies, but this development was temporary. In the eighteenth century there was a "gigantic rise of pre-nuptial conceptions." This was not "a massive violation of accepted standards in sexual behavior," but rather "a change in those standards." Stone's judgment is that:

> In the eighteenth century it looks as if the spousals again became the generally accepted moment at which sexual relations could begin, the marriage ceremony occurring later, often when the bride was quite far advanced in pregnancy. The man's honour was not damaged in the public consciousness, provided that he lived up to his promise to marry despite any possible second thoughts he might subsequently have had; and the woman's honour was not damaged in the public consciousness merely for having commenced sexual relations after the spousals but before the marriage. (1979, p. 629)

13.2.3 Reluctant virgins?

The Hardwicke Marriage Act of 1753 required registration of all marriages in England and Wales, and set up a bureaucratic apparatus for doing so. Betrothal ceased to have any legal force. Verbal contracts or pledges were no longer regarded as binding. The stigma of illegitimacy attached itself to children whose parents had not been through a wedding ceremony. Gone was the transitional phase from singleness to marriage.

Obligatory virginity The upper and middle classes borrowed the earlier Puritan conception of marriage and used it to distinguish their own practice from the less formal, more traditional alternatives. By the mid-eighteenth century they were able "to impose their will on the established church."

> They were now convinced that the legality of betrothal together with the church's toleration of clandestine marriage were, as Daniel Defoe was so fond of pointing out, crimes against both property and patriarchy: "a Gentleman might have the satisfaction of hanging a Thief that stole an old Horse from him, but could have no Justice against a rogue for stealing his Daughter." (Gillis, 1985, p. 140)

In contrast to plebeian practice where betrothal continued long after it had any legal force, in the upper class new courtship procedures required the pre-ceremonial virginity of brides, for social rather than moral reasons:

> For all women of this group virginity was obligatory. Their class had broken with the older tradition of betrothal that had offered the couple some measure of premarital conjugality and had substituted for it a highly ritualized courtship that for women began with the "coming out" party and ended with the elaborate white wedding, symbolizing their purity and status. Couples did not really come to know one another until marriage, a condition that was compensated for by the honeymoon, another of the innovations peculiar to the Victorian upper middle class. (Gillis, 1985, p. 164)

Virginity in this period had little to do with its religious meanings (see Section 11.1). Rather, the established religion reinforced the newly established opinion of it. Stone has a cold economic view of its value. Using "chastity" as a synonym for "virginity" he writes:

> The value attached to chastity is directly related to the degree of social hierarchy and the degree of property ownership. Pre-marital chastity is a bargaining chip in the marriage game, to be set off against male property and status rights. Pre-marital female sexual expression is thus built into the social system, since male and female are bargaining on the marriage market with different goods, the one social and economic, the other sexual. (1979, p. 164)

Many other changes to marriage occurred in this period that cannot be described now. Welfare legislation was frequently revised in order to discriminate against those who were not legally married. The period between 1850 and 1960 has been called "The Era of Mandatory Marriage" (Gillis, 1985, p. 229). People married earlier. Secular engagement replaced betrothal, and fixed, new, gender roles – the man the principal breadwinner, the woman the dependent wife and mother – seemed fairly established.

> *Question:* You will be very familiar by now with the claim that the churches make to base their sexual teaching on Scripture and Tradition. In that case has it struck you as odd that they now teach that marriages begin with weddings?

13.2.4 Excavating the marriage service

Contemporary church marriage services combine the two separate occasions of spousals and nuptials into a single ceremony. Macfarlane develops the point in detail:

> Behind the English wedding as it developed over the centuries there lay separate acts, one essential and one voluntary. In Anglo-Saxon England, the "wedding" was the occasion when the betrothal or pledging of the couple to each other in words of the present tense took place. This was in effect the legally binding act; it was, combined with consummation, the marriage. Later, a public celebration and announcement of the wedding might take place – the "gift", the "bridal", or "nuptials", as it became known. This was the occasion when friends and relatives assembled to feast and to hear the financial details. These two stages remained separate in essence until they were united into one occasion after the Reformation. Thus the modern Anglican wedding service includes both spousals and nuptials. (1987, pp. 309–310)

Remarkably, it is still possible to discover, in contemporary marriage liturgies, vows in the future tense, signifying the promise to marry in the future, and vows in the present tense, signifying the spouses' irrevocable consent now. I tried this out with the wedding liturgy in the Church I belong to, the Church of England. I tried an "archaeological" reading of the Common Worship Marriage Service of the Church of England (Common Worship, 2000), trying to dig deeply into it, looking for fragments of a former age. They were not hard to unearth.

There are two sets of vows which the couple must make in the presence of God, the Minister, the congregation, and at least two witnesses (who will sign that they have witnessed the vows being made). The first set of vows runs like this:

> *The minister says to the bridegroom*
> *N*, will you take *N* to be your wife?
> Will you love her, comfort her, honour and protect her,
> and, forsaking all others,
> be faithful to her as long as you both shall live?
> *He answers*
> I will.
> *The minister says to the bride*
> *N*, will you take *N* to be your husband?
> Will you love him, comfort him, honour and protect him,
> and, forsaking all others,

be faithful to him as long as you both shall live?
She answers
I will.

Did you notice the future tense of the vows (*"Will* you take ...?"; "I *will.*")? It may be doubted whether many clergy and marrying couples are aware that the future tense of these questions and answers is a tangible relic of the first millennium, when the vows, or *weds*, or *troths* were exchanged by the be*troth*ed in anticipation of their nuptial ceremony sometime in the future. *Common Worship* closely follows the 1662 Book of Common Prayer, which also requires responses first in the future, and then in the present tense. It can hardly be doubted, says one church historian, a century ago, "that we see here a survival from a time when the promise of espousal was held to be sufficiently ratified, even after a considerable time, by the nuptial ceremony following" (Lacey, 1912, pp. 48–49).

Actually, there *is* another interpretation. It is that "I will" is the *present* tense of the verb "to will." I think that the first interpretation is the more likely one. It is a genuine future tense ("I will [take]"), and a shadow of a betrothal vow. But there is no doubt about the tense of the second set of vows:

> *The bride and bridegroom face each other.*
> *The bridegroom takes the bride's right hand in his.*
> I, *N*, take you, *N*,
> to be my wife,
> to have and to hold
> from this day forward;
> for better, for worse,
> for richer, for poorer,
> in sickness and in health,
> to love and to cherish,
> till death us do part;
> according to God's holy law.
> In the presence of God I make this vow.
> *They loose hands.*
> *The bride takes the bridegroom's right hand in hers, and says*
> I, *N*, take you, *N*,
> to be my husband,
> to have and to hold
> from this day forward;
> for better, for worse,
> for richer, for poorer,
> in sickness and in health,
> to love and to cherish,
> till death us do part;
> according to God's holy law.
> In the presence of God I make this vow.

The response is not the future tense "I will," but the continuous present tense, "I take." It is the best example in the English language of a performative (see Section 2.2.1), where an utterance performs an action just by being spoken. Each of the spouses performatively "takes" the other with the words "I take you to be my wife" or husband. Yes, the future and present tenses of the two sets of vows retain a trace of the *verba de futuro* and *verba de praesenti* of another age.

This pre-modern distinction between *spousals* and *nuptials* has been forgotten. Indeed, its very recollection is likely to be resisted because it shows a cherished assumption about the entry into marriage – that it necessarily begins with a wedding – to be historically dubious. Betrothal, says Gillis (1985, p. 47), "constituted the recognized rite of transition from friends to lovers, conferring on the couple the right to sexual as well as social intimacy." Betrothal "granted them freedom to explore any personal faults or incompatibilities that had remained hidden during the earlier, more inhibited phases of courtship and could be disastrous if carried into the indissoluble status of marriage."

> *Activity:* If you are to attend a church wedding in the near future, listen to see whether the two sets of vows are retained in the service that is used. Alternatively you may like to "excavate" an online wedding service from one of the mainstream church websites, much as I have just done, and see whether it reveals traces of earlier betrothal or spousal practice.

13.3 Spousals, Nuptials, and States of Life

I hope it is by now well apparent that the widespread entry into marriage through cohabitation, from the 1990s onwards, represents remarkable parallels with marital practice in pre-modern and early-modern Britain.

The lack of stigma associated with pregnancy prior to a wedding is also a return to earlier, but still modern, ways. The broadening of possible venues for the conduct of weddings in some countries to include hotels, casinos, sports stadia, or indeed almost anywhere at all (for example, on a beach, underwater, in an air balloon) replicates earlier freedoms where wedding vows could be exchanged anywhere. Regarding parallels between early-modern and our late-modern ways of entry into marriage, John Gillis deserves the last word. Writing in 1985, his verdict is:

> Together law and society appear to have reinstated a situation very much like that which existed before 1753, when betrothal licensed pre-marital conjugality. It is also like the situation that existed in the late eighteenth and early nineteenth centuries when so many people made their own private "little weddings", postponing the public, official event until such time as they could gather the resources necessary to a proper household. (p. 310)

13.3.1 The pre-ceremonial state of life

Re-thinking "before" and "after"   Changes to marriage practice in England and Wales since the Hardwicke Marriage Act of 1753 have become so entrenched that it has become difficult even to imagine that strange and informal world of conjugality that lies behind the veil of modernity. These changes were soon exported around the British Empire. Once we get behind this Act (and for Catholics the Council of Trent in 1563), another view of marriage and the entry into it, opens up. The near-universal assumption that marriages begin with weddings is seen to be a modern one.

The earlier view is that the entry into marriage is a process involving stages. The wedding marked the "solemnization" of life-commitments already entered into, and the recognition and reception of the changed status of the couple by the community to which each belonged. The name of the Prayer Book Marriage Service of the Church of England was the "Form of Solemnization of Matrimony." The very name makes an assumption that the couple has already begun their marriage. They come to the Church in order to have it "solemnized." These stages can still be found in contemporary marriage services.

The earlier view shows how the proscription of "sex before marriage," still frenetically discussed by anxious young Christians, is shown to be a misdescription, based on a misunderstanding of the historical entry into marriage, and a confusion between marriages and weddings. The earlier view, that marriage is entered into in stages, renders those easy temporal distinctions between "before" and "after," provided by the identification between the beginning of a marriage with a wedding, superfluous.

The earlier view can be mapped by borrowing from the Middle Ages the terms that were used to track the progress of couples into wedlock. They are:

The three states of marriage

Matrimonium initiatum	This is marriage initiated or begun. Commitment has reached the point where it is exclusive, but still provisional. It is the point at which the spousals would have been conducted. Since it is a beginning of marriage, the couple can start having sex when they are ready for it.
Matrimonium consummatum	This is marriage thought to be completed or consummated the first time a couple has sex.
Matrimonium ratum	This is marriage ratified, in the eyes of God, the Church, the couple's communities, their families and friends. It is a wedding.

These old Latin terms used are beautifully simple and useable. The long period between puberty and the average age of first marriage can be 15–20 years. Since the gift of celibacy is rare, most of us will not have it. We may meet partners we are growing to love, and be years away from the possibility of setting up a home together. In situations like these, marriages may begin. Love-making in this period can be an aid to the growth of the relationship and the union of hearts and minds. The ratification of the marriage at a wedding may come years later. Sex in this period is certainly pre-ceremonial, but not necessarily pre-marital.

13.3.2 Developing yet preserving the marital tradition

Two Roman Catholic theologians have come to a very similar conclusion about the entry into marriage. Todd Salzman and Michael Lawler recall many of the features of pre-modern marital practice that have been mentioned here. But they make a straightforward proposal about reinstating a rite of betrothal:

> Our proposal is straightforward: a return to the processual marital sequence of betrothal (with appropriate ritual to ensure community involvement), sexual intercourse, possible fertility, and ceremonial wedding to acknowledge and to mark the consummation of both valid marriage and sacrament. (2008, p. 202)

The theological arguments which Salzman and Lawler use are also very similar to those here (and take further the conclusions of other recent Catholic writers – see Guindon, 1977; Legrain, 1978). They too find "the parallel between premodern, pre-Tridentine [before the Council of Trent], and pre-Victorian practices and modern or postmodern practices" to be "striking." They too observe that "Premodern betrothal led to full sexual relations and pregnancy, which in turn led to indissoluble marriage; modern nuptial cohabitation leads to full sexual relations and in turn to indissoluble marriage, with or without pregnancy." And they too make the distinction, as I have done, between *nuptial* cohabitation (I have called this "pre-nuptial") and "non-nuptial" cohabitation. We are all thinking of, and only of, "those cohabitors with an emphatic intention to marry."

Salzman and Lawler also use a formal principle of logic, borrowed from Thomas Aquinas, to underscore how traditional and so "un-novel" their proposal is. We saw the use of similar principles when querying the ban on the use of condoms even when such use is life-saving (see Section 12.6.1).

The principle this time is *Ab esse ad posse valet illatio* (Salzman and Lawler, 2008, p. 201), which means "the conclusion from actual being to possibility is valid." They use the principle to indicate a point about their use of Tradition, to illustrate that it is valid to suppose that what happened once could happen again, even at a different time. They say "From the actual historical being of the marital sequence betrothal – sexual intercourse – possible fertility – wedding, the conclusion that it could be so again, albeit in changed circumstances, is logically legitimate" (2008, p. 202).

Churches that find Tradition crucial to their practice should take heed. The proposal to reintroduce an earlier Christian understanding of marriage is logically and theologically legitimate. It is also highly appropriate.

13.3.3 The chaste beginnings of marriage

Cohabiting couples are returning to earlier ways of becoming married, unaided by appropriate ceremonies and customs, because these are no longer available. However, there is at least one important difference between the early-modern period and our own. It is about the place of children in marriages that are initiated but not ratified.

What is sometimes called the "pre-marital conjugality" of the earlier period occurred within a theological and social framework that was nonetheless strict with regard to promiscuity, which insisted on marriage as the precondition of raising children, and was fiercely insistent on fathers assuming responsibility for the welfare of the children they conceived.

Pre-industrial communities were largely self-regulating, and the full sexual experience practiced by betrothed couples was, unlike much of the same practiced by cohabiting couples today, *emphatically premised by the intention to marry*. Once a marriage had been contracted it was indissoluble, and divorce, aside from special Acts of Parliament (in England and Wales) was unavailable.

There is an obvious ready answer to this difficulty: contraception. The previous chapter provided detailed reasons why the use of these is fully consistent with leading a married life that is holy, chaste, and consistent with the will of God.

The range of contraceptives has greatly increased since the Anglican bishops approved condoms for married men in 1930 and Pope Paul VI disapproved of the Pill in 1968. There is no need to repeat these arguments. Not every act of love need be open to new life. It is natural to want sex with someone you are learning to love, and with whom you hope to share your life. It is wrong, and pastorally troubling, to greet these flowerings of love with metaphysical assumptions about contraceptive mentalities, moral deficits, daft allegations about "living in sin," and so on. The couples who are the subject of this chapter are on their way to their nuptials. They are beginning marriage. It remains their responsibility never to bring an unwanted child into the world. They need not do so.

Christian morality should not equate pre-marital chastity with the expectation that marrying couples should not make love before their wedding. Such couples will in any case be very hard indeed to find.

Matrimonium initiatum constitutes a state of life where chastity, as carefully defined (see Section 11.4.1) may be achieved and practiced.

Question: In this chapter I have suggested that there is a state of life prior to the ceremony of a wedding where sexual relations may begin. Further, these relations may be chaste. It is assumed that contraception will be used, and that straight couples should not have sex unless and until their commitment to one another embraces any children that may result from their love-making.

I have suggested that these proposals affirm and make more readily available the marital morality of the Christian faith. I have declared grounds, based on Scripture and Tradition, which support these suggestions. Opponents may think I have instead weakened marriage and undermined settled Christian principles. What do you think, and why?

References

Aquinas, T. (1920) *Summa Theologiae* (trans. Fathers of the English Dominican Province), www.newadvent.org/summa/2094.htm#article2 (accessed November 12, 2010).

Ball, L.B. (2009) Why do people still choose to marry instead of just living together? *INTAMS Review*, 15(1), 30–36.

Brooke, C. (1989) *The Medieval Idea of Marriage*, Clarendon Press, Oxford.

Brundage, J. (1993) *Sex, Law and Marriage in the Middle Ages*, Variorum, Ashgate Publishing, Aldershot, UK.

Common Worship (2000) *Marriage Service*, www.cofe. anglican.org/worship/liturgy/commonworship/texts/ marriage/marriagefront.html (accessed November 5, 2010).

Fuchs, E. (1993) Structure, ideology and politics in the biblical betrothal type-scene, in *A Feminist Companion to the Song of Songs* (ed. A. Brenner), Sheffield Academic Press, Sheffield, pp. 273–281.

Gillis, J. (1985) *For Better, For Worse: British Marriages, 1600 to the Present Day*, Oxford University Press, New York/ Oxford.

Guindon, A. (1977) Case for a "consummated" sexual bond before a "ratified" marriage. *Eglise et Theologie*, 8, 137–182.

Harcus, R. (2001) The case for betrothal, in *Celebrating Christian Marriage* (ed. A. Thatcher), Continuum & T&T Clark, New York/Edinburgh, pp. 41–54.

Institute for American Values (2009) *The State of our Unions*, www.stateofourunions.org/2009/Social_Indicators2009_ Cohabitation.pdf (accessed November 5, 2010).

Lacey, T.A. (1912) *Marriage in Church and State*, Robert Scott, London.

Legrain, M. (1978) *Mariage Chrétien, modele unique? Questions venues d'Afrique*, Chalet, Paris.

Macfarlane, A. (1987) *Marriage and Love in England: Modes of Reproduction 1300–1840*, Blackwell, Oxford.

Parker, S. (1990) *Informal Marriage, Cohabitation and the Law, 1750–1989*, St. Martin's Press, New York.

Quaife, G.R. (1979) *Wanton Wenches and Wayward Wives*, Croom Helm, London.

Rémy, J. (1979) The family: contemporary models and historical perspective, in *The Family in Crisis or in Transition: A Sociological and Theological Perspective: Concilium* (ed. A. Greeley), Seabury, New York, pp. 3–14.

Salzman, T.A., and Lawler, M.G. (2008) *The Sexual Person. Toward a Renewed Catholic Anthropology*, Georgetown University Press, Washington, DC.

Stone, L. (1979) *The Family, Sex and Marriage in England 1500–1800*, Weidenfeld & Nicolson, London.

Stone, L. (1993) Passionate attachments in the West in historical perspective, in *Perspectives on Marriage: A Reader* (eds. K. Scott and M. Warren), Oxford University Press, New York, p. 176.

Thatcher, A. (1997) Postmodernity and chastity, in *Sex These Days: Essays on Theology, Sexuality and Society* (eds. J. Davies and G. Loughlin), Sheffield Academic Press, Sheffield, pp. 122–140.

Thatcher, A. (1998) Beginning marriage: two traditions, in *Religion and Sexuality* (eds. M.A. Hayes, W. Porter, and D. Tombs), Sheffield Academic Press, Sheffield, pp. 415–426.

Thatcher, A. (1999) *Marriage after Modernity: Christian Marriage in Postmodern Times*, Sheffield Academic Press, Sheffield.

Thatcher, A. (2000) A Strange Convergence? Popes and Feminists on Contraception, in *The Good News of the Body: Sexual Theology and Feminism* (ed. L. Isherwood), Sheffield Academic Press, Sheffield, pp. 136–148.

Thatcher, A. (2001) Living together before marriage: the theological and pastoral opportunities, in *Celebrating Christian Marriage* (ed. A. Thatcher), Continuum & T&T Clark, New York/Edinburgh, pp. 55–70.

Thatcher, A. (2002) *Living Together and Christian Ethics*, Cambridge University Press, Cambridge, UK.

Williams, J.G. (1980) The beautiful and the barren: Conventions in biblical type-scenes. *Journal for the Study of the Old Testament*, 17 (June), 107–119.

14

Inclusive Theology and Sexual Minorities

In this final chapter, the theology of the previous chapters is briefly applied to sexual minorities, and to the further transformation of relations of gender. The idea of marital values is introduced in Section 14.1.1, and cautiously applied to relationships which are not legally marriages (Section 14.1.2). Marital values and the "way of justice" are commended to bisexual, intersex, and transgender people (Sections 14.1.3–14.1.6). Indifference about sexual difference is claimed to be a feature of the Reign of God (Section 14.2).

14.1 Sex

Our thinking about sex and gender in this book has been determined by several firm principles. One was the controlling importance of the Christian doctrine of God, the God who is Trinity, revealed as self-giving love in the Person of the Son. This God is the Ground of all that is, and makes human beings in the divine image. We all receive the summons of incorporation into the incarnate presence of God in the Body of Christ.

A second principle was that Christian sexual morality is a marital morality (see Section 5.1). Another principle was that there should be a focus on the *development* of Tradition at least as much as on its repetition (see Section 3.3.2). These principles are brought together in these final pages about sexual minorities.

14.1.1 Marital values

In the last chapter pre-nuptial cohabitors were brought into the institution of marriage by borrowing the time-scale of processual marriage and rolling the beginning of marriage back towards an earlier part of the couple's life-history. In the final chapter marriage is extended more broadly. Marital values are identified, and these are extended to relations that are not formally marriages.

What are the values of marriage that make it indispensable for Christianity?

Activity: You might find it useful to go back to the marriage vows described in Section 13.3 above, and note down in your own words the values that the vows express.

Comment: A short answer is likely to include deepening love, lifelong fidelity, and mutual commitment, isn't it?

Let's now make three fairly obvious observations about marital values.

First, it is clear that some marriages come to lack these marital values. If it were otherwise, there would be no divorces or social demand for them.

Second, some non-marriages nonetheless embody marital values. Some people remain committed to each other for life, having never promised to do so in a marriage ceremony. The Church used to call this *matrimonium presumptum* (presumed marriage).

Third, marriage then, as an institution, is no guarantor of the provision of marital values (anymore than the valid administration of a sacrament is the guarantor of faith in its recipients). Rowan Williams has rightly decried "the insistence on a fantasy version of heterosexual marriage as the solitary ideal, when the facts of the situation are that an enormous number of 'sanctioned' unions are a framework for violence and human destructiveness on a disturbing scale" (2002, p. 316). Sexual union, he declares, "is not delivered from moral danger and ambiguity by satisfying a formal socioreligious criterion." Some sex *within* marriage is nonetheless immoral.

These observations invite a conclusion: being married, and embodying marital values are not the same. It gives rise to a tantalizing question: wherever marital values are found should churches not be able to commend and name them, drawing the holders of them towards the One who is the self-giving source of all positive values whatsoever?

14.1.2 Extending the covenant of marriage

Arguments were offered (Chapters 9 and 10) that revision of official teaching about homosexuality is long overdue. Biblical teaching about homosexuality turns out to be about breaking hospitality rules (see Section 9.2), or about transgressing gender distinctions, or about immorality (see Section 9.3). Same-sex marriages can readily be accommodated into a developing marital tradition (see Section 10.1). The conventional proscriptions of same-sex relations based on Natural Law and on complementarity (Sections 10.2 and 10.3) were found to be particularly weak.

Can marital values exist in same-sex relationships? *Do* they exist? Even the question risks offense, for the answer "Yes" is both obvious and undeniable. Not all same-sex couples will want to marry. All couples are free to let themselves be judged by the covenant principle: do they love one another as Christ loved the Church? Is their love-making a non-retractable self-giving? Do their bodies belong to one another, wholly and exclusively? If so, then marital values are present. If, say, their love for another is inspired and deepened by the love of Christ for them both; if it is nurtured by the Eucharist, why is there a need for some further, higher standard?

At the time of writing various arrangements exist. In some countries and states, same-sex couples may marry. In other places they may register a relationship that is not technically a marriage but something else (in the United Kingdom a "civil partnership"). In yet other places no legal recognition exists, or laws forbidding any intimate same-sex contact remain. The Metropolitan Community Churches, the United Church of Christ in the United States, and in several countries, the Quakers, regard same-sex partnerships as *full marriages* and provide for the religious recognition and celebration of these.

Whether legal recognition exists, and whatever form it takes, the theological idea of a covenant is applicable to these couples. Whatever attitude Church or State may take to same-sex unions, what makes these relationships marriages, whether formally or informally, will be the marital values they embody.

Straight couples with children often find that extending their covenant to their children deepens and seals it, whereas same-sex couples will normally lack this means of enriching their relationship. Is this an impediment to the covenants of same-sex couples?

Some couples, where the law allows, will adopt or foster children. There are admirable theological reasons for providing a home for children whose biological parents are unable to do so themselves (Post, 2000; Thatcher, 2007, pp. 202–205). Assumptions that same-sex couples make poor parents are groundless. But most same-sex couples will remain childless. Their love for one another may in that case be more obviously extended outwards towards neighbors, or to work for peace and justice, or to community or church involvement. Their vows, like those of straight couples who are married, fertile, and intentionally childless, will bear fruit in the mutual support they provide for one another in their justice-making.

Lesbian and gay people remain divided regarding whether marriage is suitable for them, and lesbian and gay Christians also show a lack of unanimity about it. Part of the problem lies in the knowledge of what marriage has too often been. Straight majorities should recognize that until recently no recognition at all for same-sex unions has been forthcoming. A poor defense of marriage, that it was God's way of avoiding fornication (see Section 5.2.2), was never extended to same-sex couples, with the result that any sexual contact *at all*, remained forbidden. Marriage smacks too much of the social hegemony (see Section 8.3.1), which oppressed them for many generations.

There may be many lesbian and gay people who cannot, or cannot yet, trust the institution of marriage, even where it is available. I suggest that Farley's way of justice (see Section 5.3.1), if it is more congenial to them, becomes their way. There is a wealth of *positive* resources within the Christian Tradition that these couples may appropriate for themselves. In particular the consciousness of being both a part of the Body of Christ, and indeed a representative of that Body may be found useful (Section 8.1). Chastity (see Chapter 11) is appropriate to lesbian and gay people too!

Activity: You may wish to examine an inclusive marriage service in one of the major Christian churches. The United Church of Christ provides one on its website (UCC, 2010).

Straight couples may bring children into the world. That possibility remains a strong reason for them to practice chastity, before, inside and outside marriage. Very obviously that possibility is excluded here. While love-making will be free from the possibility of baby-making, many of the reasons for remaining chaste (including prudential ones; see Section 11.2.2) are readily applicable. The five principles for enlarging chastity, with due adaptation, may be found to be highly demanding, relevant, and applicable to lesbian and gay loving as well (Section 11.4.4).

14.1.3 Bisexual people

When I wrote about bisexuality 17 years ago I complained that "Bisexual people are almost always overlooked in discussions of sexuality" (Thatcher, 1993, pp. 155–156). Some bishops surmise that inattention to bisexual people may be due to the tendency to think "that human sexuality exclusively occurs in heterosexual or homosexual forms" (House of Bishops' Group on *Issues in Human Sexuality*, 2003; see Sections 6.3.2, 6.3, and 6.4). Perhaps I too am now guilty of overlooking them in this present work?

In mitigation I plead that heterosexuality and homosexuality are both queried as straightforward concepts and norms in this book. The bipolar distinction between them is a modern way of classifying desire, and it invites a way of classifying *ourselves* that we are free to resist. That some people respond desiringly to other people of either sex may just be an interesting fact about how some people are, but otherwise no big deal. There will be some bisexual people who may feel uncomfortable with that label, and who will not wish to identify with it.

On the other hand the term may be helpful to other bisexual people if they feel able to use it in their own "coming out," or "coming of age." It may help them to be honest in the first instance to themselves, about their desires. Other, "bi-curious" people may experiment with bisexual relationships *in order to find out whether they are bisexual* or not. This may be a case where the label itself, rather than the desire, provokes the curiosity.

Christian bisexual people should feel able to locate themselves happily within the framework suggested in earlier chapters. They should not find themselves marginalized in churches, or told that their desires are sinful, or fallen, or that they must struggle against themselves for the rest of their lives in order to be acceptable to God. They are acceptable to God already.

Bisexual people may find the image of God in them as readily as anyone else. They too may understand their bodies, should they wish it, as parts of the Body of Christ. Indeed since that Body is androgynous (see Sections 8.1.2 and 8.2) it is to be hoped that they will find their membership particularly appropriate. If their desires are "queer," so is the Body of Christ (see Section 8.2.1). All that was said in Chapter 11 regarding chastity, both as a Christian virtue and as a prudential policy for a healthy life, is applicable to bisexual people too.

In 1991, some bishops held

> that bisexual activity must always be wrong for this reason, if for no other, that it inevitably involves being unfaithful. The Church's guidance to bisexual Christians is that if they are capable of heterophile relationships and of satisfaction within them, they should follow the way of holiness in either celibacy or abstinence or heterosexual marriage. (House of Bishops of the Church of England, 1991, section 5.8)

This guidance may no longer be wise. Bisexual people do not appear to be more compulsive than other people. There are bisexual people who are promiscuous and others who are celibate; some fiercely faith-

> **Heterophile:** Literally, "one who loves the other [sex]," the bishops used it as an alternative to "heterosexual." They also used the term homophile, "one who loves the same [sex]."

ful to one person, others who have less limited and more diverse commitments. It does not follow from desiring both men and women that a bisexual person must have sex with both men and women; just as it does not follow that a married person who desires sex with someone other than his or her spouse, is free to act on the desire.

The advice to choose marriage or celibacy sounds too much like the advice that used to be given to homosexual people. In many cases it led to great unhappiness.

Too often bisexuality has been regarded as a problematic condition requiring particular self-discipline. Indeed, some bisexual people may feel uncomfortable with that label. It is possible, but surely not mandatory, that bisexual people should marry? That decision should be left to them. If they do not marry, relationships which embody marital values are open to them. They are more likely to thrive in partnerships where mutual comfort, honor, protection, and faithfulness (see Section 14.1.1) are lavishly shared. The way of justice also remains open (see Section 5.3.1). All the principles for commending and enlarging chastity (see Section 11.4) apply to them.

14.1.4 Intersex people

Intersex people have long been recognized (see Section 1.2.4). Christians are also complicit in the marginalization of intersex people, for rigid norms render "abnormal" people who cannot possibly conform to them (Cornwall, 2010). But in the theology advocated here intersex people are special people.

First, intersex people should be enabled to understand themselves as accepted and desired by God. That is likely to matter more to them than the two-sex norm that tells them they do not fit. The Kingdom of God is full of misfits.

Second, some intersex people (like lesbians and gays) may be able to accept the parody of themselves and their bodies as "queer" (see Section 2.2.1). Others may not. If they can, there is a body to which they obviously belong – the Queer Body of Christ. Since there is neither male nor female there (see Section 8.4), who cares about distinctions of sex, Christ least of all? Any need to identify with one or the other is dumped, rendered irrelevant. Since distinctions of race, class, and gender are removed "in Christ," the reinvention of them undoes the work of Christ in saving us from them.

Third, the example of eunuchs (see Section 8.3.2) may show that sex-ambiguous and gender-ambiguous bodies may act as special signs of the coming Reign of God. They are signs that all sex and gender roles are relativized as God's Reign comes. Can they not be thanked for showing us that the two-sex binary does not finally tell the truth about ourselves? However, this suggestion is offered only tentatively. It may be unhelpful to intersex people to suggest that their value is principally as an example to someone else.

Fourth, the bodies of intersex people are obviously included in Paul's teaching that the body is "a temple of the Holy Spirit," and they, like everyone else are to "honor God with your body" (see Section 8.1.1). Theology cannot tell intersex people how they are to do this. It may however release possibilities that have been slow in coming. Whatever bodies we have, we are all made to give and receive love.

Fifth, why cannot people whose bodies do not seem to fit the typical definitions of male and female, be seen not as deformed or deficient, but positively *blessed*? As having an overplus of possibility? As Cornwall observes, "Some intersexed people insist that their ambiguity or 'in-betweenness' is itself given by God, and that it should not be considered problematic or illegitimate by other Christians" (2010a, p. 25). Is there not a capacity for love and an understanding of the self that remains closed to the sexual majority, but is wonderfully opened by their experiences unavailable to the rest of us?

For some individuals and couples having children will be difficult if not impossible. But, like lesbian and gay couples, childlessness is no impediment to the making of a marital covenant. Self-acceptance will be greatly assisted by a partner whose love and loyalty is unswerving and unconditioned by a non-conforming body.

14.1.5 Transgender people

Straight majorities generally find empathy with sexual minorities difficult. They may remind us of the shifting nature of desire, and in some cases of bodily "ambiguities" that undermine a rigid male/female distinction. Transgender people (see Section 1.2.4) like other minorities require of us a duty of empathic listening. It is a simple matter. Intersex and transgender people are our neighbors, requiring our love. But in turn there is much to learn from them.

Transgender people experience acute tensions in their personal lives – these must be acknowledged and honored even if they are not fully understood. We decided Experience was a source of Theology (see Section 3.1.4). There is much to learn from the experience of transgender people. They require a social environment where sexual binaries and norms are not felt oppressively.

Any theological thoughts *about* transgender people, rather than by them, must also acknowledge that past theological efforts too easily resulted in inflicting more pain upon them, in failing to honor real difference, in reinforcing gender norms and condemning behavior that threatened these. Is the idea of an overplus of experience absurd to people who experience a sharp duality between the shape of their bodies and their sexual identity? What man has never imagined what it might be like to be a woman? And conversely. Among transgender people the sexes really do come together as one. Can some people have the remarkable experience, hidden from the great majority of us, of what it is like, on earth, to transcend the binaries between male and female, and so to anticipate a future state depicted traditionally in the picture language of heaven and the angels?

The desire for gender reassignment surgery indicates that at least some transgender people regard their predicament as intolerable. Would not the pain be less if such people were honored as Two-Spirit people are honored in the cultures where they have a rightful place?

Again membership of the queer Body of Christ ought to be a liberating, transforming experience. Here is a body that is truly androgynous, with men and women each performing both masculine and feminine roles, in a Body that represents the suprasexual God and the suprasexual Christ (see Section 7.1).

Cross-dressing   Cross-dressing has been around for centuries (Hotchkiss, 2000). Can it really be a theological or moral problem today?

We have already examined the law of Deuteronomy 22.5 that "A woman must not wear men's clothing, nor a man wear women's clothing, for the LORD your God detests anyone who does this" (see Section 9.2). This was a mixing of kinds, and mixings of kinds are no longer relevant in the Reign of God. And if they were, we would be taking care not to plant two kinds of seed in our vineyards (Deut. 22.9); not to plough with an ox and a donkey yoked together (Deut. 22.10); and not to wear "clothes of wool and linen woven together" (Deut. 22.11). Women today wear jeans, trousers, suits. Men find it more difficult to wear women's clothing publicly, although some skirts (if their wearers are from Scotland or other Celtic societies and the skirts are called something else – kilts) are acceptable. Women dressing as men crossed the gender divide, challenging or usurping the hegemony of the male. For this they might receive some public sympathy, and on the stage cross-dressing remains commonplace in pantomime.

People who cross-dress in order to give expression to the selves that are for the most part hidden commit no sin, no moral outrage, no acts of violence, no misdemeanors. Their differences and their yearnings should be honored and as far as possible, understood.

My first introduction to cross-dressing occurred when I was a minister and a young man who had locked himself in his bedroom sent a message that he wanted to talk to me. He had been discovered by his mother dressed up in her underwear. The family was plunged into a crisis from which it may never have fully recovered. He and I became good friends. I understood little of his desires, but felt instinctively that the invitation to guilt and remorse for this apparently shocking and inexplicable behavior should be shunned, and that this good person needed encouragement to discover more about himself and about the God who affirmed and accepted him as he was.

14.1.6 Marital values and justice

I have not mentioned many other people with different and pressing needs, although I hope they will find a welcome in the theology outlined in these pages. Disability Theology reminds us of the needs, including sexual needs, of disabled people, and by means of the idea of *The Disabled God* (Eiesland, 1995). Disability Theology achieves a memorable solidarity between the being of God and the being of disabled people. Vulnerable bodies find their spiritual home in the crucified Body of Christ.

Whether sexual needs in all cases are to be met by marriage will vary. Marriage may not be possible. The principles of chastity clearly apply, and especially if couples are straight, fertile, and having sex. If the covenant of marriage is unsuitable, then the principles of justice may apply instead. I hope these paragraphs have shown that a marital morality is capable of extension to situations where there is no formal marriage, even if it applies better in some cases than in others. (For the application of marital values to non-traditional families, see Thatcher, 1997, pp. 113–141.)

14.2 Gender

14.2.1 The indifference of sexual difference

The Christian performance of gender is inseparable from Christian beliefs about God. The belief that God is suprasexual (see Section 7.1) is particularly relevant. The image of the suprasexual God is locatable in men and women, equally but differently. Some recent accounts of the image of God in male and female confidently assume the image is located in the *relations* between men and women. In that case, where is the power located, and how are these relations to be conducted?

I claim sexual difference is a matter of indifference in the Reign of God, and ought to be a matter of indifference in the churches. This idea is often met defensively. It may be taken, absurdly, to advocate the sameness of the sexes; or that all men and all women are expected to perform all the roles traditionally assigned to each; or that the human ideal is androgynous. What then does it mean?

It means that with regard to many, but not all, of the social roles we human beings perform, it simply does not matter whether a man or a woman is the performer. What matters is that, when everyone has the opportunity to reach their full potential, the role is performed by the person who is best equipped and enabled to perform it. There are tasks currently better performed by men than by women, and other tasks better performed by women than by men. In such cases gender is relevant. In families the tasks may be allocated by negotiation between the members. Women are discovering they are at least as good as men in doing many things men and women did not think women could do. And men are discovering they too can be good at doing things only women used to do (like becoming primary carers, primary school teachers, or nurses).

In the churches, sexual difference is far from being a matter of indifference. The time is coming when it will matter no more, and it will rightly elicit instead a big yawn. No one will worry. But Christian thought, if it develops the doctrinal sources it has at its disposal, is able to make a big contribution to gender-justice, instead and outside the churches. We do not need to encumber ourselves with ancient gender theories and then mix them up with Gospel. There are at least three elements of this contribution.

First, the difference that really matters is *divine*. The advice of Miroslav Volf (2003) was well taken: "Instead of setting up ideals of femininity and masculinity, *we should root each in the sexed body and let the social construction of gender play itself out guided by the vision of the identity of and relations between divine persons*" (p. 170; emphasis in original: see Section 8.4.2). The divine Persons of the Trinity are co-equal, and the relations between these different but co-equal Persons is always one where difference is conducive to love, where giving and receiving are mutual and reciprocal. Divine difference enables the expression and accumulation of love. Human difference is too often an occasion for suspicion, division, domination, violence. The power of God is the power of communal Love, not the power of one Person over others.

Second, "in Christ there is neither male nor female" (Gal. 3:28). While the diversity of interpretation of this text was acknowledged, a contextual case was made (see Section 8.4.1) for preferring the reading that has Paul deploring the state of universal sinfulness that jeopardizes salvation of Jew and Greek alike. The Christ is the One who overcomes these structural evidences of sin as they are embodied in distinctions of race (Jew and Greek), class (slave and free), and gender (male and female). Differences remain, yet in remaining, they no longer possess their sinful edge. They no longer dominate, or exploit, as the manifestations of structural sin that they are, or once were. It took the Church a long time to admit to the structural sin of slavery. The structural sin of patriarchy is taking even longer to address, but it is slowly happening.

Third, the New Testament understands Jesus as the prototype of a new humanity, or new creation. This idea was mostly expressed in this study by means of the metaphor of the Body of Christ (see Sections 8.2 and 8.3). In this Body gender difference is clearly irrelevant. Anyone, everyone, can belong to it. It is gender-inclusive, androgynous, queer.

14.2.2 Transforming masculinity and femininity

In the Reign of God, "real men" are redefined. We learned how the followers of Jesus specifically undercut or subverted Roman masculinities, by redefining what it was for male Christians to be "real men" (see Section 8.3.1). Real men go the way of the Cross, renounce violence, give themselves in service to God and to neighbors. This power-shift or power-reversal invites application in the realm of male–female relations. These are no longer governed by the old model of dominance and submission, for there is now a better one, that of sharing power and shared empowerment. The old gender stereotypes, described several times in these pages, fall away. A new and better social body has been inaugurated, the Body of Christ.

Women too, freed from the responsibility of passivity, subjection, and obedience to men, can rise to the full development of their personhood. It is a sad feature of the last century that the social and political gains made by women received little encouragement from any of the churches. But theologians and Christians today are under no obligation to read gendered texts as their forefathers and mothers did. The danger for women, especially at a time that is coming to understand itself as "post-feminist," is that they may continue to see themselves as reflections in the male mirror. The equality some women seek with men extends to the worst excesses of male behavior, or expresses itself in becoming the sex objects that macho men wish them to be.

In some countries male power and gender imbalance costs lives (see Section 12.6). There will always be a need for social hierarchies, and for some people to have authority over others. How else would the armed forces, civilian police, hospitals, corporate companies, and so on, work? Where leadership and authority is influenced by gender, special cases will need to be made (and reviewed). But there is no longer any reason for gender hierarchies to govern personal relations. There is a better way of living and loving, and the theology of this work represents a way into it.

References

Cornwall, S. (2010) *Sex and Uncertainty in the Body of Christ: Intersex Conditions and Christian Theology*, Equinox, London.

Cornwall, S. (2010a) Between the lines. *All God's Children*, 2 (2), 24–26.

Eiesland, N. (1995) *The Disabled God: Toward a Liberatory Theology of Disability*, Abingdon Press, Nashville, TN.

Hotchkiss, V.R. (2000) *Clothes Make the Man: Female Cross Dressing in Medieval Europe*, Routledge, London/ New York.

House of Bishops of the Church of England (1991) *Issues in Human Sexuality: A Statement*, Church House Publishing, London.

House of Bishops' Group on *Issues in Human Sexuality* (2003) *Some Issues in Human Sexuality – A Guide to the Debate*, Church House Publishing, London.

Post, S. (2000) *More Lasting Unions: Christianity, the Family and Society*, Eerdmans, Grand Rapids, MI/Cambridge, UK.

Thatcher, A. (1993) *Liberating Sex: A Christian Sexual Theology*, SPCK, London.

Thatcher, A. (1997) Postmodernity and chastity, in *Sex These Days: Essays on Theology, Sexuality and Society* (eds. J. Davies and G. Loughlin), Sheffield Academic Press, Sheffield, pp. 122–140.

Thatcher, A. (2007) *Theology and Families*, Blackwell, Malden, MA/Oxford.

UCC (United Church of Christ) (2010) *Order For Marriage – An Inclusive Version*, www.ucc.org/worship/pdfs/323_346i_order-for-marriage-inclusive.pdf (accessed November 5, 2010).

Volf, M. (2003) The trinity and gender identity, *Gospel and Gender: A Trinitarian Engagement with being Male and Female in Christ* (ed. D.A. Campbell), T&T Clark International, London/New York, pp. 155–178.

Williams, R. (2002) The body's grace, in *Theology and Sexuality: Classic and Contemporary Readings* (ed. E.F. Rogers, Jr.), Blackwell, Malden, MA/Oxford, pp. 309–321.

Index of Authors

God, Sex, and Gender: An Introduction, First Edition. Adrian Thatcher.
© 2011 Adrian Thatcher. Published 2011 by Blackwell Publishing Ltd.

Index of Biblical References

God, Sex, and Gender: An Introduction, First Edition. Adrian Thatcher.
© 2011 Adrian Thatcher. Published 2011 by Blackwell Publishing Ltd.

Index of Subjects

Page numbers in **bold** type refer to the definitions that are presented in the text margins.

God, Sex, and Gender: An Introduction, First Edition. Adrian Thatcher.
© 2011 Adrian Thatcher. Published 2011 by Blackwell Publishing Ltd.